Lucas Delattre

BETRAYING HITLER

THE STORY OF FRITZ KOLBE
THE MOST IMPORTANT SPY
OF THE SECOND WORLD WAR

Translated by George A. Holoch, Jr

Atlantic Books
London

First published in English as *A Spy at the Heart of the Third Reich* in the United States of America in 2005 by Atlantic Monthly Press, an imprint of Grove/Atlantic, Inc.

First published in Great Britain in hardback in 2005 by Atlantic Books, an imprint of Grove Atlantic Ltd.

This paperback edition published by Atlantic Books in 2006.

Originally published in French in 2003 by Éditions Denöel, France, as *Fritz Kolbe: Un Espion au Coeur du IIIième Reich*.

1 3 5 7 9 8 6 4 2

A CIP catalogue record for this book is available from the British Library.

ISBN 1 84354 387 7

Printed and bound in Great Britain by Bookmarque Ltd

Atlantic Books
An imprint of Grove Atlantic Ltd
Ormond House
26–27 Boswell Street
London WC1N 3JZ

BETRAYING HITLER

INTRODUCTION

In September 2001, the German weekly *Der Spiegel* published an article about Fritz Kolbe, whom it described as an "anonymous hero" of the Second World War. He was profiled as an example of those Germans who opposed Nazism and who "fought with no internal or external help, driven solely by the stirrings of their conscience." Fritz Kolbe was an unknown minor official in the foreign ministry of the Nazi period, so one wonders how the two authors of the article, Alex Frohn and Hans-Michael Kloth, had discovered him. The answer lay in the archives of the Office of Strategic Services (OSS), the predecessor of the CIA, just opened by the United States government in June 2000. These documents, which had been inaccessible for more than fifty years, had just been declassified in accordance with a law passed under the Clinton presidency in 1998, the Nazi War Crimes Disclosure Act. They included 1,600 German diplomatic cables classified "top secret" that had been delivered to the Americans by Fritz Kolbe, alias "George Wood," between 1943 and 1945.

To read these documents is to understand why Kolbe was described by Allied leaders in 1945 as the "prize intelligence source of the war." In his memoirs, published in April 2003, Richard Helms, former director of the CIA, pays tribute to him by emphasizing that "Kolbe's information is now recognized as the very best produced by any Allied agent in World War II."

As *Der Spiegel* noted with surprise in September 2001, no one in his own country knew Fritz Kolbe's name. This man, who had taken enormous risks to fight Nazism, had completely disappeared from German memory after 1945. German public opinion never recognized the merits of this "traitor," even though the "traitor" had chosen the camp of democracy and freedom. To be sure, the official history of the Federal Republic of Germany (FRG) extols the virtues of a few illustrious opposition figures, such as Count Stauffenberg, originator of the failed assassination attempt against Hitler in July 1944. But it has no room for all those who, like Fritz Kolbe, demonstrated by their actions that everyone might have done something against Nazism. As George Steiner has said, "the great 'no's' to barbarism came from those so-called simple people." The article in *Der Spiegel* portrayed Fritz Kolbe as an ordinary German, the equivalent of Dutilleul, the hero of Marcel Aymé's *Passe-Muraille*. However, if all the Reich's minor officials had, like him, attempted the impossible, Hitler doubtless would not have been in power for long.

PROLOGUE

In the second week of January 1944, President Franklin Delano Roosevelt was personally informed by General William J. Donovan, the head of the OSS, of the existence of a pro-American German spy in the heart of the Reich. "We have secured through secret intelligence channels a series of what purport to be authentic reports, transmitted by various German diplomatic, consular, military, and intelligence sources to their headquarters. The source and material are being checked as to probable authenticity both here and in London. We shall submit later a considered opinion on this point. It is possible that contact with this source furnishes the first important penetration into a responsible German agency." General Donovan's memorandum was dated January 10, 1944.

"First important penetration" behind the scenes of the Nazi regime: The announcement was calculated to give the White House great satisfaction. Since the United States had entered the war against Germany and Japan in December 1941, Washington had been trying to make up for lost time in the field of intelligence. The British secret services were far in advance of their American colleagues, who had in no way foreseen the Japanese attack on Pearl Harbor on December 7,

1941, an event that had been a wake-up call hastening the establishment of the OSS a few months later.

General Donovan had been given a free hand to construct a worldwide intelligence network, but he had no spies in either Germany or Japan. Of course, a few Germans spoke to Americans when they traveled abroad, but this was sporadic. There was no secret agent in Berlin or Tokyo: the risks of capture were too great, the prospects for success too slender. The principal source of available intelligence on the Axis powers was the decoding of intercepted enemy telegraph or telephone communications. This procedure could not replace the quality of human intelligence, which was extraordinarily difficult to obtain.

The ideal spy had perhaps just been unearthed in Berlin: No one could be more useful than a well-informed German official, close to the center of power and decision making, and inclined to transmit his knowledge on a regular basis. For all of these reasons, his subordinates felt that the president of the United States should be personally informed of the existence of a German agent working at the German Foreign Ministry. In his January 10, 1944 memo, the head of the OSS informed Roosevelt that these documents would thenceforth be classified under the title of "Boston series"—a name that, like most used by the OSS, was probably chosen at random—and distributed to a very small number of people at the head of the government.

Attached to General Donovan's memorandum were fourteen very brief notes developed on the basis of elements supplied by the enigmatic spy, notes that contained a certain number of greatly significant facts. One German diplomatic dispatch dated October 6, 1943 explained that the head of the Gestapo in Italy, SS-Obersturmbannführer Herbert Kappler, had ordered the deportation of the Jewish community of Rome to the north with a view to "liquidating" it. A message from Ernst von Weizsäcker (ambassador to the Vatican since the spring of 1943), dated December 13, 1943, reported a conversation with Pope Pius XII, who expressed the wish that Germany "would hold out on the Russian front" and hoped that peace was near "or else communism would be the only winner." Still in Italy, Marshal Keitel (in the name of the führer) had given the order to execute without trial Italian officers who went over to the enemy (12 September 1943).

The most invaluable intelligence in Donovan's memo had to do with the Reich's communication channels. Berlin had installed a clandestine transmission post in Dublin. The German ambassador to Turkey, Franz von Papen, had a "mole" in the British embassy in Ankara. And most important, the Germans had an informer in the entourage of the vice president of the United States, Henry Wallace! Everything had to be done to plug the holes and prevent further leaks. The Germans might already be aware of the Allies' plan to land in France.

Roosevelt probably never learned the identity of the author of these revelations. Even the code name of the mysterious informer in Berlin, "George Wood," was kept secret. Only one or two people knew his real name and position: Fritz Kolbe, born in 1900, official in the central administration of the Foreign Ministry of the Reich in Berlin.

1

Señor Fritz Kolbe

Madrid, September 1935

It was ten in the morning in Madrid, and the city was bathed in the soft light of late summer. After eating his breakfast while reading the papers, Ernst Kocherthaler left home and headed for the German embassy. It was some distance, about three quarters of an hour away, but Kocherthaler walked quickly. As he walked beneath the locust trees, passing in front of still-deserted cafés, he could not stop thinking about the article he had just read in *ABC:* "Nuremberg, 15 September 1935: The National Socialist Party is going to pass several laws depriving Jews of full German citizenship. One planned law provides that marriages between Jews and German citizens will be prohibited. Extramarital relations between Jews and German citizens will also be prohibited." Phrases like "protection of German blood and German honor," and "survival of the German people" were repellent to Kocherthaler. He was extremely tense when he reached the embassy. He had the slight consolation that he did not yet have to see the swastika hanging in front of the building. The façade still displayed the traditional flag of the Reich (black, red, and white), but not for much longer. The Nazi Party had just decided in Nuremberg that its emblem would become the flag of the entire nation.

At the entrance, he asked for the consular service. His papers were not even checked, since he was known as a friend of Count Johannes von Welczeck, the ambassador. Count von Welczeck and Ernst Kocherthaler met often, publicly and privately. Sometimes they even spent summer vacations together, in San Sebastian, Biarritz, or Hendaye. The ambassador lobbied the Spanish authorities in support of his friend's investment proposals and liked to talk with him about economics, politics, and business. Kocherthaler owned shares in the copper mines of Andalusia and handled major energy concerns. He represented the interests of large hydrocarbon companies in Spain and was the co-president of the national federation of oil traders. Kocherthaler knew many people and was one of the most prominent figures in the Spanish capital.

Kocherthaler was led through the high-ceilinged corridors of the palace, a beautiful building that had been the Prussian embassy in the nineteenth century, to the visa and passport office in the consular section. He was shown to a seat in a waiting room, next to a little table with newspapers on it. There were a few copies of the *Frankfurter Zeitung*, still a relatively respectable paper, and certainly less painful to read than the *Völkischer Beobachter*, also available for visitors, along with various pamphlets by Joseph Goebbels. "How can Welczeck allow this propaganda in the embassy?" thought Kocherthaler, who, despite his personal friendship with the ambassador, resented him for giving in to the dictates of the Nazi Party.

By May 1933, all German diplomatic offices abroad had received a detailed document from Berlin designed to answer questions about the fate of Jews in Germany. German diplomats in Madrid had been seen at evening receptions launching into long arguments on the "Jewish question," explaining the specifically German concerns involved, and trying to put together arguments about its "universal character." The party and its ideas were infiltrating everywhere, including the German-Spanish Chamber of Commerce, where, as a non-Aryan businessman, Kocherthaler was already no longer welcome.

Leafing through the paper, Kocherthaler lifted his head and looked around. He saw an old engraving of the Brandenburg Gate. There was also a poster of the "Strength through Joy" organization, depicting two young blond women sitting on the white sand of a Baltic beach. The picture reminded him of Rügen Island, where he had spent all his childhood summers. Finally, there was a portrait of the führer with a little girl giving him a huge bouquet of flowers.

The door of the office facing him opened a few minutes later. A short official, only about five feet three inches tall, appeared in the doorway. He had a round face with prominent ears. His bald crown was as smooth as his perfectly polished shoes. The man did not have a typically German appearance, looking more like a Slav or someone from southern Europe. He was soberly but elegantly dressed. The tone of his voice was clear, and his elocution as distinct as the text of a Prussian law. His general appearance was quite pleasant, and he seemed to have a certain charm.

"What can I do for you, Mr. Kocherthaler?" he asked, pointing to a chair. Kocherthaler remained standing. The consular agent, much shorter than his visitor, was forced to look up in order to talk to him. His politeness surprised Kocherthaler, who had noticed a certain decline in German good manners since the Nazi accession to power. Minor embassy officials, most of them already Nazi Party members, seemed to have taken advantage of the new state of affairs to adopt authoritarian airs or unwelcome and excessive familiarity. This man was different.

The businessman, still standing, spoke with the solemnity of an officer of the Imperial Guard: "I have come to take the necessary steps to renounce my German citizenship." Ernst Kocherthaler asked the official to inform the authorities in Berlin that he was withdrawing from the national community and that he had taken steps to become, immediately, a Spanish citizen. "This decision is irrevocable," he added after a brief pause, his eyes downcast and his voice slightly trembling with emotion.

A little taken aback by the tenor of the statement, the consular agent seemed not to understand. He asked the visitor to explain the

reasons for his action. Kocherthaler mentioned the persecution of the
Jews in Germany, the daily humiliations to which they were subjected,
the boycotting of Jewish shops, the constant undercurrent of terror.
"The Jews have been excluded from all professions and from all pub-
lic places. The only thing they have left is their driver's licenses. This
Germany is no longer mine!" said Kocherthaler.

The laws that had just been adopted in Nuremberg had finally convinced him: He could no longer be a citizen of a country in which he
was relegated to second-class status. He himself had converted to
Protestantism before 1914, but both his parents were Jewish, and his
family tree was officially considered "impure." "I am a citizen of the
Reich, and nothing else," he said, clenching his fists. He had volunteered during the war, and, he told the official now, he maintained his
status as a reserve officer. The black, red, and white ribbon on his lapel
indicated that he had received a distinguished war medal. "Did you
fight? Do you know what it was like?" Kocherthaler asked.

The consular agent, a little surprised by the question, answered that
he had been too young to fight, that he had not been recruited until
the very last months of the war, into a Berlin battalion that had never
been sent to the front. Ernst Kocherthaler had already been in his office for more than half an hour. In the waiting room, other visitors were
growing restive. Among them was a young Spanish Falangist who
wanted a visa for Germany, and who now made a noisy display of his
impatience. But the businessman was in no hurry. He spoke of his love
for Germany, that he had left well before the rise of National Socialism. "After the war," he recalled, "I understood that there was no
longer a place for me in Germany. I was considered with contempt
either as a nasty banker or a wicked Jew, or both at once."

After three-quarters of an hour, he handed his passport to the consular employee and asked him to tear it up. A few seconds went by.
The passport remained on the table, an old one without a swastika.
The silence, barely disturbed by noises from outside, became almost
oppressive. Finally, the consular official spoke. "You should maintain
your nationality," he said to his visitor in a decisive tone. "There may
be a way of not giving up your status as a German citizen. Your war

medal could be used as an argument. In any event, here the Nazis can do nothing against you. I'm going to find out what can be done . . ."

Ernst Kocherthaler sat down and discreetly wiped his forehead. "I have no greater desire than to remain German. But on condition that I can officially declare my opposition to National Socialism in a document that will have to be rapidly transmitted to the highest authorities in Berlin." The ambassador, he thought, would no doubt approve this step. How could he refuse to allow a friend to make this gesture?

The consular agent promised to deal with the matter swiftly and to keep him informed. The visitor stood and left his business card: *Ernst Kocherthaler, Russian Petroleum Products Company, Madrid.* The official rummaged for a few moments among the papers covering his desk—some of the documents written in French, the customary language of diplomacy—and handed him his card, on which could be read: *Señor Fritz Kolbe. Secretario de Cancilleria. Embajada de Alemania. Madrid.*

Ernst Kocherthaler learned a few days later that the ambassador had not approved his action and had not transmitted his petition to Berlin. Deeply vexed, he renounced his German nationality, trying to persuade himself that the freedom of exile was better than domestic servitude. He silently reproached von Welczeck for not having the daring of Friedrich von Prittwitz und Gaffron, the German ambassador to Washington before 1933, the only German diplomat to resign on the Nazi accession to power. About his friend von Welczeck, he thought: "Not writing 'Heil Hitler!' at the bottom of your official correspondence does not make you part of the resistance."

Kocherthaler also thought again of the consular secretary who had received him. What a strange figure—Kolbe had not once used the slightest anti-Semitic expression. At one point, he had spoken of the "Nazis." No one used that epithet except opponents of the regime (its adherents would use the more dignified "National Socialists"). Kocherthaler found it strange that an obscure member of the embassy staff could openly show his distance from the party. The National Socialist Party (*Nationalsozialistische Deutsche Arbeiterpartei*, or NSDAP) recruited a substantial part of its troops from among second-level officials who, like Kolbe, had no university education. The others, the higher officials whom Kocherthaler knew well, tended to behave like nihilistic power elites, making fun of the Nazis while continuing to serve them.

Kocherthaler learned that Fritz Kolbe was the only official in the German embassy who had not joined the party. This information intrigued him, and he took the liberty of resuming contact with the chancellery secretary, curious to get to know this unusual man a little better.

Fritz Kolbe was surprised by this, since, having worked for several years on economic matters with the commercial counselor of the embassy, he knew Kocherthaler to be one of the most important people in the German community of Madrid. "Why would such an important personality want to see me? What can we possibly have to say to each other?" he wondered, after agreeing to a meeting the first Sunday in October at the Café Gijón on the Avenida de los Recoletos.

Madrid, October 1935

When the day came, Fritz Kolbe almost turned back before he reached the Café Gijón. He arrived a little early, sat on the terrace, set his white hat on his lap, and ordered a lemon *granizado*. Through the evening air drifted scents of mint and shellfish. The café was crowded that night, and the waiters were slow in filling orders.

Kocherthaler arrived, smiling, looking relaxed. The natural gentleness of his gaze and his warm handshake immediately put Kolbe at ease. He ordered a vermouth. After a few purely polite exchanges, the two men fell into an unexpectedly spontaneous rapport. Ernst Kocherthaler had ideas about everything and, it seemed, a broad experience of life. He spoke with ease, with a certain detachment, but without intimidating his companion. Even though Kocherthaler was involved in big business, Kolbe sensed that money was not the essential value for him. Kocherthaler was a cultivated man. He spoke of the

Mediterranean as the "sacred cradle of our civilization" and regretted that the Germans "now want to separate themselves from it" by seeking nourishment for the national imagination in Nordic myths. "There was a time when Germany defended freedom of conscience and welcomed all the refugees of Europe. . . . All that is long in the past!" He thought that the world was divided between those who were ready for "deeds and sufferings and sacrifices" and those who were content "with eating and drinking, coffee and knitting, cards and radio music."

As he was talking, Kocherthaler wondered to which of the two categories Fritz Kolbe belonged: his external appearance was nondescript but he saw a certain spark in his gaze. Confessing his curiosity, he asked Fritz Kolbe why he had not joined the party. Some diplomats opposed to the regime, in high positions or not, had agreed to sign up in order not to be noticed and to avoid suspicion. Why not him?

Kolbe, who was not expecting to have to talk about this sensitive subject, tried to take refuge in banalities. "I'm only a minor official in the embassy," he said, going on to say that it seemed sufficient that he had sworn an oath of loyalty and obedience to Hitler like all agents of the state. The NSDAP already had more than two million members, "so one more or one less, what does it matter?" he added, reasoning a bit maliciously that perhaps he had not been considered reliable enough to join. Many officials had submitted applications for membership to the "Brown House" in Munich, which was automatically suspicious of diplomats.

Kocherthaler wanted to know more. He was well enough informed about his interlocutor to understand that he was a rebel, but was curious about his background, wondering how a modest German official could resist the attractions of National Socialism. For his part, Fritz Kolbe had never been asked to explain his attitude, though it had not developed overnight. He was flattered that someone was interested in him but embarrassed to dwell on his personal choices. He explained that the NSDAP attracted primarily dull minds and invoked the values that had been passed on to him by his father: the refusal to obey anyone blindly, loyalty to himself, and the love of freedom. To make his point, he quoted classic maxims, such as: "Always be loyal and true, until the cold grave," or: "For what is a man profited, if he shall gain the whole world, and lose his own soul?" Fritz Kolbe had learned this passage from Matthew from his mother's lips and had never forgotten it.

Ernst Kocherthaler did not accept these trite answers. He wanted to know whether Kolbe was anti-Nazi out of Christian conviction or because he had socialist or even communist sympathies. To put him at ease, he told Kolbe that he had many professional contacts with the Soviet Union and that he had had a "splendid" time there in 1931. Kolbe acknowledged that he had indeed been raised Christian, but that he was not a churchgoer or even a believer. "You have nothing against the Jews?" Kocherthaler asked him abruptly. "Why should I?" answered Kolbe. "For me, between an Aryan and a Jew, the only difference is that one of them eats kosher food and the other one doesn't."

As for communism, he had always had deep suspicion of indoctrination, though his belief in the traditional "Prussian virtues" of order, work, and discipline gave him a certain fellow-feeling for the socialists. Friedrich Kolbe, his father, had voted faithfully for the Social Democratic Party. He had been a saddle maker in Berlin and had always told his son to "do good" and "never fear the future."

The Kolbe family came from Pomerania in northeastern Germany, a traditionally Protestant region. The Pomeranians had the reputation of being simple people, as solid as country wardrobes, provincials who were always lightly mocked for their *plattdeutsch* dialect. The Kolbe family had been part of the great migration to Berlin after 1871. Millions of people from the borders of the empire had settled in the new capital of the Reich in the hope of finding work. Fritz Kolbe had inherited an unshakable drive for upward mobility.

It was in this spirit that his father had encouraged him to become a government official. In debt, like so many other small craftsmen, he had suffered the humiliation of having to close his workshop and had become a worker in an industrial factory. Rapid industrialization was marginalizing craftsmen. The army, the principal client for the leather industry, preferred large suppliers. Fritz's childhood neighborhood of

Luisenstadt in Berlin had been full of barracks, and every morning he was awakened by military trumpets.

Of all the "Prussian virtues," blind respect for authority was the one that Fritz appreciated the least. "My father always told me that the principal defect of the Germans was their submissive spirit," he said. Of the few books he had been given to read as a child, he remembered particularly *Michael Kohlhaas,* the story of a rebel fighting to the death to obtain justice, which had made quite a mark on him.

Ernst Kocherthaler was beginning to get a better sense of Fritz Kolbe. This man, with his typical Berliner's caustic air, was hostile to all forms of authoritarian pomposity and display, Kocherthaler thought. In the course of the conversation, he was finally amused by Kolbe's adolescent side, the suppressed energy that showed itself in lively little gestures, his twinkling eyes, and a sometimes sharp tone. He often struck his left palm with his right fist. He seemed a determined person, not at all cerebral. Indeed, Fritz referred to himself as a "go-getter."

Feeling for his part that he could trust Ernst Kocherthaler, Kolbe took a few family photographs out of his wallet. He showed him a picture of his wife, Anita. She had a gentle face, with blue eyes and large sad lids. She had been suffering from pulmonary tuberculosis since 1933, which forced her to spend long periods in a sanatorium in Germany. A son, Peter, had been born in Madrid in April 1932. Kolbe told of meeting Anita in 1918, in a Berlin military hospital.

Another photo showed him in his 1918 soldier's uniform. He had belonged to an engineering battalion. The photo showed twenty other young men, and Kocherthaler noticed that they were all looking at the camera, except for one, who had his eyes fixed on an invisible spot in the distance. That was Fritz Kolbe.

In another, he could be seen doing calisthenics and wearing shorts. Kolbe was passionate about physical training. He did not smoke, drank very little, and got a lot of exercise—swimming, gymnastics, running—almost to the point of obsession. To celebrate the birth of his son he had run a marathon alone in a Madrid stadium.

The idea that one had to have a healthy body, live simply, and give priority to physical health was instilled in him during a formative child-hood experience, his time in the *Wandervogel*. This German equivalent of the Boy Scouts was where, he said, he learned "the secret of a suc-cessful life," "inner truth." He told Kocherthaler now that his time with the *Wandervogel* had been one of great freedom.

Kocherthaler listened to this story with a puzzled look. This naïve and generous overgrown boy scout seemed to him frankly a little fool-ish, and in the course of the conversation, he had caught an expres-sion about "international high finance" that had sent a chill down his spine. Scouting, in Kocherthaler's mind, with its veneration of youth and *völkisch* ideology, seemed a precursor of the Hitler Youth.

Kolbe was taken aback by the suggestion that his passion for sports was comparable to the Nazi cult of the body and violence, and though some of his old friends had joined the Freikorps following the war, and some had even become "arrant Nazis," "others became communists," he pointed out.

Kolbe explained to Kocherthaler that the *Wandervogel* had enabled adolescents to escape from the burdens of prewar society: school, fac-tory work, the army. . . . Even as a youth, he knew people were stifled under Wilhelm II and detested the bourgeois conformity and pomp-ous militarism of the imperial age. He was fourteen when he joined, just at the outset of the First World War. During the war, he had not been in the trenches, but had wandered down forest paths and slept in hay barns. The events of the outside world had not much affected him. He was a patriot like everyone else, but he felt himself above all a member of the human race. For him, the war had represented the collapse of the present and the promise of a rebirth. This hope was soon buried when he saw the thousands of wounded men who re-turned from the front to populate Berlin with their ghostly presence. What he loved was nature, escape, harmony with everything alive, which had nothing to do with the Hitler Youth! With some hesitation, Ernst Kocherthaler accepted this explanation, although he remained a bit skeptical.

The *Wandervogel* had also introduced him to boys from different social backgrounds—the sons of teachers and lawyers from Steglitz and other wealthy Berlin neighborhoods—and taught him "to think for myself," explained Fritz.

One unforgettable moment of his life among the scouts was still fresh in his mind. In the winter of 1920, Fritz and his friends had gone cross-country skiing in the Harz Mountains. "We were following each other without speaking. In the snow, the silence among the trees was profound. Our little group was looking for its way, when a solitary skier came out of the edge of the forest." He was an Englishman. "A real gentleman in any case, a little older than we were, and who spoke perfect German," Fritz recalled. He had read the works of Baden-Powell and told the young Germans, who were dumbfounded, about the adventures of the great English "chief scout" in Afghanistan, India, and South Africa. He explained some techniques for survival in hostile terrain that Baden-Powell had brought back from his journeys and set out in the book *Scouting for Boys* that had had great success in England. It taught how to light a fire without matches, how to find your way in the jungle, identify the cardinal points, administer first aid to a wounded friend, and the like. Fritz remembered the Englishman's story as though it were a revelation.

The next day, Fritz realized that he had just met a foreigner, for the first time in his life.

Madrid, November 1935

Fritz Kolbe and Ernst Kocherthaler saw each other again several times during the fall of 1935. Spain had felt civil war coming for at least a year. Rebellions in Asturias and Catalonia had been bloodily put down. The Falangists were parading in the streets, and the right increasingly resorted to violence. Rumors of a coup d'état were circulating. The camp of moderate republicans, to which Kocherthaler felt closest, could no longer find a place in a context of widespread radicalism. The era, even in Spain, was growing extraordinarily tense.

Nazism brought its enemies together, especially outside Germany. There is nothing more favorable than a crisis atmosphere for uniting expatriates. One day in a café Fritz Kolbe told his new friend that the local NSDAP cell in the embassy had just summoned him to question him about his refusal to join the "movement" and to actively support the National Socialist "Revolution." He had long been under friendly pressure, but now the situation was becoming more threatening. The head of the local party cell had learned through the indiscretion of a secretary that Kolbe had called Mussolini a "pig." He had told him threateningly that he risked being kicked out of the consular service. Fritz Kolbe denied some of the accusations and had for a time stuck to rather vague answers. He learned that he was criticized for associating with "Jewish" or "Marxist circles." Apparently, his meetings with Ernst Kocherthaler had been observed. His superiors wanted to know why he had been absent from the small celebration for the führer's birthday on April 20, 1935. Fritz Kolbe answered that his associations were his business, and above all that the state of his wife's health deprived him of any desire to celebrate. "I'm an official, I do my work well, but I would not like to look like an opportunist by joining the party now, when I was not a member before the NSDAP came to power," he told the three interrogators who came to see him. The Nazis had been visibly embarrassed by this rather wily answer. Fritz recalled that at the end of this painful discussion, he had been asked what was his "vision of the world" (*Weltanschauung*). "I pretended not to understand anything," he explained to Ernst Kocherthaler. "I told them that I did not know what a 'vision of the world' was and that I could therefore not give them an answer. I beat around the bush so much that they finally left, looking exhausted. They probably thought I was simpleminded."

Ernst reassured him: It was better to be an object of contempt than of suspicion. Solitude, all things considered, was better than prison. Kocherthaler himself felt deeply isolated. "My friends are becoming increasingly rare," he said. "Sometimes, I'm looking for a word, a quotation, and there is no one to help me. I have the impression that I am unlearning German. The worst thing is that now in Madrid we're exposed to denunciation and ill will from some members of the German community. Informers are everywhere. As though the Nazis had nothing better to do than to spend their time persecuting émigrés! I've learned that they are spreading falsehoods about me. I'm suspected of selling arms to the communists."

Kocherthaler had decided to take his three daughters out of the German school, where the atmosphere was oppressive. Despite his friendship with the ambassador, he had noticed that he was impotent in the face of the growing influence of the party. "Our friendship, dear Fritz Kolbe, is for me as unexpected as it is pleasant! You are the only German I want to talk to now," he confessed.

The rapport between the two men was sealed. Fritz began to call his friend "Ernesto" or "don Ernesto." He could not follow everything that Ernst Kocherthaler told him (particularly when he spoke about political economy or about Keynes, one of whose books he had translated into German). But he was thoroughly charmed by the man and thought that—after the Englishman in the Harz Mountains—this was the second "gentleman" whom he had had the opportunity to meet.

The rapport between the two men was all the more surprising because their lives to this point had been very different. Everything separated them: age, social background, culture. Before the war, Kocherthaler had carried on advanced studies in law and economics. At the time, Kolbe was attending primary school in a working class neighborhood of Berlin. In 1917, when one was nursing his wound from the battle of the Somme, the other was leaving secondary school prematurely to fulfill his military obligations as a young civil agent with Wolff, the German press agency of the time.

After his four months of service in 1918, Kolbe had in January 1919 taken a position as a trainee administrator in the Berlin office of the German railroads. He thought that this path would open the way to a career in Africa, "an old childhood dream," he admitted with some amusement. Unfortunately for his plans, Cameroon and Togo were no longer colonies of the Reich after the Treaty of Versailles. Chance dictated that Kolbe soon found himself in the accounting division of the German railway system. "How boring!" he acknowledged.

Fritz wanted to get out of this dead end. He took evening classes to complete his secondary education. Once he had his diploma, he decided to take concentrated courses in a business school to learn economics and languages (English, French, and Spanish). By doing this, he counted on improving his status in the railway administration. The wager paid off: In 1922 he was put in charge of the freight department of a large Berlin station. In February 1922, he was promoted to the title of "chief station, freight, and currency administrator." But he soon grew weary of counting locomotives, train cars, and boxes of freight.

Finally he had the opportunity to join the Foreign Ministry in March 1925. The ministry had positions open in consular services. Fritz Kolbe applied, took a test, and was accepted. After a few weeks of an internal training course and after being declared fit to serve in all climates, including the tropics, he was sent to Madrid.

The Spanish capital was beautiful, with a quality of life far superior to that in Berlin. The expenses of a long stay abroad—particularly moving costs—were, to be sure, far from negligible, but the ministry was generous and often advanced money if requested. Of course, inflation and the 1929 crisis had spared no one. Fritz Kolbe's salary was paid in marks; he had deposited his savings in the "bank for German officials" and had lost everything at the end of the 1920s. But the cost of living was lower in Madrid than in Germany, the atmosphere less oppressive than in Berlin, and family outings in the Pyrenees or on the Catalan coast were a taste of paradise. As for the advantages of the job, they were significant: Fritz traveled throughout Spain and even into France. On several occasions, he had replaced the vacationing German consul in Seville. He had taken the opportunity to visit Andalusia and was amused often to be taken there for a native of Moorish origin.

Madrid, December 1935

A kind of intimacy developed, in their Spanish exile, between Kocherthaler, the upper-class German of Jewish ancestry, and Kolbe, the minor consular employee. By the end of 1935, the two men were no longer meeting in Madrid's large cafés; it was too dangerous for Fritz, who was afraid that he was under surveillance, so they met at

Kocherthaler's home. One Sunday, toward the end of 1935, Fritz, Anita, and their young son Peter, then aged three, were invited to visit in the late afternoon. The family was rarely together; since 1933, Fritz was often alone in Madrid. Anita spent part of the year in a sanatorium in Germany, and little Peter in Berlin, living part of the time in his grandmother's apartment and part of the time in a Red Cross shelter.

The day they had tea with the Kocherthalers, Fritz put on his best flannel suit. Although they were in Spain, the tea and cakes were definitely German. The apartment was spacious. Old master paintings on the walls (a Goya, a Canaletto) and the many antiques decorating the apartment made it look like a museum.

Ernst Kocherthaler had a passion for history and ancient mythology, with a particular predilection for Egypt. He explained to his guests that he was working on a project for a book on the theme of the "original God." Fritz was a little distracted. He had just learned that he was being transferred to Warsaw and that he was going to leave Madrid early in 1936. He regretfully declined the invitation extended to him and his family to spend a few days vacation on Kocherthaler's property in Malaga. Tea that day had a taste of farewell. Anita was pale and seemed only distantly connected to the conversation. She soon went to rest on a chaise longue. When Ernst sat down at the piano to play an andante from a Beethoven sonata, the apartment was suddenly filled with deep sadness. Fortunately, Ernst's wife Martha, an elementary school teacher from Switzerland, cheered things up a bit. This was the first time that Fritz had met her. She too had been in the scouting movement as an adolescent and was passionately interested in discussing pedagogy.

Unfortunately, Anita Kolbe was exhausted and asked to go home.

2

RETURN TO BERLIN

Cape Town, October 20, 1939

The port of Cape Town was crowded. Hundreds of Germans were leaving South Africa because they had become undesirable in the country. England and France were at war with the Reich. The member countries of the Commonwealth (India, Australia, and New Zealand) had joined the conflict on September 3. South Africa, after a few days' hesitation and a serious government crisis, had decided to side with London on September 6. General Smuts, in favor of joining the war against Germany, had taken over as prime minister from General Hertzog, who had favored neutrality.

The German community of South Africa was under strict surveillance. Dozens of arrests had already taken place. Many preferred to return home rather than risking internment on the charge of "intelligence with the enemy." But the German liners of the Woermann Linie were no longer authorized to drop anchor in the ports of the Union of South Africa. The great repatriation was thus taking place under a neutral flag. That evening the *Bloemfontein*, a ship of the Holland Africa Line sailing to Antwerp, was mobbed by people wanting to leave. On the deck of the Dutch ship could be seen Germany's acting consul in Cape Town, Fritz Kolbe. He waved a final farewell to his son. Standing on the dock, the seven-year-old child was dressed in Bavarian style, with gray-green lederhosen and a baggy white shirt. He held the hand of a young woman, and then he hung onto the skirts of an older woman (perhaps his grandmother). The little boy seemed to be saying: "Why are you leaving me?" His gaze was firm and he held back his tears. Fritz knew that he would never forget that look.

The ship headed for the open sea on a journey that, if all went well, would last about two weeks. But submarine warfare was raging between Germany and England, and crossing the English Channel would be dangerous. A naval escort had been provided for the end of the voyage. Anxiety prevailed on board. The passengers gradually went belowdecks. Many went to the radio room to listen to the latest news from Europe. Kolbe remained alone, leaning on the rail. He did not know when he would see his son again. "Was I right to leave?" he asked himself with a pang, but it was too late to reverse his decision. The port had already disappeared over the horizon.

Fritz wondered how he could ever leave South Africa behind. As he watched the splendid shore of the bay drift by, he took with him images of flowering bougainvillea, and he caught a glimpse against the clear night sky of the flat summit of Table Mountain. When he had left Madrid at the end of 1935, he had felt himself to be Spanish. Now he had become an adopted Cape Towner. For the last time he identified the rocky peaks overlooking the sea, the Lion's Head, the Devil's Peak, the Twelve Apostle mountains—a landscape he had traveled through many times at the wheel of his superb automobile, a 1935 Horch 830 convertible. This was a luxury car ordinarily used by members of German high society, and acting consul Fritz Kolbe had used all his savings to buy it. Of all his possessions in Cape Town, his Horch was the only thing that he had insisted on shipping to Berlin (he did not yet know that he would soon have to give it up because of restrictions due to the war).

Fritz thought again of the long drives he had taken in the region, and breathed one last time the warm wind coming off the African veldt. In July 1939, he and a friend had explored the vast territory of South-West Africa and the Kalahari Desert in an all-terrain vehicle. The former German colony of South-West Africa (Südwestafrika or Südwest) was a paradise for antelope hunting. Recalling it now, Fritz remembered the exquisite taste of the wild game, but already a smell of sadly European vegetable soup was rising from the ship's kitchens.

As the African coast slipped by that evening, Fritz Kolbe thought about the harshness of fate. Young Peter's mother, Anita, had died in June 1937. She had never seen Warsaw (where Fritz had stayed for only three months), or South Africa. Fritz had remarried in the fall of 1937; his new wife was Lita Schoop, from Switzerland. Because the ceremony took place in Zurich, they had not received the copy of *Mein Kampf* now given to all newlyweds in Germany. It was a marriage of reason rather than love: Fritz had been looking primarily for a replacement mother for his son. The couple had come to live together in Cape Town early in 1938. The marriage had not lasted long; they had already been separated for some time when Fritz left Africa. The tension in the couple, evident after only a few months of life together, continued to build during their time in South Africa. One day, Lita had even threatened to denounce her husband's anti-Hitler convictions to the consul. Fritz's immediate superior was a dedicated Nazi by whom Fritz took care to remain unnoticed. After that incident, Fritz had invited a friend home so that he could spend an entire evening feigning obeisance to the "party line" in the presence of his own wife. What an unbearable charade! Very soon afterward, he had slammed the door on the marital home in the upscale neighborhood of Camps Bay (a handsome detached house with a garden), taking his son with him. Lita and Fritz had not seen each other since then. He merely knew that Lita had decided not to return to Europe (he would later learn that she had been interned as a German citizen in a British camp in East Africa).

If Fritz Kolbe had decided to leave, this was purely out of loyalty to the head of the German legation in Pretoria, Rudolf Leitner, who had asked him to return with him. Even though the diplomat was a member of the party, Kolbe respected him as a human being. He was pleased to see him on board the *Bloemfontein*. The two men knew each other well: In 1936, when Fritz had briefly returned to Berlin after a short stay in Warsaw, Leitner had been his superior in one of the departments of the ministry (Kolbe had been recommended to him by Count von Welczeck, the former ambassador to Spain). Leitner, a good-natured Austrian Catholic, particularly appreciated Kolbe for his habits, "worthy of the finest Prussian administration." Fritz was a veritable workhorse, having no hesitation in working overtime and spending the night at the office when necessary. As for Kolbe, he liked to chat with Leitner, particularly when he talked about America, where he had been posted for more than ten years. As the former consul in Chicago in the mid-1920s, he knew a huge number of amusing anecdotes about Al Capone and the hidden history of prohibition.

When Leitner had been sent to Pretoria at the end of 1937, he had not hesitated to fight to have Fritz Kolbe appointed to the consulate in Cape Town. The mission he had assigned him was to restore order to the consulate's finances, which were in a sorry state after several years of mismanagement. Kolbe had been appointed in spite of the initial hesitations of the powerful liaison office between the Foreign Ministry and the NSDAP, which controlled all foreign appointments. Leitner had had to use all his influence for Kolbe's professional qualities to trump his politically questionable status in the eyes of the liaison office.

Kolbe was something of a "protégé" of Leitner's, and Fritz would have been very distressed to compromise him. If he had decided to stay in South Africa, as some of his friends had advised, he would have been interned until the end of the war—that was one thing—but above all he would have put his immediate superior in difficulty. In Berlin, Rudolf Leitner would have been criticized for having supported a "deserter," which would have put an end to his career. Kolbe decided to return to the ministry, with an aching heart.

It was a sad voyage. Fritz Kolbe had never felt so alone. He did not reply when an unknown traveler suggested they have a drink. He was suspicious, because the ship was full of informers, cheaters, and professional gamblers. Late at night, he could still be seen strolling on the promenade deck, lost in thought. He was trying to imagine Europe at war. He resigned himself to returning to a Berlin under the Nazi yoke.

The capital of the Reich, he thought, must be gloomier than ever. Fritz had heard that the Gestapo had veritable carte blanche to eliminate whoever it wanted with no legal accountability. Patrols would harass passersby on the slightest pretext. Building managers were now in service to the party, ready to denounce the slightest suspect behavior. Fritz remembered the day in 1937 when he had had the misfortune to pass a Nazi leader's car on a broad Berlin avenue. The eminent figure's chauffeur (was it Göring, he wondered?) had given him a threatening look and followed him for a while, as if to record his license plate. Fritz anxiously anticipated a summons from the Gestapo. Nothing had happened in the end, but he had slept badly for two weeks.

Even if the war was far from popular, a majority of Germans remained in favor of Hitler and thought that he "was going to come through it," as always. How, he wondered, could millions of people see the approaching catastrophe without reacting? How could they accept the curfew and the obligatory food and clothing ration cards? Fritz told himself that it was probably already too late—military hostilities were right around the corner, and public opinion would unite behind the regime out of a patriotic reflex.

The ministry to which Fritz was returning was, worst of all, under Ribbentrop—the man who had just signed a pact with Moscow after having denounced for years "the Russians, our sworn enemies." Fritz had never seen him but had a fairly clear idea of him. The foreign minister had earned the nickname "Ribbensnob" since he had purchased the right to put a "von" before his surname. He was one of the most mediocre leaders of the regime, known for his pathological obsequiousness toward the führer and his brutality to his subordinates. It seemed that the atmosphere in the Wilhelmstrasse offices had seriously deteriorated in the last two years. Everyone was said to be at the mercy of outbursts of anger from the minister, who insulted his interlocutors, not hesitating to call them "idiots" or "wimps." Generally speaking, Ribbentrop—a former sparkling-wine merchant—detested most career diplomats. He wanted to make the Foreign Ministry into a "powerful National Socialist instrument at the service of the Führer," and to do this he had taken control of the ministry by placing reliable men in the key positions. Half of the five hundred high officials in the ministry were already members of the party, and one in ten belonged to the SS.

The shock waves of events in Germany had spread as far as South Africa. In the German consulate in Cape Town, Fritz Kolbe had observed a gradual deterioration of the climate. Afrikaner nationalism seemed to have grown wings thanks to Hitler, and the atmosphere had become electric. The Afrikaners imitated fascist spectacles commemorating their own history. One evening in the fall of 1938, on leaving the consulate, Fritz had encountered a small troop of Grey Shirts, a fascist league modeled on the SA. The young men had greeted him with a Hitler salute. Fritz had pretended to have forgotten something in the building in order to avoid having to talk to them.

The militants of the Afrikaner cause, as always, had chosen the German camp out of hatred for the British. This had already taken place during the Boer War in 1899, and again in 1914. Since Hitler's accession to power, the descendants of Dutch immigrants thought that once again the fate of the Afrikaner *volk* was in the hands of Germany and more or less openly praised all the victories of the Reich in Europe.

Fritz had seen all kinds at the consulate. Sometimes they had talked to him as though he were a personal representative of the führer. The most moderate of his visitors argued in favor of South African neutrality: "After all, Hitler is no threat to our interests," he often heard. Others openly wanted an alliance with the Reich and proposed returning the colony of South-West Africa to Germany in order to seal this agreement in the name of peoples oppressed by "British imperialism."

The worst had come when Fritz had had to organize a visit to Cape Town by an NSDAP delegation that had come from Berlin to meet with South African counterparts from the New Order (a movement founded by Oswald Pirow), who defended a "Christian nationalist"

ideology based on the ideals of blood and soil. This had happened early
in 1939. Fritz had been unable to get out of participating in an evening
"among comrades" at the city's German club. The reception, naturally accompanied by large quantities of German beer, had featured
various songs drawn from the Nazi repertory.

Lüderitz, October 22, 1939

Lüderitz, a port of South-West Africa, was named for a tobacco merchant from Bremen who had set up a trading post there toward the
end of the nineteenth century. Liners sailing to Europe called there
twenty-four hours after leaving Cape Town. From the deck that
morning, Fritz watched the swarm of activity on the pier: herds of
sheep, horses, and the transport of freight—impressive quantities of
bales of wool, rifles, agricultural equipment, cases of schnapps. Europe was distant, but German was spoken here, and the architecture
as well displayed its clearly German origins.

The former colony of the Reich, half desert, had maintained majority German-speaking enclaves like Lüderitz and Swakopmund, popu-
lated by Catholic missionaries from the Rhineland, merchants from the
Baltic Sea coast, and transplanted German farmers. The Nazis were
naturally interested in this region, which they contemplated reconnect-
ing to the Reich in the context of a vast colonial project. Berlin had already appointed the "shadow governors" of the future African empire.
The agitation of the Afrikaners in South Africa was vigorously encouraged by certain German circles in the Südwest. Toward the mid-1930s,
NSDAP cells had been set up throughout the territory. Swastika flags
had been raised here and there. Leaders of the Hitler Youth had come
from the Reich with the intention of training overseas imitators. Fritz
knew by reputation the German consul general at Windhoek, Walter
Lierau, who had arrived in 1939: he was the first diplomat of the Foreign Ministry to have been a member of the SS.

Fritz thought about his son; this was the region where little Peter
was going to live during his father's absence, with his adopted family.

The child was to live with Otto and Suzi Lohff, a German couple who lived in the town of Keetmanshoop, 250 kilometers in the interior, who were soon to move to Swakopmund, very close to another port, Walvis Bay. Otto Lohff worked for the Metje and Ziegler company, one of the largest German firms in South-West Africa, importers of supplies for construction and public works. Because the local economy needed him, he had not been interned by the South African authorities.

Otto Lohff had rather nationalistic opinions, but he was not a Nazi. Fritz was especially close to Suzi (nicknamed Ui), Otto's wife; in fact, she had become his mistress. After separating from his wife, Fritz had lived in the small boarding house in Cape Town run by Ui's mother, Frau Kahlke. She thought of herself almost as little Peter's grandmother. Fritz found "granny Kahlke" marvelous, knowing everything about his relationship with her daughter and never committing the slightest indiscretion in front of the deceived husband. As a result, he had forgiven her a good deal, starting with her naïve admiration of Hitler ("She has not set foot in Germany since 1914," he said to himself, "she cannot understand what is happening"). Fritz had promised Ui that he would come for her after the war and take her to live in Germany.

For now, he returned to Berlin alone, because he wanted to spare his son the misfortunes of war and allow him to escape from privation and hunger, of which he still had terrible memories from his experience in Berlin after 1918. Nor did he have any intention of entrusting him to the schoolmasters of the Nazi regime. He knew that the Hitler Youth now called the shots in classrooms. There was no question of leaving Peter in the hands of some brigade, nor any question of seeing him forcibly enlisted in the "Reich labor force" to repair roads or cut wood in the forest.

Sailing toward Europe, Fritz knew that he had already crossed the line in his opposition to the Nazi regime. In Cape Town, he had committed his first illegal act: He had agreed to forge some passports at a friend's request, to save some anti-Nazi refugees from Germany. This friend may have been Toni Singer, an engineer of Austrian origin, a company head, and member of a Masonic lodge. Thanks to him, Fritz had penetrated the secret society a bit and had begun, clandestinely, his personal initiation. He had particularly appreciated the idea that man had to reform himself before attempting to reform the world. Self-improvement should be intellectual as well as physical. "Only mastery of the body opens up the fullness of being," according to a Masonic precept to which Fritz fully subscribed.

Fritz realized, on the ship taking him back to Germany, how estranged he had become from his own country. He was incapable of mixing with the German passengers, some of whom were noisily celebrating the losses inflicted on the British by the U-boats and singing: "Today Germany belongs to us / And tomorrow the entire world." Alone in his cabin, frequently nauseated because of the stormy sea, he thought that there was perhaps already a Gestapo file with his name on it, like those he had personally handled in the Cape Town consulate ("unreliable element, to be watched, regularly socializes with Jews and Freemasons"). In Berlin, he would be forgiven not a single false move. In the best case, he risked being sent to the front. Fortunately, he was appreciated. The invaluable protection of Rudolf Leitner must not fail him. But Fritz was weary of pretending in order to avoid trouble.

There could be no question of fighting against the Nazis. During his preceding stay in the capital of the Reich in 1936 and 1937, he had seen up close the cost of protesting the regime: One of his friends had lost his job with the Berlin city government, two others had been sentenced to two and three years in a concentration camp, another, arrested for "illicit possession of printing material," had committed suicide after being tortured. So many others, whose names he did not know, had disappeared into the camps.

At the same time Fritz knew that it was always possible to "do a little something" in silence and anonymity, as other Germans were doing here and there, each one according to his means. All things considered, it was perhaps better to stay in Berlin and have a foot inside the system rather than choose exile and observe events from the outside. He had spent a little time with German émigré circles in South Africa and had soon wearied of their interminable discussions and their contagious bitterness. But up to what point could he fulfill his obligations as a government official without selling his soul?

To give himself courage, Fritz recalled an expression that he had heard somewhere, although he could not remember exactly where: "Life is not like the game of chess. There are not only black and white pieces. There are gray figures, solitary knights, and equivocal characters who never get caught."

Berlin, November 1939

At seven-thirty in the morning, on November 9, 1939, Fritz Kolbe took up his duties at the ministry. He walked shivering through the capital, a harsh winter looming, and was surprised to observe that life seemed to be going on more or less normally, though the silence on the streets of Berlin was eerie. Shortages, particularly of coal, were beginning to make themselves felt, but there was plenty of bread and potatoes, and people were dressed normally. The Nazi leaders seemed to have prepared well for their war. Submarines were engaged in a violent but distant *Kriegsspiel* along the British coasts and in the North Atlantic, but Berlin felt rather far from events.

What had changed in Berlin was the color of the city. Apartments and offices were perpetually plunged in darkness. It was now mandatory to cover windows with dark paper in case of enemy bombardment, even if English planes were not flying over the capital and were merely dropping leaflets over the Ruhr. Even by day, windows remained covered. Headlights of buses and automobiles were darkened with black paint except for a one-by-five-centimeter slit. "Darkening" was the key directive in wartime. Posters stuck up everywhere indicated that whoever did not obey the orders to "darken" was subject to severe penalties. Because of the literal darkness, household injuries were on the rise (objects dropped on feet, heads banging against doorways, and so on). The present and the future were also shrouded in absolute obscurity. Everything was done to prevent information from circulating. No one had the right to listen to foreign radio stations (in this case too, offenders were subject to long prison terms). The war could not be seen, but could be listened to in secret. People strained their ears to catch scraps of the BBC's German language broadcasts.

There was no way to escape from the ubiquitous propaganda. The walls were covered with pro-war slogans. "The day when proud Albion collapses will be a day of joy for us," were the first German words to greet Fritz Kolbe at the border, on the train trip from Antwerp to Berlin. New expressions had appeared in everyday speech: Fritz quickly learned that the male population was divided into those with a "u. k. post" (unavailable to the army) and those who were considered "k. v." (available). He hoped with all his heart that he would be considered "u. k.": these two letters were for him the initials of happiness.

Going to the office, Fritz did not yet know what his new assignment would be. He was a little apprehensive about the meeting that soon awaited him with the head of personnel of the Foreign Ministry. Going through Pariser Platz, across from the American embassy, he looked up at the roof of the Adlon Hotel, where an antiaircraft battery had been set up. With his head in the air, he almost collided with a group of passersby having an animated discussion. He caught a few scraps of the conversation: "attempt against the führer," "Munich," "hall." He knew nothing more when he went in at Wilhelmstrasse 76, one of the three entrances to the Foreign Ministry.

One of Fritz's colleagues, encountered by chance in a corridor, quickly brought him up to date. The night before in Munich, a bomb had exploded in the beer hall where the führer had given a speech every year to commemorate the failed putsch of 1923. Seven were dead and sixty wounded. But, contrary to his usual pattern, Hitler had left the room a little earlier than planned. The bomb had exploded at 9:20, only thirteen minutes after he had left.

At the ministry, as everywhere else, the attack was all that was talked about. The flags were at half-staff. There was word of a march in Munich in honor of the seven people killed in the attack. Radio programs were frequently interrupted by special bulletins. The nasal voice of Goebbels commented on the event on the spot and presented the official version of the facts: "Unquestionably, this ignoble act, probably committed by German traitors, bears the signature of the British secret services."

Lost in thought, Fritz wandered through the corridors of the ministry. His eyes went wide when he saw at a distance a junior minister in a dark blue uniform covered with stripes and gold buttons, and wearing a ceremonial dagger on his belt. Aside from that odd surprise ("you'd think we were in an operetta," Fritz said to himself), nothing had changed since 1937. He glanced into the dreary offices of the Foreign Ministry, and found them as dilapidated and underequipped as when he left—still the same brass lamps with green shades, old oil lamps remodeled into electric ones; the same worn carpets on the floor; the same musty odor of old documents—and yet something had changed, an apparently very minor detail: the typewriters had been replaced. They now had a new key so you could type "SS" in Gothic script.

Fritz crossed paths with several old acquaintances, who whispered a word or two about the life of the foreign ministry at war. He learned that Ribbentrop had been consumed by remorse since, contrary to what the minister had anticipated (and loudly proclaimed), England had declared war on Germany. He was told that a legation adviser, Eduard Brücklmeier, had been briefly arrested by the Gestapo for "defeatism," before finally being released. A colleague complained about the fact that foreign diplomats had deserted the ministry. "We only see a few representatives of friendly or neutral countries," he said. "We spend our time trying to understand what is expected of us," added another. "Jurisdictional disputes with other ministries take up all our energy."

After walking down long corridors, Fritz Kolbe finally arrived at the office of the head of personnel, Hermann Kriebel. In the waiting room, he came across one of his old acquaintances, Hans Schroeder, Kriebel's assistant. Schroeder had joined the Foreign Ministry when Fritz had, in 1925. The two men were about the same age and had had their first diplomatic training together. But since then, Schroeder's career—he was wearing the party insignia on his lapel—had been much more dazzling than Fritz's. "Kolbe! How have you been all this time?" cried Schroeder in a sonorous voice, warmly shaking his hand. Fritz was not taken in by the familiarity. He thought he could catch a slight glimmer of satisfied contempt in the eyes of his interlocutor. Briefly, he reported on his eleven years in Spain, his two years in South Africa, and his forced return following the outbreak of the war. "Good, very good," said Schroeder, smiling broadly. "It so happens that I've heard that they've saved a magnificent post for you: consul at Stavanger in Norway. A quiet country! No rationing, a normal life, an interesting post! What do you think?" Fritz was surprised. He had not been expecting such an attractive offer. Rudolf Leitner must have intervened in his favor, or else such a promotion would not have been offered to him. "But you see," Schroeder continued, "there's a small problem: You're not a party member. A few years ago, we could have turned a blind eye to that, but now it's no longer possible. Frankly, don't be an idiot! All you have to do is get your card, and then make a little courtesy visit to certain people who would like to know you better. In short, it's not very complicated: the matter is entirely in your hands, my friend!"

After having what Schroeder said confirmed by the head of personnel, Fritz was stunned. He who had sworn never to become *Pg* (party member) was now being offered a very handsome post on condition that he deny his convictions! He took two days to make up his mind. With a heavy heart, he decided not to accept the offer, wondering if he was not making a monumental mistake. He knew that nothing interesting would now be offered to him, and he saw himself stagnating for the rest of his life in some obscure back office in the ministry. Worse, he feared his gesture would be interpreted as an affront by Rudolf Leitner. He risked losing in him his only protector. From then on, catastrophe seemed inevitable.

And indeed a few days later Leitner called Fritz into his office. A great surprise awaited him. His former superior in Pretoria had called him in to encourage him to go to Stavanger and to try to persuade him to join the party. Fairly quickly, considering Fritz's arguments, he nevertheless showed some understanding and even seemed to hint at his respect. One might say that he was saluting, without really daring to say it, Kolbe's constancy. "The problem," he said, taking the trouble to escort him to the door of his office, "is that now you are going to be offered something much less interesting, and for now I can't do much for you."

Reassured by Leitner's attitude, Kolbe felt a bit more lighthearted. Staying in Berlin, he would be able to see old friends and take care of his aged mother, who detested the Nazis and could use the company. The priority was to remain himself, "defenseless but not without honor." Walking through the Berlin streets on the way to his hotel— a temporary residence until he could get settled more comfortably— Fritz Kolbe felt torn between pride and despair, between his desire to flee to Norway and the personal integrity he prized. As he walked, he wondered about his fate. He thought with disgust about a Berlin doctor who had just divorced his wife after thirty years of marriage because she was Jewish and "he had not realized what that meant."

Fritz had never felt so deeply nostalgic for foreign capitals. He remembered a mission to Paris in the late 1920s. He had been there for only a few days to deliver diplomatic correspondence, but he had preserved an undying memory of the city. At this very moment, he would have dearly loved to talk to Ernst Kocherthaler, his old friend from Madrid. It was too bad that it was no longer possible to see Don Ernesto. The Kocherthaler family had settled in Switzerland shortly after the beginning of the Spanish Civil War. They had not totally lost touch, of course. They continued to exchange letters, but the postal censorship in Berlin imposed a good deal of discretion. Fritz thought again of the question that Kocherthaler had asked him in the course of one of their conversations in Madrid: "Are you ready for exploits, suffering, sacrifice?" He regretted not knowing how to answer at the time. Now he knew what he would say: Yes, he was ready to make sacrifices, for example, giving up a post as consul. It might not be a spectacular act, but he had remained true to himself.

Fritz had understood, since the interrogation to which he had been subjected in Madrid in late 1935, how useful it could be to appear to be an idiot in order to preserve your freedom. Since that day, the party informers had left him relatively in peace, and suspicion toward him had faded to some degree. Rather than displaying feigned support for the established authorities (like a certain number of senior diplomats more or less opposed to the regime), Kolbe preferred to adopt an ingenuous attitude that fit well with his modest rank. He told himself that by cultivating his image as an obtuse but efficient minor official he would perhaps be left alone, and that the most insignificant post would enable him at least to maintain his dignity.

Berlin, November 21, 1939

Fritz Kolbe had been in his new position for a few days. He was now assigned to the visa and passport section of the ministry, which was under the jurisdiction of the legal affairs department. His mission consisted of delivering authorizations to leave German territory to members of the foreign ministry who had to go abroad. Kolbe had fewer and fewer regrets about the post of consul at Stavanger. Even if his new assignment was not very interesting, it enabled him to remain informed about events and to keep in contact with colleagues. The foreign ministry was a mine of invaluable information. With respect to the coming offensive in the West, Fritz had learned in the course of October 1939 that sixty to seventy divisions of the Wehrmacht had been transferred from Poland to the Rhine. There had also been rumors in the last few weeks that the SS had committed atrocities in Poland.

The name of the man who had attempted to assassinate Hitler in Munich had been made public. He was a thirty-six-year-old carpenter named Georg Elser. Arrested on November 8, the man had confessed after several days of interrogation. The bomb used in the attack was very primitive in design but effective. Heinrich Himmler, the Reichsführer SS, had reaffirmed that the British secret services had been behind the attack. A little later in the day, it was learned that the Gestapo in fact had arrested two high-ranking British espionage agents on November 9 near the town of Venlo on the Dutch-German border. Posing as opponents of Hitler looking to arrange for support from London, its agents had lured the English into an ambush, killing a Dutch intelligence officer in the process. The two British agents had been brought to Germany for interrogation.

Reading this news, Fritz Kolbe was not the only one who thought that Himmler was probably the brains behind the Munich assassination attempt. He thought of a setup. The Nazis, he said to himself, know that this war is unpopular and want to distract the Germans by making them think that the English want war and that the führer is a demigod protected by supernatural powers. On the other hand, if the SS was really behind this faked assassination attempt, how could Hitler have taken the risk of placing himself next to a ticking bomb that might have gone off a few minutes too soon? Suppose Georg Elser had acted alone, as he claimed. Fritz Kolbe would have liked to talk about the event with some of his friends in the ministry. But he was soon made to understand that it was better not to speak openly on the subject, especially if you called into question the analysis authorized by Goebbels.

The Ministry of Propaganda in fact had taken advantage of the event to put on a grandiose spectacle. November 11 had been declared a "day of national mourning." In Munich, ten thousand people had marched in silence past the Nazi-flag-draped coffins of the seven people killed in the attempt. The ceremony had been broadcast live on the radio. The event served more than one purpose, because the party had taken advantage of it to settle some internal scores. Fritz thought of Georg Elser, the young Swabian carpenter who looked like a bum. He then remembered what Toni Singer had said to him in South Africa in the course of his brief Masonic initiation. Toni Singer had spoken to him of the symbolism of the tarot and had told him that the only card without a number, hence excluded from the game, was the Fool. This card was the symbol of the authentic initiate, able to see a world inaccessible to ordinary mortals. It pictured a vagabond, holding a staff in his right hand, his pack over his left shoulder, pursued by a dog trying to bite him, with his eyes turned toward the sky.

3

WHAT IS TO BE DONE?

Berlin, May 10, 1940

The offensive in the West had begun. The Wehrmacht was in Holland and was heading for Belgium. Walking toward the Kottler, a restaurant and café on Motzstrasse in the Schöneberg neighborhood, Fritz Kolbe could not help showing his agitated state: He kicked every pebble he saw and muttered incomprehensible words under his breath. Passersby turned their heads to look at this lunatic walking at full speed, but he kept going, paying no attention to his surroundings. With his black leather coat and his eyes glowing beneath the brim of his hat, he might almost have been taken for an agent of the Gestapo.

The Café Kottler was a place of relative freedom. It was possible to have quiet discussions there because the tables were set in alcoves and discreetly lit with candles. The privacy of discussions was ensured by the music of the zither player who livened up the atmosphere every evening. In short, it was a safe place. The owner was a trustworthy man, a Swabian who pretended to admire the regime but had his own opinions. Above the bar he had hung a sign intended to lull the

Gestapo's curiosity: *Der Deutsche grüsst mit 'Heil Hitler!'*, next to an ad for Dörnberg liqueurs.

When he reached the café, Fritz went directly to the table in back, in a little quiet corner where he usually sat. The table had been reserved, as always, in the name of a more or less fictitious "sports association" created by Fritz Kolbe—a method enabling him to avoid awakening the suspicion of the authorities, particularly because Fritz truly was an exercise enthusiast and he trained several times a week in various individual and team sports. The "association" assembled old childhood friends, most of whom he had met on *Wandervogel* hikes, with whom Fritz now played chess at the Kottler when they were not running in the Grunewald or Wannsee woods. Among them was Walter Girgner, his closest friend, a bon vivant with a talent for business (he had founded a clothing company that was now obliged to work for the Wehrmacht), Kurt Arndt, a police captain, and Kurt Weinhold (nicknamed Leuko), an engineer at Siemens. Even though he had set up house with a certain Lieschen Walter (about whom nothing is known), Fritz was leading the life of a confirmed bachelor.

"What's gotten into you, Fritz?" said Walter Girgner, seeing his friend's distressed look. "This time, the war has entered an irreversible phase," said Fritz. "We are in Holland and Belgium. And then what? France? England? Where is all this going to end? What revolts me is the knowledge that my own ministry has put the cream of its intelligence at the service of this new offensive. For months, the jurists of the Foreign Ministry have been assembling so-called evidence to demonstrate that Holland and Belgium are not maintaining their neutrality. Did you hear Ribbentrop's press conference this morning? To make sure that our neighbors do remain neutral, we invade them! What cynicism! They call it a 'protective measure'! If I had been consul at Stavanger, God knows what role that would have had me play in this history of madmen."

Fritz and his friends agreed that enough was enough and that something had to be done, but what? Since they had renewed their acquaintance in November 1939, they had asked themselves this question every week, and they always ended up feeling as though they were going around in circles and about to go mad ("Sometimes I was doubting who was mad, whether all the others or myself," Fritz explained after the war).

"Speaking for myself, I can no longer tolerate these lies," said Fritz. "We have to do everything to prevent this band of assassins from continuing to act. Have you read the latest news? A couple has just been taken away by the Gestapo after being denounced by their own daughter! A chicken thief has been sentenced to death by a special court, in the name of the new provisions of war legislation and the fight against 'parasites of the people.' But it's the Nazis who are a band of vermin and crooks. Everyone agrees, speaking like me and saying that this war is insane, so why doesn't anyone do anything, why?"

There was an awkward silence. Fritz had an idea. The group ought to distribute anonymous leaflets, write counter-propaganda to denounce the official lies. Tomorrow, he would set to work at home. Writing with his left hand and wearing gloves, in capital letters, he would set down expressions like the ones that circulated in the Café Kottler at night: "What is pessimism? Not winning the war and maintaining Nazi power. What is optimism? Losing the war and seeing the Nazis go." Or else, inspired by a popular song: "Everything flees and everything leaves / Soon the end of Hitler and the party." These little squibs would be sent to big companies, big stores, and other places likely to ensure that their content was widely disseminated. They would be accompanied by a little note along these lines: "If you don't agree with this message, please bring it to the nearest police station." The idea was to stir up trouble in people's minds. Above all, they could not get caught. They would have to multiply precautions when carrying the leaflets, never send them more than once from the same place, learn to hug the walls at certain late hours.

Pleased with his resolution, Fritz did not talk about it immediately to his friends. He preferred to wait until there were fewer customers in the room and he had only familiar faces around him. While waiting, he began to recite aloud a few words by Friedrich Schiller: the knights' song from *Wallenstein's Camp*, which he knew by heart because he had sung it often when he was a *Wandervogel*: "Till life has been staked for the rise or the fall / Your life will never be won at all." Fritz noted with satisfaction that these words had a certain effect around him. He knew that Schiller was looked on favorably by the Nazis (unlike Goethe, whose Masonic inclinations made him suspect), and he was taking no risks by quoting some lines aloud. He called to the zither player to ask if he could play the melody of the knights' song. The musician agreed for a small tip. The little group, followed by the whole café (including policemen in uniform who were among the customers that evening) intoned the martial air, too well known to be suspected of the slightest subversiveness: "Freedom has vanished out of the land, / Only masters and slaves will you find; / Deceit and treachery now command / Among craven humankind."

While the rest of the café continued singing happily, Fritz's small group of friends drank a toast in their corner, whispering conspiratorial words: "for the king," instead of "to your health," and "devil take them!" Going home that evening, Fritz had the impression that he had become the leader of a little seditious group. His friends had enthusiastically welcomed his plan to distribute leaflets. They would soon meet at Fritz's apartment on Klopstockstrasse to write them. The danger of underground action was exciting. "In battle, man still has his value," Fritz said to himself, thinking about a line from Schiller.

Berlin, June 1940

German troops entered Paris on June 14, through the Porte Maillot. Hitler had won his bet and now had himself called the "greatest general of all time." The order to hang out the flags came to all the cities of Germany two days later. The triumphal display was extraordinary. Each parade was succeeded by another, and brass band followed brass band. The voices of children could be heard singing songs with joyous refrains. The people thought that the war was over and saw that Hitler had gotten everything he wanted: Danzig, Memel, the western regions of Poland, Alsace-Lorraine, Saarland, Eupen, and Malmédy, not to mention Austria and Sudetenland. The shame of the Treaty of Versailles had finally been washed away. It would finally be possible to live in peace. Even the most skeptical generals had come to believe in the führer's genius. For all those like Fritz Kolbe who had hoped for a gradual weakening of the regime, this incredible victory over France meant dismay and profound bitterness.

After eight months at the ministry, Fritz observed with a mixture of satisfaction and dread that he provided complete satisfaction to his superiors, in professional terms. He was beginning to feel like a little soldier caught up in an immense war machine. "Am I meant, finally, to work with them?" he asked himself in anguish. He remembered a hurtful remark by Ernst Kocherthaler: "You could have been a Nazi!"

Speed, precision, discretion, these were the qualities attested to by his superiors. As a result, one of Ribbentrop's closest associates, Martin Luther (no relation to the father of the Reformation), had brought Fritz into his office to handle a task with which he had experience: processing requests for visas for foreign travel. This time he was not dealing with internal ministry files, but with requests presented by people outside the foreign ministry, notably party members, high government officials, and other eminent public figures. The multiplicity of authorizations that had to be obtained made Fritz Kolbe's work truly exhausting.

Martin Luther was not a career diplomat. He came from the "Ribbentrop Office" and enjoyed the minister's full confidence. With his round glasses, slightly pudgy face, sniggering smile, and bull neck, he in no way resembled the classic appearance of the foreign ministry. He was a member of the SA and, in fact, one imagined him much more at ease in street fights than in composing diplomatic cables. He was known as the "moving man" because he had been the head of a moving company in the 1920s (he had in fact met the foreign minister when he moved Ribbentrop's furniture to the embassy in London). A specialist in financial manipulations, Luther had an extraordinarily extensive list of contacts.

He was one of the most feared figures in the ministry. The "German" department of which he was in charge had been established in

May 1940 and was the exclusive umbrella department for many highly sensitive matters: relations with the NSDAP and all its subsidiary organizations (in competition with the "Organization of the Party for Foreign Countries" or *Auslandsorganisation*, also housed in the ministry); relations with the SS and various secret services of the Reich; the "Jewish question," "race policy," foreign propaganda questions (in competition with Goebbels's ministry), matters related to foreign workers conscripted by force to work in Germany, and so on. As though more clearly to establish the independence of the "German" department from the rest of the ministry, its offices were not located on Wilhelmstrasse but in a building some distance away, on Rauchstrasse.

Fritz Kolbe detested Luther. He also hated his subordinates, notably one named Franz Rademacher, whom he sometimes encountered in the canteen. Pudgy, even a bit fat, Rademacher did not have the savoir faire of a high-ranking diplomat. He was the specialist on the "Jewish question" on Ribbentrop's staff. In the spring of 1940, the "settling" of that question was a matter of intense reflection at the foreign ministry, which was attempting to secure a position of leadership in the matter and wanted to show that it put forward ideas for how to implement "the annihilation of the Jewish race in Europe." All proposals were centralized in the "D III" (Deutschland III) office of Franz Rademacher, who had the diplomatic rank of secretary of the legation. Inside the ministry, Rademacher's office was simply known as the "Jewish desk" or *Judenreferat*, just as there was a "French desk" and a "Russian desk."

When Fritz Kolbe took up his duties in the "German" department, Franz Rademacher was totally absorbed in the "Madagascar plan." This plan envisioned the deportation of the Jewish population of Europe to that Indian Ocean island, then a French protectorate. Fritz Kolbe, suddenly at the heart of the regime, had a hard time behaving himself. On several occasions, important figures had occasion to complain about him to Martin Luther. "Who is that petty official who doesn't even give the Hitler salute when we come in?" Exasperated by these remarks, Martin Luther appeared one day without warning in Fritz's office and gave him a warning as brief as it was threatening:

"Kolbe, I wanted to tell you that I will not stand for one more lapse from you. You wouldn't be the first to disappear."

Fritz felt a chill run down his spine. From that moment on he became more careful and faded into the background. He decided to make himself known exclusively for his inordinate love of the game of chess. He was sometimes seen replaying for himself great matches of the past, using a handbook and a pocket chess set. He scribbled descriptions of the greatest tournaments on little scraps of paper that he never wearied of rereading. Once he was even heard to recite by heart—as though it were a poem—the opening of one of the great matches between Wilhelm Steinitz and Emmanuel Lasker at their celebrated 1896 Moscow tournament: "1. d4 d5, 2. c4 e6, 3. Nc3, Nf6, 4. Bg5 Be7, 5. e3 0–0, 6. Qb3 Nbd7, 7. Nf3, c6, 8. Bd3 dc4, 9. Bc4 b5 . . ." Fritz established an amateur club that met in the ministry canteen. He did not hesitate to play matches with the most hardened Nazis. He took his revenge in the game, and once again he was taken for a likable eccentric.

Fritz's office door was always open. He saw an enormous variety of people. The Nazi occupations in Europe caused a huge movement of specialists of all kinds and a proliferation of requests for foreign visas. There were lawyers traveling to supervise and manage the confiscation of Jewish property in the occupied countries, experts in the history of art who went to select works in France. Some ministers, like Ribbentrop, Göring, and Rosenberg, had teams specializing in foreign "requisitions" (works of art, horses, wine). There were representatives of every profession: journalists appointed to set up a pro-German press throughout Europe, directors of cultural institutes sent to conquered territories, archivists, lecturers, architects . . .

One day toward the end of the spring of 1940, a pretty woman entered Fritz Kolbe's office and asked for a visa for Switzerland. It was rare for a woman to appear in the corridors of the Foreign Ministry. Fritz Kolbe gave her a form to fill out and had her sit at a little desk facing his own. While she wrote, he took the opportunity to scrutinize her. The visitor had style: dressed in white, she had entered the room wearing an elegant wide-brimmed hat. It was immediately apparent that she was a woman of quality, even displaying a certain distance from the people she addressed, the antithesis of a "Lieschen Müller," the generic name for a Berlin shopgirl. She wrote quickly, crossing words out. Obviously, she was swamped with work and in a hurry to leave. About forty years old, like Fritz, she introduced herself as a personal assistant to Professor Sauerbruch. "Not someone likely to have children," thought Fritz as he looked at her. He had immediately understood that she was one of those modern ambitious women who had difficulty seeing themselves in the role of housewife reserved for them by the Nazis.

As he watched her fill out the document, Fritz managed to read from a distance what she was writing. He learned that her name was Maria Fritsch, that she was unmarried, and that she was born in 1901 in Bütow, in Pomerania. A Kashubian woman, straight and even a little rigid like many people of the region, Prussians who had become a little Slavic because they lived in mixed German-Polish territory. "Pommerland?" he asked her in the local dialect, and he added—still in *plattdeutsch*—a famous line of poetry to make her notice him: "*Wo de Ostseewellen trecken an den Strand?*" ("Where the Baltic Sea waves kiss the beach?"). The woman's face suddenly became more cordial. "*Dor is mine Heimat, dor bün ik tau Huus*" ("There is my country, there I am at home"), she countered immediately, still in low-German dialect. An onlooker would have had difficulty understanding much of the exchange that followed. It sounded like a slightly drunken conversation in untranslatable dialect. Only a few words, used by Fritz in an ironic way, could be recognized. He imitated a speech by Hitler in *plattdeutsch*, barking out *Dütschland!*, *Föhrer!*, *Vaderland!*, making his visitor burst out laughing.

Already, she was getting up to leave. Fritz managed to delay her a little longer: the form was incomplete, a letter had to go with it. She hastened to write it, but hesitated for a moment before giving it to him. "Should I sign with '*Heil Hitler*'?" she asked him, her pen still uncapped in her right hand. Fritz Kolbe did not answer. She looked up, worried, and encountered an almost threatening look. "Look here, don't think of it," he finally said, "do you know where we are?"

A quick exchange of smiles and there was now complete trust between the two.

Fritz wanted to see her again. He asked Maria Fritsch whether it would be possible to make an appointment to see Professor Sauerbruch. He did a lot of sports—boxing, running, bicycling—and always felt severe pain in his knees, despite a surgery he had had in 1933. "I'll see what I can do," she answered, "he is swamped, but I'll try to slip in an appointment for you." With that, she disappeared down the corridors of the ministry.

Ferdinand Sauerbruch was a great doctor. The surgical procedures that he invented were recognized around the world. In particular, he had conceived a revolutionary method for opening a patient's rib cage without provoking a collapse of the lungs (the patient's torso was placed in a low-pressure chamber, while his head remained in the open air). He had also created an artificial hand that could be moved at will.

Independently of his enormous talent, Sauerbruch was to the medicine of the Third Reich what Gustav Gründgens (the man on whom Klaus Mann modeled his character Mephisto) was to the theater of the time. Like him, he probably would have emigrated and would have become a fiery antifascist "if only he had been given attractive offers abroad," according to Klaus Mann. Instead, the professor had chosen to pursue his career in Germany as though nothing had changed. At the age of sixty-five in 1940, the "Professor Doktor" was a prince of medicine, covered with honors, not lacking in self-importance or even vanity. He was head of the largest hospital in Berlin, the Charité. He sometimes exercised his art like a chess champion, carrying on several operations at the same time in different operating theaters. He taught in amphitheaters filled with students and admirers of both sexes. He was asked for his opinions throughout Europe, and he counted several crowned heads among his patients.

Sauerbruch had never taken care of Hitler, but the dying Marshal Hindenburg had called on him for his prostate, Goebbels for his appendicitis, and Robert Ley—head of the "Labor Front," which replaced the dissolved unions—his hemorrhoids. Sauerbruch had contacts high up in the Reich chancellery. One of the doctors closest to the führer, SS-Obersturmbannführer Karl Brandt (in charge of the euthanasia program for the mentally handicapped), was one of his former pupils. In charge of medical matters for the principal scientific institutions of the Reich, Professor Sauerbruch supported some of the worst medical experiments carried out in the concentration camps.

The Nazis needed to keep on their side major intellectual and artistic talents like Ferdinand Sauerbruch. Not affiliated with the Nazi Party, the surgeon was an emblem of respectability for the regime, which granted him great freedom of speech and action. He was a member of the prestigious "Wednesday Club," an independent intellectual group that continued to hold regular meetings despite the war. It was one of the few forums for discussion where one could still escape from the surveillance of the Gestapo. They didn't engage in politics at the Wednesday Club, although they did not avoid various subjects related to the present time. Among the figures who were members of the club were both the biologist Eugen Fischer, one of the major theorists of eugenics, and General Ludwig Beck, former army chief of staff, who had resigned in August 1938 to protest against Hitler's planned invasion of Czechoslovakia.

Fritz Kolbe did not yet know, when he met Sauerbruch for the first time, how useful he would find the Charité hospital and the protected status of the surgeon.

4

IN THE WOLF'S LAIR

Between Berlin and East Prussia, September 18, 1941

In the train taking him to Hitler's headquarters in East Prussia, Fritz Kolbe read the newspapers and glanced through a few dispatches that he had to hand over the next day to the führer's diplomatic staff. Since his departure from the Berlin-Grunewald station, he had been alone in his compartment. The car was reserved for officers and government officials headed for the front or on missions to the reserve lines. Since the beginning of the Russian campaign in June 1941, the führer's headquarters had been in the "wolf's lair" (*Wolfsschanze*) at the eastern edge of the country. Fritz was carrying a large quantity of documents, most of which were classified "secret Reich business" (*geheime Reichssachen*, the highest level of confidentiality for the Nazis). Under no circumstances was he to be separated from the briefcase containing them. The documents were intended for his superior, Ambassador Karl Ritter, one of the highest officials in the Foreign Ministry, who was in consultation with military headquarters.

Born in Bavaria and trained as a lawyer, Karl Ritter had been the undisputed specialist for economic questions in the Foreign Ministry since the 1930s. Since the beginning of the war he had headed a key department in the ministry, political-military affairs (Pol I M). He had a typical title for the time: he was an "ambassador on special mission," which meant that he was there to bypass on an ad hoc basis the traditional decision-making networks of the ministry. Although he was a career diplomat, he enjoyed Ribbentrop's complete confidence. Ritter dealt in particular with the "economic aspects of the war," as well as high-level relations between the Foreign Ministry and the Wehrmacht. Since the beginning of the war he was almost always away from the ministry. This skilled professional negotiator was known for his unscrupulous intelligence, cold cynicism, and strength of character, all qualities that made him able to impose himself on Wehrmacht generals, even though he himself had no military experience.

A party member since 1938, but never having been in the SS (nor in the SA, like Luther), Ritter had no illusions about the criminal character of the regime. He had nevertheless chosen to serve the Nazis out of professional conscience, with an attitude of indifference. "Here, at least, you travel," he said one day in Fritz Kolbe's presence. He held Ribbentrop in contempt, although he never showed it openly (on the contrary, he behaved toward him with almost obsequious deference, which caused extreme annoyance to his subordinate Fritz Kolbe). Appointed ambassador to Rio de Janeiro in 1937, he had been expelled in 1938 by the dictator Getulio Vargas, who considered him a dangerous pro-Nazi agitator.

On his return from Rio, Ritter had wanted to resign on the grounds of age—he was slightly under sixty—but Ribbentrop, who needed his talents, had insisted that he remain in the service. Karl Ritter had finally agreed because he had been offered a key post endowed with broad responsibilities. From that moment, he had been at the heart of his country's principal diplomatic negotiations, like the Munich agreements of September 1938, but above all the Nazi-Soviet pact in August 1939. This agreement between Hitler and Stalin, which was unexpected, to say the least, had in part been drafted by him, in close cooperation with Friedrich-Wilhelm Gaus, the ministry's chief lawyer and another Weimar man who had learned to adapt to circumstances.

Like Gaus, Ritter had complete command of the science of treaties. He knew Russia well from his experience supervising major German industrial programs there in the 1920s (following the 1922 Rapallo
agreements). In order to follow through on the Hitler-Stalin pact, and
in particular to monitor the exchange of raw materials and armaments
between the two countries, he had even lived in Moscow between
October 1939 and March 1940. When he spoke of Stalin, with whom
he had been in close contact on several occasions in connection with
that mission, Karl Ritter did not conceal his very great admiration for
the man.

Fritz Kolbe had been Karl Ritter's personal assistant since late 1940
or early 1941. This promotion had been due to the intervention of
Rudolf Leitner, the former head of the German legation in Pretoria,
who had been a member of Karl Ritter's cabinet since his return from
South Africa. Rudolf Leitner had never let Fritz drop, and Fritz was
deeply grateful to him for making it possible for him to leave the "German" department and its stifling atmosphere. But now, he found himself assistant to the chief of political-military affairs in the midst of
the war! "It's really farcical," Fritz had been telling himself since he
assumed his new duties. "I hate the Nazis and I can't manage to get
out of the highest circles of power!"

The work for Karl Ritter was interesting. Instead of stamping passports and visas, every morning Fritz Kolbe received dispatches from
German diplomatic posts abroad, sorted them according to their importance, and summarized them for his boss. Kolbe was to destroy the
documents already read by Ritter. Summaries of conversations between high officials of the ministry with foreign diplomats posted to
Berlin also came across his desk. Finally, Fritz received and read the
foreign press (with a few days' delay, because the English and American press, for example, came through Lisbon) and summarized its
content for Ritter. "In a short time, I became one of the best informed
officials in the ministry," Fritz wrote a few years later. By early 1941,
Fritz was one of the first to know of the secret preparations for the
Russian campaign: Karl Ritter's role was specifically to prepare the

movement of German troops toward Russia through its allied countries in central Europe (Finland, Hungary, Romania).

In personal terms, Fritz had no complaints: Karl Ritter was not very likable, but he was fair to his subordinates. And he was a man of the world, not at all like the coarse Luther with his brutal manners. Ritter had always been at the heart of German social life and besides, he clearly had panache, with his twinkling eye, his careful language, and his elegant hands (Luther had often had dirty fingernails). Ritter spoke most European languages, he knew most of the big industrialists in the country, he frequented art openings, he went to the opera.

The relationship between Ritter and Fritz Kolbe was essentially professional, and since both men were workhorses, they got on fairly well together. Both were short, a detail not without importance. On a few occasions, their conversation took a personal turn. When Kolbe had joined Karl Ritter's staff, Ritter had let him know that he knew of his reputation as a "hothead." He tried to reassure Fritz by telling him that here, what counted was above all competency and work done well. To set him at ease, he said that the Nazis didn't like him either. "You know I have a reputation as a *democrat* in this house. The authorities know that I drafted almost all the commercial treaties of the Weimar period. I spent all my time in the Reichstag. Since my drafts were passed by the SPD or the Zentrum, that was enough to sabotage my reputation in some eyes."

A little later, Ritter had questioned Fritz Kolbe briefly about his experience in South Africa. "I too know Africa well," he had said. "Some of my studies were at the Colonial Institute in Hamburg, where I learned many fascinating things: tropical hygiene, applied botany, colonial law, and even Swahili. Just before the Great War, I was appointed to a position in the imperial government in Cameroon. The war put an end to that adventure, and I had to return to Berlin."

When Karl Ritter had learned where Fritz's family came from, he had spoken to him spontaneously of the Pomeranians of Brazil, entire families of whom had gone into exile there to escape famine and poverty. Though Brazil might seem unlikely, in fact there were already German colonies in the south of the country, established early in the nineteenth century.

Fritz Kolbe recalled these scraps of conversation as he headed for the führer's headquarters on the night of September 18, 1941. This mission was something new for him. Ritter wanted his mail to be delivered personally. The ambassador had lost confidence in the diplomatic mail services. At the end of August 1941, he had complained about the careless way in which confidential documents were sent to him. "My mail was found in the headquarters kitchen, another time at the telephone switchboard!" he had informed his Berlin office. As a result, he wanted his subordinates to be their own telegraph operators.

Fritz was not overjoyed with this trip. Of course, it gave him an opportunity to leave Berlin, but he had no desire to get closer to Hitler, Ribbentrop, and the top generals of the Wehrmacht. He had been dreaming of exile for months now, but not to the East. He pined for Spain and South Africa (sometimes he thought of Switzerland, which had the virtue of being a neutral country and seemed to have been spared by events). From time to time, he looked out the window of his compartment. The German-Polish plain with its endless birch forests exuded melancholy, despite a splendid sunset shining through the woods. Autumn and the climate of war enveloped the landscape in matchless sadness.

Having nothing else to do, Fritz plunged into reading the newspapers. The press was entirely subject to party propaganda, but the most important facts could be found in it: "The wearing of a yellow star is obligatory for Jews beginning this month of September 1941." News from the front was more difficult to decipher. The triumphant communiqués of the army high command (the OKW, or *Oberkommando der Wehrmacht*) hardly made it possible to get a precise idea of the real situation. "Siege of Leningrad, imminent fall of Kiev": that was about all that could be learned from the day's papers. There was no need to try to find out more, the rest was merely a long lyrical and indigestible outpouring on the theme of the "heroic action of the soldiers of the Wehrmacht" or on the battle of Kiev, "the greatest of all time."

Everyone knew in the fall of 1941 that there could no longer be any question of a quick end to the war. Fritz recalled the rumors heard in Berlin: there were more and more frequent whispers that Hitler had had terrible outbursts of fury. The führer was said to have an increasingly pronounced tendency to lose his composure in the face of the enemy. He had been heard to howl with anger when Rudolf Hess went to England in May 1941, and when Churchill and Roosevelt offered assistance to Stalin in mid-August 1941, making possible for the first time a coordinated war on two fronts. According to an unverifiable rumor, sometimes Hitler would bite anything at hand: his handkerchief, a cushion, and even the curtains!

In the train taking Fritz to the "wolf's lair," the night was very dark: it was traveling through what used to be the Danzig corridor with all lights out, for fear of bombardment or sabotage by the Polish resistance. At break of day, following the instructions he had received, he put on the uniform that he would have to wear at the führer's headquarters, a *feldgrau*-colored uniform provided by the ministry. He had difficulty recognizing himself in the mirror. He hesitated particularly before putting on the headgear: a peaked cap with a double strand of aluminum above the visor and a badge representing an eagle holding a swastika in its claws.

Fritz arrived in the early morning at Gerdauen, a little town that looked like a border post, sixty kilometers southeast of Königsberg. A Foreign Ministry car was waiting to take him directly to Karl Ritter. They went through the countryside of Masuria and the forest of Rastenburg (still more birch woods), with silvered lakes and magnificent glades, but also marshes and peat bogs. "The region is infested with mosquitoes," warned the driver, advising Fritz to cover his hands and neck with Dr. Zinsser's lotion, made in Leipzig, "excellent as a preventive measure."

After the little town of Angerburg, they plunged again into the forest. There was no way of telling where they were, no indication of the "Führerhauptquartier." If the road signs were to be believed, the car was headed toward an enigmatic factory supposedly belonging to a celebrated precision instrument maker (Askania Werke). "Askania?

That's all nonsense. That lets them conceal the real nature of the place," the driver told Fritz in answer to his question about the meaning of these strange signs.

After half an hour had passed, and they had gone through several guard posts at the entry of various "forbidden zones" protected by high fences, barbed wire, and patrols, they could see the first wooden huts and half-buried bunkers. They finally arrived at a clearing where three trains were standing. They could not be seen from a distance because they were thoroughly camouflaged, like the railroad track, with nets covered in fake foliage. And yet they occupied a space as large as a marshaling yard. One of the three trains held the "field offices" of the foreign minister. Next to Ribbentrop's was Göring's—the most beautiful of all, a veritable palace on wheels—and finally Heinrich Himmler's. This had been the first "railroad headquarters" to see the light, and since then all the high officials of the regime had wanted to have, like the Reichsführer SS, their private train (*Sonderzug*) close to the front. The three trains were equipped with everything necessary: private salons, radio room, dining car, toilets, and showers (and even a screening room in Himmler's train). At the ends of the cars were antiaircraft batteries in case of enemy attack.

It was after ten in the morning and the heat was stifling, even in the shade. A smell of tar drifted through the air. Fritz was brought to one of the cars of Ribbentrop's train, where he was asked to wait for a few minutes. Karl Ritter was not yet there. While waiting for his boss in a little compartment that resembled an antechamber, Fritz glanced outside. There were patrols with dogs. Fritz also noticed a small group of officers having a conversation, each with mosquito netting around his head. Fritz held back his laughter.

Soon, an armored car arrived, stirring up the dust. This was Karl Ritter's car. At Ritter's right, Fritz thought he recognized Walther Hewel, a close confidant of the führer. Hewel, a Nazi stalwart from the early days, ensured constant contact between Ribbentrop and Hitler. There were also a stenographer and a few officers of the high command of the Wehrmacht whom Fritz did not know. Everyone was in uniform. Karl Ritter looked even smaller than usual when he was seen next to Walther Hewel, a strong man with a powerful presence. Hewel did not at all correspond to the clichéd image of the Aryan man (he was dark-haired), which had not prevented him from becoming an SS-Brigadeführer, the equivalent of a brigadier general in the elite order of the Nazi regime.

Karl Ritter looked irritated when he came into the train car, soon followed by his colleagues, and sat at a table covered with campaign maps. He had not seen Fritz, who was hidden by a door ajar at the other end of the compartment and who was waiting to be called before showing himself. "Where can the minister be?" Ritter asked in an exasperated tone. "We had an appointment for ten o'clock!" "Mister Ambassador," said Walter Hewel, "the minister usually gets up late, you know that very well. Right now, he is probably being taken care of by his personal barber in his private apartment," he added, with a little ironic smile. Like many others, Walther Hewel detested Ribbentrop. He made no attempt to disguise his disregard for him, since Hewel was one of the few historic companions in arms of Adolf Hitler, and had personally participated at his side in the failed 1923 Munich putsch.

While waiting for Ribbentrop's arrival, Karl Ritter questioned Walther Hewel about the evenings with Hitler in "forbidden zone number one," a few kilometers from there. "It's cold," replied Hewel, "the führer never heats the rooms where he is. No one dares to speak for fear of being ridiculous. When he invites us into his 'tea house' after dinner, he spends the entire evening carrying on long monologues while drinking a brew made of fennel. He is attentive only to his dog Blondi. Sometimes he doesn't seem to realize that there are ten people around him thinking only of going to bed. Last night he spoke for more than an hour about vegetarian cooking and the nausea meat makes him feel. He detests the idea that animals are killed so they can be eaten!" Karl Ritter displayed a sneering attitude and asked if it was allowed "at least to play bridge" (one of his favorite pastimes) at the führer's evenings.

In Adolf Hitler's circle, neither bridge nor any other game was played. The führer preferred long discussions in front of a skimpy fire.

Walther Hewel described how, the night before, the führer had spoken at length of his plans for Russia, and that he had seemed very
optimistic about the conquest of Moscow, "which shouldn't take long
to fall after Kiev." He explained to his audience that once Moscow
and Leningrad had been captured they should simply be wiped off the
map. Russia would be a vast agricultural province and a source of raw
materials from which Germany would take everything it needed.
"When we have conquered the territory," Hewel went on, "the führer
thinks that it will not take much effort to control it. A bit like the
British in India: an administration of 250,000 men should suffice, and
a few divisions to put down possible rebellions." The Russian, Hewel
asserted, had a slave mentality: "The Russian, at bottom, is a kind of
rabbit," he said. "He doesn't have the ability to transform himself into
a 'bee' or an 'ant,' as we Germans can. There is no point in trying to
make the Russian more intelligent than he is." The Russia of tomorrow, Hewel continued, would look like something new: "German
towns, and all around them countryside where Russian peasants will
work. A little further on, there will be large territories for our army
training." There was a proposal to settle on the borders of this "oriental
empire" peoples close to the Germans by blood, such as the Norwe-
gians, Danes, and Swedes, who would protect Germany from the "Asi-
atic hordes." The führer thought that in the future Europe would be
entirely united against America. "Even the English will be with us
once we have conquered the Russian landmass and all its natural
resources!"

    "You really believe all this talk? You think that Moscow is easy to
capture? Believe me, I know Russia, and everything you tell me is very
pretty but not very realistic!" remarked Karl Ritter, who trusted
Walther Hewel enough to tell him frankly what he thought. Hewel,
who respected Ritter, and retained some degree of independent
thinking, had a contemplative air. "But after all, what does it matter?"
Ritter continued. "Right now, let's talk about urgent matters. I would
like to have details about what is to be done with prisoners of war.
We've settled the question of political prisoners, who have to be liq-
uidated. Do you have figures on the number of political commissars in

the Red Army already killed? And where are we in reference to ordinary prisoners?"

Walther Hewel turned to an OKW officer to ask for more information. The officer took from his briefcase a recent circular and read a few passages: "Bolshevism is the mortal enemy of Germany. For the first time German soldiers are facing an enemy trained not only as a soldier but as a political agent in the service of Bolshevism. He has learned to fight against National Socialism with all available means: sabotage, demoralizing propaganda, assassination . . . The Bolshevik soldier has thereby lost the right to be treated as an ordinary combatant according to the provisions of the Geneva Conventions."

"What does that mean exactly?" asked Karl Ritter, whose mission was to translate the führer's orders into carefully chosen terms. "Well," answered the OKW officer, "that means, for example, that a prisoner who shows the slightest inclination to disobey orders should be shot without warning."

In the antechamber of the railroad car, Fritz listened aghast to this incredible dialogue. He knew that horrors had taken place since the beginning of the war in Poland and Russia, but until now he had not known that transgression of the laws of war was coldly encouraged by the highest leaders of the state and the army. The fact that his own boss, Karl Ritter, was associated with this kind of wrongdoing only increased his indignation. He strained his ears to continue to capture the conversation when he heard that an aide de camp had informed Ritter of his presence. "Kolbe is here!" exclaimed Ritter. "But what is he doing here, not saying anything? Send him in right away!" Fritz was led into the room. He made a Hitler salute to everyone and handed Ritter a thick sheaf of documents from his briefcase. Ritter did not have the time to consult these papers right away. He quickly dismissed his assistant and made an appointment with him for the following day after asking briefly about news from his Berlin office.

It was noon. Fritz was taken to an attractive hunting lodge ten kilometers away that was used as a residence for employees of the Foreign Ministry. On the edge of a forest and overlooking a large lake, it had been built for the 1936 Olympics as a residence for competitors

in the ice boat event. The inn provided comfortable conditions unknown in Berlin. There were bouquets of flowers on the tables, fine
wines, and plentiful supplies of liquor and cigarettes. A French chef
selected by the occupation forces in Paris had been installed in the
kitchen ("the food is much better at Ribbentrop's than at Hitler's,"
Fritz told himself that night as he savored a dish of game with berries).
A Volksempfänger radio broadcast through static the latest Wehrmacht
reports and popular songs, such as *Das kann doch einen Seemann nicht
erschüttern*" ("That can't frighten a sailor") and "Lili Marlene."

In the following days, Fritz had a lot of free time. He took advantage
of it to go for long runs around the lake that the windows of his room
looked out on. Ten days at Hitler's headquarters; Fritz had not expected
to stay that long. Busy with countless different tasks, Karl Ritter took
time to write answers to the dispatches brought from Berlin and have
them signed by Ribbentrop (who always signed in green ink).

One of Ritter's missions was to assist the admiralty in choosing
combat zones for submarine warfare. It was also his responsibility to
draft Berlin's official reactions in the event of a "blunder," notably
when a neutral country complained about German aggression. Among
the dispatches that Fritz had brought from Berlin were vigorous protest notes from Washington following attacks without warning by
German U-boats against American ships. On each occasion, President Roosevelt had increased the intensity of expression of his
anger. In a message to Congress in June, he had denounced the sinking of the *Robin Moor* as "an act of piracy." And in a fireside chat on
September 11, referring to the Nazi leaders, he had said: "But when
you see a rattlesnake poised to strike, you do not wait until he has
struck before you crush him," and noted that it was "the time for
prevention of attack."

Walking by the lake, Fritz Kolbe was surprised that he did not feel
comfortable. He should have been enjoying the magnificent country,
but he had only one wish, to leave the "wolf's lair," its poisonous atmosphere, and its mosquitoes. He was finally authorized to return to
Berlin with a satchel full of documents signed by the minister. Time

was short. His return this time was on board a military plane, a Junkers
Ju 52.

Berlin, November 1941

"Do you control / Yourself? Are you the master of yourself? / Do you
stand free amid the world as I do / So you may be the author of your
actions?" (*The Death of Wallenstein*, Act 3, Scene 2).

   Back in Berlin, Fritz had plunged into Schiller and was meditating
on these words of Wallenstein. Since his trip to the "wolf's lair" and
the astounding conversation that he had overheard between Karl
Ritter and Walther Hewel, he had decided to leave Germany. He saw
no other way to remain true to himself. He could no longer defend his
country now that he knew it was guilty of such injustices and unspeak-
able abominations. What had happened since late 1939 exceeded in
horror everything that had been seen between 1914 and 1918. Fritz
was beginning to understand that the "war of extermination" conducted by the Nazis was leading to an apocalypse. Whatever the outcome—victory or defeat of Germany—nothing allowed the slightest
hope for the future: either Germany won the war and multiplied its
criminal power, or it lost and found itself outcast from the civilized
world.

   On returning from his stay at Hitler's headquarters, Fritz had heard
of the activities of "mobile task forces" of the secret police headed by
Reinhard Heydrich (the Einsatzgruppen) in the rear of the Russian
front. The mission of the Einsatzgruppen was to massacre Jews, on
the pretext of "forestalling the risk of spreading epidemics behind the
front lines." The foreign ministry had received very precise reports
stating that men, women, and even children had indiscriminately been
machine-gunned, had their throats cut, been burned alive, or sometimes murdered with blows of a pickax or a hammer.

   Fritz was beginning to think that if he continued to rub shoulders
with evil he would end up being its accomplice. He had had enough

of behaving like the good soldier Svejk. Playing the stupid and narrow-minded petty official led to nothing, except protecting himself. He sometimes saw himself in dreams in a foreign uniform, bearing arms, fighting against the men of the Wehrmacht. He immediately reproached himself for denying his own people. After all, German soldiers had not wanted, for the most part, to be involved in this kind of criminal adventure. The only ones who deserved to be eliminated were the leaders of the country. These questions tormented him. In that fall of 1941, it was not uncommon for him to wake up in the middle of the night with violent cramps in his stomach. In addition to the multiple pains he suffered from his constant excessive exercise, Fritz was beginning to hurt everywhere.

By chance, since he had met Professor Sauerbruch's assistant in the spring of 1940, Fritz had easy access to the Charité hospital. At the request of Maria Fritsch, the famous surgeon had agreed to treat Fritz's knees and had prescribed a thermal cure at Bad Brambach in southern Saxony, where he had spent three weeks at the end of the summer of 1940.

Fritz gradually developed the habit of going to the hospital once or twice a week for no medical reason. Located not far from the Foreign Ministry, the hospital was a veritable enclave in the city, with fifteen red brick buildings with neo-Gothic façades. There were even hothouses for the cultivation and wintering of plants and trees. Fritz went to see Maria on leaving his office and spent a good bit of time chatting with her at the hospital. One evening, he even played her an old song from the *Wandervogel*, accompanying himself on a guitar that happened to be sitting in a corner of the room. He sang well, with a warm voice, and the words of the song were a declaration of love. "Come, let's go into the fields, the cuckoo is calling us from the pine forest / Young girl, let yourself go in the dance." Maria had been unable to conceal her emotion.

From that moment on, the two were inseparable. They met in the restaurants of Charlottenburg, then went to the cinema. Fritz felt all the more comfortable at the Charité because he had the feeling of being protected from prying eyes. At the Foreign Ministry, he knew that he was under surveillance and had to be constantly careful not to say one wrong word. This wasn't true at the hospital, which was like an island protected from the outside world, even though it was in the heart of the capital of the Reich. The Gestapo did not penetrate there, and Fritz did not feel he was being spied on. On the contrary, he was the one in an observation post, trying to identify the figures who came to see Professor Sauerbruch. And there were many of them. You might encounter the surgeon in the company of a doctor in an SS uniform, and then the next day with a man who was under heavy surveillance by the regime.

Fritz's frequent comings and goings to see Maria Fritsch did not long go unnoticed by Sauerbruch. After hearing his assistant laugh during the evenings she spent with Fritz, the surgeon asked Maria to introduce her friend to him formally. The two men hit it off well. In this wartime period, lively minds like Fritz's were welcome. He had a gift for diverting his audience by telling anecdotes from behind the scenes in the ministry or reporting the latest comical details about Ribbentrop's life. And Sauerbruch adored gossip. He picked it up everywhere and spiced it up in his style in order to shine in Berlin salons. He liked Fritz a good deal and invited him home several times.

One evening at the surgeon's house toward the end of November 1941, Fritz noticed a clergyman dressed in black, noticeable by his wrinkled suit, his thick glasses, and his slightly dirty white collar. The unknown man had drawn his attention from the very beginning of the evening. He and Ferdinand Sauerbruch had carried on an apparently interesting conversation in low tones. Fritz had been unable to catch the slightest scrap of it, but he had immediately seen that the churchman was an enemy of the regime. Those things could soon be felt. It took only a glance or a way of pitching one's voice to be identified. Fritz wanted to know more about this figure. He learned that this was the prelate Georg Schreiber, former Reichstag deputy under the Zentrum label, the pre-1933 Catholic party. A theologian, university professor, and also a political man, Schreiber had been a very influential figure during the Weimar Republic. In his special fields of political action (church questions, culture, education, foreign policy, and science), he was an unquestioned authority. Since the Nazis had come to power they had subjected him to constant affronts. Research institutes and other learned societies over which he had presided had been forced to close down. For the leaders of the Third Reich, Georg Schreiber was the embodiment of the despised "old system."

Schreiber had been protected by Sauerbruch on more than one occasion. The two men were personally very close. The prelate often came to rest at the Charité where he was treated for "abdominal troubles." Fritz Kolbe was curious to meet a man of the cloth who had not compromised with the regime (it hardly mattered that he was a Catholic). He introduced himself.

After exchanging a few banalities about life behind the scenes in the Foreign Ministry and current sports (two areas in which Schreiber was well versed), Fritz dared to bring up politics. "What did you think," he asked, "of Clemens von Galen's recent speech against the elimination of the mentally handicapped? Why aren't there more men of the church like him who dare to denounce the crimes of the Nazis?" Schreiber, after making certain that no one was listening to their conversation, expressed his full support of the bishop of Münster. He revealed to Fritz that Professor Sauerbruch had information that the Nazis had already eliminated seventy thousand of the mentally handicapped since 1939 (including many children), and that they intended to kill "old people, the tubercular, the war wounded, and others unworthy to live (*lebensunswerte Menschen*), as they say."

This revelation startled Fritz. Now sensing that he could trust his interlocutor, he dared to ask the prelate to help him resolve his problems of conscience: "How can I continue to serve this regime? I want to leave the country, but that is not possible. If I stay, am I morally tainted by my status as an official? After all, I took an oath in the name of the führer, like all the others . . ." Georg Schreiber looked very serious and took him aside to answer him. The conversation lasted for more than an hour. No one knows exactly what Schreiber said that evening. In any event, Fritz retained the following message: "Do not leave Germany! Fight against the Nazis with the resources that you have. If you are in this post, this is because God willed it for one reason or another."

Berlin, 1942

Germany could only be reborn—from the Nazis' ashes. Fritz had known that since 1933. But for the regime to fall, Germany would have to lose the war. It took Fritz time to recognize that it was not shameful to be a "defeatist," that a quick surrender was in fact in Germany's best interests, but it took root in Fritz like a painfully obvious fact between late 1941 and early 1942. Not all his friends, far from it, could follow him into this way of seeing things. He himself sometimes began to doubt. Throughout all of 1942, he felt more alone and isolated than ever.

"You must opt for a party in the war . . . I have / No choice. I must use force or else endure it," Fritz repeated to himself as he read *The Death of Wallenstein* (Act 2, Scene 1). He made the following argument: One could not wish for a Nazi victory. In addition, the defeat of Germany was foreseeable once the United States had entered the war against Germany in December 1941 and Japan on its side took no steps to attack Russia and establish a second front in the Far East. Finally, the longer it took Germany to lay down arms, the weaker it would be at the end of the conflict. This situation of weakness would risk throwing it into the arms of the Communists.

Since the early 1930s, Fritz had been almost as vehemently opposed to the Communists as to the Nazis. To be sure, he had for a time been attracted by the revolutionary language that cut through the perpetual compromises of the Social Democrats. After October 1917, he had not been impervious to the "great light in the East." He had a few happy memories from that period of his life. For example, he still liked to sing, when he was in good company, songs of the radical left, full of mockery for the Social Democratic moderates: the "*Revoluzzer*" by Erich Mühsam was one of his favorite songs. But the dictatorial practices of the KPD had quickly snuffed any temptations in that direction. The possibility of the USSR invading Germany depressed him almost as much as that of Hitler attaining victory.

Even though Schreiber had advised him against engaging in dangerous activities, Fritz continued to write anti-Nazi leaflets throughout 1942. He left letters with "defeatist" content, supposedly written by a "soldier back from the Russian front"—a role with unassailable credibility in Germany at the time—in telephone booths. Fritz contemplated taking even bolder steps. He and two of his friends came up with the idea of blowing up a railroad bridge at Werder am Havel, a small town about thirty kilometers southwest of Berlin. But the plan, for unknown reasons, was never carried out.

This excited state, although dangerous, was pathetic and a little naïve. With the position he occupied and the information at his disposal, Fritz had long known that he could do much better: provide information to the enemies of his country. From his time as a *Wandervogel*, he knew that espionage was very much an act of war, and that he would "have to be very clever at passing news secretly from one place to another," as Baden-Powell put it. He had been one of the boldest speaking out against the Nazis among the chatterers at the Café Kottler, and he had never lacked courage in writing anonymous propaganda against the regime, but this was something entirely different. *Sharing intelligence with the enemy:* these terrifying words frequently echoed in his mind, although he was unable to tell whether it was simple common sense or lunatic recklessness that had put such ideas into his head.

For some time Fritz had already been acting on the edge of "high treason" (*Hochverrat*), by counterfeiting passports in South Africa and by distributing anonymous messages. These were very great risks. But in the event he were to provide information of a strategic nature to the Allies, he would be guilty of genuine "treason to his country" (*Landesverrat*), which meant not only a death sentence but also dishonor in the eyes of generations to come.

On every occasion, it was the words of the prelate Schreiber that enabled him to orient his compass: "Do not leave Germany! Fight against the Nazis with the resources that you have." On one occasion, he attempted to establish contact with an American diplomat posted in Berlin whose name had been given to him by a friend. But with the American entry into the war in December 1941, the United States embassy closed its doors and the American diplomatic corps left the capital of the Reich. On two or three occasions in 1941 and 1942, Fritz tried to secure a mission as diplomatic courier in order to go to Switzerland. He explained first that he wanted to take a well-deserved leave, then he claimed that he had to go to Switzerland to settle the formalities of his divorce, since his second wife—who had remained in Africa and from whom he was de facto separated—was from Zurich. This was only a pretext: Once in Bern, he would have tried to speak to his old friend Ernst Kocherthaler, who knew many people and who would no doubt have been able to help him contact the Allies. It was a wasted effort: every time, the request was refused without explanation, and in fact, Fritz learned that his refusal to join the party was the real reason for the rejection. He did not insist, for fear of awakening suspicion, but, weary of the battle, he was once again tempted to flee the country. Fritz was torn between his desire for exile, his will to resist, and his new passion for Maria.

What he did not know was that at the same time some Nazi leaders themselves were discreetly beginning to doubt Germany's victory. Of course, German offensives on the Russian front continued to be victorious. The Wehrmacht had reached the Volga, in the heart of the Caucasus, and was approaching the oil wells of Baku. In North Africa, Rommel's troops marched into Egypt and were preparing to advance toward the Suez Canal. In the Atlantic, Allied convoys were suffering heavy losses because of German submarines. But the most perceptive minds did not allow themselves to be blinded by these events and made longer-term calculations. Well-informed Germans (of whom Karl Ritter was one) knew that the economic and military potential of the United States was at least comparable to that of the Axis powers. They knew that there was a tendency to overestimate the power of Japan and to underestimate American power. The proliferation of fronts was making a German victory increasingly problematic. And since Hitler had had to give up his plan of taking Moscow before the winter of

1941–42, it was clear that Russia would not fall "like a house of cards." The likelihood of a long war was now in everyone's mind. The theater of operations was beginning to shift dangerously toward Germany itself, with the increase of bombing by the Royal Air Force of major German cities (Cologne had been very severely damaged in May 1942). Paradoxically, lucidity was greatest in Heinrich Himmler's circle. The regime's principal killers were the first to sense the wind shifting, toward the middle of 1942.

Unlike the SS leaders, Kolbe wanted to see the Nazi regime disappear and not merely limit the damage of a foreseeable defeat. Kolbe wished for the total defeat of his own country. Once this had been accomplished, it would be possible to sweep away the past and contribute to the birth of a new, more just, and more democratic Germany. As for the means of getting there, he merely dreamed of them. He had contacts with none of the small German opposition groups. He had not yet heard of Goerdeler or of the Kreisau Circle. He had no concrete plan. In the spring of 1942, he wanted to leave Karl Ritter's staff and find a post abroad, but he was made to understand that there was no point in trying.

He continued to perform his duties conscientiously. After his first visit to the führer's headquarters in East Prussia, Fritz returned there several times in the course of 1942. The mission became routine: He had to transmit to Karl Ritter the documents that Ritter did not want to entrust to the official mail services. Fritz went to the "wolf's lair" between late January and early February, in early April, and shortly before Christmas.

Every time, Fritz took the train at the Grunewald station. One day in the spring of 1942, looking out the window of his special compartment, he saw a train into which the police were forcing dozens of Jewish families (recognizable from their yellow stars). In October 1941, the government began deporting the Jews of Berlin to the East. At the time, the Reichsbahn was not yet using freight cars for deportations; this was a perfectly ordinary passenger train. No one knew where exactly they were going—nor did Fritz Kolbe, but he knew that the passengers in that train would not be coming back to Germany.

5

Decisive Encounters

Berlin, February 1943

In early 1943, Fritz Kolbe awaited a call from destiny. He did not know what to do and yet he wanted to take action. He sensed a reason for existing. He was no longer satisfied with "peddling his principles without taking the trouble to, or even dreaming of, put them into practice.... Great things are not done only on impulse, and they are a sequence of little things combined into a whole."

Others than he had for a long time been attempting the impossible. Resistance networks had been set up. Kolbe had no precise knowledge of the existence of these little groups, even though he was vaguely aware of the fact that "actions" were being plotted here and there. Allied bombs were now threatening all of Germany. The reign of violent death had been decreed everywhere. Sirens were now heard night and day in Berlin. At the Foreign Ministry, their sinister wail was blended, oddly, with the sound of a large gong that was used during every air raid (after the war, Fritz would not be able to hear the sound of a gong without shivering in fear).

During this time, far from the bombs, another war was going on, much less noisy, much more discreet, and yet decisive: the intelligence war. Fritz was waiting only for the opportunity to join it. He imagined it in a rather fuzzy way, not knowing what the "great game" looked like. What he knew boiled down to two or three simple ideas: neutral countries (like Switzerland, but also Sweden, Ireland, Portugal, and Turkey) were, as between 1914 and 1918, hotbeds of espionage. If you had good information in wartime, you had more power than an ambassador. Whether you were a banker, an industrialist, or even an obscure nonentity, you had every likelihood of influencing the course of events.

The time was, less than ever, one for hesitation. Fritz Kolbe felt in the air a call for the impossible and the incredible. Eager to act, he felt prepared to commit unprecedented deeds. "Treason? So be it," he said to himself after a point that cannot be precisely located (probably late 1942 or early 1943). Fritz described this personal transformation in a document written just after the war: "I had reflected inwardly on this question (treason or *Verrat*) and I had ended by overcoming it. Hitler had come to power through force and deception and had plunged Germany and the entire world into war. From my point of view, no one was obligated to loyalty and obedience to the Hitler regime."

From the beginning, Fritz had thought that the only way of acting effectively was through intervention from outside. The Allies had the power necessary to get rid of the regime. This force, he told himself, must be supported by well-placed elements at the heart of the system.

This prospect was beginning to give him the strength to act, because he, the solitary minor official, could now make himself useful, if he was able to make contact abroad, to gather trustworthy friends around him, and above all if he was lucky. From chess, Fritz had learned two lessons: A straight line is not necessarily the shortest path between two spaces, and a pawn used advisedly can sometimes transform a game.

While Allied bombs were raining on Berlin, a strange feeling of serenity took hold of Fritz Kolbe. He was happier and happier, and ever more relaxed, as though he were flourishing because of the inner anger that inhabited him. Taking advantage of the air raids, he spent a good deal of his time chatting with his colleagues, in the corridors of the ministry or in its underground bunker, one of the safest in the city, located under the Adlon Hotel a few steps from Wilhelmstrasse, not far from the Brandenburg Gate. With bombing becoming more frequent, the Adlon had been transformed into a kind of salon that favored encounters. It was one of the only shelters in Berlin where one did not have to fight to get in. No crush or excessive panic; these were civilized people, though of course you had to be careful to avoid indiscreet ears. "The enemy is listening to you" (*Feind hört mit!*) could be read on matchboxes of the time—an expression that had to be taken literally in all circumstances. However, it was easier to exchange confidences there than elsewhere, even if in an undertone.

Berlin, spring 1943

Thanks to his perpetual comings and goings during this time between his office, underground shelters, and the Charité hospital, Fritz Kolbe had some encounters that would soon have a decisive effect on his plans. He met up again with Karl Dumont, formerly posted to Madrid, who was now in charge of relations between the Foreign Ministry and the Wehrmacht's weapons procurement organization. Long-standing friends, Dumont and Kolbe completely trusted each other.

A little later, probably in the spring or summer of 1943, he met Count Alfred von Waldersee at Professor Sauerbruch's. Major Waldersee was almost the same age as Fritz (he was born in 1898). He had been posted to France and then fought in the battle of Stalingrad, from which he had had the good fortune to be evacuated because of a wound. Waldersee had close ties to the aristocratic and military circles that were the most ferociously opposed to Hitler. His friends, Fritz knew, had no hesitation in using the words "assassination attempt," "coup d'état," and even "revolution."

We know almost nothing about this connection, except that Count Waldersee made the first move toward Fritz, with the obvious aim to get firsthand information from the Foreign Ministry. Waldersee seems to have been important for Fritz, and presented him in various documents written after the war as a close friend, even an accomplice. A minor official a friend to an aristocratic officer: war, like sports, breaks down many social barriers.

Since late 1942, Fritz had also been in contact with a surgeon from Alsace, Professor Adolphe Jung, whom he had met at the Charité hospital. Professor Jung was one of Professor Sauerbruch's colleagues. He had had to leave annexed Alsace to serve in the hospitals of the Reich, which were flooded with patients and wounded soldiers and suffering from a severe shortage of qualified personnel. He lived in a small room in the Charité's surgical clinic, just below Maria Fritsch.

Fritz made the first move toward Dr. Jung. His approach was a little provocative. "Do you have courage? Are you daring?" he said at their first meeting (probably in late 1942). Jung said nothing, afraid of falling into a trap. Then Fritz revealed something, as though to test him: "Warn your friends in France. Otto Abetz, the German ambassador to occupied France, wants to arrest Cardinal Gerlier, the archbishop of Lyon." Just in case, Jung decided to transmit the message through his brother, the manager of a large store in Strasbourg, but he was mistrustful. Who is this Fritz Kolbe? he wondered. Jung later wrote:

> Because of my functions and in the milieu to which I was transplanted I was brought into contact with the most notorious anti-Nazi elements, and I had the opportunity in particular to meet K., a fierce enemy of the regime and a secretary in the Foreign Ministry. . . . When I arrived in the capital of the Reich, alone in enemy country, how could I know whom I was dealing with? When an individual uttered threats against the Nazi authorities, how could I know whether he was in good faith or whether he was only an agent provocateur for the Gestapo endeavoring to discover enemies of the regime? I knew nothing about him. He was German, and he had a very visible position in the Foreign Ministry. He told me that he was not a member of the National Socialist party. And yet, I

said to myself, he keeps his official post! Shouldn't I be doubly distrustful? I observed him during the visits he made to an employee of our clinic whose fiancé he claimed to be. He told me that he had lived abroad for a long time, had learned to like and admire the English, the Americans, and the French. He loathed militarism and uniforms. He was sensible, level-headed, and cautious, although bursting with energy. Gradually we came closer together. Suddenly, after a few months, we were decided. We had to help one another, we had to work together.

Fritz was charmed by this elegant Frenchman, who also knew the United States from having studied there. Transferred by force to the interior of the Reich in March 1942, Adolphe Jung had worked first in the Lake Constance region, and then joined Ferdinand Sauerbruch's staff in Berlin. He had arrived in Berlin in October 1942. The appointment was a stroke of luck for him, enabling him to work with a leading doctor. At the Charité hospital, he treated chiefly Professor Sauerbruch's private clientele.

From one air raid to the next, Fritz and Adolphe Jung got to know each other better: "In the shelter where we met during Allied air attacks," Jung wrote after the war, "we usually passed each other by without speaking. If possible we stayed in separate compartments of the shelter. But what joy shined in our eyes when Allied successes saddened the pale faces of the Nazis surrounding us. K. tightened all the muscles of his face, struck his left palm with his right fist, and constantly repeated: 'What are they doing? What are they waiting for? Berlin has to be bombed over and over! We'll die, so what, but let them come!' We were agreed, K. and I, that they had to come. But can I be blamed for confessing that just thinking about it made a chill run down my spine?"

When she heard Fritz use this kind of language, his lover Maria couldn't stand it. "Now keep quiet, keep quiet. Are you mad?" she asked. Turning to Adolphe Jung, she exclaimed, "He's mad, isn't he? He doesn't know what he's saying! He laughs stupidly like that, to

himself, when the sirens wail and warn us of another thousand bombers from the RAF or the U.S. Air Force, what is that all about?" "K.
was not mad," writes Jung, "but very intelligent, very aware of all the
dangers. Perhaps he was sometimes a little too excitable, but that was
his temperament. He was well served by a vigorous imagination which
enabled him to find in a flash the right solution or the right reply in
the most difficult situations. His hatred of Nazism was real. For the
Germans he had only disdain. 'They'll die,' he said, 'they'll get what
they deserve.'"

In the spring of 1943, Fritz met an exceptional woman who was to
be of great help in his plans. A little cold at first sight, slightly older
than Fritz (she was approaching fifty), this woman looked like a rather
austere old maid, which did not keep her from being refined and
elegant. Her name was Gertrud von Heimerdinger, and she had a
decision-making position in the diplomatic mail service (office 138,
Wilhelmstrasse 74–76). She had the power to recommend one diplomat or another for a particular foreign post. Fritz had an intuition that
she shared his opinions. He had a few very precise ulterior motives for
approaching her. He had not given up his plan to go to Switzerland,
and he counted on making her into an ally.

Gertrud von Heimerdinger was the daughter of a Prussian general
who had served under Emperor Wilhelm II. That no doubt explained
her rather austere appearance. But Fritz felt from their first encounter that she was a trustworthy person, cultured, belonging to the aristocratic milieu that detested Nazism because it was coarse, vulgar, and
opposed to the elementary values she had learned at a very early age.
Prussian aristocrats like her were both very conservative on some
points and very liberal on others. They had nationalist convictions that
did not keep them from being instinctively attached to the rule of law.
Fritz was beginning to tell himself that women definitely had more
character than men, in this Germany that had been cut adrift.

In the Adlon shelter, in the canteen, or in the corridors of the ministry, Fritz arranged to cross paths with Gertrud von Heimerdinger,
and each time he said a few words to her, nothing more. The conver-

sation did not go much beyond an exchange about the weather and similar banalities. One evening when he met her in the subway, he made a little friendly sign. The charm offensive finally had the desired effect: After a few months, there was a tacit confidence between them. Fritz very soon understood that Gertrud was well disposed toward him. There was nothing political in this.

During one of their encounters in the spring of 1943, Gertrud von Heimerdinger promised to help Fritz Kolbe secure a mission to Switzerland as soon as possible. As he had done regularly since 1940, Fritz repeated that he had to go there to settle the formalities of his divorce. His second wife, Lita Schoop, was of Swiss nationality, and his marriage had taken place in Zurich. "If I manage to get you out, you can take care of your personal affairs, and then you will escape from the bombing, at least for a few days," Gertrud told Fritz. It seemed that she had decided to take him under her protection.

From that day on, Fritz could not stay still. Although his duty was to destroy the diplomatic cables that his boss had read, he began to collect conscientiously the most interesting among them. He put them in his safe, in order to make use of them as soon as the opportunity might arise.

Berlin, summer 1943

The war had reached a turning point, and the Wehrmacht was retreating on all fronts. In North Africa, German ambitions had just ended with the fall of Tunis (May 8, 1943). There was talk of "Tunisgrad" to point to the magnitude of the defeat. The Italian ally was starting to vacillate. The Allies were now not very far from the coast of Sicily. Mussolini had little time left. In the East, the prospects were hardly better. The Reich was shifting to the defensive. The period that was beginning was full of danger and disillusionment. People sensed the coming debacle, which would soon take the form of "a long retreat punctuated with halts and recoveries, wild counterattacks as before

Kursk and Orel in July 1943, where, in the largest tank battle of the entire war, the Wehrmacht showed its teeth for one of the last times."

During these decisive months, in Berlin, like everyone else, Fritz expected the worst. For the last little while he had been living in a little apartment at Kurfürstendamm 155, in a building also housing writers, an actor, and a business owner. Until then, between 1940 and 1943, he had lived with friends like a stowaway: first near the Tiergarten, then near Adolf Hitler Platz, north of Charlottenburg, finally near Tempelhof airport. Since meeting Maria, he had wanted to settle somewhere for good. He had found a few rooms in a large apartment to sublet.

There was no point in looking for his name on the door or his telephone number in the Berlin directory. Fritz remained a secretive person and gave his address only to very rare close friends. He lived on the second floor. The bell in the lobby was labeled Herr von Jaroschevitsch and Herr von Rohde (a colleague from the Foreign Ministry). The telephone number was 976.981. This was the first time since his return from South Africa that he had had the heart to set up a space for himself, furnished with sobriety but elegance. Despite the black paper stuck on the windows to block the light, the place was welcoming and warm. But as he saw a new personal life taking shape, around him the world was collapsing.

On his way to the office, almost every morning he met homeless people, entire families who had left burning houses in the middle of the night. Most often, these people had been able to take nothing with them, except sometimes a pillow or a blanket. Fritz also encountered crews of foreign workers who had been assigned to clear away the ruins. "We are stoic in the ordeal, no hysteria and no panic. The more we are attacked, the stronger we are," said the weekly *Das Reich* on July 2, 1943. But at the end of the month, from July 24 to 30, the terrible bombing of Hamburg caused thirty thousand deaths and was a devastating blow to the morale of the German population.

The regime sank into a megalomaniacal and repressive autism with no end in sight. Informers were everywhere. In December 1942 children were taken from their parents' care because they refused to make the Hitler salute at school. Prisons and camps were filling up. There was a risk at any moment and on the slightest pretext of being "taken away."

One evening, in fact, strangers knocked brutally on Fritz's door. "Open up!" they said harshly. Fritz had no choice. He already saw himself in the cellars of the Gestapo. In fact, it was only two minor local officials in charge of antiaircraft defense who ordered him to darken his windows more thoroughly, nothing more serious. Nevertheless, daily life had become a perpetual nightmare. The sinister shadow of Plötzensee prison hovered over the city. In this fortress near the great industrial warehouses of Berlin, extra butchers' hooks had been installed in December 1942 to be able to hang several people at once without wasting time.

6

ALLEN DULLES

Bern, spring 1943

The quiet city of Bern, capital of the Swiss Confederation, seemed barely touched by the events in Europe and the rest of the world, but it was impossible to guess from mere appearances how the city was swarming with activity. Fake diplomats were putting together embryonic counteralliances, and professional spies of all nationalities and all political persuasions had set up their headquarters there. Bern was the privileged place for thwarting the enemy's stratagems, trying to foresee the ends and the means of the opposing camp, and exchanging false rumors for true secrets.

Switzerland was not only a nest of spies, but also, thanks to its status as a neutral country in the heart of Europe and at the gates of the Reich, the best extraterritorial platform that could be imagined. This had been even truer since November 1942. With the occupation of the southern zone by the Germans, France had been closed off to the Allies. Switzerland had become the only base for observation in the heart of Europe, planted like a triangle between Nazi Germany, Fascist Italy, and occupied France.

A mysterious figure had been living since November 1942 in a handsome old house in Bern, located not far from the cathedral, at Herrengasse 23. He could often be seen walking rapidly, the pockets of his coat full of hastily folded newspapers, between the railroad station and his downtown house. He liked the neighborhood, with its medieval fountains with multicolored sculptures, its sidewalks beneath arcades, and its ancient paving stones. From the windows of his large apartment on the ground floor of a building that had four stories, he had a magnificent view of the mountains of the Bern Oberland.

In the morning, to get to his office on Dufourstrasse, in the embassy district, he crossed the Kirchenfeld bridge over the Aare (a metal bridge forty meters above the river). At noon, he had lunch at the Theater Café, where the waiters seemed to know him very well. He could very often be seen at the Hôtel Bellevue, where foreign diplomats met Swiss politicians for dinner. Most of the time he went on foot. But sometimes he could be seen in the back seat of a Citroën driven by a personal chauffeur, and smoking a pipe. He was a tall man, with a mustache, who wore glasses with rather thick lenses that made him look like a college professor. He dressed in corduroy, flannel, or tweed. He usually wore a bow tie. Elegant without being stiff, he had a habit of wearing his hat toward the back of his head, which gave him an air of studied negligence. Some people thought he was English. In fact, he was an American.

Allen Welsh Dulles was officially the special assistant for legal affairs of the U.S. ambassador to Switzerland. The son of a Presbyterian minister, a member of the East Coast establishment, this 1914 Princeton graduate knew Europe remarkably well. In 1917 and 1918 he already was an attaché at the American embassy in Bern charged with gathering intelligence about Germany, Austria-Hungary, and the Balkans. He then spent a few months behind the scenes at Versailles during the treaty negotiations, with other young diplomats who had recently graduated (most of them from Princeton), whom President Wilson liked to have around him. Dulles felt all the more at ease in these surroundings because Robert Lansing, the secretary of state, was his uncle, and because his grandfather, General John W. Foster, had held that post a few decades earlier. During the negotiations, and in the years following the restoration of peace, the young Allen W. Dulles had traveled extensively through France and Germany devastated by the war. He was convinced that a solid alliance between the United States and Germany would make it possible to create a solid rampart against the spread of Bolshevism.

Although he had given up a diplomatic career to become a Wall Street lawyer, Allen Dulles had continued to be of service to the State Department. In 1933, in the course of a diplomatic mission to Germany, he had met Hitler in person. Although he felt nothing but disgust for the Nazis, Dulles was a friend to Germany.

In November 1942, Dulles was back in Bern. At the last moment, he had crossed through France from Spain, just when the German troops were seizing the southern zone. He had been able to reach Switzerland only through the providential assistance of a not overly scrupulous French customs agent who had not informed the Gestapo of his passage. Once there, Dulles had not attempted in the slightest to conceal his arrival or especially hidden the nature of his work. In the Swiss press, an article presented him as the "personal representative of President Roosevelt," charged with a "special duty." From then on everyone knew that Mr. Dulles was a key figure in American espionage in continental Europe. In fact, he had been appointed by the Office of Strategic Services, the American intelligence organization that had just been established by President Roosevelt in June. Oddly, the publicity around his name did not trouble him in the least, whereas it irritated some of his English counterparts, who were a little suspicious of this "dilettante" intruding on their preserve.

Dulles's notoriety and his natural charm, but also the rather substantial financial resources he had at his disposal, meant that large numbers of people came to see him. Everyone who had information to offer (or to sell) came to knock at his door. Every night, after curfew, shadows slipped furtively beneath the arcades leading to his house, and left through the back garden, which sloped steeply toward the River Aare, hidden from prying eyes. Among these night visitors were double agents, manipulators, charlatans. Over a drink, Dulles listened to them more or less attentively. He usually put people at ease by seating them before a fire, and let them talk while he stirred the embers and smoked his pipe. "The Swiss knew very well that their country was the scene of all manner of intrigues; agents of the secret service, spies, revolutionaries and agitators infested the hotels of the principal towns": this description of the country in 1914 by Somerset Maugham in *Ashenden* applied to Bern in 1943. Dulles had enough confidence in his own instincts to be able to sort out the true from the false.

His mission was to gather all the intelligence possible about occupied Europe, particularly about Germany, but also relating to France, Italy, and other countries allied to the Reich. Among other things, he had been asked to "establish and maintain contacts with underground anti-Nazi movements in Germany." Dulles personally would have liked to provide active assistance to those movements, but he could not because of a lack of political support in Washington.

The British were of course his privileged interlocutors, even though some old intelligence veterans complained about his casual manner. He was considered an eccentric, but they recognized his talent. The French agents of the Deuxième Bureau in Bern were all prepared to work for him since the Vichy regime, in November 1942, had lost its last illusions about its sovereignty. The French agreed to be financed by the OSS in Bern, which helped them send intelligence to the authorities of Free France, now based in Algiers. Within a very short time, Dulles thus had an excellent observation network at his disposal in occupied France. The Poles also offered him their services: Dulles soon made the acquaintance of Halina Szymanska, the widow of a Polish officer based in Bern, who was the mistress of Admiral Canaris, chief of military intelligence (Abwehr). Not infrequently, when Admiral Canaris wanted to "let slip" a piece of intelligence intended for the Allies, he confided a secret to Mme. Szymanska (for example, in June 1941, Hitler's imminent invasion of Russia). Several diplomats from Axis countries stationed in Bern, wishing to establish relations with the Allies, also became preferred sources. Baron Bakach-Bessenyey, the Hungarian envoy, was notably among them.

Things were more difficult with the Swiss. The authorities in Bern were intent on maintaining equal distance from all the countries involved in the conflict. But the reality was entirely different: the majority of the population sympathized with the Allies. Dulles soon had his own network of trusted men inside the Swiss intelligence service, led by Lieutenant-Colonel Roger Masson.

At all times, one had to be wary of the Germans. Among the countless networks of informers present in the country, those working for Germany were particularly effective and well established on the ground thanks to the existence of a large German community. German newspapers had numerous correspondents in Bern. And there were Swiss Germanophile circles, particularly in the army. For years, this small world had been receiving active support from the German legation. In addition, the German consulates in Switzerland were more often than not headed by men from the Abwehr or the SD (Sicherheitsdienst, foreign intelligence services).

Hitler had given up the idea of invading Switzerland in 1940. He needed a solid economic and financial conduit bordering Germany, and Switzerland provided Germany, in exchange for gold, the currency it needed to procure raw materials indispensable for the war. Nevertheless, Hitler judged that, sooner or later, Switzerland would become a part of the "Greater Reich." Rumors of a plan of attack constantly came to the ears of the authorities in Bern. The threat grew as the new strategic context became clear in late 1942 and early 1943, marked by the advance of Allied forces in North Africa and the weakening of Italy. Was Germany not going to "swallow" Switzerland in order to strengthen its southern flank? Living with the perpetual threat of invasion, the authorities of the Swiss Confederation were in a state of maximum alert. From time to time they expelled one foreign diplomat or another when his activities seemed to exceed the terms of his mission. All citizens of countries involved in the conflict were subject to strict surveillance. The Allied intelligence services were more tolerated than their German counterparts, but neutrality was not to be trifled with in light of the knowledge that Berlin needed only a pretext to invade Switzerland. The entire country lived in fear of a fifth column.

Allen Dulles thus found that his work was naturally handicapped. Nevertheless, his address book was filled every day with new names, and his scanty knowledge of German did not prevent him from communicating with all kinds of people: anti-Nazi exiles from all milieus (political, cultural, union), diplomats and intelligence agents of all nationalities—including Chinese—lawyers, bankers, industrialists, publishers, journalists, churchmen, and even German bargemen authorized to travel on the Rhine between Germany and Switzerland. He met fairly frequently with Carl Gustav Jung in Zurich, who presented his analysis of the psychology of the Nazi leaders and of the "collective unconscious" of the Germans.

Allen Dulles had very good informants in Geneva. One of his most interesting contacts was the Dutchman Willem A. Visser't Hooft, general secretary of the Ecumenical Council of Churches. He was also well acquainted with William Rappard, former rector of the University of Geneva, who had also represented Switzerland at the League of Nations. Through one or another of his friends, he entered into contact with Adam von Trott zu Solz in January 1943. This young and brilliant German diplomat, an eminent member of the Kreisau Circle, wished to obtain American aid for the underground opposition movements in Germany. "Support us or we will be tempted to turn to the Soviets," was the substance of his message in a conversation on Swiss territory with one of Dulles's close collaborators. Allen Dulles had instructions to promise nothing to anyone, especially since the policy defined by Churchill and Roosevelt was the "unconditional surrender" of Germany (a formulation that Dulles personally considered a "catastrophe" because it stifled any impulse toward resistance in Germany). The German diplomat thus left empty-handed.

At about the same time (mid-January 1943), Dulles was visited by Prince Maximilien Egon Hohenlohe von Langenberg, one of his old acquaintances from the time of the First World War. Prince Hohenlohe was a German aristocrat with roots in Sudetenland, who divided his time among Germany, Spain, and Mexico—where his wife, a Spanish marquise, owned large estates. He himself had a passport from Liechtenstein, a neutral country like Switzerland, which enabled him to travel almost everywhere in the world. He was in contact with very high officials throughout Europe (the Aga Khan was among his friends), but especially in Berlin, and notably with Heinrich Himmler. "Help the SS; they are the only ones who can protect Germany against communism and maintain order in the country," Hohenlohe had told Dulles. The prince encouraged a simple solution: elimination of Hitler, a seizure of power by the SS, a separate peace with the West, and a united front of Western democracies against the Russians. No one knows precisely what Dulles answered, but it seems that the American spymaster left all doors open in order to maintain contact for the future.

It was not easy for Dulles to communicate with Washington, particularly with complete security. Since the end of the unoccupied zone in France, Switzerland had literally been cut off from the rest of the world. Diplomatic mail was suspended. All connections with the outside had to be by telegraph or telephone. Telephones were of course tapped, and nothing confidential could be said over that channel. For telegraphy, a very secure system of encryption had to be used because the only lines available were those of the Swiss postal and telecommunications service. As a result, this work required two full-time employees out of the small OSS Bern crew, which numbered only about fifteen. Dulles and his colleagues were not exceedingly cautious. As a method of encryption, they used simple transpositions of letters, a technique as old as the hills that consisted of changing the order of letters by constructing more or less sophisticated anagrams.

In the spring of 1943, Allen Dulles learned that the Germans had succeeded in deciphering a series of dispatches that he had sent from Bern to Washington. That day, he had used—for convenience—the coding system of the State Department, normally used by the American legation in Bern. This method was even less secure than that of the OSS. This technical failure might have been very costly to the Americans if the leak had concerned sensitive information.

From that day onward, Dulles was encouraged to strengthen the security of his communications. He multiplied encryption keys by using systems with double or triple transpositions. This did not save his system from remaining rather rudimentary in comparison to the complexity of the German Enigma code.

The man who had informed Dulles of the leak was a German. Six feet five inches tall, myopic (the lenses of his glasses were as thick as bottles), his appearance was not very prepossessing. "He looks like a Latin teacher," thought Dulles when he met him for the first time during the first few weeks of 1943. This was Hans-Bernd Gisevius, vice-consul of the Reich in Zurich, but above all member of the Abwehr, the military intelligence service. After carrying out a long and very meticulous investigation of this obscure figure, Dulles had agreed to enter into contact with him.

Gisevius had long been a friend of Hjalmar Schacht, former economics minister of the Reich. He was also close to Admiral Canaris and to General Oster, the mysterious heads of the Abwehr. Finally, he said that he had close contacts with the Protestant circles opposed to the regime. Gisevius had a Nazi past and had even been a member of the Gestapo in 1933 and 1934. Having gradually become an opponent of the regime, he had a mission to make contact with the Allies for the purpose of obtaining support for the plots that were being hatched against Hitler. The English were suspicious of him and had refused to take him seriously. But by revealing to the Americans a technical secret of great importance, Gisevius had given them a token of his good faith. He soon became known as "Tiny," as a joke on his great height. He became "512" in the internal nomenclature of the OSS.

Dulles and Gisevius met fairly often, at night after curfew, in Bern or Zurich. Gisevius was (along with a few others) one of the first to reveal to Dulles the existence of long-range German missiles designed to be fired on London. In February 1943, he explained that these rockets were being built "somewhere in Pomerania." In June, Dulles learned from another source that this "somewhere" was in fact Peenemünde, a Baltic Sea resort. The information provided by Gisevius was hence of the highest quality. Thanks to him, Dulles was also able to transmit to Washington precise details about the state of mind of the German population and the balance of power inside the Nazi regime. Gradually, the head of the American secret services in

Switzerland was beginning to become a serious competitor of his British colleagues.

In Washington, however, Dulles did not have an excellent reputation. In late April 1943, the head of American intelligence in Switzerland received the following telegram from his superiors in the OSS:

It has been requested of us to inform you that "all news from Bern these days is being discounted 100% by the War Department." It is suggested that Switzerland is an ideal location for plants, tendentious intelligence and peace feelers but no details are given. As our duty requires we have passed on the above information. However, we restate our satisfaction that you are the one through whom our Swiss reports come and we believe in your ability to distinguish good intelligence from bad with utmost confidence.

7

A VISA FOR BERN

Berlin, mid-August 1943

Sunday, August 15, 1943, at around seven in the evening, Fritz Kolbe went to the Anhalter Bahnhof in Berlin. He was to take the 8:20 train for Basel. Fritz arrived early. The distance between the Foreign Ministry and the station was not great (it took only a half hour walking toward the south). The city was bathed in soft summer light. The shadows of the few passersby stretched out on the ground. This neighborhood of government offices at the end of the day seemed immobile and curiously calm. After leaving his Kurfürstendamm apartment, Fritz had stopped at Wilhelmstrasse to pick up the files that had to be turned over to the German legation in Switzerland. The assignment was a routine operation: The transmission of diplomatic mail from Berlin to Bern took place twice a week, leaving Berlin on Sunday and Wednesday evenings. The task was rotated among mid-level officials and never given to a woman.

In his inside jacket pocket, Fritz had carefully placed his diplomatic passport and his orders. The latter document would serve as his pass at every checkpoint. It was an invaluable talisman, highly prized in the ministry and in German diplomatic offices throughout the world. There were many candidates in Berlin for trips to the capitals of neutral countries, particularly to Bern, which was reputedly a very pleasant city.

In the diplomatic mail office, Fritz had been given a leather briefcase containing a thick envelope with a wax seal. The envelope was rather large, forty by fifty centimeters. Fritz did not know what was in it, except that it included official mail for the head of legation and his colleagues, the latest official memoranda, and various confidential messages (including those of the secret services, which sometimes created friction between Himmler and Ribbentrop). He was not to open it on any pretext. The briefcase was at no time to be left unguarded.

A little earlier in the day, the rest of the diplomatic pouch had already been brought to the station. Even though Fritz Kolbe was not personally carrying this second transmittal, he was administratively responsible for it. It consisted of several bags or cases containing nonsecret documents or voluminous objects. These packages, stamped "official dispatch," were not examined by customs (no more than was the envelope containing diplomatic cables). This part of the diplomatic pouch had to be deposited at the station before noon. The members of the ministry took advantage of this system to send private letters or gifts to friends and relatives in Switzerland. Officially, the diplomatic pouch might weigh no more than one hundred kilograms. In fact, it was often twice that, despite official warnings.

Before leaving the ministry building, Fritz went to his office and carefully closed and locked the door behind him. He opened the metal safe in which he kept the most important documents and removed from it two gray envelopes, which were not sealed. Then, after closing the safe, he took off his pants, wrapped the two envelopes around his thighs, and fastened them with sturdy string. He tied several knots that he had learned in the *Wandervogel*, made certain that the arrangement was solid, and put his pants back on. He left his office, went down the large empty staircases of the ministry (since it was Sunday, almost no one was there), and came out into the street. This peculiar operation—which obviously had had no witnesses—had lasted for only a few minutes.

At this time the next day, Fritz would be in Bern. It was the first time after two years of asking that he had received authorization to go abroad as a diplomatic courier. Gertrud von Heimerdinger had done things well. Her push in the right direction had been necessary for Fritz Kolbe's name to be placed on the list of the privileged authorized to spend a weekend of semivacation in Switzerland. Ambassador Karl Ritter had not opposed the trip. He had seen it as a way of compensating his faithful assistant, whose energy and devotion he still appreciated. To enable his subordinate to leave, he had had to guarantee his political reliability in writing. Fritz himself had had to promise, also in writing, to return to Germany at the conclusion of his mission.

Fritz was lucky and yet he was in a feverish state. "Have I forgotten something?" he asked himself as he walked down Wilhelmstrasse. He passed in front of the Reich Chancellery, at the corner of Vosstrasse, with its cold and imposing colonnade. The area was calm and almost lifeless. The entire street seemed deserted. Only a few armed sentinels stood guard at the entry to official buildings. At every street corner, Fritz felt as though he was being watched.

Across the street from the Reich Chancellery was the Ministry of Propaganda. Several people could be seen working there even though it was Sunday. The ministry had its work cut out for it right now in commenting on the series of debacles of the Wehrmacht. For several days the press had been hailing the "triumphant retreat" of the German army in Sicily and congratulating its leaders for having limited the losses of men and materiel in their "magnificent" maneuver of withdrawal to Italy. "We have avoided total annihilation," was the uniform headline for the editorials. These victorious proclamations could not mask the essential: German radio had announced Mussolini's fall on July 26.

Continuing on his way, Fritz passed in front of Göring's Air Force Ministry. Huge black limousines were parked in the courtyard. A little further along, he passed the buildings of the RSHA (the Gestapo and the other security services of the Reich) and could not repress a shiver. Himmler's empire occupied a whole stretch of Wilhelmstrasse, between Prinz-Albrecht-Strasse and Anhalter Strasse. It was common knowledge that inside the walls of these palaces from the imperial period, people were assassinated and tortured. Fritz walked faster. He turned to the right and saw the station. Finally, a neighborhood with a little more life! Opposite the large Anhalter station was the Askanischer Platz. Despite the war, the plaza had remained welcoming, with its large hotels, its commotion, and its numerous restaurants and beer halls.

Fritz saw a large crowd at the entrance to the station. There were many families leaving to seek refuge far from the city. It had been strongly recommended that the women and children of Berlin leave the capital of the Reich to get away from the bombing. It was a head-long flight. "What is most striking walking in the streets of Berlin today is the huge crowd that forms from time to time in certain neighbor-hoods around certain stations of the Stadtbahn. People are heading for an unknown destination without noise, I even often have the im-pression without a word. Even in the most crowded rush hours for the métro, I never saw such a compact crowd in the streets of Paris," wrote Adolphe Jung in his diary of Berlin at war.

On the way to his train, Fritz noticed in the shop windows on the plaza facing the station the first tangible signs of the beginnings of shortages. There was not a single razor blade to be found; special-ized stores offered to sharpen used blades. Continuing through the mass of departing travelers, Fritz saw young boys in military uniforms: the draft age had just been lowered to seventeen. The ogre of the Wehrmacht was devouring the youth of the country. Perhaps Fritz thought of his son, who was now eleven. He had received one or two postcards from him, mailed from South-West Africa, but he had not answered. (Why this silence? Perhaps to preserve the boy and avoid attracting police attention.)

Fritz entered the station building. He was holding the timetable, which showed on one side the "schedule valid from November 1942 on," and on the other an advertisement for the Dresdner Bank. Inside the building, the huge glass-lined hall multiplied the echoes of human voices and steam locomotives. The place was rather grandiose. This early August 1943, the locomotives were decorated with swastikas and propaganda posters: "The wheels of our trains must roll in the direction of victory." Other very large posters were hanging on the walls of the station: one sign indicated the direction to the air raid shelter in the station basement, another asked the traveler to avoid any unnecessary trip.

As night began to fall, the station was plunged into semidarkness. There was no longer any real lighting on the platforms. The bulbs in the lampposts had been painted blue in order not to attract the eyes of enemy pilots. Everywhere, pylons had been covered in white paint up to two meters from the ground so that travelers would not bang into them. On platform 1, the train for Basel was beginning to fill up. Fritz went into a special compartment reserved for travelers on official missions, in the front of the train.

The train left Berlin punctually at 8:20. Fritz did not sleep, or barely. The car was full throughout the journey through Germany, but few travelers were going as far as the Swiss border. The night passed without incident. Apart from routine verification of tickets on leaving Berlin, there was no checking on the passengers. Fritz watched stations go by throughout the night. Halle, 10:35. Erfurt, 12:25 A.M. Frankfurt am Main, 4:34. Heidelberg, 6:27. Karlsruhe, 7:22. Freiburg im Breisgau, 9:40. During the trip, there were several long halts; this was not because of air raid warnings but because the locomotive was changed several times. Finally, they arrived in Basel, German station (Basel DRB, for *Deutsche Reichsbahn*), close to the scheduled time, 11:11. It was Monday morning, August 16, 1943.

The "German station" in Basel was an enclave of the Reich in Switzerland. Fritz had heard that this border station was a favorite observation post for the Nazis and a nest of German spies. As he left the train, Fritz looked around him, not very reassured. At a bank counter, he was given the regulation ten marks (no more) to which every German leaving the Reich had the right. Then he approached the border post, where he managed more or less to conceal his nervousness as he presented his papers. His heart was beating like mad. If there had been a body search, he would have had no hope of escape.

Fritz Kolbe's papers were in order: he had an authorization to stay for four days (until Friday, August 20). As could be verified inside his passport, he had a German visa furnished by the Foreign Ministry (visa no. 4235), and a Swiss visa, provided by the Swiss legation in Berlin (visa no. 519). The German customs officer, with a look as cold as a statue, signaled him to move on. The hardest part was over. Fritz was in Switzerland. He felt an immense relief.

After taking a shuttle to the Swiss station in Basel (Basel SBB), Fritz got on another train, for Bern. He took a deep breath. Perhaps he had seen in the Basel station German trains full of coal or military materiel moving slowly toward Italy through the Gothard tunnel (the route connecting Rome and Berlin). But he suddenly felt transported into another world. Switzerland was a strange country, both very close to and very far from Germany. A country where you could find German political refugees, Jews, resistance fighters from around Europe trying to lie low, German, Italian, and Austrian deserters, escaped prisoners of war, Allied airmen who had survived missions in Germany . . .

Bern, Monday, August 16, 1943

On his arrival in Bern, Fritz was immediately picked up by a diplomatic vehicle that took him to the German legation in fifteen minutes. He was astonished by the beauty of the site and at the same time surprised to discover the modest size of the Swiss capital. He soon noticed that Bern had absolutely no road signs and that it was thus very easy to get lost if you didn't know your way around. He found out that the road signs had been removed because of the prospect of a German attack: Everything had to be done to make the invader lose his way. He also noticed that the car in which he was riding did not display a Nazi flag.

On leaving the station, Fritz had had the time to leave his personal belongings at his hotel, which was not far from the station. This was the Hotel Jura (on Platz Bubenberg), a modest hotel, but quite comfortable. He had taken the opportunity to hide the documents he had concealed beneath his pants. The day passed in consultations with his colleagues in the German legation, which was located in a villa in the Brunnadern district, in the southern part of the city (Willadingweg 78). Perhaps Fritz had a brief conversation with Otto Köcher, head of the legation, whom he had known well since Spain.

Crossing through the city by car, he had seen the handsome residences of the Kirchenfeld district. All the diplomatic missions of the world were there, to judge from the flags decorating the façades. What was striking, coming from Berlin, was the idyllic nature of the place. There was a liveliness and an apparently gentle way of life, which was no longer known in Berlin, even if Fritz was a little disappointed by the absence of chocolate and pastries from the store windows in the center of town. Getting out of the car that deposited him in front of the German legation, he felt surrounded by calm and silence. Just the sound of the wind in the trees and the "pock" of tennis rackets hitting a ball nearby.

That evening, Fritz was invited to a diplomatic reception. He had the time to go back to his hotel to change, and it was probably then that he managed to reach his old friend Ernst Kocherthaler from a public telephone. Kocherthaler had been living in Switzerland since September 1936. After fleeing the civil war and the Falangists (who suspected him of having supplied arms to the Republicans), he had settled with his family in Adelboden, a little mountain village in the Alps near Bern, an hour and a half south of the capital. Fritz knew his telephone number ("146 in Adelboden," he said to the operator). This was the first time that the two men had spoken in eight years. They were moved by the reunion, but the poor quality of the telephone line made it impossible for them to speak for long. They arranged to meet in Bern the next morning.

Bern, Tuesday, August 17, 1943

No one knows the name of the restaurant or café in Bern where Fritz Kolbe and Ernst Kocherthaler met. All the newspapers of the day

carried the headline that Sicily had come entirely under Allied control. For Fritz, this was good news. But Ernst Kocherthaler greatly
feared that this event would lead to the German invasion of Switzerland. Despite worries about the future, the two friends were happy
to see each other again. Kocherthaler was delighted to rediscover
Fritz's outspokenness and good humor. He immediately questioned
him about rumors he had heard from an industrialist friend in Berlin:
"There is talk of plans of a coup d'état against Hitler, a suggestion of
a military government headed by Rommel. What is Himmler doing
about it? They say he's more powerful than ever."

Fritz told Ernst about the atmosphere in Berlin, about the bombing,
and about the general feeling of extreme lassitude ("Many Berliners,"
he said, "have only one wish: to sleep"). In the summer of 1943, more
and more Germans were becoming pro-Russian, because of a very simple
argument: At least the Russians were not bombing German cities.

After a few minutes, the two men began to speak in lower tones.
Fritz informed his friend of the reason for his coming to Bern: He
wanted to transmit information to the Allies. "Ernst, you can certainly
help me meet someone, I'm sure you know names and addresses."
Ernst Kocherthaler started, taken aback. He had been expecting anything but that. He had already met the head of the British legation,
Clifford Norton, at a reception. Would he remember? There was nothing to keep him from trying, but he would have to act quickly because
Fritz was going back to Berlin on Friday. "What do you have to offer?"
asked Ernst. It was then, after furtively looking around to make sure
that no one was watching them, that Fritz took from his briefcase a
little bundle of secret documents he had taken from Wilhelmstrasse.
"Here, see if that may interest someone and tell them that I have other
things with me."

What happened next has given rise to many different versions. After
1945, the facts were reconstructed by the principal protagonists on
the basis of often foggy memories. The truth suffered from more or
less conscious or voluntary approximations. Indications of dates are
often contradictory and most of the time false. Only Fritz Kolbe's
passport makes it possible to locate fairly precisely the unfolding of

events in the week from August 17 to 20, 1943. According to a version frequently reported, Fritz went himself to see a member of the British legation. He is said to have told him that he had information to offer and that he was prepared to collaborate with the Allies without compensation. The English diplomat, still according to legend, showed him out with the following words: "You're probably a double agent, or else some kind of cad!"

In fact, things did not happen in quite that way. That Tuesday, August 17—probably in late morning—it was Ernst Kocherthaler who presented himself at the British legation of Bern, located on Thunstrasse (a long street running through the Kirchenfeld district, along which one would travel from the center of town to the German legation). Without an appointment, he asked to see the head of legation in person, or, failing that, his deputy, "for a matter of the greatest importance," and he showed a German diplomatic cable in order to indicate the purpose of his visit. As was to be feared, he was told that it was impossible to see Mr. Norton, and that the legation's number-two could not see him either. Kocherthaler insisted, refusing to budge, demanding to be presented to someone. He was made to wait for a long time. Finally, a certain Captain Reid came to see him in the lobby to see what this was all about. Once again, Kocherthaler introduced himself as a friend of the British envoy, Clifford Norton, showed his German diplomatic cable, and said that he had a "friend in a high position in the Foreign Ministry in Berlin, who is now in Bern, and who is offering to work for the Allied cause by providing firsthand information."

Finally, Colonel Cartwright agreed to talk to him, but briefly. Colonel Henry Antrobus Cartwright had served as military attaché since September 1939. He was not the ideal interlocutor. His principal mission in this period consisted of debriefing British pilots who had managed to hide in Switzerland after being shot down over Germany. He then tried to evacuate them to London. He would have done better to meet the air force attaché, Freddie West, an intelligence specialist, but he was not necessarily in Bern that day, and Kocherthaler had no time to lose.

Colonel Cartwright did not listen to him for long. He realized rather quickly that Kocherthaler, who claimed to be in touch with Clifford Norton and the legation's number two, Douglas MacKillop, knew neither one very well. He did not trust this man claiming to serve as an intermediary for a mysterious German diplomat who said he was prepared to turn over information for nothing and whose name he refused to reveal. He soon dismissed his visitor, politely refusing his offer. He did not even tell his colleagues in the secret service about the visit.

Cartwright had just passed up a historic opportunity, but his caution was understandable. The English were very suspicious of secret (or supposedly secret) offers coming from Germany. They had received very strict instructions from the Foreign Office, which had warned them against traps. And then, English diplomatic circles were hesitant as a matter of principle about any contact with the German resistance. The reason for this was simple: they were afraid that the Russians were doing the same thing and were seeking to sign a separate peace with Germany, behind the backs of the English and Americans.

Ernst Kocherthaler left the British legation annoyed. He immediately thought of contacting a representative of the United States, but did not know how to go about finding the right door to knock on and an attentive ear. It occurred to him to get in touch with his friend Paul Dreyfuss, a banker in Basel. Kocherthaler knew that Dreyfuss had an address book even larger than his own. So he called and told him briefly what he wanted to do.

At the same time, Tuesday evening around six, in Bern, Colonel Cartwright crossed paths with Allen Dulles in the street. The scene took place in Dufourstrasse, very close to the American legation (which was a little further along, at Alpenstrasse 29 and 35). Dulles came by, as always, with his coat pockets full of newspapers and his pipe in his mouth. Cartwright spoke a few words in passing, before going on his way (the colonel had no time to dawdle, someone was with him): "You'll probably receive a call from a German I just met. I don't remember his name. A name with 'tal' in it: Knochenthaler or

Kochenthaler, something like that. I think this cove will turn up at your shop in due course, so you should be on the lookout for him."

Bern, Wednesday, August 18, 1943

The American diplomat Gerald (Gerry) Mayer got an early-morning phone call. It was 7:30. It is not known whether he was still at home or already in his office on Dufourstrasse. At the other end of the line was Paul Dreyfuss. The two men did not know each other very well. Paul Dreyfuss was calling the American to recommend to him one of his friends who wished to see him to talk to him about an "extremely important" matter. Who is he? "A Spanish citizen of German origin," Herr Kocherthaler, who was going to call him at nine that morning.

At nine o'clock on the dot, the telephone rang in Mayer's office. A few minutes later Kocherthaler was in front of Gerald Mayer and set before him a sheaf of diplomatic cables from Berlin (accounts vary on how many documents: three, sixteen, twenty-nine?). He offered him a meeting with a diplomat friend from the foreign ministry, "a devoted anti-Nazi, prepared to work for the Allies by providing information." This meeting would have to take place "before noon on Friday."

Kocherthaler did not know Gerry Mayer, an elegant man (thin mustache, twinkling gaze, half-smile) who, like Allen Dulles, bore the title of "special assistant" to the American envoy in Bern, Leland Harrison. In fact, Mayer was the local specialist for American propaganda, employed by the Office of War Information (OWI). In that capacity, he worked in close collaboration with Allen Dulles and the OSS, whose offices were in the same building as his, Dufourstrasse 26. Dulles was very appreciative of his young colleague at the OWI, particularly for his extensive knowledge of Germany.

Not knowing that his interlocutor spoke German, Kocherthaler spoke to Gerry Mayer in English. The conversation was not long. It remained vague enough so that nothing confidential came out. The name of Fritz Kolbe was not mentioned, nor his position—Kocherthaler merely said that he was a "rare bird"—but the purpose of the offer was clear. There was something concrete on the table: a pile of copies of German cables stamped "top secret" (*geheime Reichssache*). Gerry Mayer leafed through them distractedly. He adopted a cool attitude, as though he had seen others like them, but he was beginning to find this very interesting. He asked his mysterious visitor to wait a moment in the anteroom.

Now everything would move very quickly. Mayer rushed to Allen Dulles's office on the floor above and told him of the surprising offer from his "German visitor," a "man with the air of a Prussian general, clean-shaven, as straight as an I." Dulles listened attentively, his pipe in his mouth. He asked Gerry Mayer to give him an hour or two, mindful that the day before, he had heard of Kocherthaler purely by accident from Colonel Cartwright. Before going back down to the ground floor, Mayer put the cables from Berlin on Dulles's desk. It was a series of exceptional documents. Each one of them was signed by a German ambassador and personally addressed to Foreign Minister Ribbentrop. In one of them, Otto Abetz, ambassador of the Reich in Paris, spoke of the Vichy regime setting up a network of pro-German agents behind the Allied lines in North Africa. In another, the former minister Constantin von Neurath, now plenipotentiary in Prague, described the rise of anti-Nazi resistance in the Czech population. From Ankara, the German ambassador, Franz von Papen, sent an alarm signal about British agents, more and more of whom were entering Turkey through Istanbul. Based on these documents, Allen Dulles asked Gerald Mayer to maintain contact with Kocherthaler and to let him know that they would call him back later that day.

Once Mayer had left his office, Dulles picked up the phone and called Colonel Cartwright at the British legation. "Can I come to see you right away?" The colonel could see him in half an hour. It was 11:30. Dulles went to see the British military attaché, who offered him a whiskey and told him about the interview of the day before with Kocherthaler, encouraging him not to take the offer seriously.

When he got back to his office, Dulles weighed the pros and cons. With his pipe in his mouth, he looked distractedly out the window, entirely lost in thought. Was Kocherthaler an agent provocateur? Were the Swiss laying a trap for the Americans, so that if they were caught they could be expelled from the country? That would show the Germans that the Swiss were as harsh with Allied as with Axis intelligence agents. In that case, Dulles would be taking a big risk: Espionage was illegal in Switzerland and he could not fall back on diplomatic immunity. It could also be a trap set by the Germans themselves, handing him information without importance so they could decipher American code when he sent it to Washington. A classic trick. It was all too good to be true, Dulles concluded.

But Dulles remembered an experience that had shaped his professional life. When he was posted to Bern the first time in early 1917, he had been sought out by an obscure Russian revolutionary who wanted to meet him. It was a Sunday. Dulles hadn't even taken the trouble to talk to him, preferring not to cancel the tennis game he had scheduled that morning with a beautiful woman. A few weeks later, he had realized that the man who had wanted to see him was none other than Vladimir Ilyich Ulyanov, known as Lenin. From that day on, Allen Dulles had promised himself that he would never again turn down any meeting with an unknown. Without going that far back in his memories, he thought of a pronouncement made a few months earlier by General Donovan, the head of the OSS: "Every man or woman who can hurt the Hun is okay with me."

He had to agree to see this diplomat from Berlin. It was a risk that had to be taken as a professional duty. Back in his office, Dulles let Gerry Mayer know that he wanted to meet the German and his intermediary, Dr. Kocherthaler, as soon as possible. "Between now and then," Dulles added, "do a little investigation of this Kocherthaler."

Bern, Thursday, August 19, 1943

There are contradictory versions of subsequent events. According to the most common, "a meeting was set for midnight in the apartment of Dulles's assistant [Gerry Mayer] in the Kirchenfeld district. Dulles, in disguise, was to meet them at half past twelve. When he arrived,

Dr. O. [Kocherthaler] and the secret courier, a man in a black leather jacket, were already there. Dulles was introduced as a Mr. Douglas, Mayer's assistant."

Fritz Kolbe and, very likely, Ernst Kocherthaler (although his presence is not absolutely certain) arrived at Gerald Mayer's apartment. Fritz Kolbe was wearing a black leather jacket, probably a little warm for the season. The two men were wearing hats. The atmosphere at the beginning was rather tense. They were evaluating, "sniffing" one another. No one had shaken hands in greeting. For an hour or a little more, Ernst and Fritz conversed with Gerry Mayer in German. After a while, Allen Dulles entered the room. The mood became a bit more relaxed. Even though everyone remained wary, Dulles's presence tended to create a pleasant atmosphere around him. The man seemed benevolent and his words were often punctuated with a strong, infectious laugh.

"Mr. Douglas" looked like a giant next to Gerald Mayer and Fritz, who was charmed by this man with the air of a gentleman. He saw some traits in common with Ernst Kocherthaler: same class, same warm ease, and same imposing height. But Dulles spoke very bad German, his accent was deplorable. He had Gerald Mayer translate some of Fritz's statements. Before anything else, he looked at this small man from Berlin and silently analyzed Fritz Kolbe's face. "He was short, stocky, and bald. He looked more like an ex-prizefighter than a diplomat. His eyes were sharp and searching, with a look that Dulles considered honest determination." Dulles, who for the moment followed his intuition, did not make an initially negative judgment on the unknown man.

At that moment, Fritz took a large brown envelope from his inside jacket pocket, with a red wax seal stamped with a swastika. The envelope was open, the seal already broken. Fritz took a sheaf of documents out of the envelope. He set the stack on the table.

A stunned silence greeted this unexpected gesture. Dulles began to look through some of the cables. Some of them were carbon copies of original documents (or at least presented as such by this unknown man whom he still greatly mistrusted); others were almost illegible handwritten notes. Fritz Kolbe's handwriting was particularly difficult to decipher. One of the cables dealt with the morale of German troops on the Russian front, another drew up a provisional summary of sabotage actions by the anti-German resistance in France, yet another dealt with a secret conversation between Foreign Minister Ribbentrop and the Japanese ambassador in Berlin.

A long conversation got under way between Dulles and Fritz on Germany, Berlin, what went on behind the scenes in the regime. Fritz described the atmosphere in Berlin, the growing sense of fear, the German-language programs on the BBC that people listened to secretly. He described in detail the mini-"putsch" of Deputy State Secretary Martin Luther and answered questions from the two Americans about the strength of the SS apparatus. He described the morose atmosphere of the German legation in Bern ("morale in Bern legation is bad").

One of the highlights of the evening came when Fritz set out to describe very precisely the location of Hitler's headquarters in East Prussia, and made a sketch of it in pencil, with the help of a map spread out on a coffee table. "The East Prussian German HQ is located on the east shore of a small Lake Schwanzeitsee . . . Headquarters are established about 7 kilometers east of Rastenburg and 28 kilometers south of Angerburg. Everything is extremely well camouflaged. Here is Hitler's bombproof hideout situated underground . . . Here is Ribbentrop's train . . . there are railroad sidings where Himmler and Göring set up quarters . . . A restaurant for diplomats, Jägerhöhe, is located 300 meters to the north . . ."

The tension relaxed. Drinks were served. Fritz continued to provide revelations of the greatest importance. The Germans, he explained, had managed to decipher an American diplomatic message sent from Cairo on August 7, 1943. Dulles and Mayer thus realized that the State Department's cipher had probably been broken. It was urgent to warn Washington of this security breach threatening the United States's secret communications.

And that was not all. Kolbe was like a magician pulling dozens of surprises out of his sleeve. Strategic revelations ("how the Spanish are delivering tungsten to the Germans," "planned retreat of German troops as far as the Dnieper," "German and Japanese submarines at the Cape of Good Hope"). Indications on the location of industrial sites worth bombing ("the Telefunken factory in Lichterfelde, near Berlin, which provides precision equipment to the Luftwaffe"). Details on the increasing disorganization of the German industrial system ("Long-term planning has completely disappeared in German war industry. Plans are made from day to day and subject to constant change. As a result many newly appointed women employees are advised to come to work but to bring their knitting because they might be without work for days on end").

At some point late in the evening, Fritz Kolbe indicated that the Germans had a spy who had first-hand information coming from London (code name "Hector" or "Hektor"). The source had direct access to Stafford Cripps, the minister of aeronautic production. In Dublin, another German spy, a "Dr. Götz," was flourishing, and the Germans had a clandestine radio transmitter in the Irish capital. At the other end of the world, the Portuguese colony of Mozambique was an important German observation post. The consulate of the Reich in Lourenço Marques in particular regularly provided precise information about the movements of Allied ships in the southern oceans. The Americans were extremely interested. If they were true, these pieces of information were of vital importance for the future course of the war.

To crown it all, Fritz gave the details of the cryptography used by the German Foreign Ministry. It was a very effective coding system. He explained its functioning: "A normal cipher book is used. Every word has a number group. In addition to this the outpost and the Foreign Office have identical pads, each page of which is usable once only. These pages are covered with numbers in 48 groups of five. These numbers are added to the original cipher number at the transmitting end and deducted at the receiving end. Sum total, without adding decimals, is received at Foreign Office, their pad additions are subtracted, and original cipher results." This was known as the "one-time pad" system, which was much more secure than the American coding methods (where each letter corresponded to a given number). Unfortunately, Fritz could not say more about it. Codes changed constantly, and the Americans could not make much concrete use of these revelations. They sent the details provided by Fritz Kolbe to London for another evaluation.

The Americans asked the unknown man from Berlin to tell them his name and to talk about himself. Fritz Kolbe laid his cards on the table, revealed his identity, told the story of his life, talked about the *Wandervogel,* and described his work for Ambassador Karl Ritter. He did not consider that he was in any way under suspicion and cited as proof of this that he worked in the Political/Military Department. He provided dates, gave a summary of his career, and supplied details on the subversive activities he had carried out in secret since the beginning of the war. In particular, he described the fraudulent use of passports brought back from Cape Town, which he said he had given to Jews to help them flee Germany. He told them that his earnings at the outbreak of the war were 700 marks monthly, plus 200 marks special confidence bonus. He even talked about his son and gave them his address in South-West Africa ("c/o Ui and Otto Lohff, in Swakopmund") to establish his credibility and serve as a guarantee. He also mentioned the name of Toni Singer, his best friend in Cape Town. They asked him about his motivations. Did he want money? Fritz Kolbe said no, explaining the reason for his decisions: "What I do I do for an ideal, I ask for no remuneration except possibly for reimbursement of modest expenses."

This remark surprised the two Americans. "Is this a joke?" they both said. Ernst defended his friend's good faith: "He thinks it is not enough to clench one's fist and hide it in one's pocket. The fist must be used to strike." Fritz in turn added a few words: "It is not only one's right but one's duty to fight such a government. . . . My wish is to shorten the war. And at the end of the war, Nazism, fascism, and all the other isms of the totalitarian states should end. We will need American help against the Russians tomorrow in our and in their interest, but we must help them now. That is why I wish to establish contact with the Western democracies. All we ask as payment for our services is help and encouragement and support after the war." "The war," said Dulles, "must first be won. It is too soon to speak of what comes afterward."

Despite the late hour (it was three in the morning, according to Dulles's memoirs), they continued to bombard Fritz with questions: Could he provide other information? Did he come to Bern often? Fritz answered that he might come back, but that it was not certain. A system of communication between Berlin and Bern had to be organized. In order to finalize all these practical matters, a second appointment was made for Friday morning, again in Mayer's apartment. The four men took leave of one another. When he returned to his hotel that night—as he was to say later—Fritz felt "deep satisfaction." He nevertheless wondered if he had not been in too much of a hurry to reveal everything he knew. "Perhaps this haste was judged badly," he thought. For their part, the two Americans, still in Mayer's apartment, briefly shared their first impressions of the man whose name they pronounced as Fritz Colby. They agreed in observing that the German had asked practically no questions and had not tried to lead the conversation into any specific subject. This was a rather good sign, but they shouldn't allow themselves to be lulled by what might be a trap wrapped up in a remarkable performance.

Back in his hotel room Fritz did not go to bed immediately. He sat at the small dimly lit table facing his bed and wrote down his last will and testament, which he intended to give to the Americans before he left. These few lines (a page and a half) were to be given to the appropriate person, "in the event of . . ."

"If I leave this life in one way or another," wrote Fritz, "I would like little Peter to be placed in good hands. . . . Peter should be brought up in my spirit. Do not instill in him hatred of the enemy nor hatred of those who may assassinate me, but rather the unconditional will to fight and to defend our ideals. . . . No one can deny that my action is guided by ideals. Does existence have any meaning when you no longer have freedom, as is now the case in Germany?"

Fritz then gave a list of people to whom his son might be entrusted: If he wishes, Peter may stay with the Lohff family in Swakopmund in South-West Africa, or else return one day to Berlin to stay with one of

Fritz's close friends ("Walter Girgner, Lankwitz, Leonorenstrasse," or "Leuko," a nickname for Kurt Weinhold, his friend the engineer at Siemens). Maria Fritsch ("nicknamed 'little rabbit,' assistant to Professor Sauerbruch"), might possibly "become a good mother" for him. "In any case," Fritz added, "I would have married her eventually." Peter might also be raised by Ernst Kocherthaler: "This man," he wrote, directly addressing his son, "may in particular take care of your needs and finance your education." Fritz than asked Peter to "pay attention to Grandma Kolbe," Fritz's mother. "She is old but she has a surprisingly good and just sense of reality." And Fritz added a sentence about his brother Hans, "with whom I have sometimes quarreled, but who is still a good brother."

The recommendations to Peter then became very precise: "About your future profession, my dear Peter! I have always thought that you might become a sports doctor if that is something that would interest you. Perhaps your gift for mathematics will enable you to become an engineer. That would suit me, or you might be a lawyer. In any case, try above all to become an upright man, keep your youthful enthusiasm, and keep your heart pure! Respect women. The finest of them all was your mother. Always think of that when you're with a girl. And always fight for truth and justice. Even when that seems hopeless to you. Go to meet the enemy with the same weapons that he has and do not forget the goal: our final victory [*Endsieg*]."

In conclusion, Fritz paid homage to his own father ("I feel united with him in the respect for what is right"), and asked his son to do the same with him ("ask my friends about my motives"). The will concludes with a moving appeal to Peter: "I remain your papa. Speak to me at night, as I have done to you so often in the last few years."

Bern, Friday, August 20, 1943

The next day they met as agreed in Gerry Mayer's apartment at eight in the morning. Fritz was probably free of professional obligations and at liberty to stroll around Bern. Despite the risk of being seen, he had agreed to this morning meeting in the midst of the American diplomatic district. He may have been discreetly deposited by a taxi. Gerry Mayer and "Mr. Douglas" (Allen Dulles) were there. Fritz had figured out that the mysterious Douglas was not a simple assistant in the legation, but he did not yet know his real name. Ernst Kocherthaler was probably present.

At the request of the two Americans, Fritz had used Thursday to gather some pieces of information from his diplomatic colleagues in Bern about the German espionage network in Switzerland. This network, Fritz explained, was divided into two departments, the collection of intelligence organized by Himmler's services (SD, *Sicherheitsdienst*), and counterespionage (KO, *Kriegsorganisation*) under the Abwehr. The Americans certainly already knew that, but they took notes all the same.

Fritz then gave some names of diplomats who he thought were spies in disguise (for example, "legation adviser Frank"), but he did not seem very sure of himself. Fritz then stated with certainty that "the Germans have well-placed men in each of the enemy legations in Bern," but in this case too, he gave no names (probably because he didn't know any).

"Who might possibly work for us?" the two Americans asked him. Kolbe believed that "the Chief Commercial Attaché, Consul General Reuter, a Nazi by necessity rather than by conviction, was approachable. Reuter was a bachelor and liked the ladies. A second man mentioned was Kapler, Consular Secretary, who had lived in the United States for ten years and was also a lukewarm Nazi."

Time passed quickly. Allen Dulles proposed that they move on to technical details: How could they organize future collaboration between Fritz and his new "friends" in Bern? They needed a password, in case Fritz were to travel to the capital of another neutral country, which would enable him to contact the Americans again. "Let's take the figure 25900, since that's your date of birth," proposed Dulles, who went on: "If you come back here you only have to introduce yourself as Mr. König." They brought up the possibility of reestablishing contact in Stockholm, in case Fritz were to be sent there as a courier. At

another point, the name "Georg Sommer" was suggested, for no better reason than that it was the middle of the summer. Finally it was
decided that when Fritz tried to establish contact with the Americans,
he would use the name "George Merz." And then, if by chance the
Americans wanted to contact Fritz in Berlin, the agent would claim to
be "Georg Winter" ("Anita Winter," if it was a woman).

For the moment, they left it at that. Would they ever see one another again? Before taking his leave, Fritz gave the Americans an envelope from his hotel (the Hotel Jura) containing the two pages of his
will—he had made a copy that he kept with him. He asked them if he
could dictate the text of a telegram for his son in Swakopmund. The
Americans strongly discouraged him from exposing himself in that way:
"It's madness, don't do it." Fritz did not insist.

When they left him, the two Americans gave Fritz a relatively large
sum of money: two hundred Swiss francs. Fritz accepted the money
to "cover his present and future taxi fares," but also to buy cigars and
chocolate, which would give great pleasure to his superiors at the ministry in Berlin. In Dulles's view, this money should serve to maintain
relations with Gertrud von Heimerdinger, who held the key to Fritz's
future trips to Bern.

The three men separated around 10:30. "Come back soon and bring
us as many cables as possible": this was, in substance, the farewell
message of the two Americans to their new friend from Berlin. When
he left Mayer's apartment, Fritz Kolbe had a feeling of great success.
The Americans were taking him seriously and were counting on him.
It was up to him to feed their curiosity.

Fritz did not have much time to wander around the center of Bern,
look in the shop windows, or go into the stores. Knowing that he did
not have the right to keep foreign currency, he had given most of the
two hundred Swiss francs to his friend Ernst Kocherthaler. With the
rest, he had made some purchases so that he could bring back a few
small gifts to Berlin. He took a train around noon. The same route as
the preceding Sunday, in the opposite direction. The express for Berlin left Basel in the middle of the afternoon. Fritz's passport was
stamped by German customs at the Basel station at 4:46. The trip was

fast, but he had had the feeling of being observed during the journey from Bern to Basel. The man watching him had looked neither Swiss nor German. Was it an American? "Don't they trust me?" he asked himself anxiously. After crossing the German border, he felt lighter. As on the way there, there were few checks on the train. He arrived in Berlin the next morning at 7:41 (track 9, Anhalter Bahnhof, according to the timetable in force since November 1942). The first thing Fritz did when he got off the train was to buy a newspaper. That morning, there was an editorial by Goebbels in the *Berliner Lokalanzeiger* about the debacle in Sicily and Allied bombing of Peenemünde, the manufacturing site for the V-2. "Sometimes," wrote Goebbels that August 21, "as we are moving toward final victory [*Endsieg*], we may find ourselves in the midst of a sunken lane where we can no longer see the goal of our march. But that does not mean that it is lost."

8

"George Wood"

Swakopmund, September 1943

Meanwhile, little Peter Kolbe was living out his childhood in the distant land of South-West Africa. His happy, carefree existence was that of a "free child of Summerhill" before the fact. In Swakopmund, he lived in the house of "Granny Kahlke," his adoptive grandmother, who was extraordinarily kind and did not have the strength to impose the slightest discipline on him. His adoptive parents, Otto and Ui Lohff, came to see him every weekend and on Sunday night returned to Walvis Bay, thirty kilometers away, where they lived during the week. Peter spent his time playing in the dunes and riding his bicycle along the huge Atlantic beaches. He would ride his bicycle far from the city, often alone in wild nature, with a small supply of dried meat (*biltong*, still well known in present-day Namibia). One of his favorite pastimes was to watch whales in the ocean. Desert animals were never far off. One day in the distance he saw a lion that had come to cool off at the edge of the water. He loved this landscape, "hard as locust wood, with dry river beds, and cliffs roasting in the sun." At night, he devoured the novels of Karl May (the adventures of the Indian Winnetou). He read very late, hiding a flashlight under the sheets. Sometimes at night he also quietly left the house to go fishing on the seashore, after making sure that his grandmother was peacefully snoring. On one wall in his room, there was a photo of a boy playing a drum, dressed in the uniform of the Hitler Youth. The picture had been hung there by Granny Kahlke, who naïvely idealized the führer ten thousand kilometers away.

Events in Europe seemed very distant. The Germans in South Africa did not have the right to own a radio. News circulated by word of mouth. A few radios listened to in hiding made it possible to get scraps of information from the Reich. Peter Kolbe remembers that he jumped for joy every time a U-boat sank an Allied ship (the event was announced on German radio by the striking of a gong, and there were as many strokes as ships that had been sunk). All that did not keep him from going to soccer matches where German friends a little older than he played against British sailors on shore leave.

Peter had no news from his father. Gradually, he forgot him, even though, at the insistence of his guardians, he occasionally sent him an impersonal letter to tell him that he was making progress in the German school and that he behaved well in class. Because he played an important role in the local economy, Peter's adoptive father Otto Lohff was spared from being sent to a camp by the South African authorities, unlike most of the Germans who had remained in the commonwealth. Almost every one of Peter's classmates had an interned father, while their mothers continued to take care of the family farms.

One day in September 1943, when Peter (age eleven) came home from school, he encountered two South African plainclothes police at his grandmother's house. For a German family at the time, it was not uncommon to receive a visit of this kind. The authorities in Pretoria collected all the information possible about this population, which was by definition suspect. After questioning Granny Kahlke for a long time, one of the policemen turned to the child and asked him a few precise questions: "What is your name? Who is your father? Where is he? Who is your mother?" Terrified by this unexpected interrogation, Peter believed that he had been identified as a bad boy. He had broken a window in a nearby house with a slingshot a few days earlier.

But the interrogation had no consequences. After a few weeks, Peter and his adoptive grandmother managed to forget this unpleasant episode. It was only much later, after the war, that Fritz's son realized that this episode had a connection to his father's clandestine activities in Berlin and Bern. Allen Dulles, with the help of his British and South African colleagues, had wanted to verify the statements of Fritz Kolbe. It was necessary to confirm the existence of the son, see if the address was correct, ask him about his life, verify the dates, and cross-check the information with counterespionage experts.

Bern and London, late August 1943

By August 20, 1943, in Bern, Allen Dulles and Gerry Mayer had in fact launched as precise an investigation as possible into their visitor from Berlin. No stone could be left unturned, all indications had to be assembled, and every hypothesis written down. A long labor of verification began. In order to do this, they asked for help from their colleagues in counterespionage (department X-2 of the OSS). All the data on the new agent were centralized in London, the European headquarters of the organization, and the Americans had no hesitation in calling on their British colleagues in MI6, who had a substantial lead over them on Germany thanks to their own network and their exceptionally abundant archives. The British also put at the Americans' disposal their transmission lines between Switzerland and London, because the security of their communications was better. It was through the British coding department in Switzerland that all the documents dealing with Kolbe's biography reached London; these sensitive details had above all to be kept out of German hands.

In Bern, the "Fritz Kolbe" file had been created even before his departure for Berlin. As early as the evening of August 19, Allen Dulles and Gerry Mayer set to work and put down on paper everything they had remembered from their conversation with him. Allen Dulles wrote several memos between August 19 and 31, with the intention of drawing a profile of the man and evaluating his credibility. First of all a code name had to be found for Kolbe: after thinking of calling him "König," "Kaiser," or "George Winter," it was finally decided that he would be "George Wood." The reason for the choice of this name is a mystery. To ensure the protection of their agents, the Americans chose nicknames by chance, with no relation to the context. George Wood was the name of a celebrated lawyer in New York in the nineteenth century, and perhaps Allen Dulles thought of him. In addition, like all Dulles's other sources in Bern, "Wood" was given a number: from then on he would be "674" (and sometimes "805," two numbers being better than one). This too was a purely random choice.

The first entry, dated August 19, is merely a summary description of the man. Date and place of birth of Fritz Kolbe; schooling; scouting ("Wood belonged to a German 'Hikers' club called *Wandervogel* which he claimed had been basically anti-Nazi"); career and postings; marriage; details about the son who had stayed in South Africa; second marriage with Lita Schoop ("a Swiss girl"), daughter of Ulrich Schoop, who lived in Zurich; very precise details about Lita's brothers and sisters who also lived in Switzerland: One brother was married to an American, a sister was married to an Englishman serving in the British army. It was also noted that Fritz Kolbe had worked with Rudolf Leitner ("Botschafter, with ten years' service in Washington"), and that he was a trusted subordinate of Karl Ritter ("once lukewarm towards Nazism and known to have proposed to the daughter of Ullstein, has now become thoroughly corrupt"). The document contained errors that would later gradually be corrected. Fritz's date of entry into the Foreign Ministry, in particular, was wrong. The Americans had noted 1935 instead of 1925.

A preliminary physical description of Fritz Kolbe, alias George Wood, was rapidly sketched:

As to description, we generally agree. Gerry would put his height at 5'7" and adds baldish. What hair he has is clipped short and brownish. Typical Prussian-Slavic features. Eyes wide apart, blue grey, frank expression in eyes. Unworldly, but acquired ease in conversation through his travels. Shape of head round, ears not large but stood out from head. Gerry only differs from me here in the color of the hair, but that made no great impression on me, as he didn't have much of it. As to the ears, we both agree that they were not abnormally large, but they certainly were abnormally prominent.

As for Fritz Kolbe's personality, the diagnosis was formulated in these terms: "Kolbe made the impression that he was somewhat naïve and a romantic idealist. He does not appear to be very intelligent or cunning. He wanted, for example, to send an en clair telegram to the housekeeper who is in charge of his son in South Africa, giving messages, addresses and so on, and he has also left with Dulles a letter addressed to his son 'in case he is shot.'"

OSS headquarters in London very quickly set to work on the first elements sent from Bern. Colonel David Bruce, chief of OSS London, didn't know exactly what to do with this file. He immediately had it sent to the British. Lieutenant-Colonel Claude E. M. Dansey was approached in person. Vice-director of the Secret Intelligence Service (SIS), Sir Claude Edward Marjoribanks Dansey was not only the number-two of the British intelligence services, but he was also a man of extremely strong character. Universally detested by his subordinates for his brutal and contemptuous manners, he nevertheless had recognized mastery over everything that had to do with Germany. In order to observe the Reich, he had set up his own espionage network in Switzerland before the war ("organization Z"). The file that was submitted to him by the OSS contained four pages in all: two on Fritz Kolbe's biography and two of official German cables summarized in English as examples of the "material" offered by Kolbe. One of these cables came from "Hektor," an Abwehr agent based in Stockholm, and said this: "JOSEPHINE reports June 24th: Notable increase loading English West coast June 11th to June 21th Liverpool. June 14th to June 15th departure 2 Panzer regiments destination Middle East. During this period total 25,000 men embarked mainly for Middle

East." The other came from Dublin and spoke of an attempted escape of "Götz," a German agent in Dublin.

It took Dansey only a few days to produce a preliminary assessment of the file. The judgment was negative, pending further information.

> I believe we have a trace of this man KOLBE, and not a very satisfactory one at that. . . . It seems possible that Wood is identical with a "Wood" who joined the German Navy in 1917. In 1924 this person was known as "Captain Wood" when he was in command of German Coast defenses and was concerned with a Lieutenant der Marine who was known to belong to the German I.S. in passing false reports through an intermediary to the Inter-Allied Commission of Control in Germany. In 1927 he left the Navy as a result of an accident and went to Brazil as an aviator. He returned to Germany about 1930, when he was given employment in the German I.S. In the beginning of 1931 he was attached to the Kiel office of the German naval and military intelligence service where he held the rank of Oberleutnant z. See a. D.

Dansey had mixed up some files. He was confusing Kolbe with a man of the same name whose physical description was similar (both were about 5'7" in height and suffered from fairly advanced baldness). Dansey's word carried some weight, and this first expert opinion on Fritz Kolbe certainly troubled the Americans. Claude Dansey, for his part, detested the men of the OSS and Allen Dulles in particular. He thought of Switzerland as his private domain, so much so that it "had become a fierce proprietary obsession." He was probably not displeased to be able to demonstrate that the Americans, those amateurs, had hit a snag.

In reality, Dansey was furious. "The sight of the Berlin papers must have been a severe shock to him. . . . It was clearly impossible that Dulles should have pulled off this spectacular scoop under his nose. Therefore, he had not. The stuff was obviously a plant, and Dulles had fallen for it like a ton of bricks." These are the observations of a far from unknown figure, Kim Philby. He was at the time the number-two in the British counterespionage service (Section V of the SIS), and was asked to review the Kolbe file by his chief, Felix Cowgill. Cowgill showed great interest in the potential of "674" (Fritz Kolbe). But he did not want to do anything that might antagonize his superiors. "Dansey and Cowgill," according to Philby, "had contented themselves with skimming the paper cursorily in the search for implausibilities and contradictions to buttress their advocacy of the plant theory." For them, the information provided by "Wood" was "chicken feed," an enticing means of sending the Allies off on the wrong track.

As for Philby, who was already working behind the scenes for the Soviets, his secret mission was to inform the Kremlin of any contact between the Germans and the Anglo-American forces. Through him, Moscow was probably aware, by the end of August 1943, of the existence of a German diplomat working in Berlin who wanted to work for the Americans.

Kim Philby decided to keep an eye on the "George Wood" file. He hastened to send significant excerpts to the experts of Bletchley Park (specialists in decoding German communications), in order to see whether any information provided by the mysterious agent in Berlin might be of some use to Moscow. The heads of the British secret services had for their part decided that "George Wood" was an impostor, even if some of his information was noted with great interest. Who were Josephine and Hektor, they wondered, when they found out that important leaks from London had passed through Stockholm.

But they could not accept that a volunteer agent like Kolbe could be serious. "On the whole, SIS prefers to have agents on its payroll, since the acceptance of pay induces pliability. The unpaid agent is apt to behave independently, and to become an infernal nuisance. He has, almost certainly, his own political axes to grind, and his sincerity is often a measure of the inconvenience he can cause," explained Kim Philby. There was no lack of agents drawn by money, particularly in Switzerland, among Germans who had left the Reich for one reason or another.

In his memoir, Kim Philby devoted a few pages to Fritz Kolbe (without mentioning his name or his alias, George Wood). He remembered with what lack of interest the existence of the agent in Berlin had been greeted in London.

> By the end of 1943, it was clear that the Axis was headed for defeat, and many Germans began to have second thoughts about their loyalty to Hitler. As a result, a steady trickle of defectors began to appear at the gates of Allied missions with offers of assistance and requests for asylum. . . . One day, a German presented himself at the British Legation in Berne, Switzerland, and asked to see the British Military Attaché. He explained that he was an official of the German Foreign Ministry, and had brought with him from Berlin a suitcase full of Foreign Ministry documents. On hearing this staggering claim, the Attaché promptly threw him out. . . . It was barely credible that anyone would have the nerve to pass through the German frontier controls with a suitcase containing contraband official papers.

In Bern, Allen Dulles's views were diametrically opposed to those of Kim Philby. "'If you have to pay an agent, you might as well not use him,' he would tell recruits. . . . A potential agent should at the very least be driven by some other motivation—hatred, passion, or revenge." Nothing could be more desirable than a community of interest between the agent and his case officer. Conversely, a venal agent was capable of betraying everyone, as the history of Colonel Redl on the eve of the First World War in Austria-Hungary had demonstrated. "Strong faith is more important than high intelligence. Moral force is the only force that can accomplish great things in the world," was a maxim in the Dulles family, steeped in Presbyterian culture. Unlike most of the British, and particularly his colleagues in the secret services, Allen Dulles believed in the existence of "two Germanys," one good and one bad. From the beginning, the head of the OSS in Bern had analyzed the challenge of the world war as a struggle for the conquest of German souls. With a little luck, Fritz Kolbe would turn out to belong to the "good Germany," but his good faith had to be ascertained by means of a thorough investigation.

Dulles's opinions about Germany were rather heavily influenced by his daily conversations with a German who had emigrated to Switzerland and whom he had hired in late 1942 and made into one of his closest collaborators in Bern. Gero von Schulze-Gaevernitz (b. 1901) had much that Dulles would find attractive: broad culture, a cosmopolitan spirit, a great capacity for friendship. This financier, devoted to sports and philosophy, who divided his time between skiing and reading Seneca, was the son of a German economist who had been a Democratic Party deputy in the Weimar Republic. Dulles had known him well in Berlin in the 1920s.

The Gaevernitz family had always been in favor of an alliance among Germany, Britain, and the United States in order to stand in the way of Soviet Russia. But they were equally opposed to Nazism. Although connected to the most influential circles in the country (his sister had married a member of the Stinnes family), the young Gero had left Germany to take refuge in Switzerland in 1933. His mother was Jewish. He himself, who had lived for several years in the United States, had renounced his German citizenship and defined himself as a "liberal Christian." He would not accept the slightest compromise with the Hitler regime.

"Gaevernitz was deeply motivated by the conviction that Germany had never been so thoroughly permeated by Nazism as many were inclined to believe and that there were people in Germany, even in high positions in both the civilian and military administration, ready to support any workable undertaking that would get rid of Hitler and the Nazis and put an end to the war," Dulles stated in one of his memoirs.

At the OSS in Bern, Gero von Schulze-Gaevernitz worked on most of the files concerning Germany. He regularly received informers or emissaries who had come from Berlin. Kept busy by his contacts at the highest levels, he was not directly concerned with Fritz Kolbe, and it is not certain whether Dulles informed him in detail about this extremely unusual case. However, by chance in a conversation on Tuesday, August 31, 1943, it turned out that Schulze-Gaevernitz knew Ernst Kocherthaler well.

Dulles immediately took notes, because he knew nothing about this mysterious figure who, as an intermediary for Fritz Kolbe, represented an important piece in the puzzle he was putting together. According to Gaevernitz, Kocherthaler was a man who could be trusted. "A man of excellent reputation and of considerable business standing in Switzerland," he explained. "Von G. spoke highly of K. . . . [who] was at one time with Warburg & Co, Hamburg . . . According to von G. K. is Jewish, or partly Jewish, by race, Christian by religion and in fact very active in religious circles. Known to the Visser't Hooft group in Geneva and has apparently done some work with respect to the establishment of a Christian University in Switzerland for the post-war education of German teachers." Allen Dulles noted that Gero "seemed completely confident of [K.'s] consistent anti-Nazi position," and he transmitted these details to his colleagues in London in order to assist the ongoing investigation.

Berlin, late August 1943

Back in Berlin on Saturday, August 21, 1943, Fritz was greeted by one of the most terrible bombardments that the capital of the Reich had ever experienced. Between August 20 and 23, the Charlottenburg, Steglitz, and especially Lankwitz neighborhoods were very heavily damaged. Sunday evening, he was in fact in Lankwitz at his friend Walter Girgner's when a huge roar of engines was heard: It was the RAF planes. Fritz was in the middle of recounting his trip to Bern and his meeting with the Americans. Also present was Hans Kolbe, Fritz's only brother.

There was a deluge of bombs. None of the three friends had ever experienced anything like it. Like all Berliners, they could recognize by sound the different types of bomb (explosive or incendiary). But now they didn't have the time to indulge in that exercise. Suddenly, lightning seemed to be striking them. The entire neighborhood seemed to be sinking beneath the earth in a deluge of fire. The two houses adjacent to Girgner's were hit before their eyes. The three men took refuge in the cellar. At five in the morning, when the planes had left, Fritz and his friends came out of their hole and were stunned to see that an explosive bomb that had fallen very close to Girgner's house had not detonated. They had had a narrow escape. The Lankwitz neighborhood was destroyed.

Fritz went home on foot, passing through scenes of desolation, amid the cries of survivors and the heat of burning ruins. The rescue services were overwhelmed by events. He took more than an hour to get back to the Kurfürstendamm, not knowing whether the house he lived in was still standing. *Gott sei Dank*, he said to himself when he got there. The building was still there, and most important, there was still running water on every floor. He quickly took a cold shower and went to the ministry at nine o'clock.

That same morning, his friend Karl Dumont came to see him in his office. Speaking in a low voice, he wanted to know everything about the trip to Switzerland. Of all Fritz's colleagues in the Foreign Ministry, Dumont was the only one who was aware of Fritz's real intentions. Since they had known one another in Madrid, there had been perfect rapport between the two men. Dumont had been absent because of illness the week before. He thought that his friend had failed and was ready to bury him in reproaches. At the moment, Fritz could not tell him the details of his trip, but he met him again in the late afternoon, at a time when the offices were already largely deserted, to give him a detailed report of his visit to Bern.

Bern, September 1943

By early September 1943, Allen Dulles had completed the first phase of his investigation of Fritz Kolbe. He had not yet eliminated the theory that it was a trap. He was waiting to see whether and how his informant would show himself again. It was a letter addressed to Ernst

Kocherthaler, written in Berlin on September 16, 1943, that revealed that Fritz had not said his last.

The letter contained reading material for the Americans: a few copies of cables, a new map of Hitler's headquarters (the same as in August, with a few errors corrected), and the schedule for the daily train between Berlin and Rastenburg, the "wolf's lair" in East Prussia. It also contained a few details about the results of the Allied bombardment of the ball bearing factory in Schweinfurt a few weeks earlier. Fritz took the liberty of suggesting other targets and provided a personal opinion about German secret weapons, which he erroneously claimed was "the greatest bluff ever practiced on the German people."

At the end of his letter, Fritz had hastily scribbled a few words in his unreadable handwriting: "I write these lines in wild haste, scanning the material with one eye and typing it with the other hand." In conclusion, he took leave of his readers in Bern by sending them "greetings from Hektor" (an allusion to the Abwehr agent based in Stockholm), and signed "George M.," for "George Merz," the provisional pseudonym adopted during his August visit.

How had this message reached Bern? Mystery. Given its content, it could not have gone through ordinary mail. It was probably mailed in Bern by a colleague of Fritz's carrying the diplomatic pouch—a routine expedition that took place every week, exactly like the one Fritz had made in August. Every time a diplomat went abroad for a mission of this kind, he took out and brought back dozens and dozens of private letters and packages having nothing to do with his professional duties. These packages were placed in the train's baggage compartment, were entitled to diplomatic immunity, and were not checked at the border. From Germany to Switzerland, people sent books, radios, phonographs . . . It is probable that if Fritz Kolbe had given a personal letter to a colleague on assignment to Bern, the "mailman" was totally ignorant of its contents.

Another hypothesis can be suggested: Fritz knew a trustworthy person who, because he was a surgeon, could easily travel between Berlin, annexed Alsace, and sometimes even Switzerland. This was Albert Bur, a friend of Adolphe Jung's, former chief surgeon of the hospital of Sélestat, dismissed in late 1941 for being a "Francophile." Albert Bur lived in Obernai (Ober-Ehnheim in German). He was a specialist in photography and devoted a good deal of time to the emerging technique of color photography and its medical applications. In this connection, he frequented chemical industry circles, particularly the Agfa company. Fritz had naturally gotten on well with him. The two men shared a passion for sports: before the war, Bur had been president of the Sport Club of Sélestat.

Doctor Bur was prepared to take risks for the Allied cause. He was in contact with French Resistance circles and with British agents active in France. His wife was an American born in Chicago. He naturally became an intermediary for Fritz in order to transmit information, in particular about "Josephine," and even tried to convince him to travel secretly to London. This was too dangerous, in Fritz's judgment, but he nevertheless decided to involve his friend closely in his plans. Thanks to his frequent travels, Albert Bur was a rare jewel.

Bern, October 1943

On October 10, 1943, the OSS in London received a mysterious telegram from Bern: Allen Dulles cabled cryptically that he "had just got some 200 pages of *alpha* and since they were no longer sure of *beta*, it would take weeks to handle. [He was] fully convinced of *delta* after yesterday's *gamma* and from internal evidence." The key to this strange message was not received in London until the following day. It was revealed that *alpha* meant German two-way secret Foreign Ministry cables, *beta* meant the security of the communications channel, and *delta* the particular value and authoritative quality of this material. Finally, *gamma* meant Wood's cross-examination.

Fritz Kolbe had arrived in Bern a few days earlier in the course of a new assignment as diplomatic courier. Fräulein von Heimerdinger had shown herself very capable in securing this second mission for her protégé. The small gifts brought back from Bern in August may have facilitated matters. A cigar here, a box of chocolates there; Fritz Kolbe had been generous. Why not do him a favor and let him breathe a little bit abroad? In Berlin in October 1943 it was impossible even to pretend to live normally. The bombardment by Allied planes was added to the increasing harshness of the regime. There was not only the constant fear of bombardment hanging over everything, but the slightest misstep could send you to the gallows. How many people had already been executed for making "defeatist" statements?

The day before he was to leave for Bern, Fritz had narrowly escaped death. It was in the evening in the midst of an air raid. As a ministerial official, Fritz had a pass giving him the right to move around during curfew. He was coming back from the Charité hospital on his bicycle (he had gone to say goodbye to Maria) and was on his way to his office to file some documents. Sirens began to wail; it was an RAF attack. One could see the approach of white flares from the magnesium incendiary bombs. Just at the moment when the alarm began, Fritz was at the corner of Unter den Linden and Wilhelmstrasse. An armed warden ordered him to stop and not to cross the street. Fritz got off his bicycle and showed his pass. The warden examined the document with his flashlight. At that moment, a projectile fell less than fifty meters from the two men, a little further down Wilhelmstrasse, knocking them violently to the ground. After a few seconds, they staggered to their feet, stunned, covered with debris, but unhurt. Fritz warmly thanked the warden for having stopped him at the corner. Had he continued on his way, he would have been at the point of the bomb's impact, where there was now a large smoking crater. He took one of the Havana cigars he had bought in Switzerland out of his pocket, gave it to the warden as a token of thanks, and went on his way to the ministry. The warden smiled with pleasure.

The next morning, he made preparations for departure. Fräulein von Heimerdinger, as she had the first time, gave Fritz a sealed envelope containing the diplomatic mail for Bern. After signing the registry indicating that he was now responsible for it, he went to his office to complete his packing with the personal documents intended for the Americans. This time, he had no wish to fasten documents around his thighs. It was a dangerous method and not worthy of him, he thought.

But what else could he do? After returning from his first trip, in September, he had managed secretly to get hold of an official ministry seal, in exchange for a box of Swiss chocolates. Petty dealings of this kind were very common and attracted very little attention. The sealed envelope that had just been given to him could be slipped inside a slightly larger pouch containing the other documents. All he had to do was to properly seal the new envelope, even though it had become thicker than the original. Instead of a trunk with a false bottom, he had a pouch with a false top.

Fritz carried out the entire operation by manipulating the papers in a drawer of his desk hidden from prying eyes. Unfortunately, the wax caught fire and the operation almost turned into a disaster. He just managed to save his package and put out the flames. After wiping his forehead and opening the window to dispel the odor of burnt paper, Fritz went back to work with his heart pounding. Finally the package was ready. Fritz was not dissatisfied with the result: the seal marked with the eagle and the swastika had a rigorously authentic appearance. As for the weight of the package, he knew that diplomatic pouches were never weighed, neither going nor coming.

Fritz took the early evening train on Wednesday, October 6 from the Anhalter Bahnhof, as he did the first time (departure at 8:20). Ordinarily, the trip from Berlin to Basel took sixteen hours. But because of air raids, delays had become very frequent, and the trip might last as long as three days. Once he was in his compartment, he called the attendant of his car aside and, handing him a handsome tip, asked to be the first to be warned if there was an alert. "I am terrified of bombs and I would be a bit reassured if you were to warn me in advance," he said. In fact, Fritz wanted to have time to get rid of his documents in case of danger.

At four in the morning, the porter rapped sharply on the door of his compartment. "Blue alert, sir," he said. That meant that an attack was imminent. It was not yet a "red alert," but he had to act quickly. The train had stopped. Fritz had kept his clothes on. He quickly got off the train holding his briefcase close to himself. The spot was deserted. They were in the middle of the woods, "probably between Frankfurt and Karlsruhe." The moon lit up the rails. Then the other passengers began scrambling out of the train. A baby cried. A man yelled that he had lost something in the confusion. Fritz took cover in a ditch below the tracks.

At that point a plane headed directly for the train. It was a light English bomber, a Mosquito, an isolated plane flying low. The plane fired a few salvos at the locomotive. There was no answering fire: a passenger train like this one had no antiaircraft guns. The plane soon disappeared. But a few moments later, a huge explosion was heard a few hundred meters in front of the train. The plane had dropped a bomb on a trestle. Although not completely destroying it, the bomb had seriously damaged the track, making it impossible to continue the trip. There was a long wait before another train could replace the first one, on the other side of the trestle. Night passed, morning, and after-noon. Finally the journey could continue. The passengers had to cross the trestle over a precipice on foot, which took a long time. Fritz was irritated that he had lost an entire day from his schedule.

Going through customs in Basel was nerve-wracking. As much as, if not more than the first time, Fritz had violent stomach pains and was perspiring so profusely that he was afraid of attracting the attention of the customs agents. He knew that in the event of a thorough search, he would have no hope of escape. Nothing was worse than this pre-cise moment. A German customs agent was looking at him with a par-ticularly suspicious air. Did he suspect? Fritz tried to maintain all the composure at his command. He looked directly into the eyes of the man in uniform, attempting to keep his gaze as cold as possible, keep-ing his pouch in plain sight under his arm ("above all, appear to have nothing to hide," he said to himself). The official motioned him through.

Even though he was still in the "German station" of Basel, Fritz was now in Switzerland. He headed for the men's room and locked him-self in a toilet. He tore open the outer envelope and removed the documents not intended for the German legation in Bern and put them in his coat. The official envelope was replaced in his briefcase. He burned the now superfluous envelope and flushed the ashes down the bowl. He went out and took a taxi across the Rhine to the Swiss station of Basel (Basel SBB), where he caught the train to Bern. Before getting on the train, he found a telephone booth from which he called 146 at Adelboden, Ernst Kocherthaler's number. The Americans were immediately informed that "Wood" had arrived.

It was Thursday, October 7, late at night, when Fritz arrived in Bern. His friend Ernst was already in town. The next morning, after delivering the diplomatic mail to the German legation, he and Fritz met at a café, as they had the first time. Ernst informed Fritz that the Americans had impatiently been waiting for his return and that they wanted to see him that very evening. "At 11:30 tonight, Gerald Mayer will pick you up in his car on Kirchenfeld bridge. It's a Triumph sportscar. You will wait in the shadows at the southern end of the bridge. To identify himself, he'll switch on his headlights once he's in the middle of the bridge. They are blue because of the curfew."

That evening the meeting took place as planned. At 11:30, Fritz jumped into Gerry Mayer's car. "Glad to see that you made it back again," he said in a friendly voice, adding that they were going to see Mr. Douglas. Fritz admired Gerry Mayer's handsome Triumph, wanted to talk to him about the Horch that he had had to give up because of the war, but unfortunately the trip was very short. After taking a few narrow cobblestone streets in the old city, Mayer steered his car onto a road along the River Aare. The Triumph was going very slowly, with no lights. Soon it reached a point below the Kirchenfeld bridge whose metal outline could be seen forty meters above. The height seemed dizzying. Mayer turned off the engine. At this very dark spot, there were few passersby and it was easy to pass unseen. Mayer asked Fritz to get out alone and explained how to get to Dulles's house through the garden in back, up a steep path through dense shrubbery. "Go on alone. I'll rejoin you up there in a little while. You're expected."

A few minutes later, Fritz Kolbe was in Herrengasse 23. Glass in hand, he savored this moment of stolen freedom and appreciated the very "old England" comfort of the ground floor living room. The principal lighting in the room came from a large fire in the fireplace. Allen Dulles—a poker in one hand, his pipe in the other—frequently stirred the fire and added logs when necessary. Gerald Mayer arrived a few minutes later. Dulles contemplated the sheaf of documents that Fritz had just deposited on a coffee table. There were two hundred pages of documents, half copies of cables, half Fritz's handwritten notes in German, in a cramped handwriting that only Ernst Kocherthaler was able to decipher. Dulles did not have time to read the documents in detail that night. Out of curiosity, he skimmed through the "delivery."

The ambassador of the Reich in Paris, Otto Abetz, gave a list of the French whom he suspected of sympathizing with the Allies and whom he recommended should be arrested. From Spain, there was a message that the Falangist authorities had agreed to make new deliveries of "oranges" to Germany. The "oranges," as Fritz was to explain a short time later, designated tungsten, a strategic material that the German armaments industry desperately needed. From Latin America came information that a particular Allied sea lane was threatened by U-boats in the Atlantic. Was Dulles interested? He let nothing show.

The conversation continued late into the night. Even more than the documents he had brought from Berlin, Fritz's opinions seemed to intrigue the Americans. They asked him even more questions than in August. He indicated on a map of Berlin some sites that, according to him, were worth bombing. "This particular Telefunken plant produces precision instruments for the Luftwaffe. . . . There in the Lichterfelde district is the enlarged SS barracks, housing the Leibstandarte SS, Hitler's personal guard."

Fritz had time to dwell at some length on his motivations, his family, his opinions. The Americans wanted to gather information, but they also wanted to determine whether Fritz contradicted himself and whether his explanations were plausible. They spoke again of the *Wandervogel,* and at length about Madrid and Cape Town. Fritz was made to understand that no detail was superfluous. Dulles and Mayer were interested in everything, including details that might seem useless. "Where are the principal shoe factories in Germany?" they asked him in the course of the conversation.

Life in Berlin and the general atmosphere of the capital of the Reich seemed to interest them just as much as revelations of a political or military nature. Fritz was asked to speak of his friends and contacts in Berlin. He naturally mentioned his friend Karl Dumont in the ministry, but also Count Waldersee, the Wehrmacht officer whom he had met in Professor Sauerbruch's circle, with whom he had hit it off in the summer of 1943.

Between Friday, October 8 and Tuesday, October 12, the date of his departure for Berlin, Fritz came to see Dulles several times, using all possible tricks to avoid being followed. He slipped furtively through the arcades of the old city, plunged into shops that had back doors, and multiplied zigzag movements, always arriving at the back door of Herrengasse 23. Most of the time, meetings took place late at night. In his nocturnal movements through Bern, Fritz wore his hat pulled low on his forehead and used a different coat from the one he wore during the day. To avoid attracting the slightest suspicion, he accepted all dinner invitations from his colleagues in the legation. Dulles and Mayer never saw him arrive before eleven at night and did not let him leave before two or three in the morning. He came to see Dulles in company with Ernst Kocherthaler. The two friends had stopped meeting during the day, because they thought that their connection might attract suspicion.

This nocturnal activity was harmful to Fritz's reputation. The managers of the Hotel Jura looked at him strangely. Obviously they were suspicious of him. Was the hotel in contact with the Gestapo? To avoid any unpleasant surprises, Fritz decided to pass himself off as a Don Juan. In his discussions with colleagues from the German legation, he frequently spoke teasingly of the "pretty Swiss women, who were not all that timid." One night, he spent a few hours in a brothel in Bern (Café Colombine), after which he made an appointment with a local doctor who specialized in venereal diseases. At the end of the visit, he was presented with a bill, which he carefully preserved in order to have concrete evidence available in the event of a later interrogation.

On Tuesday, October 12, 1943, Fritz had to leave for Berlin. Before his departure, the Americans agreed with him about ways of improving their future collaboration. It was not certain whether Fritz would be able to return to Bern anytime soon: Diplomatic courier assignments were handed out sparingly. Could they figure out a secure and regular means of communication? Sending mail to Ernst Kocherthaler, as Fritz had done with his September 16 letter, was much too dangerous for everyone. "You have to be much more cautious!" the Americans admonished him.

One idea was decided on: Fritz could from time to time send to a third person based in Bern a perfectly innocuous message on an ordinary postcard. Alerted by this signal, the Americans would know that Dr. Bur had brought home to Obernai "material" provided by Fritz in Berlin. An American agent could come to get the package in Alsace a few days later. The envoy would be introduced as M. or Mme. König. It was decided that Fritz's "mailbox" in Bern would be that of Kocherthaler's brother-in-law, Walter Schuepp. A librarian by profession, Walter Schuepp was, according to Fritz, a "good Swiss citizen" who was perfectly ordinary. He had the twofold advantage of being completely unnoticed in the local scene and of living very near the OSS offices in Bern (his address was Gryphenhübeliweg 19). Even though they were not really very close, Ernst Kocherthaler trusted him enough to involve him in this delicate enterprise.

And suppose the Americans wanted to contact their agent in Berlin? Fritz proposed a scenario: "One of your contacts in Berlin just has to call me at my office (telephone number: 11.00.13) claiming to be 'Georg Merz.' We'll arrange to meet at my apartment on Kurfürstendamm." Dulles and Mayer carefully noted this proposal. What Fritz did not know was that apart from him, the Americans had no contacts in Berlin. Even if they had, they never would have sent one of their agents to Fritz's apartment, not yet being able to state with certainty whether he was a sincere friend of the Allies or a double agent working for the Gestapo.

Fritz was delighted with these secret arrangements. The more schemes and complicated tricks there were, the happier he was. He insisted that he be informed by certain coded signals whether his messages had in fact been received. Thanks to his contacts in business circles who were constantly going back and forth between Switzerland and the Reich, Ernst Kocherthaler could have food parcels sent to Fritz, containing sardines, butter, coffee . . . These parcels, Fritz suggested, could be sent at regular intervals but would contain coffee only if the messages from Berlin had been received in Bern. The Americans and Kocherthaler were not enthusiastic, but they promised Fritz that they would do as he wished.

Before leaving, "Kaiser" wanted to repay the 200 Swiss francs that he had been given on his first trip by Allen Dulles. In order to do this, he had brought with him two gold rings (probably the wedding rings from his two marriages). He wanted to exchange them for money at a jewelry shop in Bern. The Americans dissuaded him, telling him that he should use his time for more useful things. They nevertheless agreed to keep the two rings as mementos of him.

Fritz asked the Americans if they could give him a revolver, but Dulles and Mayer thought that a firearm would only worsen his case if he were caught. Fritz was disappointed, but in any case he had what he needed in Berlin—in a drawer at home he kept a little revolver that he had brought back from South Africa, and he counted on using it on the day when the Gestapo came to arrest him.

The return train trip from Bern to Berlin went off without incident or air raids. He left on Thursday afternoon and arrived in Berlin the following morning. Among the diplomatic cables he was carrying in his briefcase was one from the chief of the German legation in Switzerland, Otto Köcher, telling Ribbentrop that Swiss neutrality would be preserved at all costs. "Switzerland cannot join the Allied cause," he wrote in this cable of October 7, 1943. It was known in Berlin that the Americans were putting pressure on Switzerland, whose airfields they wanted to use for raids on Germany. Otto Köcher was well informed: The leaders in Bern had no intention of quarreling with Germany.

London, November 1943

Colonel David K. E. Bruce, head of the OSS in London, was a multi-millionaire, a Democrat, and the son of a senator and son-in-law of Andrew Mellon, the American steel magnate and former secretary of the treasury. All information coming from Europe passed through him and his services before being communicated to OSS headquarters in Washington. In late November 1943, David Bruce received a note from Norman Holmes Pearson, his colleague in charge of counterespionage (X-2) in London. This eight-page note concerned Fritz Kolbe ("Subject: Wood case"). This was a synthesis of everything that had been written by the Americans and the English since early August about "George Wood."

The document was full of mistakes, including in the presentation of facts: "On 16.8.43 an individual known as Wood appeared in Geneva carrying a diplomatic bag from the German FO. . . . His first approach was through a German Jew named Kochenthaler." In this note, Fritz Kolbe was presented as a "somewhat naïve and romantic idealist" who "made no special effort to find out which of the cables were of special interest," but who "made no attempt to lead the conversation into any particular channels."

Dansey's theory, according to which Kolbe was a navy officer who had been a double agent in the 1920s, was reiterated as a plausible hypothesis. What could be concealed behind "George Wood"? A German attempt to decipher the OSS Bern messages? To avoid this risk, everything had been done to confuse matters: none of the cables transmitted by "Wood" had been transcribed and "sent in the German text or even a literal English translation summary of the original cable," in communications between Bern and London. Every proper name had been changed, whether of people or places. "We are keeping close watch on cipher security in re-wording," Dulles wrote in one of his secret messages to Washington. In accordance with these elementary precautions, the word *Grand* meant the German foreign minister, *Porto* designated a German foreign embassy or legation, *Grimm* was used for Germany or German, *Zulu* was the equivalent of the United Kingdom, *Red* was France, *Storm* designated the German legation in Bern, *Vinta* was Ribbentrop, *Apple* was Otto Abetz, *Fat Boy* was Göring . . . Hitler had no alias.

Another hypothesis: "Wood" was working for a sophisticated operation aimed at drawing the Americans into a trap. He came to Bern only to awaken their interest in order to be in a better position to deceive them a little later on. That could not be ruled out. But an analysis of Wood's messages did not provide anything, for the moment, to support that hypothesis. "To the contrary, a certain amount of interesting material from an X-2 [counterespionage] point of view has been revealed."

In particular, Fritz Kolbe had provided material to help identify "Josephine," a mysterious mole well placed in London who was providing high-class information to the Germans. Thanks to "Wood" and the Ultra machine, the British identified the spy, about whom they knew that he was supervised at a distance by the Abwehr office in Stockholm. The British secret services discovered that "Josephine" was the Swedish naval attaché in London, Johann Gabriel Oxenstierna, a diplomat who was particularly well informed about the movements and preparations of the Royal Navy.

Count Oxenstierna was not himself an agent of the Reich, but his professional mail was read at the defense ministry in Stockholm by a secretary who was working for the Germans. The Abwehr's liaison agent in Stockholm was Karl-Heinz Krämer, known as "Hektor" in the secret German documents. In September 1943, London demanded that the Swedish authorities recall the naval attaché. They reacted sharply and took several months to accede to the demand. Finally, Count Oxenstierna was expelled in the spring of 1944. A certain number of high British officials, who had been particularly talkative in their discussions with "Josephine," were disciplined.

Fritz Kolbe's credibility was no doubt increased by the discovery of "Josephine." However, in early November, the number-two of the British secret services, Claude Dansey, asserted that "there is nothing in them [Wood's cables] which could affect the course of the war." Others, beginning with Allen Dulles, were less categorical. Fritz Kolbe had enabled the Americans to put pressure on Ireland to put an end to German espionage activities in that country. The Dublin authorities had been urged to confiscate a clandestine radio transmitter, the existence of which Kolbe had revealed. Moreover, Kolbe made it possible to verify the impact of some of the Allied bombing of major German cities. For example, he provided the official Nazi report of bombings on October 2 and 3, 1943: "EMDEN: 20 bombs struck the Nordsee Werfte. MUNICH: IG Farben has been severely hit, also Dynamit AG, Allgemeine Transport Gesellschaft, Metzeler Gummi Werke . . . Slaughterhouse and main railway station were also hit. KASSEL: damage was done to Panzer locomotives and howitzers at the Herschel Werke. Junkers factory was not hit."

In order to determine whether "Wood" was trustworthy, each document that he provided was closely scrutinized by the OSS in London. The files were transmitted to Washington with long commentaries. Paragraph by paragraph, word by word, everything was gone over with a fine-tooth comb and weighed against information derived from other sources. "Paragraph 1 is probable but hard to verify," "paragraph 2 had been verified, its content is accurate," "paragraph 3 is correct," and so on. While the Allies had still not ruled out the possibility of a trap, they nevertheless thought it less and less likely. Nothing in "Wood's" attitude led them to detect suspect behavior. If this was a game of deception, "it will have been far and away the most elaborate deceptive strategy so far known either to British or American counterespionage services," wrote Norman Pearson in his November 23, 1943 memorandum.

"Wood's" motivations seemed to be purely individual. "On the whole," Pearson went on, "it seems likely that whether or not Wood is acting as he does from the ideological motives he professes, and despite the fact that he is unwilling to receive any money for his services, he is at the same time not unaware that after the Defeat some special consideration might be accorded to him." The conclusion was chilling: "The habits of rats on sinking ships are well known."

9

THE "KAPPA FILES"

Ankara, October 1943

"Gentlemen do not read each other's mail," U.S. Secretary of State Henry Stimson had said in 1929. This deep disdain for espionage was very widespread in English and American diplomatic circles. Sir Hugh Knatchbull-Hugessen, British ambassador to Turkey since 1939, and a diplomat of the old school, shared that way of thinking. Intelligence was outside the scope of his work and he did not want to hear it talked about. This indifference was close to negligence—he had an Albanian servant named Elyeza Bazna, of whom he had no thorough investigation made, though the man came to him out of the blue, and the ambassador never suspected that he had hired a dangerous spy in the pay of Germany.

In late October 1943, Bazna decided to contact the Germans to offer them secret documents from the British embassy. He had managed to steal the key to the personal safe of Ambassador Knatchbull-Hugessen while the ambassador was sleeping. He had had a copy made and was thus able to get his hands on confidential documents of the greatest importance. He immediately thought of making them available to the enemies of England in exchange for hard cash. On the evening of October 26 he went to the German embassy on Atatürk Boulevard, where he met Ludwig Moyzisch, a former journalist from Vienna with the official title of commercial attaché, who was in fact a permanent agent of the intelligence services. In their conversation, Bazna spoke French and claimed that his name was Pierre. He said that he hated the English, who had "killed his father." He offered documents of "exceptional quality" in exchange for money, although he had nothing to show for the moment. He was asking for fabulous amounts (twenty thousand pounds for two rolls of undeveloped film). "Pierre" gave Moyzisch two days to think about it, letting him know that he would not hesitate to look for a better client—for example, the Soviets—in the event of a German refusal.

Moyzisch, somewhat skeptical, informed the ambassador, Franz von Papen, of this astonishing offer. Von Papen was very fond of all kinds of intrigue and believed in the virtues of combining diplomacy with espionage. Because of the scope of the affair, von Papen referred it directly to Foreign Minister Ribbentrop in Berlin, who turned the file over to his assistant, Horst Wagner, liaison officer between the ministry and the SS. The file was soon turned over to Walter Schellenberg, head of foreign espionage. He decided to pay the twenty thousand pounds "to see," and was not disappointed by the result. The first "delivery" from the Albanian servant contained many details about conversations at the highest level between British and Turkish leaders. These negotiations dealt with a highly strategic question: Was Turkey finally going to abandon its de facto neutrality? Would it shift into the Allied camp, and if so, at what price? Its strategic interest was to remain outside the war, even though it secretly dreamed of a dual defeat: first of the Soviets and then of Nazi Germany.

Ambassador von Papen could use the documents photographed by the Albanian valet to attempt to thwart the maneuvers of the Allies. Always one step ahead thanks to the information provided by his spy, he was in a position to put very targeted pressure on the Turkish authorities in order to force them to maintain their neutrality. He decided to name this exceptional spy "Cicero," because of the particularly eloquent nature of the material supplied. In Berlin, Walter Schellenberg hoped to use Cicero to decipher the English secret codes. On November 4, 1943, a plane from Berlin landed in Ankara with the sum of two hundred thousand pounds sterling on board. This treasure was to pay the spy for several months. It turned out much later that these were counterfeit bills expertly produced by a secret agency of the Reich's espionage services.

In the course of the fall of 1943 and the following winter, Cicero turned over large quantities of invaluable information to the Germans. Ambassador von Papen considered him a first-rate source and used him daily to supply material for his diplomatic cables to Berlin. He informed Hitler in person of the existence of the Cicero file when they met in November 1943. But Foreign Minister Ribbentrop, who detested von Papen, whom he saw as a rival, had every interest in minimizing the importance of the affair. "Too good to be true," he told Ernst Kaltenbrunner, chief of the German secret services. A trap could not be ruled out. It is thus not certain that Berlin drew all the benefit possible from the information provided by the spy in Ankara.

However, Cicero had enough to feed the curiosity of the leaders of the Reich. In particular, he provided rather detailed reports of the major summit conferences of the Allied camp in Cairo and Teheran in November and December 1943, about which Turkish leaders knew a good deal because of their close contacts with the British. Thanks to Cicero, the Germans were able to grasp the broad outlines of their enemies' diplomatic strategy: Churchill wanted to open a front in southeastern Europe by trying (without success) to include Turkey in a vast Mediterranean offensive against Germany. The Americans did not share this view. Roosevelt was relatively uninterested in Turkey and was concentrating on an invasion of the European continent from Great Britain. Despite some not insignificant differences of opinion, the Allies' determination to crush the Axis forces was absolute. Those German leaders who paid attention to Cicero's revelations could have no illusions on that subject. "Cicero's documents described with clarity the fate that awaited Germany," Franz von Papen wrote in his memoirs after the war. "I trembled with emotion before the spectacle of the vast historical prospects opened to me by those stolen documents," Ludwig Moyzisch wrote many years after the events.

Bern, December 1943

The Allies learned of the existence of the spy in Ankara thanks to "George Wood." The first mention of Cicero in an Allied document followed another visit to Bern by Fritz Kolbe, which took place over the Christmas holiday. Kolbe brought to the Americans from Berlin a series of cables, some of which came from the German embassy in Ankara. Among the documents that Allen Dulles transmitted to Washington, several mentioned the existence of Cicero.

On December 29, OSS Bern sent to Washington headquarters a coded message mentioning the name of Cicero, with no explanation of the nature of this mysterious source. A few days later, in a cable sent on New Year's Day 1944, Allen Dulles provided details for his Washington colleagues, referring to a series of documents "on which Milit [Ambassador von Papen] clearly placed great value and which, seemingly, were taken from the Zulu [British] Embassy through a source designated as Cicero." These details, Dulles added, had been immediately turned over to the British intelligence services based in Switzerland (designated as 521 in OSS language), for transmission to London.

On learning of the content of the information provided by Cicero, the leadership of the Allied intelligence services felt a chill: the spy had given his German contacts a list of documents prepared by the "Zulu ambassador" (Sir Hugh Knatchbull-Hugessen) in preparation for the second Cairo conference of early December 1943, a conference that had unsuccessfully considered Turkey's entry into the war on the side of the Allies. Also included in the "deliveries" by the Ankara spy was a Foreign Office memorandum dated October 7, 1943 with the title "A Long-Range View of Turkish-British Policy." All the steps taken by the English to encourage Turkey's entry into the war were set out in detail. These ultraconfidential materials had been transmitted by von Papen to the Foreign Ministry in Berlin (*Grand*), between November 3 and 5, 1943.

The identity of Cicero, and what exactly the Germans knew through him, were questions that reached the highest levels of the Allied command during the first weeks of 1944. But the British were slow to react. They waited until the end of January before asking Dulles to ask his Berlin agent for "additional available messages from the Cicero sources." Almost a month later, they asked for more details about the exact time of the November cables. On January 10, 1944, OSS Bern informed London and Washington that "Wood is ignorant of the identity of Cicero." Several weeks later, in late February 1944, Dulles wrote: "We are informed by Wood that there is no way of finding out who Cicero is or where the information about Cairo and Teheran originated. He suggests, in connection with this, that the leak might have come from an Albanian-born private secretary of Inönü whom the President took with him to Cairo." Although fairly close to reality, these details were not sufficient to identify the spy.

Feeling the vise tighten around him, Elyeza Bazna left his position in March 1944. Since mid-January 1944, the British had been actively looking for the source of the leak. At the very moment that Allen Dulles had informed Washington and London of the existence of a mole in the British embassy in Ankara—at the very beginning of January 1944—Ambassador Knatchbull-Hugessen had learned from his Turkish interlocutors that von Papen "knew too much to be honest." Two British counterespionage agents were sent to Ankara to carry out an investigation in his entourage. In Bern, Allen Dulles had asked them to be discreet and to behave as though the visit were a routine inspection. His concern was to protect his source, Fritz Kolbe, who might be identified by the Germans in case the network were dismantled. The two British agents also had to deal tactfully with the extreme sensitivity of the British ambassador, who could not understand how his embassy could be under suspicion. The detectives questioned Elyeza Bazna but found him too stupid and too ill at ease in English to consider him a suspect.

The Cicero affair could have been a disaster if the leak had not been discovered in time thanks to "George Wood." "Nothing indicates that the Germans got from Cicero the slightest detail about the plan for a landing in Europe, except perhaps the code name of the operation: *Overlord*," Dulles wrote after the war.

Berlin, December 1943

After his October visit to Bern, Fritz thought that it would be a long time before he would be able to come back. Nor did Allen Dulles expect to see him again. It had been agreed that Fritz would thenceforth send what he knew through his friend Albert Bur, the surgeon from Alsace. This complicated means of transmission was probably never used.

Berlin was in a state of chaos. The bombing was more and more terrible. Late November was particularly hard, with thousands of dead, more than two hundred thousand people made homeless, and tens of thousands of buildings destroyed. The central neighborhoods of Alexanderplatz and Charlottenburg (Fritz's neighborhood) were the most heavily damaged. Railroad stations were one of the favorite targets of the flying fortresses. Even the zoo was hit. A bomb landed directly on the crocodile house during the night of November 23. There were rumors of wild animals roaming through the streets of the city.

The Foreign Ministry was the target of several destructive raids. Only the offices on the second floor could still be used. That winter some of the chandeliers in the ministry began to resemble fountains. The carpets were saturated with water. Pieces of cardboard were hung in the windows in place of glass. It was cold. The diplomats worked with their coats on. Some of the ministry's departments were evacuated to Silesia. But most heads of departments remained in Berlin, and Fritz Kolbe, as a result, also stayed in the capital of the Reich.

The Charité hospital, where Maria Fritsch lived, had not emerged unharmed from the rain of fire. "All the windows were broken," wrote the surgeon Adolphe Jung in his notes for December 1943. "Most of the window frames and doors were torn out. Curtains and camouflage cloths for the windows, torn out as well. Cabinets opened and overturned. Plaster fallen from ceilings and walls. A strong wind full of smoke and soot blew through the corridors and the rooms open on all sides. . . . All the patients were in the cellars. The laundry and storage rooms were emptied out and the patients' beds set out in them. Long rows of beds were in the corridors, men, women, and soldiers all mixed together."

Basic goods and services were growing increasingly scarce. Life was constantly punctuated by collections for the community: cloth, old paper, shoes, materials of all kinds, including animals (particularly dogs, requisitioned for the army). Coal was in short supply. It was forbidden to run water during air raids; it had to be kept in reserve to fight fires. But this was not always enough: "Here and there a fire hose, handled by soldiers or firemen, threw jets of water on the houses," wrote Adolphe Jung. "The water came from the Spree through long pipes in the depths of the river, because, of course, the usual pipes, less than an hour after the bombing, had no more pressure. Even in cellars, you could barely get a small quantity of water."

Half the time, Fritz Kolbe and his close friends were in the shelters. "Life in a bunker," he said himself of the winter nights of 1943 spent in underground shelters with stale air. You could never be without your civil defense kit, the content of which was strictly determined by the administration: a suitcase containing clothing, extra linen, shoe care products, a sewing kit, a bar of soap and a package of crackers for each person, a container of milk, sugar, oatmeal, a bottle of water, a small saucepan, plates and utensils, and matches. A pitiful set of provisions. In any event, the shelters provided only relative safety: "Cases of violent death were reported when the outside of a shelter was hit by a bomb with no damage to the interior. Some people are said to have fallen, bleeding from the nose and the mouth, dying from a fractured skull. This was caused by the impact transmitted directly to a head leaning against the bunker wall," according to Adolphe Jung.

Berliners thus lived from day to day, in the expectation of imminent death. But life continued nevertheless. Professor Sauerbruch and his friends in the Wednesday Club continued to meet to discuss various subjects once or twice a month. In addition to a noteworthy presentation by the physicist Werner Heisenberg on "The Evolution of the Concept of Reality in Physics" (June 30, 1943), the year was marked by a presentation by the former ambassador to Rome, Ulrich von Hassell, on "The Personality of King Alexander of Yugoslavia" (December 15, 1943). The members of the club appreciated more than ever the friendly atmosphere of their meetings. One evening at Sauerbruch's, the austere Ulrich von Hassell even stood unsteadily on a table and started singing old student songs.

A distinct relaxation of social constraints began to be noticed almost everywhere. After the summer of 1943, with the massive movement of families to the countryside, Berlin had become a city of bachelors. From boozy evenings to passing flirtations, men had decided to take advantage of life. "If their wives only knew!" wrote the journalist Ursula von Kardorff. Money no longer had much importance; tips had never been so generous in the cafés and restaurants that were still open. The center of this slightly decadent social life was the Adlon Hotel, near the Brandenburg Gate. In addition, a large foreign population had given the capital of the Reich a new face. Forced labor had brought people from around Europe to replace the Germans who were at the front. From workers to doctors, all professions were represented. Berlin was in the process of becoming a kind of involuntary melting pot.

The leaders of the Reich no longer knew what to come up with to mobilize the population for a "fanatical" drive toward "final victory." In December, a directive from Goebbels required journalists to banish the word "catastrophe" from their vocabulary.

Bern, late December 1943

Meanwhile in Washington and London, "George Wood" began to be of real interest. Some secret service figures wanted to ask the Berlin agent questions on precise points. But Dulles informed his OSS colleagues in Washington: "Impossible now to ask 805 more questions without incurring risk, unless he comes back, which is not likely." For his part, Fritz was furious at not being able to transmit regularly to Bern everything that passed through his hands.

Suddenly, a letter written on December 18, 1943 informed the Americans of the imminent arrival of their friend from Berlin. As had been agreed in October, the message was sent in the form of an innocuous letter to Walter Schuepp, Ernst Kocherthaler's brother-in-law. "Dear Walter, I wanted to tell you that we are still alive despite the latest bombing. Apart from a few broken windows, nothing happened to us. I take the opportunity to tell you that I will probably be at your house on 27 December. So, save a piece of the Christmas goose for me! Say hello to Ernesto and his family. Merry Christmas!" Fritz had written this letter, signed "Georges" (*sic*), in Berlin but had given it to a diplomatic courier on assignment to Bern, and it bore a Swiss postmark of 21 December. As soon as he received it, Walter Schuepp passed it on to Ernst Kocherthaler, who immediately sent a telegram to Gerald Mayer: "I have heard from a friend abroad that he will probably be in Bern on the 27th . . . Since I should by no means miss him, I'm going to be there then, at 13:09. If you could be there too we could talk over our pending business."

Fritz had managed to secure an assignment to Switzerland. This was his third visit to Bern since August. Because of the holidays at the end of the year, there was no other candidate for the trip. By going, he was doing a service for Fräulein von Heimerdinger, to whom he confessed that he was going "to talk to German émigré circles in Switzerland," no longer attempting to justify his trip by the formalities of his divorce. The only difficulty was to provide a motive for this new absence to his boss, Karl Ritter, who finally signed his orders and asked Fritz to bring back a box of good cigars from Brazil, which he paid for, as usual, in advance. It took Fritz two days to travel from Berlin to Bern. The Anhalter Bahnhof had been bombed: the building was still standing but all the tracks had been destroyed. He had to go to Potsdam to take the train.

Fritz stayed in Bern over the holidays. Every night, he saw the Americans for many hours. It was on the occasion of this trip that he gave Allen Dulles von Papen's cables alluding to Cicero, along with many other things. Allen Dulles and Gerald Mayer had never had to absorb so much information all at once. Fritz had brought more than two hundred documents, not only copies of cables but also handwritten notes that only Ernst Kocherthaler was able to decipher.

In the course of this third meeting with Kolbe, the Americans gathered information of all kinds. Night after night, Fritz unleashed a torrent of information. Revelations of a military nature were particularly interesting. Kolbe indicated the location of a Junkers factory where engines for the new Messerschmitt 262 were assembled, the first jet plane in the Luftwaffe (in Dessau, south of Berlin). He also provided one of the places where the new secret German rockets were stored. Fritz Kolbe did not know the name of these weapons, but Professor Sauerbruch had spoken to him of a site where he had seen launching pads aimed at England when he was traveling in Belgium. This was probably Helfaut-Wizernes, near Saint-Omer in the northern part of France that had been annexed to Belgium. The position was bombed some weeks later (from March 11 to September 1, 1944), although it is not known whether the information provided by Fritz had helped to identify the target.

Fritz Kolbe was well informed about the results of the most recent Allied bombing in Germany and the rest of Europe. He spoke at length about the ruins of Berlin and described daily life in the capital of the Reich. He revealed that the oil fields of Ploesti in Rumania had resumed production after being heavily bombed in August 1943. He also spoke of atrocities committed in the occupied countries. A cable from Athens dated January 2, 1944 revealed, for example, that as reprisal against the resistance, all the male inhabitants of the village of Kalavrita in the Peloponnese had been massacred, including young boys.

The most substantial information provided by Kolbe concerned the international relations of the Reich, particularly its links with the members of the Axis and with neutral countries close to Germany, such as Spain and Portugal. It was clear from reading the dispatches from Berlin that that Europe was beginning to fall apart and was now held together only by force. Even fear of the Soviets was no longer a sufficient adhesive force.

With reference to Italy, the cables brought by Fritz sketched an image of a defeated country, torn in two, under the iron grip of the Nazis (the north and the capital had been occupied by the Wehrmacht since September 1943). One dispatch reported recent discussions in Belluno, in the Italian Alps, between Mussolini and the German ambassador to Rome, Rudolf Rahn. "Mussolini attacked the German scorched-earth policy in a recent discussion with Rahn. The former said that this policy would make the Italian people so angry that it would result in preventing any effective Italian cooperation in fighting alongside the Nazis."

On Spain, one dispatch described in a few words the state of relations between the two countries: "Conti [Franco] still wants Germans to win. . . . Unfavorable news from battlefront bothers Conti who wants news of military developments from HQ." To be sure, Spain was continuing to supply strategic materials to Germany—one dispatch provided the tonnage of tungsten delivered by Spain to Germany between January and September 1943 (more than seven hundred tons). These exports were disguised as "shipments of sardines," sometimes as "shipments of oranges," and a little later as "shipments of lead." But Franco's ministers were not all in agreement about continuing these exports and some were beginning to think that it was time to shift to the side of the Allies. At the same time, Baron Oswald von Hoyningen-Huene, the Reich's envoy to Lisbon, was warning Berlin that Portugal intended to increase the prices for its raw materials (tungsten, especially) shipped to Germany.

The Americans were probably a little disappointed that Fritz had brought so little material coming from Japan. But there was an interesting cable from Tokyo, dated December 20, 1943, in which the German ambassador reported that he had heard that "Stalin has recently been a victim of 'Herzasthma' and his physicians have urged that he take a rest."

The hesitations of central European countries that were allied with Berlin appeared openly. All of a sudden, thanks to Kolbe, it was possible to see the gradual crumbling of Hitler's alliances, prelude to a direct assumption of power by the Reich authorities. Bulgaria and Rumania seemed to be the first to want to change sides. Sofia, October 29, 1943: "The state of mind of the Bulgarian population is growing much worse." Bucharest, November 1943: "The situation in Rumania is becoming serious. The arms supplied by Germany remain in the country and are not used in the fight against Russia." Indications of gradual detachment by each of these allied countries proliferated in the press (there were no more attacks on Stalin, war propaganda grew weaker, and there was better treatment of the Jews, according to the documents provided by Kolbe). With reference to Hungary, Fritz delivered more ambiguous reports. "Hungary remains firmly on the side of the Reich. What can the Americans offer us? Guarantee our borders?" explained Otto Hatz, a high official in the Hungarian intelligence services in mid-December.

Many documents had to do with France. Fritz Kolbe allowed them to see, almost day by day, the serious crisis of confidence in the fall of 1943 between Vichy and the Reich, which would lead to increased control by Berlin over the regime and the gradual establishment of a "militia state." In late October 1943, the German ambassador in Paris, Otto Abetz, revealed to Ribbentrop that Pétain was trying to make contact with the Allies. The marshal's immediate entourage was subject to intensified suspicion on the part of the Germans. Conversely, Pierre Laval enjoyed the confidence of the German authorities and was constantly seeking Berlin's support in his struggle for influence against Pétain. In addition, in a conversation with Roland Krug von Nidda, Otto Abetz's representative at Vichy, on October 27, 1943, "he requested that he be allowed to undertake the job of cleaning up Pétain's group of associates." Another cable signed by Otto Abetz on December 3 considered the possibility of forcing Pétain to resign without directly offending French public opinion. "For French consumption," Abetz wrote, "it is essential to show that Pétain failed in an historic mission and led the country almost to ruin. . . . Inside France, the Pétain regime produced national stagnation and reaction."

Abetz wrote again on December 14, 1943: "The increasing poverty of the French laboring masses has created the fear of a gradual shift toward communism." And on December 16: "Doriot's headquarters imply that they do not wish to participate in the government unless the Cabinet is selected by Doriot himself." And on December 19, a dispatch provided a statistical summary of attacks committed by the French Resistance. The figures gave evidence of a continuous increase.

And then there was an astonishing document dated December 24, 1943: a list of thirty-five prominent French personalities that the Gestapo proposed to have arrested, although it had not been able to reach its goal, "the various German authorities not having succeeded in coming to an agreement" on those arrests. As a consequence, Otto Abetz decided to send the list to Berlin in order to get definitive instructions from his ministry. The list, presented in alphabetical order, contained no names of political figures, except for that of a former minister, Lucien Lamoureux, characterized as an "active radical-socialist" but defended by the German military authorities against the Gestapo. Principally targeted were the mayors of a certain number of French towns characterized as "opponents of collaboration," "pro-Jewish Gaullists," "Freemasons," or even "members of the Rotary Club." The mayors of Caen, Rennes, Rouen, Poitiers, Abbeville, Lunéville, Versailles, Fontainebleau, Chartres, Pontivy, and even Vichy were suspected. There were also some prefects (Alpes-Maritimes, Hérault, Calvados). But in every case Ambassador Abetz or the military occupation authorities pointed out that there was no evidence of an offense and refused to authorize the arrests. There were also important figures from the world of finance, such as Henri Ardant, the influential president of the Société Générale (the Gestapo denounced his "anti-German attitude," but the military authorities defended him) and Yves Bréart de Boisanger, governor of the Bank of France (called "disloyal" by the Gestapo, but Hans-Richard Hemmen, the Reich's delegate for economic and financial questions to the French authorities, opposed his arrest. There were also several actors: Jean-Louis Barrault, Marie Bell, Béatrice Bretty ("the embassy expresses reservations, because they are politically insignificant; very much appreciated as artists"), and personalities of the intellectual world like the publisher Jean Fayard, whom the embassy defended because he had "published books favorable to National Socialism before the war." In the end, the composition of this "blacklist" had no consequences. The weakness of the accusations, the competition among the different occupation authorities, and the complexity of the protective networks were stronger than the Gestapo.

Bern/Berlin, early January 1944

Because of the holiday at the end of the year, Fritz had stayed an entire week in Bern. He returned to Berlin on Sunday, January 2. Later, speaking of this trip, he remembered that he had returned home in a state of advanced fatigue, "not at all rested or rejuvenated, but pale with exhaustion, having gone without sleep for several nights, and always a little nervous." The last adjective is a euphemism: Every time he returned to Germany, Fritz was terrified at the idea of being picked up by the Gestapo when he got off the train. But this time again, he could return home as though nothing had happened.

In Bern, the Americans were staggering under the workload. Every night between Christmas and New Year's Day had been spent talking with Kolbe. During the day, Allen Dulles and Gerald Mayer wrote summaries that they immediately turned over to their technical staff for coding. Dulles made several reports to Washington after each of his conversations with "Wood." He used some general elements of analysis to supply material for his telephone conversations with Washington headquarters, which took place every evening in the form of news flashes. Cables went off day and night. On the basis of the "secret cables of the Reich" (*geheime Reichssachen*) brought by Fritz, the Kappa messages were developed for London and Washington. Once there, they would be reworked and summarized under the name of "Boston series." As usual, the OSS Bern experts had to be particularly careful to disguise all proper names. Von Papen became *Milit* and Sükrü Saracoglu, the Turkish prime minister, *Harem*. Numan Menemencioglu, the foreign minister, was *Penni*. Otto Köcher, the German envoy to Bern, was called *Lomax*, and Switzerland was designated as *Rasho*. In the period from Christmas to the middle of January, OSS Bern was working at top speed. It took at least two weeks after every visit from Kolbe to digest all the documents that he had brought.

To get the materials from "George Wood" to London and Washington, the Americans had had access to a new means of communication since the fall of 1943. Of course, the telegraph remained the favored means of transmission—there was nothing faster or more secure. But since the liberation of Corsica in October, Allied troops were no longer very far from Switzerland, and OSS contacts in the Resistance made it possible to transmit documents through Geneva, Lyon, and Marseille to Calvi or Bastia. This system was useful for conveying copies of original documents or maps. Files were first microfilmed. Then the precious little package was given to a locomotive engineer on the train between Geneva and Lyon. The railroad man placed the package in a little hatch above the boiler, ready to destroy it quickly in case of an untimely visit from the Gestapo. In Lyon, a "friend" received the envelope and carried it to Marseille by bicycle. From there, a fishing boat took it to Corsica, where it was put on board a plane for Algiers, then on to London and Washington. Between the departure and the arrival of the package, ten to twelve days went by.

The quantity and quality of documents supplied by "George Wood" in the course of this Christmas visit considerably increased his credibility. Even before Fritz's departure for Berlin, Allen Dulles had taken up his pen to sum up their third encounter: "I now firmly believe in his good faith and am ready to stake my reputation that they are genuine. I base my conclusion on internal evidence and on the nature of the documents themselves," he wrote on December 29, 1943 to his usual correspondents in the OSS. In Washington as well, they were beginning to become convinced of the good faith of the Berlin agent. "Seemingly authentic and vastly more interesting," was now the word in General Donovan's entourage (telegram from Washington head-quarters to the OSS London office, 7 January 1944).

On January 10, the head of the OSS decided to present the first fourteen Kappa/Boston cables to President Roosevelt. The file was extremely confidential, and its distribution correspondingly restricted: There was a copy for the White House, another for the State Department, one for the War Department, and one for the Navy. And then a few selected items were given to one or another department of the OSS, especially counterespionage (X-2), but also the research and analysis department. A few fragments were communicated to the army intelligence services (G2). In all, no more than about ten people were kept informed of the revelations from "George Wood."

Berlin/Bern, February–March 1944

It was impossible for Fritz to return to Switzerland after his long stay at Christmas. Too many absences would have been noticed. To get around the difficulty, he approached a colleague who had had the good fortune, in early 1944, to be placed on a list of regular couriers for Bern. A member of the Nazi Party, Willy Pohle had all the requisite qualities for the position. But Fritz trusted him, knowing that he could give him his personal correspondence with no fear. Fritz even dared to tell him, as he had already confided in Fräulein von Heimerdinger, that he wished to inform certain "German émigré circles in Switzerland" about what was really going on in Germany. Willy Pohle willingly agreed to be of service to him. After all, this kind of small gesture was common in the ministry. Fritz was able to show his gratitude. He asked his colleague to go to see Walter Schuepp in person in Bern (Gryphenhübeliweg 19), to withdraw the sum of fifty Swiss francs "due from a friend" (not telling him, of course, that this was left over from the two hundred francs given to him by Dulles). Fritz suggested to Pohle that he use some of that money for his personal expenses and that he buy cigars with the rest, in order to be able to offer some to Karl Ritter.

Professor Sauerbruch also had occasion to go to Switzerland from time to time for conferences or surgical operations. Most of the time he went to Zurich. When the opportunity arose—as it did, for example, in mid-February 1944—Fritz asked him to mail a letter to Walter Schuepp. The explanation that he gave to the surgeon was the same one he had given to Pohle: He said that he had regular connections with "German émigré circles." Fritz would never have dared to tell the surgeon the truth.

"Sauerbruch doesn't know what's in the letter. If you should be in contact with him don't give me away. He would be deeply hurt," Fritz wrote in a letter that he passed to the Americans through Ernst Kocherthaler toward the middle of February 1944. This was a letter of eight crowded pages, seven in tight script and one typed single-spaced. Once again, Kocherthaler had to be enlisted to transcribe the script. It was cast in the form of a dialogue between two fictional figures who agreed that the outcome of the war was already decided, and it supported this thesis by a sort of survey of the world situation in which the evidence was drawn from diplomatic cables supplied by Fritz and other sources of inside information. Fritz had no doubt wanted to amuse himself by using a fictional register. Had the purpose been to conceal the nature of his message, the device was not very prudent: If a letter like this one had been opened, it would have led him to the gallows. "I passed many sleepless nights when the 'material' was on its way," Fritz confessed after the war. The letter ended hurriedly: "I have to stop. Too bad. What good are these air raids?"

In Bern, this letter troubled and confused Allen Dulles: "It is hard to decipher all the cases as well as to differentiate . . . Foreign Office documents or policy from Wood's own opinions," he cabled to his Washington colleagues on February 21. A few days later, Dulles explained that "this letter was written in a hurry and part of it was apparently composed during an air raid. These facts may explain the inconsistencies."

Despite a few false notes, Allen Dulles managed to draw out of Fritz's letter a series of interesting indications on certain very sensitive matters. German agents stationed in Ireland were providing a series of precise observations about military sites in England (air bases, arms factories, munitions dumps). Other passages reported a rein-forcement of the Atlantic Wall in France. It clearly appeared that the preparations for a vast invasion of the continent, "between April and June 1944," were known to the Germans. But the leaders of the Reich were ignorant of the location of the future landing ("there is talk of Holland," reported the spies based in Ireland), and nothing indicated that they knew its date.

This was not all. For the first time, Fritz provided information about Japan (*Scarlet* in the Kappa cables) on the basis of facts collected by the German embassy in Tokyo. He revealed in particular that Tokyo was secretly encouraging its Berlin ally to make peace with Moscow. He also transmitted information on certain Japanese positions in the Pacific (Burma and New Guinea).

Early in March, a postcard from Fritz arrived at OSS Bern through the usual diplomatic circuit. It pictured a bouquet of narcissus along with a few spring buds. At first sight, it was a warm birthday greeting addressed to Walter Schuepp, but he was born on April 28 and the card had been written on February 22—so it would seem that Fritz had been particularly early with his card. In fact, the greeting contained a hidden message. An assemblage of apparently incoherent letters had been typed on the right side of the card: *D xzrfgx aqh ADX Thfokf tlhjlnkva hcy Htvkpz Alml Gsyfji Oxsuch Wkmybdcebzp*. Was this simply bad typing? Fritz apologized. "A child was playing at typing just as the card was about to be sent," and Fritz added that "unfortunately [he] had no other card available."

This strange message was deciphered by the Americans through the code to which Fritz had given them the key during one of his previous visits to Bern. It said: "Yolland of OWI in Ankara is discussing defec-tion to Germany with Consul Wolff in Ankara." Fritz had not even taken the trouble to put the card in an envelope. He was confident in the indecipherability of his personal secret code. He was right. The card arrived at its destination without provoking the slightest suspi-cion. It had been mailed in Bern, as usual, by Willy Pohle or another of Fritz's colleagues on a mission to the German legation in Switzerland.

Fritz's mail was now arriving regularly in Bern. His correspondence might be hidden in a pair of shoes or in clothing, but mailings always arrived for Ernst Kocherthaler's brother-in-law in the diplomatic pouch. Another letter soon arrived for Walter Schuepp (it had been written on March 6, 1944), with, once again, dozens of excerpts from confidential cables. "Poor fellow who has to read all that! I had real good opportunities, and I didn't waste any of them!" Fritz wrote. Among the several "pearls" of this springtime delivery, the Americans found the summary of a conversation between the German envoy in Bern, Otto Köcher, and Marcel Pilet-Golaz, the chief of the Swiss diplomatic corps. The latter considered probable, in case of a failure of the Allied invasion, an "Anglo-German agreement" aimed at preventing the installation of a Soviet regime in Germany. Numan Menemencioglu, the Turkish foreign minister, expressed exactly the same opinion (according to a cable sent from Ankara on February 12, 1944).

Fritz Kolbe relayed certain rumors reporting tensions between the Allies. In a letter received in February, he had revealed that the German diplomatic service was interested in the anti-Soviet attitude of a certain "Dallas," the key man in the American legation in Bern. This was, of course, Allen Dulles, whose remarks about the "excess of Soviet power" had reached the ears of Otto Abetz through Jean Jardin, former cabinet secretary to Pierre Laval who had been posted to Bern since the fall of 1943. In addition, in his letter of March 6, Fritz thought that he could say, on the basis of a recent cable from von Papen, that Roosevelt had been extremely critical of Stalin during the Teheran conference (November 28 to December 1, the first summit meeting among Roosevelt, Churchill, and Stalin). German diplomatic circles seemed not to exclude the possibility of a break between the Americans and the Russians, a prelude to a "compromise peace" between the Germans and the Anglo-American forces.

In relaying this kind of information, was Fritz expressing political intentions, and was he acting on behalf of a high Berlin official who wished to remain anonymous? The OSS people naturally asked themselves this kind of question. Some cables communicated by Fritz could pass for disguised political messages, such as one from January 2, 1944, written by the German envoy in Bucharest, Manfred Freiherr von Killinger. He said that, according to a Rumanian source working in Rome, "the Pope was highly perturbed and had told him that the British and Americans were paving the way for Bolshevism in Italy."

However, the letter of March 6 helped reassure the American's about "Wood's" good faith. Fritz had put a second envelope inside the first, labeled "confidential/for Ernesto." It contained four pages written in very small script. Reading with a magnifying glass, the Americans discovered a complete list of the German counterespionage service (the Abwehr) in Switzerland. Already fairly well informed on this subject, they could put this very valuable information together with what they knew from other sources and work out a nearly complete organization chart of enemy agents operating in their immediate vicinity. The most interesting was probably the information gleaned by Fritz that the Germans were unaware of the existence of the OSS office in Bern. In Berlin it was thought that the headquarters of American intelligence in Switzerland was located in Zurich.

To please Fritz and thank him for his help, the Americans answered in a code that he had himself devised. They sent to Berlin a postcard with a mountain scene, mailed from the ski resort of Parsenn, near Davos. The message was the following: "I managed to make three ski jumps. As you know, I am not a beginner. The weather is fine." The "three successful jumps" meant that the Americans had in fact received the last three letters from Fritz. "I am not a beginner" meant that they had managed to decipher his postcard of February 22. "The weather is fine": the information was useful. This was the best postcard Fritz had ever received.

10

ONE MISUNDERSTANDING
AFTER ANOTHER

Washington, January–March 1944

Although President Roosevelt had received in January 1944 some of
the cables sent by Fritz, the Berlin spy continued to be subject to
strong suspicion in American intelligence circles. "All the messages
are probably authentic. . . . Although our investigation reveals no evidence to substantiate the suspicion, colleagues here still suspect that
the whole thing may be a buildup to a sensational plant," was still the
finding of the experts of the Secret Intelligence department of the
OSS on January 22, 1944. If this way of seeing persisted so long in
Washington, this was because the Allies themselves frequently used
subterfuge and deception in their war against Germany.

On January 28, 1944, OSS headquarters in Washington decided to
test the knowledge of the mysterious Berlin agent. It sent to its Bern
office a strange message in the form of a guessing game. "What are the
present relations between Himmler and Ribbentrop? . . . Is political
intelligence collected by Himmler's outfit? If so, what agencies are
instrumental in collecting it? . . . Are the intelligence functions of the
Auswärtiges Amt and the Sicherheitsdienst coordinated? . . . What

distinction can be made between the Geheimstaatspolizei and the Sicherheitsdienst? . . . Please try to get Wood to reply to these questions the next chance you get. They are preliminary test queries to which we know the answers."

Allen Dulles paid no attention to this odd questionnaire and immediately threw the grotesque document into the wastebasket. He was gradually growing weary of all this suspicion and was impatient with the skepticism of his Washington colleagues, but minds barely changed at OSS headquarters; on the contrary, obstacles to the dissemination of Fritz Kolbe's material proliferated. As time went on, the agency headed by General Donovan became an increasingly less flexible organization, and espionage experts expanded their power, sometimes bureaucratic and nitpicking, over most ongoing operations. Beginning in late 1943, the OSS systematically asked for the opinion of the Military Intelligence Service before authorizing the dissemination of the Kappa/Boston papers to Washington decision makers. And the professionals of military intelligence were even more circumspect than their OSS colleagues. They turned the file over to the Special Branch, the department specializing in deciphering enemy messages, under the authority of Colonel Alfred McCormack, a former Chicago lawyer. Colonel McCormack's men had the means to cross-check huge quantities of German communications intercepted around the world and had privileged access to the very valuable information gleaned by the British from the "Ultra" system. For several months, Colonel McCormack and his assistants worked with the seriousness and precision of entomologists on the Kappa material. They read and reread, paragraph by paragraph, all the cables given to them by the OSS. Hundreds of documents were studied and dissected. As a result, the dissemination of the documents was considerably slowed.

Beginning in February 1944, "Wood's" information no longer circulated beyond a very closed circle, limited to the world of intelligence and counterespionage. President Roosevelt stopped being informed of the content of the Boston reports. Among political appointees, only Assistant Secretary of State Adolf Berle remained on the list of recipients. Berle was a brilliant economist close to Roosevelt, charged with coordinating all the "special files," but he was primarily concerned with the problems of Latin America. It may be asked justifiably whether he was in the best position to grasp the content of the material supplied by Kolbe.

By searching hard enough for a flaw in the "George Wood" documents, Colonel McCormack finally found one. "It's a bad fish," he said on reading a German diplomatic cable from Rome, received in Bern in late February 1944. This document mentioned a decree of Marshal Kesselring, commander-in-chief of all Wehrmacht forces in southwestern Europe. The text was as follows: "The Commanding Officer of the Southwest front has decreed that in the event of the evacuation of Rome, all the electric plants with the exception of those supplying Vatican City, all railroad and industrial plants outside of the city, all bridges over the Tiber, and gas and water tubes attached to 5 of these bridges, are to be demolished. The order does not exclude any bridge." On reading this cable, Alfred McCormack immediately thought that it was a fake. He believed that the Germans had every interest in getting this kind of information to the Allies in order to slow down their offensive in the ongoing Italian campaign. He observed that other elements of information coming from Italy contradicted the tenor of this message. Finally, he judged that Marshal Kesselring did not have the authority necessary to make a decision with such weighty consequences. The order of destruction (even partial) of a city like Rome should logically come from the führer and from him alone. The British, questioned by McCormack, also found the message suspect.

As a consequence, for many more months, everything that came from "George Wood" was read with redoubled caution. In Washington and London, people always anticipated a trap. An OSS procedural notice dated March 24, 1944 said that the reports (except those of counterintelligence import) were to be "disseminated with the explanation that they are unconfirmed and that we are desirous of comment on their authenticity." At the same time, however, Washington sent a request to Allen Dulles: could his source not provide elements of information about Japan and the Far East?

Washington's request was a call for help. Throughout the duration of the war, the American espionage network in Asia remained very weak. There was no equivalent to Fritz Kolbe in Tokyo, and Washington did not have a mole in the upper reaches of the Japanese administration. Allen Dulles was probably pleased to note that they were appealing to him, the man in Bern, to collect data from around the world. But how could he transmit the request to Fritz Kolbe in Berlin? He decided to send him a message on a postcard. A classic mountain scene would once again serve the purpose. The signature was a woman's. The message in German on the reverse was innocuous enough not to arouse the suspicion of the censors, stating that one of her friends prior to the war had kept a shop selling Japanese trinkets, toys, etc., and had found a considerable market for them. Now her friend could get them no more. In view of Germany's close alliance with Japan, was it possible to find any of this Japanese material in Germany, or to get it through Germany? Her friend wanted more of it. When he received this card mailed from Zurich, Fritz immediately understood what was involved and he began to assemble cables coming from Tokyo. He carefully stored them in his safe for transmission to Bern when the opportunity arose.

Berlin, March 1944

The scene took place in or around March 1944. We are not sure whether Fritz was at home that afternoon or in Maria Fritsch's apartment in the Charité hospital, his favorite refuge. In any event, he was not at the ministry. His colleagues had seen him at work between eight and noon, as they did every morning, but he had left his office at lunch, pleading a minor illness in order to get permission to leave for a few hours. He had taken with him in his briefcase a confidential memorandum on Hungary that he intended to summarize for the Americans. The document had been prepared by Heinrich Himmler's services. It was a detailed presentation of the anti-German activities of Miklós Kállay, the prime minister of Hungary. The Reichsführer SS had sent the file to Ribbentrop. As a matter of course, the envelope (stamped *geheime Reichssache*) had found its way to Karl Ritter, who had turned it over to Fritz Kolbe for filing. This was not the first time that Fritz had dared to risk taking documents from Wilhelmstrasse. Working at home or at Maria's, he could concentrate better on reviewing important documents. Of course, this was strictly forbidden. If he had been found outside the ministry in possession of secret files, he would immediately have been turned over to the Gestapo. But no one ever checked the contents of his briefcase.

The SS report on Hungary illustrated the fears of the Hitler regime about the Reich's satellite countries. Since the winter of 1942–43 and the rout of the Hungarian Second Army on the Don, Budapest had been plagued by doubt. "Every Hungarian soldier understands that he is being asked to sacrifice himself for interests other than his own. . . . If a nation begins to free itself from the hated yoke, the system as a whole is going to crack," wrote Ruth Andreas-Friedrich in her diary on March 22, 1944.

Since the summer of 1943, the authorities in Budapest had been trying to shake off the chains of their alliance with Berlin. The anti-Jewish measures were only laxly followed, a relatively independent press continued to appear, some opposition parties were not banned. But, above all, the Hungarian leaders were multiplying secret contacts with the Allies. In Ankara, Bern, and Lisbon, envoys from Miklós Kállay were holding discussions with diplomatic representatives from London and Washington. Starting in the second half of 1943, Hitler constantly put pressure on Admiral Horthy to change prime ministers.

These details, and many others, were in the file that Fritz removed from the ministry that morning. He thought he had all the time he needed to study the memorandum far from prying eyes. But while working in a room where he thought he could be at peace, the phone rang. At the other end of the line, a colleague spoke to him in a panic-stricken tone: "Where is the Kállay file? Ribbentrop is about to go to a meeting with Himmler. He needs the file right away." Kolbe answered that the file was in his personal safe at the Foreign Ministry. He was the only one with a key. Oddly, he kept cool (afterward, he was astonished that he did not give way to panic). He ran back to the ministry. Fifteen minutes later, he was there, out of breath, his brief-case in hand. He rushed up the stairs four at a time and swept into his office like a whirlwind. There he managed to make it appear that he took the document out of his safe and finally handed it to a colleague standing near him stamping his feet with impatience. A few minutes later, he learned that Karl Ritter, furious, had for an hour been spew-ing out violent cries of rage against his subordinates and was close to having a breakdown over the incident.

The "Kállay file" would not come into the hands of the OSS. This was a pity, because Fritz knew that the Americans in Bern were vi-tally interested in everything concerning developments in countries allied to Germany. He had already provided them, since late 1943, with information of the greatest importance about Hungary. Thanks to Fritz, the Americans knew that the Germans were aware of some of their secret conversations with envoys of the Kállay government. Dur-ing the last week of 1943, Adolf Beckerle, German envoy in Sofia, had transmitted to Berlin an Abwehr report disclosing very confidential statements made by a lieutenant colonel of the Hungarian secret ser-vices well known to the secret services in Washington. The man's name was Otto Hatz. He had disclosed to the Germans the complete contents of his discussions with an American diplomat in Istanbul. The document had come into the hands of the OSS through the good of-fices of Fritz. It was thus learned in Washington that some Hungarian interlocutors of the United States were playing a double game. Beckerle spoke of this Lieutenant Colonel Hatz as a "trustworthy man," resolutely "pro-German." In a Kappa cable sent to Washington in late December 1943, the OSS officers in Bern had pointed out that *Trude* (Otto Hatz) "is maybe pulling our legs."

This information of the highest importance was not used as it should be, and the Americans allowed themselves to be caught in a trap with terrible consequences. On March 16, 1944, a team of three American spies, equipped with a radio transmitter, was secretly para-chuted into Hungary to prepare a reversal of alliances (the operation, christened "Sparrow," was masterminded from OSS Bern). But the three agents were captured shortly after their arrival on Hungarian territory and sent to Berlin for interrogation. Furious at the secret dealings of some governing circles in Budapest with the Allies, Hitler had decided to strike a great blow. On March 19, 1944, Germany invaded Hungary and put an end to any inclination toward the emancipation of the country. In place of the Kállay government, a collaborationist government under the leadership of General Döme Sztójay was set up. The strong man of Hungary was now a German from the foreign ministry, the ambassador plenipotentiary, and SS Brigadeführer Edmund Veesenmayer, a career diplomat who specialized in carrying out the regime's dirty work (posted to the Balkans since 1941, he had been in charge of eliminating the Jews of Serbia).

Hitler knew that the Hungarian leaders were having discussions with the Allies. This was what motivated his decision to invade Hungary. The Americans knew, through Kolbe, that the Germans were closely following their negotiations with the Kállay government. But they did not take precautions to neutralize Lieutenant Colonel Hatz. If they had taken into account information provided by "George Wood," they might have enabled Hungary to escape a catastrophe: Beginning in late March 1944, the country was placed under the thumb of the SS. A merciless system of repression was put in place. The opposition was sent to concentration camps. Systematic deportation of the Jewish population began.

After the occupation of the country by the Germans, the Americans continued to be very well informed, through Fritz Kolbe, of what was going on in Hungary. In the Foreign Ministry, Ambassador Karl Ritter was the principal contact for Edmund Veesenmayer, the Reich's proconsul in the Hungarian capital. But it would appear that all of that did no good. In Washington, "George Wood" was not yet considered a totally trustworthy source.

In early spring 1944, everyone in Berlin was savoring something of a respite in Allied bombing. In late March, Fritz learned that he would soon have a mission to Bern. The prospect of resuming contact with the Americans filled him with both enthusiasm and anxiety. Border controls had been reinforced during the last few weeks. The Nazi leaders were more than ever suspicious of people in contact with foreign countries (particularly with neutral countries). They knew from their intelligence services that leaks from Hitler's headquarters were spreading through neutral countries. Fortunately for Fritz, no one thought of suspecting him in particular, but it was now not infrequent for diplomatic couriers to be subject to a body search when they crossed the border. Sometimes they even had to disclose the contents of their briefcases.

Fritz feared that his trips to Bern had attracted the attention of the Gestapo. Always well informed, the surgeon Ferdinand Sauerbruch had warned Fritz that the chief of protocol of the Foreign Ministry, Alexander von Dörnberg, was interested in his comings and goings in Switzerland. "Something is in the air," Fritz told himself with foreboding. The intuition had an even firmer basis because he was now part of an active resistance group. For the first time, he was participating in clandestine meetings attended by influential men. More and more often, he met Count Alfred von Waldersee, a former major in the Wehrmacht and an anti-Nazi, who was in the process of going into business through family connections in the Ruhr. Through Ernst Kocherthaler, he had met Walter Bauer, who was close to Carl Goerdeler and resolutely determined to take action.

An economist and an intellectual, Walter Bauer was a former student of Husserl and Heidegger at the University of Freiburg. He had worked for a large coal company in Prague controlled by a Jewish family. When the company was "Aryanized," the Nazis had offered to make him its head, but he had refused and resigned from his position. Having become independent, he remained active in industry, but he spent a great deal of time in Protestant church circles opposed to the regime. Fritz greatly admired him. He was a self-made man. He had completed his high school studies in evening courses after having been brought up, like Fritz, in the school of the youth movement. The two men were about the same age.

Walter Bauer's office, at Unter den Linden 28, was a place for meetings and discussions. Fritz was there very often. Those who frequented the address were not unknown: you could meet Goerdeler, Dietrich Bonhoeffer, and other eminent figures among the anti-Nazi Christians. Fritz had no direct contact with these major figures of the time, but he came to recognize them. He probably did not always feel at ease in the midst of this intellectual community used to wide-ranging debates. Similarly, he chose to remain in the background at the Wednesday Club when Professor Sauerbruch honored him with an invitation to address it in 1944. "Those people intimidate me," he said in explanation to the surgeon. What he didn't tell Sauerbruch was that he found the members of the Wednesday Club "too old" for his taste.

However, Fritz felt perfectly at ease with a seventy-year-old man, Paul Löbe, a major figure in the SPD and a living embodiment of the Weimar Republic. The circumstances of their meeting are impossible to specify (probably in January 1944, maybe at Walter Bauer's office, perhaps at the home of friends from prewar Social Democratic circles). Paul Löbe was the last president of the democratic Reichstag. Replaced in his parliamentary seat by Hermann Göring in 1932, he had been sent to a concentration camp in Silesia when the Nazis came to power. Abused and tortured, he had finally been released after several months' detention. A former typesetter, he had survived on three hundred marks a month (one-third of Fritz's salary) by proofreading for a Berlin publisher. Fritz was impressed by Löbe's simplicity, an eminent figure who had remained close to the people and knew how to work with his hands. Even though it is impossible to say whether the two men met often and whether they had thorough discussions, Fritz felt that they were close, and even more, thought of him as a comrade in arms.

Bern, spring 1944

Everywhere in Europe in the spring of 1944, people were beginning to think about the shape of post-Hitler Germany. In Berlin, around Ludwig Beck, Carl Goerdeler, Julius Leber, and a few others, a government program was put in place and the organizational structure of a future government already existed on paper. In Bern, the Americans of the

OSS engaged in the same kind of exercise. Allen Dulles had prepared for his superiors in Washington a list of German personalities likely to be given a principal role after the fall of Nazism. He mentioned the names of various figures exiled in Switzerland. Most of them had impeccable democratic credentials, like Otto Braun, former Social Democratic leader in Prussia, and the liberal economist Wilhelm Röpke. But there was also the name of an OSS informer, Hans-Bernd Gisevius, vice-consul of the Reich in Zurich, a former member of the Gestapo who had become a confirmed anti-Nazi in the Abwehr. If he had known of the existence of this list, Fritz Kolbe would probably not have found it unusual to be included, but his name was not there.

Among the Germans in exile in Switzerland there was a ferment of ideas and a proliferation of plans for the future. Ernst Kocherthaler, for example, wrote page after page during this period. On his own initiative, he wrote a series of brief analyses of postwar priorities for Allen Dulles. How could Germany be de-Nazified? It would be necessary above all, he said, "to create democratic universities" and help the Germans resist the attractions of communism, knowing that "only a minority among them understand the individualism of Western civilization." Kocherthaler also wrote about the economic problems of Europe and the world following the conflict. He suggested turning to the creation of a "world economic government" acting "in a spirit of cooperation rather than competition."

During this period, Ernst Kocherthaler sent Allen Dulles a memorandum titled "The Jewish Question in Post-War Europe." In it he wrote:

In Spring 1944 most of the European Jews are killed or have emigrated overseas. Between 3 and 5 million have been exterminated. In the Ukraine and Poland only those who have joined the guerrillas have survived. Of the German Jews some are still spared in Theresienstadt (Czechoslovakia). . . . With some minor exceptions, Hitler's program of extermination had full success in Central and Eastern Europe and partial success in Western Europe. . . . In the process of liquidating the remains of Nazi ideology, the anti-Semitic question is important. A whole generation of youth has been fed with a vision of a Jew who has been given in Nazi religion the place of the devil. . . . It is therefore important for the future of the fight against Nazi ideology in Germany and German-occupied countries, that the returning Jews should be well chosen and return only gradually. For the rest, a home state anywhere in the world would offer the only solution. In Palestine mass immigration of Jews would provoke a conflict with the Arabs and the Moslems all over the world, since Pan-Islamism has been strengthened during the war. . . . A Jewish home must therefore be found where only a thin indigenous population would have to be expropriated. Regions with good climate and rich enough to be suitable for economic development seem to exist, best of all in Madagascar. Here a Jewish state under French sovereignty could occupy half the island.

Fritz was far removed from this kind of thinking when he arrived in Bern on April 11, 1944, for his fourth visit since August 1943. Worn out by the train trip made in ever more difficult conditions, he had above all experienced the terror of being arrested. Arriving in Switzerland without being searched, he had felt so relieved after the last customs inspection that he dropped the key to the diplomatic pouch in a toilet in the Basel railroad station (the attendant had agreed to retrieve it for a handsome tip). Forced to spend some time with a colleague from the German consulate in Basel who had come to collect a package of dispatches, Fritz had sat with him at a table in the railroad station restaurant. He had quickly drunk several glasses of schnapps before leaving for Bern.

"Wood has arrived with more than 200 highly valuable Easter eggs," Allen Dulles wrote to his colleagues in Washington on April 11, 1944 ("What a bunny!" headquarters cabled back). Fritz's visits now followed a well-oiled routine, always according to the same pattern. At night, they met secretly at Allen Dulles's, on Herrengasse. The four protagonists of the summer of 1943 were still there: Dulles and Kolbe, but also Gerald Mayer and Ernst Kocherthaler. Among the surprises that Fritz pulled out of his bag on the night of April 11 were the famous "Japanese trinkets" requested in the postcard sent a few weeks earlier. And what trinkets! To Allen Dulles's great satisfaction, Fritz had brought from Berlin several extremely interesting cables from Tokyo. One set of dispatches stood out from the rest. It was a long report on the principal Japanese military bases in Asia, written following an investigative mission carried out between January 28 and February 25, 1944. The cables were signed by Ambassador Heinrich Stahmer, but Washington would learn soon thereafter that the text was based on reports from General Kretschmer, the German military attaché in Tokyo, and his colleague Air Force General Gronau—which changed nothing of the exceptional quality of the document.

The two men had traveled almost everywhere in Asia and all doors had been open to them. They had gone to Burma (Mandalay, Rangoon, Prome), to Formosa, Singapore, Saigon, Bangkok, to Indonesia (Macassar, Madium, Manado), to Eastern Malaya (Kuching and Labuan), and to the Philippines (Davao and Manila). At every stop on their excursion they had been given a guided tour of military installations. They had conscientiously recorded everything that they saw: the location of the various bases of the Japanese army, the strengths and weaknesses of each of them, the number of divisions stationed at each site, the names of the principal commanders of each base, the supply lines, the state of Japanese knowledge of Allied forces, the relations between the Japanese army and navy. Some cables from Heinrich Stahmer reported private conversations with Asian political leaders subservient to Tokyo: General Pibul Songgram, the Thai prime minister, seemed demoralized by the bombing of Bangkok and no longer to believe in the victory of the Axis powers. President José Laurel of the Philippines was confronted with huge economic difficulties.

For the Americans, the value of this information was incalculable. Immediately transmitted to the translation and encryption teams of the OSS office, they would require a week of work before they could be transmitted to Washington. Not a crumb of the text was left out. In its English version, the final document was more than twenty pages long, divided into more than ten sections. The OSS transcribers were so overwhelmed that they left some words in German, not bothering to translate them.

But Fritz was already talking about something else. He had other "pearls" to offer: a list of the principal members of the German espionage network in Sweden and a document of the same kind for Spain. The two documents provided many names and described in detail the reorganization measures in process (breaking up of structures intended to strengthen the secrecy of the system, since the Abwehr was now entirely under the control of the SS).

"Talk to us about Berlin's opinion of Allied plans to invade the European continent," Dulles asked a little later that night. Fritz told everything he knew: "Although the Foreign Ministry thinks that the landing will take place soon, the Nazis have just sent a little more than twenty divisions from the West to the East, because the führer thought he was short of troops on the Russian front." With respect to the location of the invasion, the German leaders "are thinking primarily of the Mediterranean—perhaps Corsica—or else Antwerp, or maybe Norway." Reassuring! What was of concern, on the other hand, was that Ireland continued to play the role of a rear base for German espionage of England. Fritz set on the table a dozen fairly well informed cables about ongoing British military preparations. All of them were signed by Eduard Hempel, the Reich's envoy in Dublin.

The two Americans filled notebooks as they listened to Fritz. They asked him about the latest developments in the Reich's armaments industry. Fritz mentioned the construction of new miniaturized submarines in the Baden region ("near Karlsruhe"). These submarines had a one-man crew and could threaten sea lanes used by the Allies. "The Army's principal worry," said Wood, "is the lack of fighter aircraft. The country cannot cope with the bombing raids, especially the daylight precision raids by U.S. planes, which are growing increasingly more successful, and this might lead to the downfall of Germany before the invasion even starts."

And the countries allied to Germany? "Rumania is disintegrating. Antonescu is in a very low state of mind, brought on by a report he received from Rumanian intelligence, stating that completely out of hand German troops were fleeing headlong back through Moldavia, looting and raping . . . bartering their arms for liquor." Among the several cables from Bucharest (signed by the envoy Manfred Freiherr von Killinger), one mentioned the conspiratorial activities of a circle of pro-Allied Rumanian aristocrats gathered around Marthe Bibesco.

Fritz then took out of his briefcase a thick sheaf of cables on Hungary. There were more than one hundred pages signed by Edmund Veesenmayer, the German proconsul in Budapest. The passage that interested Allen Dulles the most was brief and to the point: "Within the last 24 hours, I have had three long talks with von Horthy. As a result, I am more and more convinced that on the one hand the regent is an unmitigated liar and on the other he is physically no longer capable of performing his duties. He is constantly repeating himself, often contradicting himself within a few sentences, and sometimes does not know how to go on. Everything he says sounds like a memorized formula, and I fear that it will be difficult to convince him, let alone win him over."

Reading these words and adding up everything he had just learned (from Thailand through Rumania to Hungary), Dulles suddenly realized that the dynamism of the Axis had definitively been broken. He was stunned. It is impossible to say whether he paid any attention to another passage from Veesenmayer that gave a glimpse of the fate of the Jews of Hungary: "Today, decrees were issued which indicate the government is taking steps to deal with the Jewish situation. This is being done, in fact, with a degree of astuteness not common in this country. However, some of the designated punishments are inadequate, and I shall make sure that in actual practice they are more severe." A little further on was another document: "3451 Jews have been arrested up to April 1st. The towns of Beregszasz, Munkacs, and Ungvar, where there is an especially large proportion of Jews, have been segregated. Councils of Elders have been established in the towns. We note that the populace seems quite happy when healthy Jews are apprehended. Poor Jews are the object of pity."

The information provided by Fritz was so copious that it all seemed to blend together. After speaking of the fate of the Jews, the subject of the effect of recent Allied bombing of Budapest came up: "The raid which occurred during daylight on April 3rd did the damage indicated below to important plants: The Donau Flugzeugbau AG airplane works at Horthy-Liget suffered severe damage. The 'Zestörer' Messerschmitt 210 is turned out here at the rate of 50 a month. Technical experts report that it is possible for the works to be in operation once more by May 1st, at 60% of capacity." Fritz added that a chemical fertilizer factory and a refinery in Budapest had been destroyed. In Bulgaria, "the city of Sofia is practically in ruins, except for a few suburbs," wrote the envoy of the Reich, Adolf Beckerle, following the huge Allied bombing on March 30. But the German diplomat pointed out that the members of the regency council, Bogdan Filov and Prince Cyril, "are still with us."

And Yugoslavia? There too, Fritz had material to satisfy the Americans' curiosity. Cables from Belgrade and Zagreb (Agram in German) described increasing connections between General Mihailovich's Chetniks and the Germans. In Croatia, the population was showing increasing hostility to the Wehrmacht because of food shortages and because it suspected the Germans of "favoring Muslim autonomy."

Fritz was in Bern only long enough for three meetings. But he gave his American friends enough to work on for a month. When he was there, the nights in Bern were short. Arriving on Tuesday, April 11, he left for Berlin on Friday, April 14. As he left, the Americans politely let him know that his "literary" variations (of the type "survey of the world situation as seen by two Germans") were not appreciated as much as original documents. "George" was not insulted. For his part, he suggested that they now communicate with him by sending coded messages in the London *Times* (which he received with one week's delay), or else in the evening broadcasts of the BBC (password, "Peter, Peter," his son's name).

Another precaution was taken to facilitate matters: He took with him a camera provided by the Americans. The device was of high quality, a Robot of German manufacture (with a capacity of sixty exposures). Rolls of film would be easier to get through the border than kilos of paper. With the colossal volume of documents that he was now handling, this solution should make his work easier ("otherwise, it was no longer possible," Fritz was to explain a few years later). For the Americans, this method offered many advantages: Instead of sending manuscripts difficult to decipher because of his cramped handwriting, Fritz would now type his comments and photograph them.

After Fritz left, a feeling of excitement and frenzy continued to permeate the atmosphere in the OSS offices. Dozens and dozens of Kappa messages were cabled to Washington and London daily until the end of the month. Allen Dulles gave these dispatches the name "Kapril" (a contraction of Kappa and April) to clearly distinguish them from their predecessors—a useful and necessary precaution, for some recurring subjects, such as the deliveries of Spanish tungsten to Germany, generated kilometers of cables every time.

Washington, April 16, 1944

On April 16, two days after Fritz's departure for Berlin, his material reached the highest authorities in the United States. For the first time since January 10, President Roosevelt got on his desk that day a report with the Boston heading, analyzed and commented on. The OSS thought that "George Wood's" latest visit to Bern was important enough to justify sending a "Memorandum for the President" to the White House. So much for the prejudices and doubts of the experts. A copy was also sent to Secretary of State Cordell Hull, to Army Chief of Staff George C. Marshall, to the commander in chief of the U.S. Navy, Admiral Ernest J. King, to the supreme commander in Europe, General Dwight D. Eisenhower, as well as to the highest British authorities. The document was drafted by Colonel G. Edward Buxton, one of General Donovan's right-hand men.

Of all that had just been revealed by "George Wood" in Bern, neither the file on Japan nor the one on Hungary went to the president; nothing of all that, but rather what Fritz told Allen Dulles sitting by the fire, spontaneously, about the atmosphere prevailing in Germany, the state of mind of the leaders of the Reich and the evolution of the feelings of ordinary people. "Eighty percent of the German people feel opposed to the Nazis and is waiting for the day of delivery," Fritz had told his American friends, immediately adding, "yet active revolutionary action cannot be expected for the time being. Himmler controls by his spies and terrorists every one of the various police organizations and the key positions of the armed forces so thoroughly that the forces of opposition that exist even within the police do not risk a plot." Fritz had added an observation that was very troubling to the Americans: "The communist organization and propaganda have been strengthened in the last few months. As parts of the Nazi SA and even the SS have changed over to the communists, Russia disposes of a good organization in order to control the revolution by their elements, when the situation is ripe."

The Allies were fond of this kind of information, because they had no way of knowing what was going on inside the country. Germany in early 1944 resembled an impenetrable fortress. Only a very few people, one of whom was Fritz Kolbe, enabled the veil to be lifted a little. Apart from him, there were Hans-Bernd Gisevius and his friends in the Abwehr, an occasional businessman, and a few boatmen who sailed on the Rhine and whom OSS agents questioned in the cafés of Basel.

The memorandum to President Roosevelt stated, in part:

The enclosed dispatch from Bern and the accompanying evaluation of its source should, it is believed, be brought to your attention as early as possible. This cable is the evaluation by our principal Swiss intelligence representative of two hundred enemy documents (four hundred pages) that have just come into his hands. . . . A cable has been sent to the author, requesting him to review it carefully to see whether he wishes, on reflection, to modify any of its language and to report here by cable immediately. It would seem that the author, thanks to the sudden receipt of more than 400 pages of material all at one moment, finds himself in a position where he can see the whole picture rather than any single part.

The OSS then quoted at length a Kappa message written by Dulles on April 12:

Sincerely regret that you are unable at this time to view Wood's material as it stands without condensation and abridgement. In some 400 pages, dealing with the internal maneuvering of German diplomatic policy for the past two months, a picture of imminent doom and final downfall is presented. Into a tormented General Headquarters and a half-dead Foreign Office stream the lamentations of a score of diplomatic posts. It is a scene wherein haggard Secret Service and diplomatic agents are doing their best to cope with the defeatism and desertion of flatly defiant satellites and allies and recalcitrant neutrals. . . . Already Canaris has disappeared from the picture, and a conference was hastily convoked in Berlin at which efforts were made to mend the gaping holes left in the Abwehr. Unable now to fall back on his favorite means of avoiding disconcerting critics by retiring to his bed, Ribbentrop has beat a retreat to Fuschl and retains a number of his principal aides at Salzburg. The remainder of the Foreign Office is strung out all the way between Riesengebirge and the capital. Practically impossible working conditions exist in the latter, and bomb shelters are being permanently used for code work. Once messages have been deciphered, a frantic search begins to locate the specific service or minister to which each cable must be forwarded; and, when a reply is called for, another search is required to deliver this to the right place. . . .
    The final deathbed contortions of a petrified Nazi diplomacy are pictured in these telegrams. The reader is carried from one extreme of emotion to the other, from tears to laughter, as he examines these messages and sees the cruelty exhibited by the

Germans in their final swan-song of brutality toward the
peoples so irrevocably and pitifully enmeshed by the Gestapo
after half a decade of futile struggles, and yet at the same time
also sees the absurdity of the dilemma which now confronts
this diplomacy both within and without Festung Europa.

This message was considered exceptional by the heads of the OSS,
because most official analyses up to that time had concluded that the
Nazis were still solidly holding onto power. On April 3, 1944, General
Donovan had sent a letter to President Roosevelt characterizing the
morale in the capital of the Reich in these terms: "As though they were
under the influence of morphine, with no sign of collapse and yet a general despair of ever gaining the victory now." While it seemed that the
war was likely to last for a long time, Dulles's message of April 12 for the
first time suggested that the end of the tunnel might be in sight.

On April 20, 1944, a new message from the OSS landed on President Roosevelt's desk. He was informed that Allen Dulles was sticking with his analysis: Germany, he said, was at the end of its rope,
even if nothing had yet been won by the Allies:

The message from Switzerland (transmitted to you on 12
April 1944) 'should not be read as indicating that the morale
of the Nazi Army is nearing collapse (excepting probably the
so-called Grossdeutscher, Slav and other non-German elements.)' Nor does our Swiss representative think that any
important Nazi military officials are ready and willing to let us
come in through the West unopposed. He believes, rather,
that fierce opposition may be given to any invasion attempt. A
collapse of Germany might follow, however, a few months
after the establishment of a firm toe-hold in the West. He
concludes: 'the timing of the invasion attempt may be all-
important. The German people are war-weary and apathetic,
and even in Nazi circles the same kind of psychological
depression can be seen as appeared last August and September. Yet if they could stabilize the Russian front once more,

they may catch a second wind, and put up an even stronger
defense against invasion.'

Washington/Bern, April 26, 1944

On Wednesday, April 26, 1944, Washington sent Allen Dulles an encouraging message: "Particular felicitations for the Japanese data. The
military people are most appreciative. . . . Far Eastern information is
the most highly desired next to any hot invasion material." The American generals in Asia were now informed of the principal Kappa revelation concerning their theater of operations. A few days later, Colonel
Alfred McCormack presented his final report on "George Wood,"
overall cautious and reserved, but laudatory with respect to Japan:
"They contain a certain amount of new information which, if true, is
useful—notably the identification of a number of divisional commanders in Burma," he wrote.

On the other hand, McCormack did not think the remainder of the
Kappa material was of much use: "Because of the time lag between
the date of origin and date of receipt here, information that might have
been of interest had either been obtained from other sources or had
become stale. As is usual with diplomatic communications, a good deal
of the material is second-hand information upon subjects on which
first-hand information is available, or it relays expressions of opinion
made for diplomatic purposes or made by people whose opinions on
the particular subjects are of no great consequence."

At the same time, the British began to take an interest in the "George
Wood" file. An investigation in London in April revealed that only
4 percent of the information supplied by Wood was false or incorrect.
On May 12, 1944, David Bruce, chief of the OSS in London, transmitted to Allen Dulles "special congratulations" from his British colleagues
for the material on Japan. On his own initiative, Kim Philby of MI6 had
sent a copy of Fritz's documents concerning the order of battle of Japanese troops to Alistair Denniston, the head of Bletchley Park, the agency
charged with deciphering enemy messages. Denniston's services were

enthusiastic and asked for more. Soon the heads of the Army, Navy, and Air Force "all three howled for more," as Philby was to write in his memoirs. Claude Dansey, the number-two in MI6, was absolutely furious that one of Dulles's agents was having such success in London. But he calmed down when Philby explained that he had done everything possible to conceal the American origin of "Wood." "Not even our own circulating sections, let alone the departments, knew that OSS were involved. They regarded it as *our* stuff, they were asking *us* for more. It seemed that the credit would be ours." From that moment on, Dansey rubbed his hands and congratulated his young colleague (Philby was then thirty-two). Philby's career progressed, and his reputation grew in the British intelligence community. No one knew that he was working for Moscow. Philby was later to recall fondly in his memoirs: "Our German friend proved to be an intrepid operator, and paid several more visits to Bern with his useful suitcase."

In Washington, as in London, they were beginning to abandon the hypothesis of a 'trap" in the course of the spring of 1944. In the last delivery from "George Wood," there was much information that was harmful to German interests. Dulles's German informant was finally becoming a source worthy of belief.

In a message sent on April 26, 1944 to one of the heads of the OSS (Whitney H. Shepardson, known as "Jackpot"), Dulles wrote:

I appreciate danger of becoming so enamored with one's own sources that one falls into such traps. While possibility you suggest should never be excluded my present views are:

1. As yet no evidence of plant in material itself.
2. Having critically examined hundreds of these documents internal and external evidence has persuaded me of their genuineness.
3. Local intermediary is I believe above question though of course he might be fooled also.
4. Have analyzed entire scheme under which material procured and transmitted and it is logical and feasible.

All of foregoing while persuasive is not conclusive and agree with you on importance of continuing critical examination. So far only disturbing element has been some evidence of recklessness on Wood's part but this is quite usual in conspirators.

Berlin, late April 1944

When Fritz returned to Berlin, the city was bathed in magnificent sunlight. The official forecast for the third week of April predicted "weather fit for the Führer [*Führerwetter*]." The capital was nearly empty, notably on Hitler's birthday, April 20, a holiday in Nazi Germany. Goebbels's propaganda machine poured forth factitious celebrations, overblown pronouncements, and unshakable convictions. Everything was "fanatical," "heroic," or "tragic."

Fritz was bitter, almost enraged. For the first time he felt useless. The role of spy no longer suited him. He wanted to take some action. He may well have anticipated that he would be criticized after the war for having been the agent of a foreign power. Armed resistance was much nobler, but he had just grasped that the Americans would not help him go down that path. In Bern, he had proudly presented to Allen Dulles a plan that was very dear to his heart: the creation of a "people's militia" [*Volksmiliz*] assembling Germans opposed to Nazism, with himself as troop leader. He had anticipated enlisting all his friends in these shock troops. But, most important, he wanted to mobilize everyone he knew in the Social Democratic networks and those close to the old unions. The idea behind the plan was to revive the defense leagues of the Weimar Republic. In Fritz's plan, "his" militia would be able to control a certain number of nerve centers in the capital of the Reich (the airports, and some lakes in the vicinity of Berlin, such as the Wannsee and the Schlachtensee) in support of a large-scale parachute operation carried out by the Allies. The members of the brigade were to recognize each other by an armband with the initials VM (for *Volksmiliz*). The network would have been mobile, Fritz having thought of distributing bicycles to its members. "We would need machine pistols, ammunition, food rations, signal flares, helmets, and bracelets with the insignia VM," he had told Dulles. For communications, a secret code had been worked out (the password was to be George 25900). Walter Bauer's office at Unter den Linden 28 was to be the headquarters of this small underground army.

"What do you think, Mr. Douglas?" Fritz had asked Allen Dulles, his eyes glowing with enthusiasm. The American had not answered immediately. He had puffed on his pipe in silence, then he had quickly changed the subject. The only thing that had seemed to interest him in the whole story was the identity of the conspirators in the "people's militia" led by Fritz Kolbe. Fritz, a little disconcerted by his proposal's lack of effect, provided a list of his "comrades in arms": Walter Bauer, Paul Löbe, Alfred Graf Waldersee. Allen Dulles had advised Fritz to do nothing that might put his life in danger: "We need you where you are. Keep telling us what you find out at the Foreign Ministry; that is really where you are most useful for us."

Very disappointed by this rejection, Fritz had returned to Berlin with the feeling that he had been "dropped." But he had nonetheless decided to continue the game of espionage, since he had no other means of acting. Perhaps, he told himself, I just have to wait a little longer and have the patience to convince the Americans of the need for a joint action in Berlin. He was not ready to give up his idea of a "people's militia."

On his return to the capital of the Reich, Fritz Kolbe was informed (probably by Gertrud von Heimerdinger) that he would have no opportunity to return to Switzerland for a long time. New arrangements had been made to reduce to a minimum the list of people authorized to travel abroad. He also learned that the Swiss authorities were now making difficulties over granting him a visa. Fritz wondered what had happened. It was impossible to know for sure. Perhaps his nocturnal visits to certain dens of iniquity had been observed. In the worst case, the Swiss were aware of his contacts with the Americans and wanted to avoid any problem with the authorities of the Reich. After a few moments of anxiety, Fritz finally learned that the Swiss authorities had generally become fussier and that the restrictions applied to everyone.

Fritz was trapped in Berlin. If he couldn't go to Bern, he would have liked to go to Stockholm or Lisbon, but those trips were not authorized either. He would have liked to send messages through Albert Bur in Alsace (proposed password: "foie gras of Strasbourg"), but this system didn't work. That did not keep him from continuing to work for the Americans. He took some time to learn how to use the camera he had been given and continued working on paper until the fall of 1944. To send documents to Bern, he always had alternative solutions. Some of his friends were still carrying the diplomatic mail to Bern—such as Willy Pohle and a certain Hans Vogel. On other occasions, Professor Sauerbruch went to Switzerland (for example, at Pentecost in 1944).

On several occasions, Fritz asked for help from another of his acquaintances, Wilhelm Mackeben, who lived in a chalet in Bavaria, in the Allgäu region near Lake Constance. Mackeben traveled extensively around Europe as an "independent sales representative." He was a former Foreign Ministry official, politically conservative but very opposed to the Nazis. After some service in Latin America, he found himself working for Karl Ritter beginning in September 1939. It was there that Fritz had met him. But the NSDAP had finally gotten his head in 1942, when he had been forced to leave the ministry. During the spring of 1944, Mackeben agreed to get Fritz's mail to Switzerland. Apparently he still enjoyed a special status that allowed him to go through customs without being checked. He did not know what he was carrying. In any event, Fritz trusted him enough to give him Ernst Kocherthaler's address. Mackeben was delighted to meet him because he was a "useful contact," with connections in many parts of Europe. On the way there, Fritz's messages were hidden in the lining of a piece of clothing or the sole of a shoe. On the way back, the Americans' answers were concealed in packages of coffee, cigars, or cigarettes.

The first time that Mackeben went back and forth between Berlin and Bern was in May 1944. A letter from Fritz dated May 10 reached Dulles through him. In this letter, Fritz provided a list of the principal spies working for Germany in North Africa (Tangiers, Tetouan, Casablanca). It contained the names of several diplomats, members of consular services, and journalists of every nationality (including

Frenchmen, Italians, and even a former Norwegian consul). The letter contained more than just information. Fritz for the first time expressed irritation. He asked why the Americans had still not followed his advice and bombed, for example, a Siemens capacitor factory in Gera (Thuringia), the petrochemical factories of Leuna, or a communications center of the Navy command in Eberswalde (northeast of Berlin). He was also surprised to learn that nothing had been done to interrupt the flow of tungsten from Spain to Germany ("Wood comments cable speaks for itself and adds: 'are you still asleep?'").

"If you are satisfied with me, send me some Nescafé. If you no longer want me to send you information, send me a pair of scissors," Fritz had added, clearly sulking a little, no longer sure whether the Americans still needed him. "If you have things to ask me, send me cigarettes and put something in them please, because I'll smoke them myself," he added in one of the coded messages he liked to use. The letter ended with these words: "I will not fail to seize any coming opportunity to write to you, even if I have to set to work in the early morning hours after an air raid. Sorry for my disjointed writing. I'm so overwhelmed that I no longer know what I'm doing. My fiancée complains that I am neglecting her. And yet I love her!"

The Americans' answer, slipped into a package of cigarettes, tried to be reassuring: "Try to come to see your former father-in-law in Zurich. Find a pretext connected with the settling of your divorce." But Fritz did not receive the message. In late May, when Mackeben was getting ready to return to Germany with the "cigarettes" intended for Fritz, Ernst Kocherthaler received a terse telegram from Berlin: "Please no cigarettes," signed "Georg."

Berlin, May 31, 1944

There was a meeting that evening in Berlin of the Wednesday Club at Sauerbruch's. The Grunewald neighborhood was half in ruins, but Sauerbruch's house on Herthastrasse was still standing. The speaker was General Beck, who was delivering a presentation on Marshal Foch, "our great French adversary," whom he was honored to have known personally. Despite his reservations about the Versailles treaty and "the mistakes of French policy in the Rhineland after 1918," General Beck delivered a very laudatory speech about the old adversary of the armies of von Klück and Moltke. Of course, he said in substance, Foch can be criticized for having been impulsive, stubborn, and sometimes a little rigid in his approach to the offensive. But Beck was full of admiration for this man, who had always acted within the limits of what was possible and whom he described in conclusion as "a great man and a great general." The applause was warm. Then the eight guests went to the table and the conversation quickly changed to other subjects. "Sauerbruch always serves sparkling wine. And since we never have much in our stomachs, the atmosphere soon gets lively," in the words of one of the people present that evening, the philosopher Eduard Spranger.

Some members of the Wednesday Club knew that General Beck was involved with a group of conspirators who intended to eliminate Hitler, overthrow the Nazi regime, and negotiate a separate peace with the Western powers. If the plan were to succeed, Ludwig Beck was supposed to become head of state in place of the führer. Ulrich von Hassell, who was also at Sauerbruch's that evening, was the prospective foreign minister. It was here in Ferdinand Sauerbruch's house that Ludwig Beck had met for the first time a young and brilliant officer who was supposed to become secretary of state in a future ministry of war after the coup d'état: Colonel von Stauffenberg, chief of staff of the Army Supply Services. Count von Stauffenberg had been treated in Munich by Professor Sauerbruch for serious wounds suffered in Africa. Struck by a mine explosion, he had lost an eye, his right hand, and two fingers of his left hand. Stauffenberg did not take part in the meetings of the Wednesday Club. But most of its members knew him well and knew that he represented, along with Carl Goerdeler (future chancellor in the event the coup was successful), a central element in the resistance to the regime.

Through the intermediary of their friend Hans-Bernd Gisevius in Switzerland, General Beck and Carl Goerdeler had sent several messages to Allen Dulles, in early April and early May 1944. In the name of their resistance organization, which included dozens of high-ranking officers and various political figures, conservatives, and old Social Democrats, these men were asking for help from the United States in case their coup were to succeed. They proposed to the Americans the capitulation of the Wehrmacht on condition that they be able to continue the war in the East against the Soviets. They were in favor of a massive landing of Western troops in Germany and asked particularly that several American airborne divisions be parachuted into Berlin. But Dulles's reply had not been encouraging: "My orders are clear: the surrender of Germany will be unconditional and nothing can be done without the Soviets," he had told them in substance.

The plot was nevertheless closely followed by the Americans. While the British refused to accept the very idea of a "German resistance," Dulles transmitted to his superiors the names of the principal conspirators and the contents of their plans. He had for a long time now been in contact with another member of the conspiracy, who was also calling in vain for Allied help in overthrowing Hitler: the diplomat Adam von Trott zu Solz, who had gone to Bern several times in the course of 1943 and in early 1944. In the language of the OSS, the conspirators had become *Breakers*, General Beck was *Tucky*, Goerdeler was *Lester*, and Adam von Trott was *800*.

Berlin, June–July 1944

Life in Berlin was more and more dangerous for Fritz. In late June, he sent another message to Bern in which he confessed: "The last few days have been very difficult for me. Suspicions seemed to be weighing on me, but then they seem to have been dissipated. In any case, I have heard nothing further." He nevertheless continued to provide information. The quality of the "material" did not decline; quite the contrary. In late June 1944, he revealed that "the Germans are still expecting a landing in the Pas-de-Calais, even after 6 June, and are not withdrawing troops from the Belgian coast for that reason." In early July, he provided a series of details on the V-1s and future V-2s: "The flight control mechanism is produced in Gdynia, at the Ascania works, on the Baltic (near Danzig). The jets are built by Krupp in Wuppertal, additional parts which are not named are manufactured by the Siemens factories north of Augsburg. . . . Both the V-1 and V-2 models are made in the lower Danube region, in the vicinity of St. Valentin." Other electronic equipment intended for the V-2 is manufactured "in the Siemens factory in Arnstadt, in Thuringia, about forty-five kilometers west of Orlamünde." "In comparison with the V-1, the V-2 travels through the stratosphere. It is radio controlled and therefore a more accurate weapon. In addition, it possesses a longer range. This new model will be in use by the Nazis within 60 days at the outside."

Fritz helped the Americans to identify the fallback regions for all the advanced German industries: Thuringia and its deep underground shelters. Still in early July, Fritz gave the location of a factory where the first supersonic airplane in history was manufactured. He did not give its name, but it was the Messerschmitt 262. The factory was located in Kahla, in Thuringia: "near Orlamünde, between Rudolstadt and Jena. Factory in part underground. Already bombed in late June, but the damage is minimal, and the factory will soon enter the production phase."

Fritz never forgot to speak of Berlin, where an American bombing raid on June 21, 1944 was particularly devastating:

The factory manufacturing diesel engines for submarines was destroyed. AEG is still operating in some of the factories of the city; the cable plant, however, is no longer running. The Hotel Continental and a block of houses around the hotel were destroyed by fire. The Friedrichstrasse railroad station was badly damaged and the Schlesischer railroad station was hit during the raid. The Osram factory was also hit but is still operating. . . . The Siemensstadt plant is almost at a standstill. . . . The AEG factory manufacturing precision instruments for submarines and the Knorr-Bremse

plant, both of which are located at Treptower Park, were
said to have been untouched.

Dulles was satisfied, as were his Washington colleagues. What they
did not know was that Fritz Kolbe was also involved in seditious activities. The telegram from Fritz that was received on May 20 ("Please,
no cigarettes") had hinted that he was in danger. Sometime in the
spring, he was supposed to go with Walter Bauer to a secret meeting
in Potsdam with some civilian and military conspirators close to Count
Waldersee. Because of an organizational error due to faulty internal
communication, neither he nor Walter Bauer went to the meeting.
Waldersee was also absent. This was lucky for them, because the list
of people present at this secret meeting fell into the hands of the
Gestapo. A few months later, all of them were to be executed.

11

FINAL REVELATIONS

Berlin, late July 1944

After the Allied landing in Normandy, the armies of the Reich carried out a vast defensive withdrawal, but they were still fighting. Was this the beginning of the end? The failed assassination attempt against Hitler on July 20, 1944 was enough to make the enemies of Nazism lose all hope. The only virtue of the plot, despite its failure, had been "that the German resistance movement [had taken] the plunge before the eyes of the world and of history." For all those who dreamed of the fall of the regime, there seemed to be no way out but to turn in on themselves, to "love one's country in silence and in silence scorn its leaders." The most incredulous were obliged to agree that Hitler seemed to be protected by providence.

There was another miracle: Fritz Kolbe's clandestine activities remained unnoticed. Fritz had even received a promotion in early July, rising from the rank of "consular secretary" to "secretary of the chancellery" (*Kanzler*). The party, as usual, had a right of veto over this promotion. The ministry had sent a four-page form to the regional headquarters of the NSDAP (Hermann-Göring-Strasse 14 in Berlin), a document in which it was stated that Fritz was not a member of the party but that he was "of German blood" and that he "worked tirelessly and well for the National Socialist state." Even though four months had gone by before the party deigned to respond to the request, all the required stamps had been obtained and the ministry's decision had been ratified. Fritz continued to give his best efforts to his work in order to be well judged by his superiors.

However, the climate of anxiety was constantly intensifying. Although not closely associated with any of the conspirators, Fritz felt directly concerned by the slaughter that struck the ranks of the resistance during those bloody weeks. Several members of the Foreign Ministry were soon arrested and sentenced to death. Ferdinand Sauerbruch was questioned by the Gestapo because he had been in regular contact with friends of Count Stauffenberg. "Sauerbruch thinks that we are lost, he and I. He may be right," wrote Fritz in one of his messages to Bern. If someone like the professor himself was no longer safe, the worst was to be feared.

Adolphe Jung recounts how the surgeon saved his own skin:

After the failure of the assassination attempt, Sauerbruch
lived in fear. He went to the country, to property owned by
his wife, near Dresden, and spent about a week there. In fact,
he was aware of what had been attempted, although he
himself did not participate. After the fact, some allusions he
had made before the attempt relating to "events of great
importance soon about to happen" became meaningful for me.
Five people in his immediate entourage and among his close
friends had participated and were shot or hanged. In addition,
one of Sauerbruch's three sons, a career officer, who had
reached the rank of lieutenant-colonel, was a close friend of
Count von Stauffenberg. Soon thereafter, then, he was incarcerated and seriously interrogated for three weeks. Very
worried, Sauerbruch called or wrote to friends and colleagues
who were members of the party or the SS. Time was short.
With his son in prison, things could have quickly turned nasty

for him. In any event, his son would not have been released so quickly if Sauerbruch had not immediately gotten in touch with, among others, Max de Crinis, a professor of neurology, a friend of Hitler, and an important figure in the party, and with Professor Gebhardt, a military doctor with the rank of general in the army. . . . It was probably through their discreet and effective support that Sauerbruch was not imprisoned and could escape from the reprisals that followed the attempt.

Sauerbruch was spared, but many of his friends did not survive the repression of the summer of 1944. On July 12, the Wednesday Club met as though everything were normal, with a presentation by Werner Heisenberg on the history of astronomy. The session had concluded with a feast of fresh raspberries picked in the garden of the Kaiser-Wilhelm Physics Institute in Dahlem. This was the last meeting at which General Beck was present: He shot himself in the head on the evening of July 20, 1944 in Berlin. Johannes Popitz was arrested on July 21, Ulrich von Hassell on July 28. Their imminent execution was not in doubt. On July 26, the Wednesday Club convened for the last time. The meeting took place at the home of the journalist and critic Paul Fechter, who spoke about literature in a room that was three-quarters empty.

Bern, August 1944

The failure of the plot was a catastrophe for the Americans. Even though Allen Dulles mistrusted Count Stauffenberg, vaguely suspected of wanting to make a deal with the Soviets, the news of the fiasco filled him with bitterness and perplexity. "I never saw Dulles and Gaevernitz so downtrodden," according to the Bavarian Social Democrat Wilhelm Hoegner, who met them in Bern shortly after the events of July 20. If Hitler had been assassinated, the war could have been brought to a rapid conclusion. In addition, this evil stroke of fate would probably facilitate the rise to power of the hardest elements in the Nazi regime. In a message to Washington dated August 8, 1944, Dulles wrote that "Himmler and the Gestapo took advantage of the Putsch to finish off the job." Radicalization of the resistance was also predictable. On August 9, Dulles wrote: "The most efficiently organized body for work is now the Communist group." As for the military situation, it was taking a turn dangerously favorable to Stalin. In mid-August 1944, the first Soviet soldiers reached the borders of the Reich in East Prussia. The Americans, for their part, were not yet in Paris.

After July 20, the Americans heard nothing from Fritz until mid-August. Knowing his reckless character, they anxiously wondered whether he had been taken in the Gestapo's nets. But in mid-August, OSS Bern finally received a letter from Berlin through Ernst Kocherthaler. Allen Dulles was able to send a reassuring message to Washington: "His position apparently unaffected by putsch but he gives little info about it stating that notwithstanding July 20 he continues to work with Volksmiliz."

In the letter he sent to Kocherthaler, Fritz said that his greatest hope was to see a quick end to the war in the West, while it continued in the East: "Communism is not what Germany needs. . . . More and more, people here are realizing that." On the basis of this conviction, Fritz had concocted his own battle plan: "The Russians will drive to the Oder. At that time the Americans will land parachute troops in Berlin. On the critical day I'll be in position with from 30 to 100 men. Can't I get by radio advance word on when and where? Peter, Peter, say on the 9 P.M. cast? I am the only one who knows my plan in detail. I haven't let anyone in on the secret."

Ernst Kocherthaler took it upon himself to transmit to the Americans the complicated secret codes that Fritz wanted to use in his contacts with the American army: "'X Bäume wachsen' = in X/2 hours American troops will land in Berlin. 'X blühende Bäume wachsen' = A. D. with troops will land in X/2 hours. 'X Bäume blühen' = A. D. will join in X/2 hours."

Allen Dulles and Gerald Mayer probably smiled when they learned of this naïve and appealing message. What interested them in this letter of mid-August 1944 were not Fritz's personal battle plans but the invaluable information that he continued to deliver.

In late August, a new series of Kappa cables was sent to London and Washington (they were given the name "Kagust" for Kappa and August). In this new batch, there were troubling details on the exercise of Soviet power, following what had happened in Poland. Stalin had brutally abandoned his allies in the Polish National Army, and Ribbentrop had hastened to disseminate this news to the principal German diplomatic posts. A dispatch from the Deutsches Nachrichten-Büro (DNB, the official press agency) dated August 9, 1944 reported the disarmament and imprisonment of Polish units to the rear of the Russian front. The officers had been deported to Kiev. Among them, the non-communists had disappeared from one day to the next. Ribbentrop saw in the event the emergence of a new "Polish enslavement." For once, the Americans were tempted to believe German propaganda.

The other details in this "delivery" were devoted to the more usual questions of the Reich and its satellites and allies. Through "George Wood," the Americans learned in particular that the Germans intended to revive the National Assembly of the Third Republic in France in the hope of placing French institutional legality on their side. At the same time, the German authorities wanted to install the principal French institutions "in a major eastern city," perhaps Strasbourg. The Banque de France, the secret services, the radio services, the First Regiment of France, the Milice, and the *Journal Officiel* were to be moved. Surprising, and now pathetic, efforts.

Reading these documents, the Americans in Bern asked themselves a very simple question: How could they get "Wood" to come back to Switzerland? Allen Dulles wanted to use the device that had already served the purpose: Fritz's divorce. Lita Schoop, Fritz's second wife, was in detention in East Africa, like thousands of other Germans living in British territory. Using his daily professional contacts with London, Dulles tried to organize the repatriation of Lita Schoop to Switzerland, thinking that Fritz could thereby more easily justify a trip to Zurich "for personal reasons." Germany and South Africa periodically exchanged their respective nationals. During the summer of 1944, some Swedish steamships entered the port of Lisbon with dozens of German families on board. Lita Schoop was not among the passengers. Allen Dulles never found out why his plan had failed.

Bern/Washington, September 1944

In September 1944, Switzerland was plunged into a new world. Annemasse and Annecy had been liberated on August 18, Paris on August 25, and Lyon on September 3. In September, the American Seventh Army, under the command of General Alexander Patch, reached the Swiss border near Geneva. Following the Allied landings in Normandy and on the Mediterranean coast, a great breath of fresh air was rushing through the West, and Switzerland's isolation was coming to an end.

Allen Dulles took advantage of the new context to go back to Washington, passing through London. He made the entire trip in the company of General Donovan, who wanted to discuss various questions related to the future. Dulles was away from Bern between early September and late October. He spent a few weeks in New York and visited OSS headquarters in Washington, which he found hard to recognize, so great had the changes been. Now it was necessary to wear a badge in order to be authorized to enter the building, which had become a veritable fortress. The amateur spies had become professionals.

In discussing the future of the OSS with him, General Donovan expressed the view, shared by Dulles, that once peace had been restored, the United States would need more than ever a highly specialized intelligence agency, directly responsible to the president and operating around the world. The OSS was already becoming as interested in the Soviet Union as in Nazi Germany, if not more so. These new prospects made the question of the placement of the principal figures in American intelligence a matter of urgency. During the trip, there was much discussion of Allen Dulles's professional future. He wanted to become the European head of the organization, taking the place of David Bruce in London. But General Donovan had a different view: He wanted to place Dulles in charge of the German branch of the OSS as soon as Hitler's regime had surrendered.

Asked to suggest priorities for action in postwar Germany, Dulles proposed to continue the work he had carried out in Switzerland:

> Immediately contact a series of persons already placed in strategic positions in Germany whose existence is known only to us and who could be contacted only by us because of the carefully created relationships over the past two years. These persons, if they survive the German collapse, could be most helpful in obtaining secret records and files of certain German government departments and in giving us inside information as to the exact organization and location of secret government agencies and their new hideouts.

Back in Europe, Allen Dulles passed through Paris, where a major OSS office had just been established at 70, avenue des Champs-Élysées. In Bern, he thoroughly reorganized his "shop," which had been run during his absence by his assistant, Gero von Schulze-Gaevernitz. Dulles began by supplying his office with a luxurious fleet of automobiles. Before then, he had had available only a small Ford, whose use was limited by the lack of fuel coupons. After September 1944, he acquired a Chevrolet and a Packard, as well as a front-wheel-drive Citroën equipped with a gas generator. At the time, the American legation had only a single car, reserved for the envoy, Leland Harrison.

Dulles established new posts in Bern, Geneva, Zurich, and Basel. He assembled a team of new recruits charged with setting up networks in Germany, on the model of what had been done in France before the June 6 landing. A Swiss intellectual whom he had met in New York, Emmy Rado, was given the task of making contacts in the German churches. Another brilliant mind, Gerhard van Arkel, was given the same kind of mission for the working-class circles of the old unions of the Weimar Republic. Everything had to be built from the bottom up. Except for Fritz Kolbe, the OSS had no regular source of information in the heart of the Reich. Hans-Bernd Gisevius and his friends in the Abwehr had been neutralized after the failure of the July 20 plot. Those who had not been executed were struggling to survive and were no longer operational.

The OSS soon had to turn to a new kind of source: German prisoners of war. In the course of the liberation of France, the Americans had captured tens of thousands of enemy soldiers. The Allied generals wanted to take advantage of this resource. They came up with the idea of transforming some Wehrmacht officers into secret agents and sending them behind enemy lines in their original uniforms but with false identities, forged documents, and clandestine radio transmitters.

The new agents selected by the OSS in the prison camps had an exclusively operational role: They were asked to indicate the location of arms factories, Wehrmacht units, and the like. "Though no doubt our efforts in the last nine months of the war were useful, they could not replace Fritz, who after all produced intelligence of strategic importance," according to Peter Sichel, who was one of the handful of American officers of German origin assigned to select this new variety of agent. Peter Sichel came from a Jewish family in Mainz that had fled Germany in 1934. Back in Europe in an American uniform, he had arrived in Annemasse in October 1944 with the Seventh Army of General Patch. There he learned of the existence of "George Wood," "a spy who greatly enhanced Dulles's prestige," Sichel recalls.

Also in the fall of 1944, some German émigrés in London and the United States began to return to German territory in order to work secretly for the Allied cause. A Social Democrat, Jupp Kappius, was parachuted into Germany by the OSS in September 1944. Hidden in the Ruhr region, he lived in Bochum, from which he sent regular reports to the Americans. Kappius was surprised at the relative "normality" of the living conditions of the German people. The factories were operating, the mail was delivered, the telephone lines were not cut, nor was gas or electricity. Food was rationed but no one was dying of hunger. People were well dressed. "They eat butter, not margarine!" he wrote, while noting the astonishing spiritual impoverishment of the population, that was living in a state of doubt, cynicism, and the pursuit of narrow self-interest.

Rastenburg, September 1944

Fritz spent the end of August and almost the entire month of September in the "Wolf's Lair" (*Wolfsschanze*), Hitler's headquarters in East Prussia. Ambassador Karl Ritter needed him to replace an ailing colleague. Here, very close to the front, he had the unpleasant feeling of having no control over events. In Berlin he could take action. Here he felt he had become a spectator of history. There was no possibility of contacting Bern, and he had a painful awareness of the passage of time. He had no way to predict whether the war would last for another month, or another year. A few dozen kilometers away, the soldiers of the Red Army were preparing their next great offensive.

In the course of this long stay in the "wolf's lair," Fritz spent most of his time drafting reports for his boss. He was bored and wished only to return to Berlin as soon as possible. Instead of calming him down, the aromas of nature and the sound of the wind in the birch trees only increased his irritation. But he did cross paths by accident with a mysterious figure whose appearance reminded him of a composer or orchestra conductor (Fritz noticed that he had "long fingers" and a face that was "like Wilhelm Furtwängler's"). He learned that this high official frequently went to Stockholm, where he had been in contact with Soviet diplomats for more than a year. Who was this man? Fritz wondered. What was the purpose of his negotiations with the Russians? Who had asked him to take these steps: Ribbentrop or Hitler in person? Fritz was stunned to discover the existence of secret exchanges between Berlin and Moscow. He did not at the time find out what was really at stake in the discussions between the emissaries from the two capitals.

After a few days, he learned that the man's name was Peter Kleist and that he was close to Ribbentrop. Kleist had gone to Stockholm in early September to meet some Russian diplomats, but they had refused to see him. The wish to negotiate thus originated in Berlin! Fritz came to the conclusion that high German diplomatic officials were not about to abandon their efforts and that other secret attempts would be made in Stockholm. Unable to find out anything further, Fritz was nevertheless very pleased to have in his possession a piece of information of the highest importance that he would transmit to the Americans in Bern as soon as he returned to Berlin.

With nothing further to do at the führer's headquarters, he decided to make every effort to return to the capital. He faked a stomach ailment and stopped eating, despite the superior quality of the meals in the "wolf's lair." He complained of complications from an appendicitis operation he had had in 1940. His colleagues realized that Fritz was really ill when they saw him refuse cold chicken at breakfast one morning. Soon, armed with a medical certificate, he returned to Berlin around September 20, 1944. On his return, he had himself treated by his doctor friends at the Charité hospital, who agreed to prescribe fictitious treatments.

Bern, September–October 1944

"In the early part of September 1944, Dr. Bruno [*sic*] Kleist, Ministerial Dirigent of the Ost Ministerium, made a trip to Stockholm as the agent of high ranking German officials . . . in order to attempt to make contact with the Russians. In Stockholm, however, Soviet Counsellor of Embassy Semenov served notice that this action was not suitable. In spite of this, the Germans are said to be continuing efforts along these same lines. . . . Hitler has not entirely abandoned the idea of reaching an agreement with the Soviets." This OSS document was written on the basis of information supplied by Fritz Kolbe in early October 1944. It provoked disbelief among the experts in Washington who considered it "of great importance, if it is true." Colonel McCormack's staff turned up its collective nose and thought that the cable should be treated with great wariness. McCormack thought it was impossible for the German authorities to enter into contact with the Soviets, despite the fact that the Japanese wanted a separate peace with the Russians. Less negative than McCormack, Allen Dulles thought that the hypothesis of a new German-Soviet agreement was now in the realm of the possible and that everything had to be done to prevent it. He did not at all appreciate the announcement in late September of the "Morgenthau Plan," which envisaged the deindustrialization of Germany and its transformation into a vast agricultural zone. This kind of American initiative could in his view only strengthen certain pro-Soviet tendencies that were beginning to appear in the higher reaches of the German government.

The information that Fritz had gleaned in the *Wolfsschanze* reached Bern in early October. The Foreign Ministry courier Willy Pohle himself handed the confidential package to Ernst Kocherthaler. Instead of using the usual mailbox, the two men met for lunch in a Bern restaurant on October 6. In the envelope there were about thirty documents on film—this was the first time this method worked—and a handwritten note from Fritz dated October 3. This was little in comparison to the usual delivery. Fritz apologized and explained that an increasing quantity of diplomatic cables were no longer reaching the foreign ministry because they were carried directly to Hitler. The most important document in this batch was the one revealing the activities of Peter Kleist in Stockholm. But there were also very interesting details about the atmosphere in the führer's headquarters: "The climate is worse and worse," wrote Fritz, adding that "the pressure is unbelievably high." *Der Druck ist unerhört stark:* the sentence was repeated in German in the summary prepared by Allen Dulles. In addition, Fritz no longer said anything about his "militia" but asked the Americans whether he would now be more useful in Bern than in Berlin. "Recommend a reconciliation with my wife, and that will mean that I should join you."

Berlin, October 1944

The reading and processing of "George Wood's" letters were now part of the ordinary work of the Bern office of the OSS. Meanwhile in Berlin, Fritz's life was becoming ever more difficult and dangerous. To the first serious food shortages in late October was added one of the coldest winters that Germany had experienced for a long time. But above all, the danger of being discovered was constantly increasing.

Fritz was beginning to learn how to use the camera supplied by the Americans. His favorite place to work was Adolphe Jung's room in the Charité hospital. According to the French surgeon:

In the hospital, the documents were worked on until late at night. Sometimes he [Fritz] started right in to photograph them, fastening them with clips or thumbtacks onto a piece of cardboard well exposed to daylight or several electric lights. He had an excellent little camera that took extremely precise pictures two centimeters by two centimeters. I helped him as best I could. When he had to leave, he left the documents with me, particularly the ones that had not been photographed. I was often very uneasy. In my room I had only an old desk that did not lock very securely. Usually I took the papers and put them in n envelope that I sealed. On it I wrote *Manuscrit pour le Journal de Médecine* and locked it in the desk. At night I jumped when the sirens went off. I hastily dressed and went downstairs with a small suitcase and a leather briefcase containing my essential papers, into which I also stuffed the documents. Sometimes I was forced to leave them upstairs. I imagined a bomb landing on the hospital and half destroying the room, and I saw the personnel and the firemen emptying out the room to save books and papers and throwing everything in a pile. What would happen to me if I was wounded? Suppose they discovered all the documents in my possession. What would happen if one day one of the Nazis decided to search my room while I was working?

The day before the diplomatic pouch was to leave for Switzerland, on October 4, 1944, Fritz went to the mail service of the Foreign

Ministry to register one or two packages that he wished to send to Bern. He found himself facing a new employee whom he did not know, a young man full of zeal who began a thorough search of the contents of the packages—clothing supposedly left behind in Berlin by accident belonging to a colleague in the Bern legation. The suspicious employee went through shirts, trousers, and even pairs of socks, inspecting every nook and cranny. Fritz watched in terror as the young man got ready to unfold a coat, the inside pockets of which held the rolls of film he was sending to the Americans. Fritz had his hand on the little revolver that he always carried with him. But suddenly another colleague came into the room. Fritz engaged the newcomer in "an interesting conversation." The conscientious employee took part in the discussion and stopped concentrating on his work. He closed up the packages, put on the regulation seals, and put them in a large canvas sack for the next day's train to Bern. After that moment of extreme tension, Fritz locked himself in his office and drank a double cognac. "My knees were a little wobbly," he confessed many years later.

Another day in the fall of 1944, Fritz was visited at home by his *Blockwart,* the local party official assigned among other things to watch the population in the neighborhood. This routine questioning could be dangerous. Fritz did not know whether he was under suspicion after the failed plot of July 20. But he was reassured to learn that the *Blockwart* was a decent bus driver without malice or brutality. Fritz did not hide the fact that he was not a member of the party. But he denied listening to the BBC and presented himself as being neither a "moaner" nor a "spreader of false rumors." At the end of the conversation, the *Blockwart* asked Fritz for his opinion about the war: "I hope with all my heart for our final victory," said Fritz. The inspector was obviously very pleased. The expression "final victory" [*Endsieg*] had had an effect. The minor party official conscientiously wrote the expression down in his notebook and let Fritz know that his report would not be negative.

On still another occasion, while he was walking to his mother's carrying "material" (documents to be photographed), a large air raid caught him crossing Alexanderplatz. He was forced to seek refuge in a public underground shelter. On the way down the stairs, he said a prayer that he would not lose consciousness. If that were to happen, the documents might have been found and he would be done for.

Bern, November 1944

During the month of November, Allen Dulles continued to improve the working conditions in the Bern office of the OSS. The office was equipped with a radio transmitter that was installed in an attic in the Dufourstrasse buildings. For the first time, it was no longer necessary to use the Swiss mails or the "cover" of American diplomatic representation to transmit information to Washington and London. The Swiss secret services, who were probably aware of the existence of this illegal and undeclared transmitter, behaved as though nothing had happened and did not carry out a search.

Allen Dulles was gaining increased autonomy and influence. He received more and more visits in his Bern office. The time was long gone when his information was considered with some disdain by Washington headquarters. He was far from infallible, however. Dulles was excessively optimistic by nature and thought that the end of the war was near. To be sure, Aix-la-Chapelle had fallen on October 21, 1944. But Germany still had ten million men in uniform. The OSS office in Bern did not at all foresee the Ardennes counteroffensive that would begin in the middle of December.

Toward the middle of November, a new message from Fritz reached Bern. This time the rolls of film had been hidden in a box containing a watch to be repaired. The Foreign Ministry courier, as usual, was not aware of the real content of what he was carrying. One hundred pages of documents had been photographed. The most interesting messages had to do with Japan, Hungary, and the latest developments in German armaments.

Fritz revealed precise details about the V-2 rockets and added personal comments to suggest priorities for action:

There are said to be V-2 launching pads in the Eifel Mountains area. There is an assembly plant in Rübeland which is
almost entirely subterranean, on the railroad line from
Elbingerode to Blankenberg. It is felt that the bombing of
bombing of railroads and road communications would produce excellent
results for the Allies . . . A-4 is said to be the designation
applied to the V-2 bomb by the experts. It is said to be
manufactured at Saint Gallen, some forty kilometers southeast of Steyr in Austria. The parts are assembled in the Mittel
Deutsche Werke in Hartz, Germany. The buildings where
this work is done are all located underground. The smashing
of the rail shipment lines would be the most effective way to
cripple this production.

A little further on, he reported that "General Jodl sent a wire in the
first week of October 1944 to the Commander-in-Chief in the west
saying that this was not a propitious time, politically, to launch these
bombs against Paris, and that no attack should be made in that region for the present."

With reference to Japan, there were dozens of details that could be
used by the Allied armies. The Japanese were expecting an American
landing in the Philippines in mid-November, and they were preparing for a major British offensive against Rangoon, Bangkok, and Saigon.
Marshal Terauchi, supreme commander of Japanese forces in the
Southwest Pacific, was preparing the withdrawal of his headquarters
from Manila to Saigon. The Japanese authorities were beginning to
work on preparing their public opinion for a German defeat.

The information about Hungary was not of a military nature but
concerned the fate of the Jewish population. Fritz Kolbe had sent to
the Americans some cables from Budapest, one of which said the
following: "There were said to be one hundred and twenty thousand
Jews in Budapest including children who were unfit for work and
whose fate had not yet been decided. This was said to depend largely
on available transportation. The person responsible was said to be SS-
Obersturmbannführer Eichmann." Another document, based on in-

formation dating from late October 1944, indicated that "the remaining Jews in Budapest" were to be placed "in ghettos at the edge of town." For some of them, according to another document, "preparations were under way for a proposed trek on foot. The Jews were to be . . . taken to the Reich territory for work in the labor service." There was no clear mention of the extermination of the Jews, but of forced labor and "conscription." At every step there was the name of Eichmann, SS-Obersturmbannführer. This person was "not identified further," as indicated by a footnote in one of the cables of the Boston series.

By that date, the American leaders knew very well what awaited the deportees. But the Boston cables repeated word for word the vocabulary of the German diplomatic cables: "Latest available statistics showed that conscription of the province during the summer of 1944 had amounted to 440,000 people." In fact, these 440,000 Jews had been sent to Auschwitz. All that remained was the Jewish community of Budapest, which had been provisionally saved by the changing political circumstances in the city. In early July, Marshal Horthy had decided to put an end to the deportations in order to facilitate a rapprochement between Hungary and the Allies, and he had eventually announced his intention to leave the Axis. Berlin reacted harshly. On October 15, 1944, Horthy was brutally replaced by a man entirely under Berlin's thumb, Ferenc Szálasi, leader of the Arrow Cross movement. From that point on, Hungary was one of the last ramparts of the Reich, and the "final solution" was pursued there systematically, beginning with the elimination of the Jews of Budapest.

Washington, December 1944

What would become of Fritz Kolbe after the war? This question began to be asked in Washington in late 1944.

We are asked specifically what we are prepared to do in their behalf [those of German nationality who work for us behind

German lines]. In regard to offering firm guarantees of
protection and post armistice privileges to Germans whom we
recruit and who work loyally for our organization. Among
these privileges would be permission for entry into the
United States after the War, the placing of their earnings on
deposit in an American bank and the like. . . . On this we will
need authority which only you can give.

These words were addressed to President Roosevelt in a letter dated
December 1, 1944.

A few days later, the president responded negatively to the head of
the OSS:

I do not believe that we should offer any guarantees of protection in the post-hostilities period to Germans who are working
for your organization. I think that the carrying out of any such
guarantees would be difficult and probably widely misunder-
stood both in this country and abroad. We may expect that
the number of Germans who are anxious to save their skins
and property by coming over to the side of the United Nations at the last moment will rapidly increase. Among them
may be some who should properly be tried for war crimes or at
least arrested for active participation in Nazi activities. Even
with the necessary controls you mention I am not prepared to
authorize the giving of guarantees.

There would be no American sanctuary for the German friends of
the Allies. Provisions of this kind could have applied to Fritz Kolbe
and Hans-Bernd Gisevius, to whom Allen Dulles wanted to be able to
offer some postwar prospects. The intransigence of the American
president was in conformity with the policy that had been his officially
since January 1943: The surrender of Germany had to be "unconditional" and nothing should be done to encourage any hypothetical
internal resistance.

The technical evaluation of the source named "George Wood" was completed in late 1944. Lieutenant Thomas Dunn, one of the best analysts of the Kappa material in the counterespionage department of the OSS, received a summary inventory of the best deliveries of "Wood." This inventory had been prepared by Colonel McCormack. The document indicated which messages sent by the Berlin agent since his first visit to Bern in August 1943 had been of "considerable value." Files 215 to 218, which covered the reports of Generals Kretschmer and Gronau on Japan, headed the list. They were followed by the Kappa messages dealing with clandestine deliveries of tungsten from Spain to Germany (373 and 402). McCormack's inventory next mentioned everything concerning the "great game" of diplomacy in Europe. They had been able to follow the shifting alliances in central Europe (Hungary, Rumania, Bulgaria) and life behind the scenes in all the puppet regimes controlled by the Reich (particularly Vichy) with great precision thanks to "Wood." Colonel McCormack cited as an example cable number 386, which illustrated in great detail the anxieties of Berlin in July 1944, concerning Bulgaria and its inclination to leave the Axis (which it in fact abandoned in the late summer of 1944). He also mentioned cable number 388, which spoke of German plans to move some key institutions of the Vichy regime to the east of France. Oddly, Colonel McCormack did not mention any of the Kappa cables dealing with military production sites, particularly for the V-1 and V-2 rockets. Nor was there any reference in McCormack's inventory to the fate of the Jews of Rome or Hungary.

Bern, January–February 1945

Fritz Kolbe was able to return to Bern in late January 1945. He had tried to get to Switzerland for the Christmas holidays, but the confederation authorities had rejected his visa application for unexplained reasons. On January 28, 1945, Allen Dulles wrote to Washington that

"George Wood" had arrived with two hundred photographed documents. Many of them had probably been hastily done: They were out of focus and a substantial part of the film was unreadable. "These documents are harder to decipher than a crossword puzzle," Dulles wrote to his Washington colleagues.

The trip had been even more uncomfortable than in April 1944, the date of his last visit. Fritz had made the trip with a colleague from the Foreign Ministry, because the rule was now that a courier never traveled alone. The journey from Berlin to Basel had taken sixty rather than the normal sixteen hours: two days and two nights in a railroad car without a window. The line now ran through Nuremberg, Ulm, and Friedrichshafen, on the shores of Lake Constance. Fritz and his colleague had spent a night there in a hotel infested by the Gestapo. The next day, they had taken a boat across the lake to get to Switzerland.

As he had the first time, Fritz carried the documents in a little box hidden between his legs: fortunately, film was much less bulky than bundles of paper. This batch contained a series of cables dealing with recent high-level negotiations between the Swiss National Bank and the German Reichsbank. On December 10, 1944, Ernst Weber, president of the Swiss National Bank, had invited Emil Puhl, vice president of the Reichsbank, to dinner. The principal subject under discussion had been the purchase of German gold by Switzerland. For reasons of security, Weber "would take charge personally of the transfer of gold across the border." In exchange, the Reichsbank agreed to facilitate the delivery of German coal to Switzerland. The discussions had taken place in "the usual atmosphere of trust," as Otto Köcher, chief of the German legation in Bern, noted.

Some months earlier, in May 1944, Fritz had already provided the OSS with a cable from Otto Köcher revealing that Germany was selling six thousand kilos of gold a month to the Swiss National Bank. The bank's president, Ernst Weber, even said he was "ready to take even more gold than the amount fixed in the monthly quota" established by the bilateral agreement between the two central banks. Otto Köcher characterized him as a "personal friend" of Emil Puhl.

The existence of close economic and financial ties between Switzerland and Germany provoked the anger of the Allies. But there was something even more serious than the gold transactions between Berlin and Bern. A cable that Fritz brought in January 1945 revealed the existence of high-level negotiations between officials and industrialists of the two countries on weapons and advanced military technology. The Swiss wanted to acquire expertise in chemically propelled rockets and had frequent discussions with the heads of a major German company, Köln-Rottweil, part of the IG Farben conglomerate.

This information was transmitted to Washington in early February ("Jakka" messages, for January and Kappa). During his stay in Bern, Fritz did not merely share his information with Allen Dulles and Gerald Mayer. He openly made the argument for an overthrow of the Nazi regime to some of his colleagues at the German legation. At least two of the diplomats whispered to him that they agreed and that something had to be done to bring things to an end. They wanted to resign their positions, but they did not know if they could get political asylum in Switzerland. The atmosphere in the German legation had never been so gloomy. As for Fritz, he left for Berlin on February 2, 1945, making the return trip in a freight car. He used a backpack as a pillow and slept through most of the trip.

On his return to the capital of the Reich, Fritz lived through the most violent bombing he had ever experienced. The Allied raids of February 3, 1945 remained in memory as exceptionally deadly and destructive. That day, the Reich Chancellery was hit, along with the buildings of the Gestapo and the People's Court. The city was unrecognizable. The railroad stations witnessed apocalyptic scenes of hysteria. The streets were clogged with masses of refugees and with troops on the way to the front. On January 30, the Red Army had crossed the Oder, provoking the flight of millions of Germans to the west. Fifty thousand a day were arriving in the capital of the Reich, fleeing the swift and terrifying advance of T-34 tanks, mounted Cossacks, and the Russian infantry, which, rumor had it, consisted, particularly in the lower ranks, of countless pillagers and rapists.

Crossing through Berlin on his way home, Fritz felt that he was in a city under siege. Corpses were scattered everywhere, barely covered by paper bags, with heads and feet exposed at either end. On February 7, 1945, Adolphe Jung described in his diary the new face of Berlin: "People are building barricades in the streets with whatever they find there from the houses demolished by bombing. Everything is used. Large and small bricks or stone blocks from the sidewalks; wooden beams or iron bars taken from neighboring ruins. Trees, if there are any, are cut down and used. There thus arise barricades two meters wide and two meters high that almost completely close off the street."

And yet Berliners as a whole remained calm. The restaurants were full even if the menus were meager. And above all, no one spoke about the war. People seemed resigned, but not at all defeatist or even rebellious. Official Nazi propaganda recognized the existence of a "crisis," but there was as yet no talk of defeat. Goebbels's latest slogan was simple: "We will win because we must win!"

Returning to his Wilhelmstrasse office, Fritz realized that all the cables that he had carefully preserved in his safe had been destroyed by a colleague. He had been obliged to give him his key when he left for Switzerland, and the minister had ordered that "documents of no immediate interest" be destroyed in all the offices of the Foreign Ministry.

Bern, February 1945

In Bern, Allen W. Dulles was irritated to learn that the materials supplied by "George Wood" were considered by his Washington colleagues as "museum pieces" and regretted that their "full operational value" had not been obtained. He said that he "had never understood" why the "Wood" file had been treated first of all by the counterespionage service, which was endlessly concerned with verifying the authenticity of the source. Dulles finally complained about jurisdictional disputes among the army, the OSS, and the State Department. Information did not circulate, and the result was that his favorite source was treated with extreme neglect: "Again emphasize that to get full value out of this material will require staff of workers thoroughly competent German, with some background Wood material, knowledge of personalities and German diplomatic procedure plus ability decipher crossword puzzles."

In Washington, the neglect of "George Wood" was not a matter of chance. Some members of the intelligence community and the army were enthusiastic about this miraculous source, General Donovan among them, but others had mixed feelings about the general quality of the Kappa material. One of them thought: "While much of this material has been of interest and importance from different aspects, it has not seemed top-drawer save for certain few exceptions. It would seem to be more the type of communications which the old Chiefs of Divisions in the State Department used to get and give and not the information which went directly to or came from the Secretary, Undersecretary, and President . . ."

A short time later, on February 16, 1945, Dulles again complained to General Donovan: "You have requested us to have Wood concentrate on Far Eastern material and we endeavored to comply and gave transmission of this material absolute priority. I have no clue whatever whether this material proved of value to you."

Was Dulles's outburst heard? A "special unit" was soon established in the OSS to analyze the Kappa messages. The "George Wood" file was no longer under the jurisdiction of the OSS counterespionage service and was now located in the secret intelligence department. An entirely separate administrative unit was specifically dedicated to the analysis of information provided by Fritz Kolbe, including a total of fifteen people, dividing files into geographical zones, and including two colonels assigned to elucidate the most technical questions.

Allen Dulles thought that these initiatives had come too late. Since Washington had not known how to make use of the information from "George Wood," the chief of OSS Bern was now determined to take steps on his own to end the war more quickly. He was more than ever prepared to sidestep the hierarchy and act on his own hook. For example, he decided in late February 1945 not to refuse the hand extended to him by the commander of SS troops in Italy, Obergruppenführer Karl Wolff, Heinrich Himmler's former right-hand man. Wolff was acting on his own. Like other high political or military officials of the Reich, he thought that "although Germany had lost the war, it could still choose its conqueror."

After communicating through a Swiss intelligence officer and an Italian industrialist, Allen Dulles and Karl Wolff met in person in Zurich on March 8, 1945 and then in Ascona on March 19. These two meetings took place in the most complete secrecy. Contacts continued throughout March and April. In messages from Bern to Washington, Wolff was designated by the code name "Critic," and the discussions with him were given the name of "Operation Sunrise." President Roosevelt, who was already dying, did not oppose these negotiations when he learned of their existence. On April 29, 1945, the Wehrmacht laid down its arms in Italy, in a surrender without conditions. The Soviets were informed at the last minute and felt that they had been stabbed in the back. The Kremlin reacted very vigorously to this attempt toward a "separate peace" of the Western powers with the Germans. The last written contacts of Stalin with Roosevelt had to do with Dulles's secret maneuvers in Italy. The extremely harsh tone of these messages was an early sign of the coming cold war.

Berlin, March 1945

March 1945 brought general and headlong flight from Berlin. The Russians were in the process of recapturing Poland. Many people, particularly important officials of the Nazi Party, were attempting to leave the city. The others were forcibly enlisted in the *Volkssturm*, a pathetic people's militia armed with improvised weapons. Nothing was more precious at the time than a vehicle with a full fuel tank. A car could not be found, even in miserable condition, for less than fifteen or twenty thousand marks (bear in mind that Fritz Kolbe's monthly salary was nine hundred marks). The price of a liter of gasoline was forty marks or twenty cigarettes. Forged papers and passes were extremely expensive.

It was at this very moment that Fritz was given a confidential mission by his boss. Nothing professional: Karl Ritter had a mistress whom he wanted at all costs to send to safety to his house in Bavaria. She was a singer of light music, used to dressing in the latest fashion and never separated from her makeup case. She had a two-year-old daughter. Fritz was asked to drive the young woman and her child to the other end of the country in the ambassador's official Mercedes. In order to allow the vehicle to get through checkpoints, he was given orders for Switzerland, duly stamped by the relevant services of the ministry.

"In March 1945, Kolbe came to the hospital for the last time," wrote Adolphe Jung. "He had received orders to go to Switzerland. . . . All night, documents were photographed. Everything that had any importance for the American embassy was set on the stand facing the camera. He was nervous and worried. He left us knowing that Berlin would soon be literally crushed by Allied aircraft, that we would probably have to suffer through the final struggle of the Nazis against the Russian army. His fiancée was crying. I myself was worried. Would I be able to see my country and my family again? He promised to have us picked up as soon as possible on a plane by our friend D. [Dulles]." When he left, Fritz gave instructions to his three friends in the ministry, Fräulein von Heimerdinger, Karl Dumont, and Willy Pohle: "When the Americans arrive, you have to go to an American officer, claim to belong to a resistance group, and give the password 'George 25900.'"

Fritz left Berlin on March 16 or 18, 1945. Professor Sauerbruch had asked him to take his wife along, so that, including the baby, there were four people in the car. Everyone was squeezed into the front seat, since the back seat was filled with an impressive quantity of suitcases and Oriental rugs belonging to Karl Ritter and his young companion. The passengers had to shift their legs to the right so that Fritz could operate the gearshift. Comical at first, this situation soon became embarrassing.

At first, Fritz intended to leave at breakfast time, but an American air raid forced him to delay getting on the road until noon. The sky was gray, the cold biting, and there was ice on the roads. Fritz could see nothing in the limousine's rearview mirror because of everything piled in the back seat (there was even a baby carriage tied to the top of the car). The journey promised to be arduous; they had to drive early in the morning or in the early evening to avoid attacks from hedgehopping enemy fighters. The brakes on the Mercedes did not work well, and the car broke down on the very first night. They had to be towed by a truck belonging to the SS, secured through the savoir faire of Karl Ritter. The SS truck had a charcoal-burning motor and went no faster than thirty kilometers an hour, with frequent stops to clean the pipes, so that it took almost four days to get from Berlin to Bavaria. Between Berlin and Munich, there were four to six identity checks, carried out either by the army or by SS units.

Crossing the country from north to south, they had the impression that they were in a scene from the Thirty Years' War. Families of refugees were walking toward no specific destination; they could see dead animals in the fields; they came across burned-out vehicles on the sides of the road. The branches of the trees were often covered with strips of aluminum foil dropped by enemy planes to jam German radar. The singer and her baby spent the entire trip crying and screaming. Fritz was more than impatient to reach Bavaria.

When he got to the town of Kempten, in the Allgäu region of Bavaria, Fritz was finally able to rid himself of Karl Ritter's mistress, the baby, the baby carriage, the car, and the SS. Too bad about the car, he thought, but the escort was a little burdensome. Still accompanied by Professor Sauerbruch's wife, he then went to Ottobeuren, not far from there, where the prelate Georg Schreiber was waiting for him, living in hiding in a large Benedictine monastery. Fritz was able to rest for a day or two in Ottobeuren, although he continued his activities. He took the time to photograph in the monastery library some documents that he had brought with him from Berlin. Thanks to the protection of the monks, he was not obliged to register with the local police as a traveler who was passing through. The atmosphere of the cloister impressed him a great deal, especially the meals in the great hall of the monastic community. The feeling was restful, and the food in Bavaria was better than in Berlin: potatoes were not rationed.

The pause was short-lived. A few days later, Fritz Kolbe and Margot Sauerbruch took the train from Ottobeuren to Weiler, an Allgäu village that was the home of Wilhelm Mackeben, a businessman, former diplomat, and friend of Fritz. Despite the short distance, they had to change trains twice. As they were waiting for the connection at Memmingen, Fritz and Margot Sauerbruch had the terrifying experience of being stopped by a Gestapo brigade that took them into a windowless office to be interrogated. After a few frightening moments, Fritz realized that this was probably a simple routine procedure. Margot's suitcase was inspected but not Fritz's bag, which contained some highly compromising rolls of film. Fritz grew angry and demanded to be treated with all the respect due an official courier of the Foreign Ministry, pointing out that his papers were in order, including his exit visa from Germany. The policeman called the Gestapo in Munich to verify that Herr Fritz Kolbe was indeed someone from the Foreign Ministry on an official mission. They were finally able to leave without further trouble. Professor Sauerbruch, who was in the area, was reunited with his wife, and Fritz continued the journey alone.

When he reached the village of Weiler, Fritz met with his friend Wilhelm Mackeben, who kept the doors of his chalet open to all kinds of people in a constant stream: During his stay, Fritz met a Peruvian woman, an Iranian student from Teheran who had been stranded in Germany since the beginning of the war, and two German officers with whom he had a long nighttime conversation. These two Wehrmacht officers were part of a detachment assigned to transport in trucks a substantial quantity of secret documents to be hidden in southern Germany. With a knowing air, Fritz pretended to know what was involved, which allowed him to learn more. The trucks were transporting documents on the Soviet Union, the Red Army, and even a list of pro-German agents infiltrated into the USSR. They belonged to a military espionage service with expertise on Russia, and their leaders intended to use their treasure as a bargaining chip with the Allies once the war was over.

Very pleased at having gathered this information, Fritz resumed his journey to Switzerland. He went to Bregenz on a bicycle that had been graciously lent to him by Mackeben's Iranian student friend. In Bregenz, the Swiss consulate stamped his diplomatic passport without difficulty and confirmed the validity of his visa, good for a period of five days. It was April 2, 1945. The next day, he took the train at Sankt Margarethen for Zurich and Bern. The comfort was unexpected and there were no police barriers. The only check that Fritz had to go through was a medical check on entering Swiss territory: It was verified that he had neither dysentery, nor smallpox, nor scabies.

Bern, April 1945

"Wood arrived last night after laborious trip from Berlin, which he left about March 16." This was the message Dulles cabled to Washington on April 4, 1945. On that day, the final pockets of German resistance were falling in the Ruhr, and the Allies were already in the center of the Reich (Kassel, Gotha, and Erfurt were in the process of being taken). Fritz was debriefed as usual, but the Americans in Bern had less need for him. Allen Dulles was entirely taken up with his secret negotiations with Karl Wolff, Himmler's former right-hand man. This time, Ernst Kocherthaler took on the task of taking notes on his conversations with Fritz.

Fritz had a good deal to say, particularly about Japan. German Ambassador Heinrich Stahmer described the growing sense of political crisis in Tokyo and said he was convinced that the Japanese leaders were more and more unpopular among their people. In another cable, Stahmer set out in detail the latest technical developments in Japanese aviation. On the topic of Germany, Fritz provided the latest examples of the dissolution of Hitler's power.

All of that was very interesting, but for Allen Dulles, the usefulness of "George Wood" had now changed its character. The head of the Bern office of the OSS wanted to make him a permanent employee, based with the Americans and able to return to Germany to fulfill precise missions as required. At first, he wanted to send him to southern Bavaria to investigate the setting up of a "national (Alpine) Redoubt" in which Dulles was convinced the Nazi leaders would take refuge to conduct their final battle. "Almost Wagnerian," he said in his cables to Washington. Like Dulles, the leading American generals firmly believed in this scenario. For the moment, Fritz remained in Bern. Dulles asked him to investigate behind the scenes in the Reich legation, to encourage his fellow diplomats to resign, and to get hold of archive documents that might interest the Allies, notably on the financial affairs of the Nazi leaders who hoped to place their holdings in Switzerland after the defeat.

After five days in Bern, Fritz's visa was no longer valid. From that moment on, his fate was entirely in the hands of his American friends. "George Wood" had become a stowaway living under the personal protection of Allen Dulles.

Berlin, April 1945

On April 21, 1945, Walter Bauer—the anti-Nazi entrepreneur associated with Fritz—came out of prison. He had been arrested in September 1944 in connection with the investigation of the 20 July plot and subjected to inhuman treatment for several months. On the day of his liberation, the Gestapo was considerate enough to give him two subway tickets so he could go home. Three days later, on April 24, 1945, Russian troops arrived in Berlin. Pillage and rape prevailed. Maria Fritsch had remained alone in the capital of the Reich, and Fritz had no news. She left no record about this terrible period, and no one will ever know how she lived through those days of sorrow, shame, and deliverance. On every corner could be seen bodies crushed by tanks, "emptied like toothpaste tubes." The odor of death was mixed with the odor of springtime. In the midst of the ruins, birds, flowers, and fruit trees lived their lives as though nothing were happening.

The Charité hospital continued to fulfill its mission as well as possible. Doctors and medical personnel subsisted on whiskey and crackers and spent as much time in the hospital's underground shelter as on the wards, three-quarters of which were destroyed. Professor

Sauerbruch was back in Berlin. Adolphe Jung, still on his staff, recorded a constant flow of the wounded: "In the operating room, we are presented indiscriminately with soldiers and civilians, women and children, wounded. In the square in front of the hospital, despite the danger, the crowd still lines up at the bakery. A shell fell on the crowd of women and children. We have to operate without stopping" (April 22, 1945). "There are hardly any houses left in Berlin that have not been hit. Most of them have collapsed. Among those still standing, it is rarely possible to inhabit anywhere above the first floor. Of course there are no more telephones, no electricity or water, because even where the pipes are intact the pressure is so low that you can barely get a few drops in the cellars" (April 21). "Every two minutes, a large shell falls inside the walls of the hospital . . . When will I be hit?" (April 24).

On Tuesday, May 1, at 9:30 in the evening, Hamburg radio announced to the German people that serious news was about to be broadcast. Excerpts of Bruckner's Seventh Symphony were played. Finally, Admiral Dönitz announced the death of the führer the day before in Berlin. At the Charité hospital, now treating Soviet soldiers, there was not much time to listen to the radio. The Third Reich was already practically forgotten; everyone was against it, had always been against it.

12

DISGRACE

Bern, late April 1945

In late April 1945, Fritz Kolbe was given a very delicate mission by the Americans. He had no idea that this episode would strike a severe blow against his reputation and would definitively ruin his career. The war was coming to an end. The Americans were preparing the cases against German leaders whom they intended to put on trial. They were intensely interested in Nazi financial holdings outside Germany, particularly in Switzerland. But the OSS had learned that the German legation in Bern was in the process of destroying its records in view of the imminent surrender. Allen Dulles sent Fritz as an emissary to Otto Köcher, the envoy of the Reich, to persuade him to stop the destruction of documents.

Otto Köcher was extremely irritated to see Kolbe, whom he had until then considered a subordinate and who now turned out to be a traitor. He answered very curtly, stating that he would not take any orders from the Americans, even less from a German who had gone over to the Allies. But Fritz Kolbe did not give up: He attempted to persuade Köcher that it was in his interest to resign from his position.

The Americans were proposing to make him part of an embryonic pro-Allied government that could quickly put an end to the war. "You have to choose between Hitler and Germany. The whole world has its eyes on you," Fritz explained to his compatriot. Otto Köcher was angry and indignant. Unlike Kolbe, Köcher had a sense of duty and patriotism. His son was serving in the Wehrmacht. He would remain at his post until the end, in accordance with the oath of loyalty to the führer that he had taken. There was nothing further to discuss. Fritz Kolbe was unceremoniously shown to the door.

On leaving the envoy's residence, Fritz was arrested by two plain-clothes Swiss policemen who were watching the comings and goings of Otto Köcher, who was suspected of engaging in major financial manipulations for the leaders in Berlin. Some of the financial reserves of the Foreign Ministry (dozens of kilos of gold pieces) had just been secretly shipped to Bern. Was the Swiss capital about to become a rear base for the hard-core supporters of the Reich? Was the gold going to finance a pro-Nazi fifth column in Switzerland? These were the fears of the Swiss authorities, largely shared by the Americans. Thanks to the intervention of Allen Dulles, at whose home Fritz was living, the suspicions of the Swiss police about Kolbe were quickly removed. But they did not want to release him right away. They too sent him to Otto Köcher to try to get an answer to the simple question: Where is the gold of the Reich? The following evening, following orders, Fritz Kolbe made a second visit to the diplomat. Of course, he was given no information. He barely had the time to warn Köcher on behalf of the Swiss authorities against any misappropriation of funds for which he could later be prosecuted. For the second time in twenty-four hours, Ribbentrop's representative slammed the door in Fritz's face.

The visits had accomplished nothing but to worsen the position of Otto Köcher in the eyes of the Americans. They did everything to ensure that the German diplomat would not receive asylum in Switzerland after the surrender of the Reich. Köcher had strong friendships in Swiss political circles and he had been promised that he could stay in Switzerland and not be handed over to the Allies. But the combined pressure of the Allies and a portion of Swiss public opinion caused the

Federal Council to give in, and he was deported to Germany in July 1945. The former head of the German legation in Bern was placed in an American internment camp in Ludwigsburg, north of Stuttgart. The Allied military authorities began to question him about the secret relations between the Reich and Switzerland during the war. But they were unable to complete their investigation: On December 27, 1945, the body of Otto Köcher was found hanging in his cell. The "Köcher file," so promising for the investigators assigned to dissect the machinations of the Third Reich, maintained all its mysteries.

Inside the Ludwigsburg internment camp, the death of Otto Köcher provoked lively discussions among the German prisoners, some of whom were former employees of the Foreign Ministry. One of them started a rumor that would spread and cause Fritz Kolbe great harm. He said that Köcher had been betrayed by a German. A scum. A traitor who had been working for the Americans for a good while. "His name: Fritz Kolbe."

Hegenheim, May 1945

Fritz stayed in Bern until the middle of May 1945. It was there while he was staying with Allen Dulles that he learned of Germany's surrender. He did not celebrate the event as it deserved, because everyday concerns had already come to the fore again. Fritz's visa had long since expired, and he had to leave Switzerland. Allen Dulles had his agent secretly taken to an OSS barracks in Hegenheim, in Alsace, very near the Swiss border. Even though he was confident about his future, Fritz was growing bored and felt isolated far from his friends. To keep himself occupied, it was no longer enough to exercise and go running. He took English lessons and wrote various reports and memoirs for the Americans.

In April, Allen Dulles had asked him to supply a description of the state of affairs in the Foreign Ministry. The file was accompanied by a commentary by Fritz on each of its members, with good and bad marks ("This one is an out-and-out Nazi, that one might possibly be employed again at the ministry"). Before leaving Bern for Hegenheim, Fritz had been asked to write down a summary of his own history. The result was a seven-page document written in English by Ernst Kocherthaler, with the title "The Story of George." Allen Dulles placed this document in his personal archives with the intention of using it one day. In Hegenheim, Fritz continued writing, throwing down on paper more details of his life as a spy, speaking of friends who had helped him during the war, giving their names and addresses in order to recommend them to the American administration.

But Fritz wanted action. He was soon given a new mission by Dulles: He was to go to Bavaria in search of Karl Ritter and especially of Ribbentrop, both of whom had disappeared and were actively sought by the occupation authorities. He was also asked to track down the secret archives on Russia whose existence he had revealed a few weeks earlier. The Americans provided him with a jeep and a driver. Fritz left on his assignment in early June. He was helped by the prelate Schreiber, who went with him for part of the trip. But he brought back no solid information and he even unknowingly relayed some useless tips ("Eva Braun was recently arrested on the banks of the Tegernsee"). He saw the Gauleiter of Munich fleeing ("He was seen on foot, with a knapsack, near Wiessee. He then headed toward Kreuth"). Beyond that, there was no trace of Ribbentrop or of Ritter, nor of the secret archives on Russia. Fritz Kolbe thought that the former foreign minister of the Reich had taken refuge in Italy, but he was mistaken. Ribbentrop was found by the British in Hamburg and arrested on June 14, 1945.

Wiesbaden, June 30, 1945

Even though he was no longer a spy in the strict sense of the word, "George Wood" continued to be useful to the Americans. In fact, he was considered a "person of reference," whose opinion could be asked at any time to guide the actions of the American occupation authorities. In the context of the establishment of the international tribunal that was going to judge the Nazi criminals, the OSS asked him to give evidence to Judge Robert H. Jackson, who was preparing the cases for the prosecution. The meeting took place in early July in Wiesbaden, on the premises of the Henkell company (champagne, wines, and spirits), chosen more or less by chance as the new base for the OSS in Germany.

On entering Judge Jackson's office, Fritz Kolbe was introduced for the first time to General Donovan. Donovan was eager to meet the celebrated "George Wood," who had just been called "the prize intelligence source of the war" by the British secret services. "I was introduced by Allen Dulles with very warm words," Fritz wrote to his friend Kocherthaler. The discussion concerned war criminals. Judge Jackson questioned Kolbe about the personalities of Ribbentrop and his closest collaborators. Fritz told what he knew of the actions of the former minister and described the climate that prevailed in the ministry during the war. He thought that Ribbentrop's first crime had been to "persuade Hitler to invade Poland, while assuring him that Great Britain would not react." He then spoke about Karl Ritter, whom he presented as a yes-man whose role had been to encourage Ribbentrop in his worst initiatives (notably the inhuman treatment meted out to prisoners of war, especially Soviet prisoners).

Fritz Kolbe was not the only representative of the German resistance in Judge Jackson's office. Next to him was Eugen Gerstenmaier, a leader of the Protestant Church, who had barely escaped a death sentence after the plot against Hitler. Gerstenmaier was questioned about the place of religion under Nazism. He answered by saying that the churches had been the principal center of opposition to Hitler. Fritz did not at all agree with him and had no hesitation in saying so.

What was beginning to annoy him intensely was the incredible number of German figures who claimed to have played an important role in the fight against Hitler. "Whose turn is it now?" he said to himself as he met one or another of them in the corridors of the Henkell company. He had a great deal of difficulty standing for Hans-Bernd Gisevius, who was also in Wiesbaden. He thought that this preferred informant of the Americans was a veritable impostor. He had not forgotten that Gisevius had begun his career in the Gestapo in the early years of the Nazi regime.

Berlin, July 1945

On July 17, Fritz returned to Berlin on board a US Army C-47. He finally saw Maria again, from whom he had heard nothing for three months. She was in a state of total exhaustion. She had not for a moment given up her work at the Charité hospital. It was a burdensome mission: the hospital was constantly full of the wounded, refugees dying from exhaustion, and victims of the typhus epidemic that had just broken out in the capital. Professor Sauerbruch held a high office in the administration of Berlin, in the Soviet zone. Adolphe Jung had returned to France. Maria told Fritz about what was happening in the Soviet zone: widespread rape, dismantling of factories, and systematic pillage of all property. The chaos was complete. Fritz could hardly believe his ears, he who thought that the Russians—who had not bombed German cities—would be greeted as liberators by the Germans. At that very moment he realized that the page of Nazism had finally been turned. Even if the Nazi "death squads" had not completely disappeared, the danger had changed its character and was now located in the East. On July 20, 1945, there was a celebration of the failed plot against Hitler. The press was full of praise for Count Stauffenberg and his friends. Fritz was stunned at the speed with which the wheels of history were turning.

"This new life did not seem to us worth living," Maria said much later, recalling the year 1945. However, compared to most Berliners, Fritz and Maria were aware that they were in a privileged position. They did not need a ration card to live, and they were housed by the Americans. Allen Dulles, who had just taken charge of the OSS for all of Germany, lived close by, frequently asked after them, and provided them with CARE packages containing food. Fritz had the use of a car and—the height of luxury—was free to travel anywhere. He was not unhappy to have his friends benefit from his influence with the American occupation authorities. People came to see him to get a pass, a ration card, medicine, or a job. The question of his professional future had not yet arisen; for the moment Fritz was employed by the American military administration (OMGUS, Office of Military Government for Germany, United States), although he did not know how long that would last.

Although Fritz sometimes put on an American uniform when he traveled around town incognito, he did not shout from the rooftops that he was working for the conquerors. "Lackey of the Allies" and "traitor to the fatherland" were starting to become common insults. He was often looked at askance. Almost everywhere, Fritz seemed to be thought of as a "foreign body." Maria's family, in particular, regarded him with suspicion. He didn't care, but she was deeply hurt. When Fritz Kolbe was asked what his current occupation was, he claimed that with the fall of the Foreign Ministry he wanted to make use of his skills as a former railroad employee. "I am trying to set up transportation firms," he said. Only his close friends knew of his official mission. He was a member of the OMGUS office in charge of the settlement of refugees and displaced persons, but he also worked as an interpreter and driver for the Americans. A few months later, he was even accredited as a journalist to the Allied press service, which made it possible for him to interview major German political figures.

At bottom, the real nature of his work remained very vague. Everyone knew—and that was the essential point—that Fritz enjoyed a privileged position and that he had a long reach. He had people call him "George." His house in the Nikolassee neighborhood became a meeting place for a swarm of friends delighted to escape from privation, if only for one evening. One would often encounter Professor Sauerbruch, Gertrud von Heimerdinger, old childhood friends, and newcomers to the "circle," such as the industrialist Viktor Bausch and his wife Erika von Hornstein, a painter, or the popular writer Felicitas von Reznicek. Among regular visitors to the house were also a few young American OSS officers: The bon vivant Harry Hermsdorf was a liaison with Allen Dulles, and Tom Polgar, Fritz's neighbor, spent hours playing with him with electric trains.

Fritz continued to supply pieces of information to the Americans and to draft reports for them. His area of expertise was the Social Democratic Party, in which he had a rich network of contacts, particularly in the Soviet zone. He closely observed the gradual seizure of control of the Social Democratic Party by the Communist Party in the East. In the analyses that he submitted to the OSS, he did not hesitate to assimilate the "Bolsheviks" to the Nazis. He even considered the communists "more brutal and more primitive" and regretted that it had not been possible to continue the war against the USSR.

On August 7, 1945, an accident almost cost him his life. While he was riding in an American army jeep, there was a violent collision with a truck at a Berlin intersection. Fritz suffered fractures of the skull and jaw, and several broken ribs. He spent three weeks in the hospital and needed a long convalescence before he could get back on his feet.

Wiesbaden, September 26, 1945

Fritz had barely recovered when he was again called to Wiesbaden to testify before a commission headed by DeWitt C. Poole, of the U.S. State Department, who was questioning as many of the former members of the Foreign Ministry as he could in connection with the trials that were soon to begin in Nuremberg. The young OSS officer, Peter Sichel, who was now posted to Berlin, accompanied Fritz in the jeep to Wiesbaden. During the long trip, the two men spoke mostly of sports and physical exercise. Fritz Kolbe showed off a few sports medals that he had won over the years. "It was his principal source of pride," Peter Sichel recalled.

On September 26, 1945, Fritz was questioned in Wiesbaden by a member of the Poole commission. He spoke of his activities during the war. He explained that he had had about twenty "friends" who shared his convictions and had helped him to act. He again presented a precise description of every figure in the Foreign Ministry. He spoke at length of the clandestine organization of the traffic in strategic materials between Franco Spain and Nazi Germany. For the Americans, it was essential to have firsthand testimony to substantiate the prosecution in Nuremberg.

The OSS, however, feared for the safety of its protégé and did not want to provide too many opportunities for "George Wood" to speak publicly. Allen Dulles had tried to dissuade him from going before the Poole commission. Fritz had insisted, wishing as he did to participate in the work of justice being carried out by the Allies. But unlike others, notably Hans-Bernd Gisevius, he was not called to the witness stand at the international military tribunal, which began its proceedings in November 1945. Having been only a spy with no political responsibility, his testimony had to remain secret.

Berlin, 1946 to 1948

Even though he was relatively protected by his anonymity, Fritz Kolbe was not in a comfortable situation. His cooperation with the Americans made him particularly vulnerable in the context of the nascent cold war. In late June 1946, General Donovan sent a warning note to Allen Dulles: "The situation in Berlin has altered drastically since you left. There may be danger to some of those people who worked with you there. . . . There have been disappearances of many people whose names have appeared in the press as having been of assistance to the Allies during the war." In his reply, Dulles explicitly raised the question of Fritz Kolbe's future: "Certainly the possibility you suggest always exists and I understand that steps are being taken to extract 'Wood' of Boston-platinum fame and bring him over here for a cooling off period. I understand that he is still about the most useful man we have in Berlin but certain events have caused our people over here to feel that he is no longer safe."

The Americans were beginning to fear that the Soviets might kidnap Kolbe. Wasn't he as Dulles wrote, "the most useful man" for the Americans in Berlin? Fritz himself was beginning to consider living in the United States. In February 1946, he wrote to Ernst Kocherthaler that he was considering definitively giving up German citizenship and settling on the other side of the Atlantic to begin a "new life." With his usual optimism, he hoped to find "a job in industry or in the State Department." Eager to see his son Peter again, he thought it would be easier for him to get to South Africa from the United States. In Germany, it was impossible for him to get the foreign currency he needed for the trip.

But things were not that simple. It took three years of effort on Fritz's part before he could go to America. His departure was delayed at first because of his divorce, the proceedings for which were still going on. But the principal difficulty lay elsewhere. In accordance with the instructions given by President Roosevelt before his death, Fritz had been given no guarantee about his future by the American authorities. Generally speaking, Germans were suspect in the eyes of the American immigration authorities. Obtaining a long-term visa came up against huge administrative difficulties. There was always a piece missing from the file. "Details are lacking on how contact with you was established, through whom and under what guise. No statement concerning George's ideology, his reasons for entering into what is otherwise a traitorous relationship with the Allies. . . . Particularly important is your assessment of George's motivation for having cooperated with the Allies, including an attestation of his sincere desire to overthrow the Nazi regime and in the end to serve his own country by contributing to the establishment of a democratic German government." These were some of the questions to which Allen Dulles had to respond in the course of 1947.

On January 15, 1948, Dulles testified to the good faith of Fritz Kolbe in a notarized affidavit he submitted in New York. The affidavit explained that Fritz had taken "incalculable risks" in order to help the Allied cause. "Kolbe worked entirely for ideological reasons. . . . He refused any monetary reward for his work. . . . After the war was over, when Kolbe volunteered to continue to do difficult and dangerous work for us, I set aside, with General Donovan's approval, a trust account in the amount of Sw. Fcs. 20,000. This was intended largely to protect a minor son in case any accident should befall him. I understand he has not touched this money. It was set aside for him without his having requested it. . . . I volunteered that I would do everything in my power to protect and assure his future. . . . I have no hesitation in saying that Fritz Kolbe is a brave man of high principles and a sincere believer in what this country stands for. He deserves well of us." A few months later, in another notarized affidavit, Allen Dulles committed himself to Fritz's financial support in the event of any difficulties.

Fritz was not yet authorized to enter the United States, but he was determined to leave Germany. In early April 1948, Fritz and Maria moved to Switzerland, where other tedious formalities awaited them. Because of the suicide of Otto Köcher, the former envoy of the Reich in Bern, the Swiss federal authorities suspected Fritz of having played a dubious role in the final days of the war. He was subjected to extensive questioning by the Swiss police before being allowed to move freely. For a few months he worked for the Commercial Development Corporation, an import-export business that his friend Ernst Kocherthaler had just established in Zurich. When his divorce from Lita Schoop became final in July, nothing further stood in the way of his departure. The atmosphere in Germany was becoming very unpleasant. The blockade of Berlin was in full swing. But the wait lasted months longer. Fritz and Maria had the time to get married in December 1948. Finally, on March 16, 1949, they took a liner for America sailing from Cuxhaven.

New York, spring 1949

Peter Sichel was in New York to greet the couple as they got off the boat. The weather was extremely hot. In their little hotel near Washington Square, without air conditioning, the atmosphere was stifling. From the outset, the "new life" of Fritz and Maria bore no resemblance to any illusions they might have had. The State Department obviously had no position to offer to this minor German official. With only limited mastery of the English language, Fritz did not feel at all as comfortable as he had hoped. In April 1949, Allen Dulles wrote to

Fritz that he was looking for a job for him at Yale or the University of Michigan, "as a librarian or a research assistant." But these leads, modest as they were, led to nothing. By the month of May, Fritz was writing to his old friend Walter Bauer to tell him that he intended to return to Germany. Bauer advised him to stay in the United States. "In your place, with your possibilities, I would not come back at the first difficulties," he told him. Ernst Kocherthaler sent him the same message, advising him to "get hired by Standard Oil or Texaco." But Fritz disliked American society and its appetite for unbridled consumption ("People never stop eating," he observed scornfully).

Nevertheless, he tried his hand in business, thinking he had accumulated enough entrepreneurial skills working for the Commercial Development Corporation of his friend Ernst Kocherthaler. With the small nest egg he had put together with the help of Allen Dulles, he set up a small business selling asbestos. An old acquaintance from South Africa had suggested that they go into the business together. But his partner turned out to be a swindler, and he disappeared with Fritz's capital of $25,000. This was too much. Fritz and Maria decided to return to Germany immediately. They had been in the United States for barely three months. In July 1949, the couple settled near Frankfurt. "His trip here did not work out as well as one might have expected," Allen Dulles observed bluntly a few months later. As Ernst Kocherthaler said, to sum up the whole affair: "George is not a businessman type."

Frankfurt, summer 1949

The blockade of Berlin by the Soviets had just come to an end when Fritz and Maria returned from the United States. They had been away from Germany for a year, dreaming in vain of a "new life." They had lost a substantial part of their savings. They had no prospects for the future. In order to survive, Fritz did some sales work for his old friend Ernst Kocherthaler, who was involved in all kinds of business in Zurich. At his request, Fritz looked for markets for all kinds of products (diesel engines, reinforced concrete, steel, printing machinery). Preoccupied by material concerns, he had not yet tried to see his son, who was still in southern Africa and who was desperately waiting for his father to deign to take an interest in him. Peter Kolbe, who was in his early adolescence (he had his thirteenth birthday in April 1945), felt toward his absent father a mixture of indifference and resentment.

When he was still in the United States, Fritz had responded to a notice of an employment opportunity in the administration of the new Federal Republic. The new German government did not yet have an autonomous diplomatic service, but it had the right to open consulates or commercial offices abroad. Dozens of positions were beginning to open up. In his first letter of application on May 9, 1949, Fritz explained that he had the necessary language skills, the required experience, and a "political past" that made him fit for an assignment in the new consular services. To support his candidacy, he asked for help from Walter Bauer, who knew many people in the embryonic future German administration. Bauer for the moment had only an economic post and was based in Frankfurt.

That summer, Fritz sent out many unsolicited letters of application. He wrote to the SPD deputy Carlo Schmid (who did not have time to see him), to the administration of the Marshall Plan, to the foreign policy department of the Social Democratic Party. In his letters, he did not hesitate to mention the fact that he had never been a member of the Nazi Party, specifying that he had maintained close "contacts" with the Americans during the war, and that he had been a part of the "other Germany." He believed that these elements would strengthen his chances of being selected. Had he not read in a German newspaper in July 1949 that the British military governor, Sir Brian Robertson, demanded that future German diplomats be "absolutely politically clean"? Fritz Kolbe's file was probably too clean: Not only had he never joined the NSDAP, but he had never been imprisoned for acts of resistance. Imagine his surprise when he learned that his interlocutors at the Marshall Plan "did not understand why he had not been a member of the party." Walter Bauer went out of his way to help Fritz. But when he questioned the heads of the Frankfurt administration, they answered that pieces were missing from the file. "Could Fritz Kolbe name more 'references' to support his candidacy? Could he in particular provide the names of former members of the Foreign Ministry?" he was told in November 1949. Fritz Kolbe complied with the request and provided a list of people whom he hoped would speak in his favor. Among these putative "sponsors" were found Hans Schrœder (former chief of personnel of the Foreign Ministry under Ribbentrop), Count Welczeck, and Karl Ritter in person. He had to dare to use that name. The necessities of the moment required that he compromise his convictions. Fritz was convinced that Karl Ritter wished him no ill ("He changed subordinates as he changed shirts. But me he kept"). Fritz Kolbe resumed contact with him in late 1949. Ritter had just gotten out of prison after serving a sentence of four years for "war crimes" and was living in solitude in his house in Bavaria. Fritz felt that he could count on him ("We are corresponding, and he writes to me in a very friendly way").

Frankfurt, spring 1950

"We regret to inform you that the position referenced above has been given to someone other than you." This brief letter from the economic administration of Frankfurt, dated February 4, 1950, put an end to Fritz's hopes of finding a position in the consular services of the new Germany. He thought he still had possibilities at the future Foreign Ministry, whose rebirth was being actively prepared by the Federal chancellery in Bonn. In October 1949, Fritz had written to Hans-Heinrich Herwarth von Bittenfeld, chief of protocol at the Chancellery in Bonn, to ask him officially for his "readmission into the services of the Foreign Ministry." This time, instead of putting forward his status as a former "Allied contact" during the war, he had merely said that he represented the interests in Germany of a company based in Switzerland ("Maurer & Co., Bern, exporters of woolen looms," a company controlled by Ernst Kocherthaler). He had added a copy of a document that certified that he "was not af-fected by de-Nazification measures." But he never received any response to his request.

Obviously, someone was standing in his way, but Fritz never found out who it was. The reasons for the obstacles he faced, however, were clear: The old networks of the Nazi period were resuming control of the ministry and were trying everything to keep this "traitor" away. The foreign policy adviser to Chancellor Adenauer, Herbert Blanken-horn, had served in the German legation in Bern. He proclaimed pub-licly that the new members of the German diplomatic corps had to be "new men . . . democratic and pro-Western," but behind the scenes the reality was quite different.

Fritz Kolbe was without any question democratic and pro-Western. His only mistake was to have been those things before everyone else. A few months later, in May 1950, Walter Bauer spoke of the "Kolbe case" to Economics Minister Ludwig Erhard in person: "I told him that your hiring by the consular services was a problem because, apparently, they are unwilling to recognize your political activity since 1942. That deeply shocks me," Bauer explained to Fritz Kolbe shortly after this interview in Bonn. What if Allen Dulles, or his brother John Foster Dulles, U.S. Secretary of State, got wind of this story? "You can imag-ine what impact that would have on the mutual trust between Ger-many and the United States!" Bauer pointed out. Apparently, Ludwig Erhard was aware of the problem and shared this point of view. In the course of his conversation with Walter Bauer, the economics minister had turned to his secretary of state and asked him to note down Fritz Kolbe's name. The file was to be sent to the federal chancellery. The matter was to be cleared up. But that was the end of it, and the initia-tive had no consequences.

On June 1, 1950, Walter Bauer wrote to the deputy Walter Tillmans, one of the cofounders of the CDU, who had promised to help him. Walter Bauer had explained to him that Fritz Kolbe "had acted exclu-sively out of patriotism" and that it was "frightening" that his candi-dacy was blocked because of his pro-Allied activity during the war. On

June 14, 1950, Fritz—still optimistic—wrote to Walter Bauer to tell him that Dr. Tillmans seemed to be having some success: "Several deputies are said to have spoken in my favor," he explained.

Fritz Kolbe was wrong to hope. It did not take him long to understand the origin of the ostracism of which he was the target. In a letter of July 30, 1950, Walter Bauer wrote to Fritz to ask him for details on a specific episode of his biography: "I have been told that you went to the German legation in Bern shortly before the surrender to ask that Köcher turn over to you the legation's gold. I have also been told that Köcher's death is not unconnected to you. Can you tell me more about this?" The fatal misadventure had thus taken place in the last days of the war. Fritz had been wrong to play the role of emissary from the Americans to the envoy of the Reich, who had complained about him to several of his colleagues before committing suicide. Five years later, Fritz was considered not only a traitor but an assassin. The Americans could do nothing to help their former agent to get a position. In early August 1950, Allen Dulles met Herbert Blankenhorn in Bonn, but nothing concrete came out of the conversation. It was obvious that Fritz would never again have a position in the ministry.

Frankfurt, July 1950

At the end of the war, Allen Dulles and Gerald Mayer had managed to persuade Fritz to write his memoirs, even though, for security reasons, there were no plans to publish them. Ernst Kocherthaler had taken down Fritz's account and translated it into English in a seven-page document ("The Story of George"). "The important thing," Kocherthaler had said in order to persuade his friend to speak out, "is for the Americans to know that there was a positive side to Germany." Fritz had no doubts about it. He even thought that he had played the role of a "leader" in the German resistance, and he was flattered by the interest taken in him. But at the same time his pride led him to refuse to put himself forward. "What does Allen want to do with all this?" Fritz asked in May 1945. "Unlike other people, I don't want to gain fame through my story," he added in a letter to Ernst Kocherthaler in July. Observing that "memoirs of resistance to Nazism" were becoming a literary genre in their own right, Fritz had reasons for not associating himself with a huge enterprise of collective mystification.

The idea of publishing something about Fritz, however, remained alive in the mind of Gerald Mayer, who had left the world of intelligence for the movie industry (he headed the Paris office of the Motion Picture Association). In September 1949, Mayer suggested to Fritz that he write his story so that it could be made into "a film or a book." Fritz would not hear of it and refused to go to Paris to discuss the plan, as Gerald Mayer had suggested. Mayer was not discouraged, and put Fritz in contact with an American journalist, Edward P. Morgan, who wrote for the magazine *True*. Fritz was at first reticent. "Who still cares about what happened then?" he said. "All that's in the past." Finally he agreed to see Morgan. The meeting took place in early 1950 in Fritz's apartment near Frankfurt.

"In the last two years of World War II, 'George Wood' brought to the Allies no fewer than 2600 secret documents from Hitler's Foreign Office, some of them of the highest importance. Eisenhower called him one of the most valuable agents we had during the entire war." These lines introduced the article published in *True* in July 1950, under the title "The Spy the Nazis Missed." This fourteen-page article was somehow typically American, with an alluring title, illustrations worthy of a detective story, and written in a lively style. Edward P. Morgan did not mention Fritz Kolbe's real name, but the article circulated among German diplomats, who had no difficulty in identifying the figure. This was even more the case when the article was translated in full and published a year later in the Swiss weekly *Die Weltwoche*, with a darker title than the American version: "The Double Game of a Diplomat." This publication in German, which Allen Dulles had unsuccessfully attempted to prevent, helped to destroy Fritz's reputation: Instead of seeing him as a member of the resistance, most of his former colleagues considered him as an informer and a renegade.

Frankfurt, October 1950

Had Fritz been a traitor to his country? Confronting the wall of silence that faced him, he began to have reasons to question himself. Fortunately, he was not alone with his conscience. Some of his friends helped him to reflect on his past, to legitimate his action, and to preserve his personal dignity. One of them was a major intellectual, Rudolf Pechel, whom Fritz had probably met through Professor Sauerbruch. Pechel embodied the continuity of German thought: Since 1919, he had headed the editorial board of the *Deutsche Rundschau*, a prestigious monthly established in 1874, comparable to the *Revue des Deux Mondes* in France. Banned by the Nazis in 1942, it had been relaunched in 1946 by securing a British license. Fritz Kolbe became a permanent employee of the publication in October 1950. He was in charge of managing subscriptions and single-issue distribution, particularly in the Soviet zone, where the journal circulated in secret.

Although Fritz was cut off from his professional milieu, he found welcome spiritual comfort in this new work. Rudolf Pechel had unquestionable moral authority. He was not a man of the left (he came out of the "revolutionary conservatism" of the 1920s), but he had been persecuted by the Nazis, who had sent him to a concentration camp from 1942 to 1945. The *Deutsche Rundschau* published accounts by victims of Nazism and works by prestigious authors (Carlo Schmid, Golo Mann, Wilhelm Röpke) who wrote high-minded essays on the major questions of the time: resistance, treason, democracy. Through the journal, Fritz Kolbe sharpened his ideas on the themes that constantly preoccupied him. The *Deutsche Rundschau* fought in defense of the honor of the members of the German resistance to the Third Reich. It regularly denounced the return by Nazis to key positions in the Federal Republic of Germany. It gave a platform to the conspirators of July 20, 1944, who explained why their "treason" had been a patriotic gesture.

For his part, Fritz Kolbe had never doubted that he had acted as a patriot. But he needed to understand why the accusation of "treason" was sticking to him. The "right to resistance" against dictatorship was inscribed in the Fundamental Law of the new Federal Republic only in 1968. What he was reproached with, in the end, was perhaps with having supplied information that caused the death of hundreds of Germans. At the Nuremberg trial, the diplomat Hasso von Etzdorf had declared that he "had respected certain limits that mark the difference between a traitor and a patriot" and that he "had not sold Germany to foreign countries," specifying that it would have been easy for him "to supply information of a military nature to Lisbon, Stockholm, or Madrid." Hans-Bernd Gisevius, as well, had always been careful not to tell the Americans everything he knew, keeping some information to himself with the aim of saving lives. Fritz Kolbe had not had the same scruples. He had supplied industrial and military targets, aware that the Allied bombings would create many innocent victims. In the end, he had followed his job as a spy to its logical conclusion, acting as an American or British soldier would have done.

Frankfurt, September 1951

In September 1951, the daily newspaper *Frankfurter Rundschau* published a sensational investigation revealing that former Nazis were resuming power in the new German Foreign Ministry. It had been authorized to come back into existence a few months earlier under the direct authority of Chancellor Konrad Adenauer. The outcry produced by this series of articles was so huge that a parliamentary investigative committee was set up in the Bundestag.

Less than a year later, in June 1952, this committee turned in its final report, demanding much more rigor in future appointments and recommending the suspension of four high officials in the Foreign Ministry who were particularly compromised. In a Bundestag debate in October, Chancellor Adenauer did not attempt to conceal the facts and recognized that the great majority of new German diplomats (66 percent) were former members of the NSDAP. He went on to say, however, that in his view, "it was not possible to do otherwise" and that the country needed people who had "experience and skill." After being suspended for a year or two, the principal diplomats incriminated by the investigative committee were partially rehabilitated. Chancellor Adenauer appointed a new chief of personnel for the Foreign Ministry and gave him the mission of eradicating "the spirit of Wilhelmstrasse" from the ministry. The new appointee soon discovered that "it was already too late."

Frankfurt, 1953

Fritz continued working at various odd jobs. The salary from the *Deutsche Rundschau* was not enough to live on, and the Americans had stopped paying him when he left Berlin in April 1948. In early 1953, he tried to secure a position as a correspondent for a German press agency in Switzerland. His application had been accepted, the contract was on the point of being signed, but at the last moment, for reasons that he never discovered, the employer terminated discussions. Fritz was no longer surprised by anything: His name seemed to have been placed on a blacklist.

Fortunately, life was not reduced to these repeated disappointments. Fritz remained a lover of life and never complained. In April 1953 his son had reached the age of twenty-one, the age required to get a South African passport and to be able to travel to Europe. Fritz had put money aside to finance the trip. The reunion took place on July 6, 1953, in the Dutch port of Hoek. Fritz and Maria had come to pick up Peter in a car. Maria remembered that "Fritz was eager to see his son again." Peter, for his part, never thought that that was the case. The son's feelings toward the father were mixed at the very least:

> He was a complete stranger to me. I was surprised to see how
> small he was. He had an ideal, abstract image of me; he
> treated me like a child. He wanted me to put on a sweater so
> I wouldn't catch cold and he absolutely insisted on carrying
> my luggage. I hated the way he had of wanting to repair the
> damage after such a long absence. He could have written to

me after the war. But he didn't, just giving me a few very
distant signs of life. I had expected something from him
which never came.

It wasn't the presence of Fritz's new wife that troubled him. Peter
was meeting Maria for the first time, and they got on quite well together. He soon began calling her "Muschka." "If she had not been
there, things would have gone badly with my father," Peter confessed
fifty years later. Fritz could not stop lecturing his son, as though he
wanted to recover the lost years of bringing him up. "You must do your
duty every day without complaining," he said, using as an example all
the workers who got to their factories early in the morning as though
eager to begin working. This frenzy of work was impressive. There
were construction sites everywhere in Frankfurt, swarming with activity at all hours of day and night. Peter had never seen that in South
Africa.

Peter confessed that he was more interested by the trip to Europe
than by the meeting with Fritz. After fourteen years of silence, the
reunion seemed almost impossible. Peter was irritated by his father's
conduct toward women. Fritz played the role of seducer. He amused
himself by trying to pick up women with his friend Harry Hermsdorf
of the CIA. As for Fritz, he was sorry that his son was not conducting
himself in a more docile manner. When they played chess, Fritz felt a
fierce desire to win. He hoped that Peter would stay in Germany and
was absolutely determined to find a position for him in the chemical
or pharmaceutical industry. But Peter had no intention of staying in a
country that was not his own, even though he spoke the language very
well. At the end of three months, he decided to leave. He went from
Frankfurt to Venice by bicycle, then took a boat, and was back in South
Africa in January 1954.

Peter was not unaware of the fact that his father had worked for
the Americans during the war, but he did not know any of the details
of the story. "If something serious happens to you in life, speak to the
American authorities and tell them that you are the son of George
Wood," was all Fritz had said. In June 1953, Peter had been to some

parties in the American zone and had been able to see that his father had many friends in the CIA (Peter spoke English with them, pleased to see that his father did not understand everything they said). But at no time had it been possible to speak seriously with him about his past. Fritz preferred to talk about other things. He asked his son, for example, about the "prospects for the cement market in South Africa," or advised him to join the Masons. Even in the presence of his own son, Fritz Kolbe hid himself behind a smokescreen.

Washington, 1953

Allen Dulles was appointed Director of the CIA on February 26, 1953. He had left the world of intelligence in late 1945 to resume his career as a Wall Street lawyer and to head the Council on Foreign Relations. General Eisenhower had been inaugurated as president of the United States in January 1953. With the return of the Republicans to power, the Dulles family was rewarded for its commitment and loyalty: John Foster, Allen's older brother, was the new secretary of state. His younger sister Eleanor coordinated Berlin matters in the State Department. In a long portrait of Allen Dulles published in the *New York Times Magazine* on March 29, 1953, there were three paragraphs on one of the greatest "coups" of his career: During the war, Dulles had got hold of a German spy named "George Wood, the most valuable and the most prolific source of secret intelligence out of Germany." Some years later, in September 1959, Allen Dulles was presented in the magazine *True* as "America's global Sherlock," "the man who stole two thousand six hundred secret documents from the Nazi Foreign Ministry."

Since the end of the war, the reputation of Allen Dulles had rested to an appreciable degree on his encounter with Fritz Kolbe. In December 1945, when Dulles had resigned to return to the practice of law in New York, General John Magruder, one of the heads of the OSS, had written these words of farewell: "It is with a deep sense of loss that I accept your resignation. . . . As you know, the head of the British Intelligence Service credits you with the outstanding intelligence job on the Allied side in this war. That recognition would have been due as a result alone of the steady flow of intelligence from Bern and especially the Kappa-Wood material . . ." In July 1946, President Truman had awarded Allen Dulles the Medal of Merit for his good and loyal services and had particularly congratulated him for three pieces of information sent from Bern: the location of the base in Peenemünde where the V-2s were made (May 1943), the launch sites for "rocket bombs" in the Pas-de-Calais, and the regular reports of the results of Allied bombing raids on German cities. Except for Peenemünde, this information had all come from Fritz Kolbe.

Fritz was more than a little proud to see his old friend from Bern occupying a position of the first rank in the United States. The two men remained in touch, and Allen Dulles sought out news of Fritz whenever he could. This purely friendly relation was no longer based on the feeling of being engaged in the same battles. As much as he was an anticommunist, Fritz equally detested imperial and triumphant America. He was hostile to nuclear deterrence, in favor of a "middle way between capitalism and socialism," and had nothing but contempt for "the prosperity devoid of spirituality" embodied by the United States. He was not fascinated by the CIA and what it symbolized. Nothing makes it possible to determine his reaction to the coups d'état fomented by the CIA in Iran in 1953 and Guatemala in 1954. There is no surviving statement from him about the protection provided by the CIA to former Nazis or even SS officers. But he remained very close to Allen Dulles, who had never dropped him.

Stratford, Connecticut, spring 1954

In April 1954, Fritz traveled to the United States to negotiate the terms of a new employment contract. Through his friend Harry Hermsdorf, he had learned that a small Connecticut company, the Wright Power Saw & Tool Corporation, was looking for a sales representative in Europe, based in Switzerland. This company made various models of power and chain saws with pneumatic motors. It is not impossible that Allen Dulles had intervened to help Fritz secure this position.

In a letter to Rudolf Pechel, Fritz described this new experience in a few words: "I am in the technical department, where the saws are repaired. It is necessary to know things of this kind in order to do my work in Europe. But I ask myself countless questions: all this technical jargon, and everything is in English!" In a letter to Ernst Kocherthaler, Fritz wondered who on earth would buy these chain saws: "The market is not good." To get a good understanding of the material that he was going to be promoting in Europe, Fritz had to spend two months training in the forests of Connecticut. The chain saws were too heavy for him. The woods were infested with snakes.

The contract was signed in June 1954. Fritz was paid a salary of $250 a month. On this trip to the United States, he had made a detour to Washington to visit Allen Dulles. The highs and the lows of his career did not prevent him from maintaining his good humor: Peter Sichel, who put him up during his stay in the capital, recalls that "Fritz amused himself by climbing the trees in the garden to show me what he could do." Fritz crossed the Atlantic on a steamer to return to Europe. He was carrying some chain saws in his luggage.

EPILOGUE

On July 20, 1961, a plaque was dedicated at the Foreign Ministry in Bonn honoring the diplomats who had resisted Hitler. The head of the German diplomatic service at the time, Heinrich von Brentano, delivered a speech on "the force of conscience inspired by God." Ten names were engraved on the large stone panel—including Ulrich von Hassell, Adam von Trott zu Solz, Friedrich-Werner Graf von der Schulenburg—but not that of Fritz Kolbe. If he had been executed before 1945, his name might have been added to the official list of the "just."

Allen Dulles had been able to do nothing to secure the readmission of Fritz Kolbe into the service of the ministry, even though he had very good personal contacts with Chancellor Adenauer. There remained the possibility of a rehabilitation "as a matter of honor." This idea had germinated in the mind of Ernst Kocherthaler who found the injustice done to his friend intolerable. In November 1964, Kocherthaler—who had only two years left to live—wrote to Allen Dulles to ask for his support in an approach he was in the process of making to Eugen Gerstenmaier, president of the Bundestag and former member of the Protestant Church opposed to Nazism. In early spring 1965, after reading the file that Kocherthaler had sent him, Gerstenmaier signed a brief document aimed at "exonerating Fritz Kolbe from the suspicions weighing on him."

It is not certain whether Fritz had wanted to get a document like this. In a long letter to Ernst Kocherthaler dated January 10, 1965, Fritz revealed his deepest feelings:

> The members of the resistance are honored once a year, on 20 July. But a good member of the resistance is one who is dead. Whoever had ears to hear and eyes to see knew what the Nazi madness meant, even before 1933. Those who didn't want to see or understand anything continued their successful careers in the ministry. . . . My aim was to help my poor nation end the war sooner and to cut short the suffering of the people in the camps. I don't know if I succeeded. But what I did manage to do was to make the Americans see that there were people in Germany who were resisting the regime without asking for anything in return. People who acted purely out of conviction. No one has the right to give me good marks for my conduct during that period. No one can withdraw from me or grant to me my honor.

Fritz Kolbe died from gallbladder cancer on February 16, 1971 in Bern. A dozen people attended the funeral. Among them, two unknown men laid a wreath on behalf of Richard Helms, director of the CIA. Shortly before his death in 1969, Allen Dulles had written: "I always felt it was unfair that the new Germany failed to recognize the high integrity of George's purpose and the very considerable part which he played in the eventual overthrow of Hitler and Hitlerism. Some day I hope that any injustice will be righted, and that his true role will be properly recognized in his own country."

A REMEMBRANCE
OF FRITZ KOLBE

In December 1945, Richard Helms started to turn over his responsibilities as Chief of the Berlin Base of the Office of Strategic Services, which later became the CIA, to me. Dick had held this position ever since Allen Dulles had returned to the United States in the late summer of 1945. Now Dick himself was going back and I, previously head of a special unit, would be in interim charge of the entire Berlin office until a new chief was named.

Among the cases Dick turned over to me was a special one: Fritz Kolbe, alias George Wood. He briefed me on Fritz's work during the war, and the necessity of protecting him both from German reprisals and the quite real risk of Soviet kidnapping. He praised Fritz's ability to put us in touch with reliable people in Berlin, as well as Fritz's eagerness to help the prosecution of Nazi criminals in Nürnberg. He told me that we had tried to dissuade him from doing this, since it might expose him to reprisals, but that Fritz was determined to even the score.

I met Fritz shortly thereafter, in a sort of official turnover from one case officer to another, but I did not get to know him well—Harry Hersmdorf, an intelligence officer whose responsibilities largely concerned helping former members of the German resistance and their widows, had day-to-day responsibility for Fritz's case. Harry was a big, generous, and charming man who quickly became a close friend to Fritz and his companion, Maria Fritsch. He established an easy camaraderie with Fritz and his circle of friends.

Berlin was exciting and sad at the same time in this first harsh winter after the war. The city was almost totally destroyed, especially the center. Endless groups of women were involved in stacking up the stones and bricks that lay all over the landscape, at time creating virtual mountains. These *Trümmerfrauen* are an indelible memory to anyone who lived in Berlin during that period. We worked hard, but also played hard, spending evenings entertaining "reliable" Germans to get a better grasp of what had happened to them, personally and emotionally, in the long nightmare they had lived through. A good number of these Germans were friends of Fritz Kolbe, who usually accompanied them to my house, where they had a chance to be warm and have a good meal and plenty of alcohol, coffee, and cigarettes, the three things most highly valued at that period. This is how I got to know Eugen Gerstenmaier, who ultimately became a good friend, as well as Gertrud von Heimerdinger and Professor Sauerbruch. I entertained Sauerbruch quite frequently in my house as well, a complex man who consumed prodigious quantities of my cognac.

I finally got to know Fritz better only when we decided that he had to leave Berlin for his own safety. He was altogether too foolhardy to be left there on his own, not realizing what a desirable target he was for the Russians. I finally drove him out of Berlin in a Jeep, disguised in the odd uniform worn by American civilians working for the occupation authority. He also had an official document to justify his drive through the Russian Zone to Helmstedt and ultimately to Frankfurt. It was a six-hour drive, and we had plenty of time to talk—that is how we became friends. I only saw him three or four times after that. The time I remember most fondly is greeting Maria and him on their arrival in New York, which coincided with my return to Washington on retiring from the Army to join SSU (Strategic Service Unit), one of the successor organizations of OSS, which ultimately became the CIA. I spent three or four days with the two of them, showing them around

New York. They also visited Washington in 1954; we spent a lot of time together reminiscing about the war and discussing the evolution of Germany since the war.

Fritz was the easiest man to establish rapport with. He was a straight arrow, looked you in the eye, and was neither shy nor aggressive. He was happy in his skin, healthy, physically active and proud of it. He was no intellectual, no great thinker, but a great doer. To be active was everything; he simply had no end of physical energy, which needed an outlet. He had no pretense and when discussing his wartime activities, he regarded them his duty as a patriotic German. Like most great men, he was rather simple; he knew what he had to do and did not give it a second thought. Though he regretted not being able to get back into the German Diplomatic Service, he was not bitter about it. He felt that he had done his duty and he was willing to accept what fate had in store for him. He was not even much put out when the friend to whom he had entrusted his savings disappeared. Oddly enough, Fritz told me in 1954, his friend did turn up ultimately and returned the money.

I have been approached a number of times in the last fifty years by authors and TV producers who wanted to do a book or film about this man, who without any doubt was one of the greatest, if not *the* greatest, source of "human intelligence" information in the Second World War. Very little came of all this, until Lucas Delattre contacted me three years ago. It was obvious from our first contact, and his visit to Bordeaux to make my acquaintance, that finally someone understood the need to tell this story. Fortunately Lucas also possessed the other qualities necessary to do the job: intellectual curiosity, a background in German history and culture, and the professional expertise of a newspaperman. It was fun to be of a little help to him, putting him in contact with the few survivors and answering whatever questions he had. It was also great to be reminded of the many people who had a hand in this operation and with whom I had worked at one time or another during and after the war. I had long forgotten Eduard Wätjen, Eduard Schulte, Gertrud von Heimerdinger, and Gertrud's sister, who also worked on the courier desk at the Foreign Office. Neither of my old colleagues Harry Hermsdorf and Fred Stalder, who was transferred to my unit in Berlin from Bern after the war, were around to help with this story.

Finally there is an interesting lesson to learn from Fritz's story, which has been repeated many times since. Good intelligence sources are usually those who, for ideological reasons, do not agree with the policies of their government. They make contact with "the opposition" and volunteer their information. In this manner the Russians and we have gathered high-level intelligence over the last eighty years. Only rarely are "agents" recruited through subterfuge or the offer of money or blackmail. Ideology is still the great motivator and Fritz Kolbe is the ideal example of such a freedom fighter. The German government finally recognized the service he has rendered and dedicated a room to him in the German Foreign Office in Berlin.

—Peter Sichel, former Station Chief,
Central Intelligence Agency, New York, 2004

NOTES

Introduction

stirrings of their conscience: A quotation from Winston Churchill, speaking in 1946 of the conspirators in the failed plot against Hitler on July 20, 1944.

source of the war: Memorandum for the President, June 22, 1945, to President Truman from General Donovan, National Archives, College Park (entry 190c, microfilm 1642, roll 83).

agent in World War II: Richard Helms (with William Hood), *A Look Over My Shoulder* (New York: Random House, 2003), p. 37.

done something against Nazism: See Peter Steinbach, *Widerstand im Widerstreit* (Paderborn, 2001).

so-called simple people: Interview conducted by Dominique Simonnet, *L'Express,* December 28, 2000.

Prologue

head of the OSS: The Office of Strategic Services was established in June 1942 and placed under the command of the Joint Chiefs of Staff. Its role was to take charge of "unconventional warfare"—in other words, to gather intelligence and organize clandestine operations against the Axis powers. William Donovan, a Wall Street lawyer and a Republican, but above all a man of action and a First World War hero, was chosen by President Roosevelt to head the agency, which he did until 1945.

dated January 10, 1944: Memorandum for the President, National Archives (entry 190c, microfilm 1642, roll 18).

extraordinarily difficult to obtain: The distinction was already being made between the interception of enemy signals (signals intelligence, or SIGINT) and espionage based on human sources (human intelligence, HUMINT).

view to "liquidating" it: This German diplomatic cable had been transmitted to Washington on December 30, 1943, signed by Eitel Friedrich von Moellhausen, assistant to the Reich's ambassador in Rome, Rudolf Rahn. See Robert Katz, *Black Sabbath: A Journey Through a Crime Against Humanity* (London: Barker, 1969). Thanks to Astrid M. Eckert, Berlin.

"be the only winner": Message from the Swiss bureau of the OSS in Bern to Washington headquarters dated January 4, 1944, based on a cable from Ambassador von Weizsäcker of December 13, 1943. "Weizsäcker reports that the Pope hopes that the Nazis will hold on the Russian Front and dreams of a union of the old civilized countries of the West with insulation of Bolshevism towards the East." Memorandum for the President, January 10, 1944, National Archives.

went over to the enemy: Message from the OSS Bern bureau, December 31, 1943, National Archives.

United States, Henry Wallace: Memorandum for the President, January 11, 1944. The Germans knew the content of a conversation between Vice President Wallace and the Swiss ambassador to Washington, his brother-in-law. The conversation had to do with the tensions between the Western allies (Great Britain and the United States) and the USSR. The Germans apparently had a good source in the Foreign Ministry in Bern. This affair probably hastened the disgrace of Wallace, who was replaced on the November 1944 election ticket by Harry Truman.

Chapter 1

"will also be prohibited": The "law for the protection of German blood and German honor" and the "law on German citizenship" had been adopted during an NSDAP congress in Nuremberg. They laid the foundation for the total and definitive exclusion of the Jews from German society.

von Welczeck, the ambassador: Germany maintained embassies in the major capitals: Madrid, London, Paris, Rome, Washington, Moscow, Tokyo, and even Rio de Janeiro. Everywhere else, diplomatic representation did not have the title of embassy (*Botschaft*) but that of legation (*Gesandtschaft*), and the head of mission did not have the title of ambassador (*Botschafter*) but that of "envoy" (*Gesandte*).

A legation is a diplomatic mission maintained by a government in a country in which it does not have an embassy. The head of the legation, like an ambassador, is accredited to the sovereign or the head of state.

The Congress of Vienna (March 19, 1815) had distinguished two classes of diplomatic agents: ambassador (and legate or nuncio) and chargé d'affaires (accredited only to the foreign minister of the country). The Congress of Aix-la-Chapelle (November 21, 1818) added an intermediate class for resident ministers and extraordinary envoys. It is to this class that belongs a head of legation, who has the character of a plenipotentiary minister. He is addressed as "Minister," or, by custom, "Your Excellency." Thanks to Serge Pétillot-Niémetz, chargé de mission for the Dictionary of the Académie Française.

Count Johannes von Welczeck (1878–1974), ambassador to Madrid, was a diplomat of the old school. He had joined the ministry before the 1914 war, a period when a diplomatic career was still restricted to rich aristocrats able to pay their own way.

Biarritz, or Hendaye: German Foreign Ministry, Johannes von Welczeck file.

figures in the Spanish capital: Ernst Kocherthaler was vice president of the petroleum traders association in Spain. He represented the interests of major oil companies: first Shell and then the Soviet oil conglomerates favored by Madrid since the late 1920s. He was born in Madrid in 1894. His father, who came from a family of modest Jewish merchants of Würtemberg, had amassed a considerable fortune by carrying on trade between Germany and Spain. The family had returned to settle in Berlin at the end of the nineteenth century. Ernst Kocherthaler had converted to Protestantism as an adolescent. He had studied law and economics in Berlin before joining the prestigious Warburg Bank in Hamburg. In the early 1920s, he attended international financial negotiations on the stabilization of the mark as an expert. On this occasion, he met the economist John Maynard Keynes, with whom he had become rather close. He had settled in Spain in the mid-1920s. Source: private documents of the Kocherthaler family (Sylvia and Gérard Roth, Geneva).

of Jews in Germany: Hans-Jürgen Döscher, *Das Auswärtige Amt im Dritten Reich* (Berlin: Siedler, 1987).

of a Baltic beach: The *Kraft durch Freude* organization was established in November 1933 in order to organize the free time of the masses, particularly through tourism and vacation camps.

his perfectly polished shoes: "My father always had perfectly polished shoes." Peter Kolbe, Sydney, November 2001.

have a certain charm: "Fritz had a good deal of charm." Gudrun Fritsch, interview in Berlin, January 5, 2002.

become, immediately, a Spanish citizen: Source: private documents of the Kocherthaler family in Geneva. This episode of Kocherthaler's renunciation of German nationality is also reported in Edward P. Morgan's article, "The Spy the Nazis Missed," *True,* July 1950.

officially considered "impure": When Ernst Kocherthaler converted to Protestantism shortly before 1914, this was because he sincerely wanted to contribute to the assimilation of Jews and Germans, and because it was better not to be a Jew in the German army.

distinguished war medal: Ernst Kocherthaler was awarded the Iron Cross after being wounded at the battle of the Somme in 1916. Nearly one hundred thousand Jews had served in the German Army during the First World War. Their patriotism had not protected them from many forms of discrimination during and after the war.

Nazi accession to power: Döscher, *Das Auswärtige Amt im Dritten Reich.*

"part of the resistance": German Foreign Ministry, Berlin, Johannes von Welczeck file.

no university education: Franz Neumann, *Behemoth: The Structure and Practice of National Socialism* (London: Victor Gollancz, 1942).

not joined the party: Fritz Kolbe, "Course of Life," personal archives of Fritz Kolbe, Peter Kolbe collection, Sydney. See also biographical document written by Gerald Mayer and Fritz Kolbe, undated (in German, 59 pages), same collection. "Beginning in 1938, you could no longer progress in the diplomatic career if you were not a member of the party" (Hans-Jürgen Döscher, interview in Osnabrück, May 14, 2002).

German community of Madrid: "Under the authority of the commercial counselor, I worked on various economic matters: information about companies, assistance in setting up local offices, customs information, credit questions, requests for bids, etc." Curriculum vitae of Fritz Kolbe prepared after the war (undated, in German), personal archives of Fritz Kolbe, Peter Kolbe collection, Sydney.

"cards and radio music": Hermann Hesse, *Steppenwolf*, tr. Basil Creighton (1929; New York: Holt, Rinehart and Winston, 1962), p. 165.

spark in his gaze: All reports agree on this paradox: With a rather banal external appearance, Fritz Kolbe had rather strong personal magnetism and a very penetrating gaze. "When he entered a room, you could not fail to notice him," recalled Erika von Hornstein (interview of October 27, 2001 in Berlin). "There was something consecrated about him," according to Gerald Mayer (Edward P. Morgan, "The Spy the Nazis Missed").

to avoid suspicion: Most of the major names in the German resistance to Nazism were members of the NSDAP: not only the major personalities of the Foreign Ministry (Ulrich von Hassell, Adam von Trott zu Solz), but also, for example, Oskar Schindler and Stalin's spy in Tokyo, Richard Sorge.

agents of the state: Since the Nazi accession to power, the oath for officials (*Beamteneid*) had been made in the name of the führer, to whom they swore obedience and loyalty.

"Brown House" in Munich: The *Braunes Haus* had been the national headquarters of the NSDAP since 1931. It was located at Briennerstrasse 45 in Munich (the building is no longer there).

automatically suspicious of diplomats: Not belonging to the party was not necessarily a sign of resistance. Many officials wanted to join the party but were not accepted. Döscher, *Das Auswärtige Amt im Dritten Reich.*

attractions of National Socialism: Fritz Albert Karl Kolbe was born on September 25, 1900 in Berlin. "My parents were in good health, not at all rich, but lived in relative material comfort. I grew up without experiencing poverty, in harmonious family circumstances." Autobiographical document written by Fritz Kolbe on May 15, 1945 (in German, 10 pages), personal archives of Fritz Kolbe, Peter Kolbe collection, Sydney.

had not developed overnight: "He was always in the opposition. Before and after 1933, he attempted to persuade his colleagues not to join the party." Biographical document written by Gerald Mayer and Fritz Kolbe.

the love of freedom: Autobiographical document by Fritz Kolbe, May 15, 1945.

"until the cold grave": Fritz Kolbe often quoted this German popular song, the words for which are by Ludwig Hölty on a melody by Mozart from *The Magic Flute* (Papageno's aria). In German: *Üb immer Treu und Redlichkeit / Bis an dein kühles Grab."* Source: Peter Kolbe, Sydney.

had never forgotten it: Many documents mention the quotation by Fritz Kolbe of this passage from the gospel of Matthew (16:26). Biographical document written by Gerald Mayer and Fritz Kolbe, and autobiographical document by Fritz Kolbe, May 15, 1945. See also Edward P. Morgan, "The Spy the Nazis Missed."

time there in 1931: A few years later, during the Second World War, Ernst Kocherthaler had become ferociously anticommunist. He considered the USSR as "a feudal, reactionary society, totally outside historical development" (letter of Ernst Kocherthaler to Allen Dulles, April 1950, Allen W. Dulles Papers, Seeley G. Mudd Manuscript Library, Princeton).

or even a believer: "As my parents came from North Germany (Mecklenburg-Pomerania), they were Protestants, and I was baptized in the Protestant Church." Fritz Kolbe, "Course of Life."

"the other one doesn't": Biographical document by Gerald Mayer and Fritz Kolbe.

fellow-feeling for the socialists: "I had a social conscience, even though I was not a member of the Social Democratic Party." Autobiographical document, May 15, 1945. "He was not a member of any party, but his sympathies were clearly with the left." Biographical document by Gerald Mayer and Fritz Kolbe.

neighborhood of Luisenstadt: Now Kreuzberg.

"submissive spirit," he said: Morgan, "The Spy the Nazis Missed."

a mark on him: Conversation of the author with Martin and Gudrun Fritsch, Berlin, January 2002. This novella by Heinrich von Kleist, published in 1810, tells the story of a horse dealer, despoiled of his property by a nobleman, who decides to take justice into his own hands.

display, Kocherthaler thought: See Willy Brandt, *Berlin, My City.* "Berliners are clever and skeptical. . . . The Nazis could not possibly like them."

palm with his right fist: Many witnesses remember this gesture, which seems to have been a tic of Fritz's. See Morgan, "The Spy the Nazis Missed."

as a "go-getter": In German: *Draufgänger.*

Berlin military hospital: Anita Falkenhain's family came from Silesia. Her parents, former peasants, had been part of the great migration to Berlin in the 1890s, like Fritz Kolbe's parents. Anita and Fritz met at the end of the First World War. Fritz had an infected foot and had had to fight to prevent having his leg amputated. Anita, a nurse's assistant in the Berlin military hospital where he was treated, had taken care of him. Conversation with Peter Kolbe, Sydney, November 2001.

the point of obsession: "I can still run four hundred meters in less than one minute." Morgan, "The Spy the Nazis Missed."

"successful life," "inner truth": Biographical document by Gerald Mayer and Fritz Kolbe. Fritz spoke frequently about his time in the *Wandervogel.* All the autobiographical documents written after the war refer in detail to this important episode of his upbringing.

remained a bit skeptical: In a book published after the war, Allen Dulles established a parallel between the "adolescent romanticism" of the *Wandervogel* and the rise of Nazism. *Germany's Underground,* new ed. (New York: Da Capo, 2000), p. 19. Rudolf Hess and Adolf Eichmann, who belonged to the generation of Fritz Kolbe, had also been members of the *Wandervogel.*

great success in England: The book was *Scouting for Boys,* published in England in 1908 and subsequently widely translated. This book is still considered the "bible" of scouting.

time in his life: Anecdote recounted by Peter Kolbe, Sydney, November 2001.

the National Socialist "Revolution": Episode recounted in Morgan, "The Spy the Nazis Missed."

"I was simpleminded": "Always seem dumber than you are" was a method favored by Fritz to keep the Nazis off balance. The episode of the interrogation in Madrid appears in several autobiographical documents written after the war; for example,

"The Story of George" written by Ernst Kocherthaler in the spring of 1945 (personal archives of Fritz Kolbe, Peter Kolbe collection, Sydney).

translated into German: Monetary Reform was published in England in 1923 and in German translation in 1924.

press agency of the time: Fritz Kolbe left school with a certificate of completion of primary education (*einjähriges Zeugnis*). "I was not a very good student but I learned quickly." Autobiographical document, May 15, 1945.

of the German railroads: In German: *Zivil-supernumerar.*

"freight, and currency administrator": In German *Oberbahnhofs-Güter-und Kassenvorsteher.* Fritz Kolbe was in charge of the freight department of the Silesia station (*Schlesischer Bahnhof*). Curriculum vitae of Fritz Kolbe prepared after the war (undated), personal archives of Fritz Kolbe, Peter Kolbe collection, Sydney.

Ministry in March 1925: "He wanted to learn about the rest of the world and he joined the Foreign Ministry in order to be sent abroad." "The Story of George." Fritz Kolbe joined the Foreign Ministry on March 16, 1925 and was sent to Madrid in October. German Foreign Ministry, Berlin, Fritz Kolbe file.

native of Moorish origin: The details about the professional development of Fritz Kolbe are found in the autobiographical document of May 15, 1945. Many details are also found in the "Fritz Kolbe" file in the archives of the German Foreign Ministry in Berlin. Fritz replaced the German consul in Seville from September to November 1930 and from October to November 1931.

of the "original God": The project led to the publication of a book entitled *Das Reich der Antike* in Baden-Baden in 1948, which was intended as the first volume of a great "universal history" based on a "spiritual vision of history," as opposed to the materialist vision of the Marxists.

Madrid early in 1936: Because of his wife's illness, Fritz Kolbe spent only three months at his post in the Polish capital (January to March 1936) and asked for an early transfer to Berlin.

Chapter 2

Cape Town, Fritz Kolbe: "Officially, I was acting consul at the German consulate in Cape Town." Autobiographical document, May 15, 1945. Fritz Kolbe had been transferred to Cape Town in February 1938. German Foreign Ministry, Fritz Kolbe file.

never forget that look: Most of the details about Fritz Kolbe's time in South Africa are based on statements from Peter Kolbe given in Sydney in November 2001.

in Pretoria, Rudolf Leitner: Rudolf Leitner (1891–1947) was Austrian. Before joining the NSDAP in 1936, he had been consul in Chicago in the 1920s, and then a diplomatic counsellor in Washington for a part of the 1930s. He was appointed envoy of the Reich to Pretoria in October 1937. He died in captivity in a Soviet detention camp. German Foreign Ministry, Rudolf Leitner file.

former ambassador to Spain: Rudolf Leitner was then vice-director of the political department of the ministry.

years of mismanagement: Curriculum vitae of Fritz Kolbe prepared after the war (undated, in German).

controlled all foreign appointments: The liaison office between the Foreign Minis-

- no

try and the NSDAP was called the "Organization for Foreign Countries (*Auslandsorganisation* or AO). The head of this office, Ernst Bohle, was one of the most powerful figures in the ministry and held the rank of junior minister. Born in Cape Town in 1903, and having spent his youth in South Africa, he closely examined the files dealing with that country. Döscher, *Das Auswärtige Amt im Dritten Reich.*

with an aching heart: "If I had stayed in South Africa, I would have caused a good deal of harm to Leitner, who had really stood up for me." Autobiographical document, May 15, 1945. Same argument in "Course of Life."

with no legal accountability: Heinrich Himmler, head of the SS (Reichsführer SS), controlled all the police machinery of the regime through the many police tentacles of the RSHA (Reichssicherheitshauptamt, or "Central Security Office of the Reich," responsible notably for the Gestapo).

record his license plate: Anecdote recounted by Peter Kolbe, Sydney, November 2001.

brutality to his subordinates: In internal documents of the Foreign Ministry, Joachim Ribbentrop was known as the "RAM" (Reichsaussenminister, or Minister of Foreign Affairs). Ribbentrop had not joined the Nazi Party until 1932, which caused him serious problems of internal legitimacy. To compensate for this insufficiency, the minister was a member of the SS brotherhood, with the rank of SS-Obergruppenführer, equivalent to general. The esprit de corps of the SS was comparable to that of the Knights of the Round Table. Source: German Foreign Ministry, and Döscher, *Das Auswärtige Amt im Dritten Reich.*

in the key positions: Career diplomats continued to head the three principal departments of the ministry (political, economic, and legal affairs), but their real influence was in steep decline, The closest collaborators of the minister were new men who had come from the "Ribbentrop Office" (*Dienststelle Ribbentrop*), a kind of shadow cabinet set up when the head of diplomacy for the Reich was still Baron Constantin von Neurath, an opportunistic career diplomat who had been replaced by Ribbentrop in February 1938.

belonged to the SS: Döscher, *Das Auswärtige Amt im Dritten Reich.*

the Reich in Europe: There were veritable pro-Nazi mass movements in South Africa, like the Ossewa Brandwag and the Grey Shirts, that counted several hundred thousand members. These sects seized every occasion to give violent expression to their anti-Semitism, for example when the liner *Stuttgart* arrived at the port of Cape Town in October 1936 with six hundred German Jewish refugees on board. The Afrikaner nationalists denounced the "cosmopolitan network" of Jewish financiers of Cape Town, associated in their mind with the "Freemason international" and the despised big British banks.

its clearly German origins: The port of Lüderitz was built by indigenous prisoners who had survived the terrible massacres carried out by the Germans during the war against the Nama and the Herero between 1904 and 1908.

a vast colonial project: The "colonial office" of the NSDAP, directed by Franz Ritter von Epp, intended to split Africa into four zones that would have been divided among Spain, Italy, Germany, and England.

of training overseas imitators: There were even a few "Winter Assistance" (*Winterhilfswerk*) centers, a kind of soup kitchen invented by the Nazis, distributing clothing and providing meals.

member of the SS: Walter Lierau was selected for the post in Windhoek after training in agitation and propaganda as consul in Reichenberg (Liberec, Czechoslovakia) in the early 1930s. Döscher, *Das Auswärtige Amt im Dritten Reich.*

wood in the forest: Fritz explained after the war why he had not brought his son back with him to Germany: "I did not want him to be contaminated by Nazi ideology, nor did I want him to be plunged into the chaos of Europe, which I foresaw as inevitable at the end of the war." Autobiographical document, May 15, 1945.

refugees from Germany: Fritz says that he gave German émigrés in South Africa—political refugees and Jews—stateless person passports (or "Nansen passports," delivered under the authority of the League of Nations), which allowed them to avoid deportation to Germany and internment as German citizens after the onset of World War II. Memorandum of August 19, 1943 (9 pages), OSS Bern, National Archives, College Park. See also the biographical document by Gerald Mayer and Fritz Kolbe.

from his own country: Fritz loathed nationalism in all its forms. "The slogan 'right or wrong, my country' is a devil's slogan apt to kill every individual conscience." "The Story of George."

"tomorrow the entire world": In German: "*Denn heute gehört uns Deutschland / Und morgen die ganze Welt,*" from a song composed by Hans Baumann (1914–88) [*"Es zittern die morschen Knochen"*], the words of which had been slightly modified by the Nazis.

suicide after being tortured: Biographical document by Gerald Mayer and Fritz Kolbe.

"who never get caught": Freely adapted from Ernst Jünger, *Récits d'un passeur du siècle,* conversations with F. de Towarnicki (Paris: Éditions du Rocher).

subject to severe penalties: The obligatory darkening of windows was known as *Verdunkelung,* and those who did not obey this order were considered criminals (*Verdunkelungsverbrecher*) subject to long prison terms.

from Antwerp to Berlin: Biographical document by Gerald Mayer and Fritz Kolbe.

considered "k. v." (available): In German: "u. k.": *unabkömmlich;* "k. v.": *kriegsverwendungsfähig.*

to the Foreign Ministry: Wilhelmstrasse 76: this building of the old Prussian nobility, the "Pannewitz palace," had once been Bismarck's office.

dagger on his belt: Ribbentrop imposed a special dress code on diplomats on duty. The new uniforms, modeled on those of the SS, but also on those of the German navy, were designed by a stylist personally designated by the minister's wife. Ribbentrop himself wore the black SS uniform with large leather boots that came up to his knees. This code did not apply to officials of the middle rank like Fritz Kolbe. Döscher, *Das Auswärtige Amt im Dritten Reich.*

more dazzling than Fritz's: Hans Schroeder (b. 1899) had obtained the rank of "legation adviser" in 1938. A few months later, he was given the post of assistant head of personnel, with the rank of director. Schroeder was a protégé of Rudolf Hess, the head of the NSDAP, who had met him in Egypt in the late 1920s, brought him into the party in 1933, and helped him after that to quickly climb the rungs of the diplomatic career ladder. German Foreign Ministry, Berlin, Hans Schroeder file, and interview with Hans-Jürgen Döscher (Osnabrück, May 14, 2002).

"What do you think?": After the war, Hans Schroeder confirmed in writing, in 1954, that he had indeed offered the post of consul in Stavanger to Fritz Kolbe, which some people had doubted. Personal archives of Fritz Kolbe, Peter Kolbe collection, Sydney.

never to become Pg: *Pg: Partei-Genosse*, literally "party comrade."

not to accept the offer: Autobiographical document, May 15, 1945.

"do much for you": Biographical document by Gerald Mayer and Fritz Kolbe.

"but not without honor": *Wehrlos aber nicht ehrlos*: an expression used by the Social Democratic deputy Otto Wels on the occasion of the Reichstag vote granting plenary powers to Hitler on March 23, 1933. The 94 SPD deputies were the only ones to vote no.

"realized what that meant": Biographical document by Gerald Mayer and Fritz Kolbe.

undying memory of the city: Two visits to Paris (March 1928 and June 1929) are recorded in the Fritz Kolbe file in the Foreign Ministry archives.

the legal affairs department: Fritz Kolbe spent only a few months in this post. "Course of Life."

Germany for interrogation: The two agents of the Intelligence Service, Sigismund Payne Best and Richard Stevens, were to spend the rest of the war in detention in Germany. The Venlo episode led the British authorities to refuse all contact with representatives of the German resistance for the rest of the war.

settle some internal scores: Otto Strasser, an old rival of Hitler's and brother of Gregor Strasser (one of the leading figures of the SA, who was assassinated in 1934 during the Night of the Long Knives), was accused of having conspired with the British in the Munich attempt, which made it possible to remove him definitively from the circles of power.

Chapter 3

place of relative freedom: The meetings in the Café Kottler were described by Fritz to an American journalist who interviewed him after the war. Morgan, "The Spy the Nazis Missed."

"association" created by Fritz Kolbe: "The Story of George."

work for the Wehrmacht: The Walter Girgner company, established in 1932, still exists (Trumpf Blusen, Munich). It is now one of the largest shirtmakers in Europe.

of a confirmed bachelor: "In Berlin, I met up again with my friends from the youth movements. It was as though we had never been apart. All my friends, except for two, had the same political convictions that I did. Some of them were virulent anti-Nazis who wanted to take action. . . . One of them lost his post in the Berlin city administration, two others were sentenced to two- and three-year terms in concentration camps. Another, who was arrested while working on a clandestine printing press, hanged himself in prison." Autobiographical document, May 15, 1945.

explained after the war: "The Story of George." The phrase can also be found in the autobiographical document of May 15, 1945, and in the document written by Gerald Mayer and Fritz Kolbe.

"Hitler and the party": Based on *"Es geht alles vorüber / es geht alles vorbei,"* a famous song by Fred Raymond, a popular Viennese composer of the 1920s, who also

wrote "I Lost My Heart in Heidelberg." Memorandum of August 19, 1943, OSS Bern, National Archives, College Park.

at certain late hours: The episode of the anonymous letters is narrated in detail in "The Story of George," as well as in the biographical document by Gerald Mayer and Fritz Kolbe.

"Among craven humankind": Excerpt from the song of the knights, *Wallenstein's Camp* by Schiller, tr. Charles Passage (New York: Ungar, 1958), p. 40. Schiller's songs in the Café Kottler are mentioned in the biographical document of Gerald Mayer and Fritz Kolbe.

"devil take them!": Ibid.

"general of all time": In German: *Grösster Feldherr aller Zeiten* or *Gröfaz.*

superiors, in professional terms: Allen Dulles later wrote that Kolbe's "employers have an excellent opinion of him." Letter from Allen Dulles to OSS headquarters in Washington, October 30, 1943, National Archives.

"have been a Nazi!": Fritz Kolbe said that he had "continually been asked to join the party." "The Story of George." "The Nazis would have liked George to join them—they desired energetic men in their ranks—but George refused. . . . Again and again the Nazis tried to get him into their organization." Morgan, "The Spy the Nazis Missed."

to by his superiors: "During the day he worked hard at his official post, even on Sundays. Only if his activity was considered outstanding could he keep exempt from military service." "The Story of George."

father of the Reformation: On Martin Luther, see his portrait in Hans-Jürgen Döscher, *Die Braune Elite* (Darmstadt, 1999), v. 2, pp. 179–91.

visas for foreign travel: Fritz Kolbe worked for Martin Luther and the "German" department until the summer or winter of 1940 (the dates differ according to available documents). Curriculum vitae prepared after the war (undated) and biographical document by Gerald Mayer and Fritz Kolbe.

extensive list of contacts: Martin Luther had managed to avoid legal trouble after involvement in some murky affairs when he was a municipal councilor in Zehlendorf (a Berlin district) shortly after Hitler's accession to power. Döscher, *Die Braune Elite.*

away, on Rauchstrasse: It was Martin Luther who represented the Foreign Ministry at the Wannsee Conference on January 20, 1942, where a dozen high officials brought together by Reinhard Heydrich agreed in the course of an hour and a half on the practical organization of the "final solution." In Ribbentrop's name, Martin Luther secured agreement that all measures concerning Jews outside the borders of the Reich (for example, in occupied France) would require close cooperation with the Foreign Ministry, which would consequently have veto power over the question. It never made use of that power. Beginning in March 1942, Martin Luther organized, with Adolf Eichmann, the deportation of the Jews of France. Döscher, *Das Auswärtige Amt im Dritten Reich;* Christopher Browning, *The Final Solution and the German Foreign Office: A Study of Referat D III of Abteilung Deutschland, 1940–43* (New York: Holmes & Meier, 1978).

"Jewish race in Europe": "Annihilation of the Jewish race in Europe": expression used by Adolf Hitler in a speech to the Reichstag in Berlin, January 30, 1939.

and a "Russian desk": The "Jewish desk" had been established within a few months of the Nazi accession to power, while the ministry was still headed by Constantin von Neurath. Döscher, *Das Auswärtige Amt im Dritten Reich.*

then a French protectorate: The "Madagascar plan" was an old idea that had been revived in Poland in the early 1930s. The French Popular Front authorities had also thought about it (there was a fear in Paris of being submerged by Jewish immigration from Germany). The plan had also been defended by the English, who wanted to do everything to prevent German Jews from going to Palestine. With the Blitzkrieg victory over France in 1940, Germany contemplated a radical version of the plan: the expulsion of French citizens living there would have made possible the establishment of German control over the island, intended to become a large ghetto. Administration of the island was to be turned over to Reichsführer SS Heinrich Himmler. In the Foreign Ministry, Franz Rademacher worked in close collaboration with Adolf Eichmann, head of the "Jewish desk" of department IV of the RSHA (the Gestapo). Döscher, *Das Auswärtige Amt im Dritten Reich.*

"the first to disappear": Biographical document by Gerald Mayer and Fritz Kolbe.

the game of chess: Autobiographical document, May 15, 1945. Fritz Kolbe's passion for chess is also mentioned in the article by Morgan, "The Spy the Nazis Missed."

the most hardened Nazis: Morgan, "The Spy the Nazis Missed."

"waves kiss the beach?": Words from a popular song composed by a Pomeranian poet, Martha Mueller, in 1907.

corridors of the ministry: The circumstances of this first meeting with Maria Fritsch are set out in the biographical document by Gerald Mayer and Fritz Kolbe; also in a document by Maria Fritsch (October 1972), Gudrun and Martin Fritsch collection, Berlin. See also Morgan, "The Spy the Nazis Missed."

Sauerbruch was a great doctor: Ferdinand Sauerbruch was born in 1875. His career began before the First World War. In 1928, he was appointed director of the prestigious surgical service of the Charité hospital in Berlin. He was a prominent figure in German public life. A volatile and authoritarian personality, he took part in the great political debates of the time. His relationship with Nazism was ambiguous.

be moved at will: Sauerbruch had experimented with this artificial hand notably on Italian officers and soldiers during the invasion of Abyssinia after October 1935 (when Ethiopians took prisoners, it was not unusual for them to cut off right hands). Source: Pierre Kehr, surgeon in Strasbourg, former assistant of Adolphe Jung.

self-importance or even vanity: Sauerbruch bore the illustrious title of "court privy councilor" (*Geheimer Hofrat* or *Geheimrat,* a distinction presented to him at the royal court of Bavaria before World War I), and that of "Prussian councilor of state," presented by Göring in 1934. At the annual NSDAP congress in Munich in 1937, he had received the highest political-scientific distinction of the Nazi regime, the "National Prize," conceived by Hitler as an alternative to the Nobel Prize (which the Nazis hated since it had been attributed in 1936 to the dissident journalist Carl von Ossietzky). During the Second World War, Sauerbruch was appointed "doctor general of the armies" (beginning in 1942).

unions—his hemorrhoids: Ferdinand Sauerbruch, *Mes souvenirs de chirurgien,* French translation (Paris, 1952).

in the Reich chancellery: "At the time of Hitler's first battles in Munich, Sauerbruch had endeavored, without paying attention to Hitler's political aims, to do only his duty to him as a doctor, without becoming involved in the struggles of the new regime, which he did not approve in any way. Hitler is supposed to have said to him at the time: 'As long as I live, nothing will happen to you.'" Adolphe Jung, unpublished notebooks written in Berlin during the war (Frank and Marie-Christine Jung collection, Strasbourg).

in the concentration camps: Sauerbruch was head of the prestigious Surgery Society of Berlin and of the departments of medicine of the highest scientific research bodies in the Reich. At an interrogation in a de-Nazification proceeding in April 1949, he indicated that he knew nothing of medical experiments in the concentration camps. "I only did my duty as a doctor and a soldier," he said. But it now seems that Sauerbruch allowed the performance, without opposing them, of some of the worst medical experiments of the century. Wolfgang U. Eckart, "Mythos Sauerbruch," *Frankfurter Allgemeine Zeitung,* July 15, 2000. See also Notker Hammerstein, *Die Deutsche Forschungsgemeinschaft in der Weimarer Republik und im Dritten Reich* (Munich, 1999).

of speech and action: "A great doctor like him is one of the few persons to remain entirely free. He can permit himself many things impossible for others." Ursula von Kardorff, *Berliner Aufzeichnungen,* reprinted 1997.

the biologist Eugen Fischer: Eugen Fischer (1874–1967) was head of the Kaiser Wilhelm Institute of "anthropology, studies of heredity, and eugenics." He was one of the most important theoreticians of the racial doctrines from which the Nazis drew their inspiration.

General Ludwig Beck: Ludwig Beck (1880–1944) was at the center of all the circles opposed to the regime. He was to be closely associated with the preparation of the attempt against Hitler on July 20, 1944. Proposed as head of state in the event the putsch succeeded, he committed suicide when he learned of its failure.

invasion of Czechoslovakia: The meetings of the Wednesday Club took place on one or two Wednesdays each month. Each of the members played host in turn. The purpose of the association, according to by-laws dating from 1863, was to foster "scientific discussion" among a few figures of the first rank of all disciplines. The sixteen members of the club were exclusively male, chosen on the basis of co-optation, "independently of their personal orientations." See Klaus Scholder, *Die Mittwochsgesellschaft* (Berlin, 1982).

Chapter 4

Prussia, September 18, 1941: Fritz Kolbe was sent on a mission to Hitler's headquarters in East Prussia (*Wolfsschanze,* the "wolf's lair") from September 18 to 29, 1941. Foreign Ministry, Fritz Kolbe file.

Ambassador Karl Ritter: Fritz Kolbe was appointed private secretary (*Vorzimmermann*) to this high ministry official in 1940. Autobiographical document, May 15, 1945. Karl Ritter (1883–1968) had been an official at the Foreign Ministry since 1924. He had been in charge of the department of economic affairs (Wirtschaftsabteilung). In July 1937, he had been appointed ambassador to Rio de Janeiro. Foreign Ministry, Karl Ritter file.

Ministry since the 1930s: In the *Almanach de Gotha* of 1935, we find that Karl Ritter is in charge of "the national economy and reparations policy" in the "Foreign Office of the Reich."

"ambassador on speical mission,": In German: *Botschafter z. b. V. (zur besonderen Verwendung)*. After the war, Ritter claimed that he had agreed to work for Ribbentrop in 1939 on condition of not being involved in the "routine" of the ministry. He said that he had been a "free electron." Source: interrogation of Karl Ritter for the Nuremberg tribunal, July 24, 1947 (*U.S. Chief Counsel for War Crimes*, Hans-Jürgen Döscher collection, Osnabrück) Karl Ritter and Friedrich-Wilhelm Gaus (the ministry's chief lawyer), were, according to Fritz Kolbe, the only two diplomats in the ministry to "have permanent and unlimited access to Joachim von Ribbentrop." Source: conversations of Fritz Kolbe with the De Witt C. Poole commission (September 26, 1945), National Archives.

away from the ministry: Karl Ritter was always with the foreign minister, whether at Hitler's headquarters in East Prussia or at Fuschl castle near Salzburg. Boston document no. 469, National Archives.

dangerous pro-Nazi agitator: This expulsion took place after a failed putsch by the "Integralists," a Brazilian fascist movement drawn to the Third Reich and very strongly supported by a Nazi Party cell based in the German embassy with the full agreement of Karl Ritter.

return from South Africa: Autobiographical document, May 15, 1945.

"highest circles of power!": Ibid.

its content for Ritter: Memorandum of August 19, 1943, OSS Bern, National Archives.

wrote a few years later: Autobiographical document, May 15, 1945.

went to the opera: Karl Ritter was present at major German social events. He was on board the first transatlantic flight of the *Hindenburg* in May 1936, the famous zeppelin that crashed tragically a year later not far from New York. Foreign Ministry, Karl Ritter file.

didn't like him either: Karl Ritter was considered a little too lukewarm an anti-Semite. During the Weimar Republic he had wanted to marry a young woman from the Jewish Ullstein family, one of the largest newspaper publishers in Berlin. In addition, he was never a member of the SS, unlike many high officials in the ministry.

in the nineteenth century: Around 1820, demobilized Prussian soldiers were hired by Emperor Pedro I of Brazil to establish an army worthy of the name, defend the newly independent country, and make war on Argentina. This emperor married Amelie von Leuchtenberg, a Bavarian princess. There are still German towns in southern Brazil (Blumenau, Pomerode).

informed his Berlin office: Source: Foreign Ministry, Berlin.

and even the curtains!: Ulrich von Hassell, *Die Hassell Tagebücher* (Berlin, 1988).

a swastika in its claws: Internal circular of the Foreign Ministry on duty uniforms, November 27, 1942. See also Jill Halcomb, *Uniforms and Insignia of the German Foreign Office* (Crown/Agincourt, 1984).

between Ribbentrop and Hitler: Walther Hewel was one of the few high-ranking Nazis who had experienced the outside world: He had lived for several years on the island of Java, where he had managed a tea plantation for an Anglo-Dutch company. Enrico Syring, article on W. Hewel in *Die Braune Elite*, v. 2.

"all its natural resources!": In May and June 1941, the Wehrmacht high command gave orders intended to guarantee the "unprecedented rigor" demanded by Hitler with respect to Russia. Soviet prisoners of war were not treated in conformity with

the norms of the international laws of war. Between the summer of 1941 and the spring of 1942, more than two million Soviet prisoners died in German detention.

"of the Geneva Conventions": Informal conversations transcribed by Heinrich Heims at Hitler's East Prussia headquarters, *Monologe im Führerhauptquartier, 1941–1944* (Hamburg, 1980).

"sailor") and "Lili Marlene": *"Das kann doch einen Seemann nicht erschüttern"* was composed for a film by Kurt Hoffmann, *Paradies der Junggesellen* (*Bachelors' Paradise*), with Heinz Rühmann. "Lili Marlene" was composed in 1938 by Norbert Schulze, a popular composer of light music. The version sung by Lale Andersen had become the unofficial anthem of the Wehrmacht.

complained about German aggression: "Course of Life," personal archives of Fritz Kolbe, Peter Kolbe collection.

U-boats against American ships: The *Greer* was attacked off the coast of Iceland in early September 1941. A few months earlier, the *Robin Moor* had been sunk in the South Atlantic.

did not feel comfortable: "In Ritter's staff, I had the chance to see with my own eyes all the atrocities . . . of the Nazis. . . . [N]ow I could see what war really was!" "Course of Life."

plane, a Junkers Ju 52: Foreign Ministry, Fritz Kolbe file.

a pickax or a hammer: Reports from the Einsatzgruppen on the massacres in Russia circulated in the Foreign Ministry in Berlin beginning in December 1941. Döscher, *Das Auswärtige Amt im Dritten Reich.*

went to the cinema: It is not impossible that Fritz and Maria went to the Capitol cinema, near the zoo, where on October 31, 1941 the first color film from the Ufa studios was shown, a musical comedy with waltzes, fox-trots, and frills, entitled *Women Are Much Better Diplomats,* with two stars of the time, Maria Rökk and Willy Fritsch. Nor is it impossible that they saw *The Important Thing Is to Be Happy,* with Heinz Rühmann, which was shown at the Gloria Palast in the spring of 1941.

him home several times: "Sauerbruch and Kolbe became good friends." Biographical document by Gerald Mayer and Fritz Kolbe.

the despised "old system": The meeting with Schreiber is recounted in detail in the biographical document by Gerald Mayer and Fritz Kolbe. Georg Schreiber (1882–1963) was simultaneously a theologian, a university professor, and a politician. The pope had given him the honorific title of "prelate" in 1922. A Zentrum deputy in the Reichstag from 1920 to 1933, he avoided Nazi harassment with the help of Ferdinand Sauerbruch, who gave him a medical certificate enabling him to avoid a forced transfer to East Prussia. The prelate nevertheless had to give up all his duties at the University of Münster and accept a post as professor emeritus. Source: Professor Rudolf Morsey, Neustadt (former colleague of Georg Schreiber after the war).

He introduced himself: "Despite my Protestant background, we became good friends." "Course of Life."

"crimes of the Nazis?": Clemens August von Galen (1878–1946), bishop of Münster, protested vigorously against the euthanasia measures implemented by the Nazi regime in three public sermons (July–August 1941). This public intervention brought about a halt to the program of extermination of the mentally and physically handicapped.

"one reason or another": The prelate is supposed to have spoken the following words to Fritz: "It has nothing to do with high treason when you break your word given to a criminal." "Course of Life." "Prälat Schreiber . . . had confirmed [Fritz] by declaring him free of an oath to Hitler," explains Ernst Kocherthaler in "The Background of the George Story" (1964, personal archives of Fritz Kolbe, Peter Kolbe collection, Sydney). At the time of this conversation with Georg Schreiber, Fritz Kolbe had the intention of fleeing Germany by using a network of smugglers across the Swiss border. Autobiographical document, May 15, 1945.

in Germany's best interests: In May 1943, an internal circular from Ribbentrop warned the members of the Foreign Ministry that "any defeatist language will be severely punished." Officials were called on to give an example and not influence "public opinion" (*Volksstimmung*) negatively. Source: Foreign Ministry.

was never carried out: Biographical document by Gerald Mayer and Fritz Kolbe.

him by a friend: Morgan, "The Spy the Nazis Missed."

to go to Switzerland: Autobiographical document written by Fritz Kolbe in Berlin in early January 1947; personal archives of Fritz Kolbe, Peter Kolbe collection, Sydney.

the middle of 1942: One of the best-informed figures in the Reich was without any doubt the chief of foreign intelligence for the SS, Walter Schellenberg. In early August 1942, Schellenberg was seized by a great sense of uncertainty. At a meeting with his boss Heinrich Himmler in Zhytomyr, Ukraine, he offered to work for a separate peace with the Western powers, a solution that would enable Germany to maintain its conquests without weakening itself further. Himmler gave him a free hand to sound out the Western powers on condition that he spoke to no one about it. He explained that if word of this conversation reached the führer's ears, he would deny everything and would not "cover" him. Walter Schellenberg, *Mémoires* (Paris, 1957).

of his own country: "How to get rid of the Nazis? I was of the opinion that there was only one way to get there: the defeat of Germany," Fritz wrote in the autobiographical document of May 15, 1945. "Wood's opinion is that we should continue the fight until a definite military decision against the present gang is obtained. He says there is no hope of any effective action being taken by opposition groups." "Wood's oral report," OSS Bern message to Washington, April 12, 1944, National Archives.

yet heard of Goerdeler: Carl Friedrich Goerdeler (1884–1945), along with Ludwig Beck, was one of the principal figures in the German resistance. A former mayor of Leipzig, he would have become head of government if the July 20, 1944 putsch had succeeded. But the failure of the attempt against Hitler signed his death warrant. He was executed on February 2, 1945 at the Plötzensee prison in Berlin.

of the Kreisau Circle: The Kreisau Circle (*Kreisauer Kreis*) took its name from the meeting place for a group of opponents of the Nazi regime around Helmuth James von Moltke, who owned a large estate in Kreisau in Lower Silesia (now Krzyzowa in Poland).

perfectly ordinary passenger train: Source: Alfred Gottwalt, curator for railroads at the Technical Museum in Berlin.

Chapter 5

"combined into a whole": Letter from Vincent Van Gogh to his brother Theo, April 1882.

plotted here and there: A core of conspirators around General Hans Oster had been very active since 1938 in the Abwehr, the military intelligence service headed by Admiral Canaris. In the army, networks were taking steps to eliminate Hitler. In March 1943, a bomb concealed in the führer's plane flying from Smolensk to Berlin did not explode because of a defect in the detonator. A few days later in Berlin, Hitler left an exhibition early where a young officer loaded with explosives had planned to blow himself up in his presence. Another network, the "Red Orchestra" (*Rote Kapelle*), which was working for Moscow, had been brutally dismantled in late 1942. Its leaders had been executed by hanging in the Plötzensee prison in Berlin in December 1942. In February 1943, a group of young students in Munich (the "White Rose") had been arrested and all its members executed for distributing leaflets calling on the German people to overthrow the regime.

without shivering in fear: The information about the gong used during air raids comes from the archives of the Foreign Ministry. In offensive terms, Allied aviation was really operational only from late 1942 on. Beginning in early 1943, American and British planes relentlessly dropped their loads of bombs on German cities (the former in broad daylight, the latter at night). This massive deluge affected first of all the large metropolises of the Ruhr, then the rest of the country as far as Berlin. Berlin was hit for the first time in mid-January 1943. Fritz Kolbe, like all Foreign Ministry diplomats, was instructed to place a container of water in the cabinets where he kept his documents. In case of fire, water vapor was supposed to protect papers from burning (archives of the Foreign Ministry). After each attack, there were special distributions of food and an improvement in rations (cigarettes, coffee, meat).

ever, one for hesitation: On February 2, 1943, the Germans were beaten at Stalingrad; this spectacular defeat marked a turning point. The Soviet victory at Stalingrad, three months after the British victory at El Alamein, seemed to herald the end of German advances. Paradoxically, the fighting energy of the Nazi regime was strengthened. They had now entered into "total war" (the expression used by Joseph Goebbels at a rally at the Sports Palace in Berlin on February 18, 1943). No longer able to win major successes on the military fronts abroad, the murderous energy of the Nazis turned inward: the culmination of the deportations of the Jews of the Reich took place in the spring of 1943.

1942 or early 1943: Biographical document by Gerald Mayer and Fritz Kolbe.

"to the Hitler regime": Autobiographical document, May 15, 1945.

completely trusted each other: Kolbe mentions Karl Dumont in most of the autobiographical documents written after the war.

Waldersee at Professor Sauerbruch's: Alfred Graf von Waldersee (1898–1984) was a reserve officer in the Wehrmacht. He had been attached to military headquarters in France and then in Stalingrad (from which he had been evacuated after being wounded in 1942). In civilian life, he was an industrialist and businessman. His mother's family, the Haniels, owned large coal mines in the Ruhr. In April 1944, he became director of Franz Haniel & Kompanie GmbH (coal merchants and river transport). His wife was Baroness Etta von le Fort (1902–78), who had joined the Red Cross at the beginning of the Second World War. Source: Dr. Bernhard Weber-Brosamer (Franz Haniel & Kompanie, Duisburg).

at the Charité hospital: An Alsatian surgeon who stayed in Strasbourg after the Reich annexed Alsace in 1940, Dr. Jung (1902–92), as an Alsatian, had been considered a *Volksdeutscher* since 1940, that is, a member of the Germanic community without full German citizenship. Since Germany needed physicians and surgeons to replace those sent to the front, Adolphe Jung was transferred to Lake Constance and then Berlin in 1942. Source: Frank and Marie-Christine Jung, son and daughter-in-law of Adolphe Jung, Strasbourg.

"archbishop of Lyon": "The Story of George." This document notes that Cardinal Gerlier "had saved a lot of Jewish children." In the fall of 1942, Cardinal Gerlier was in fact informed of the danger of arrest hanging over him (we do not know whether the signal came from Fritz Kolbe, but it's not impossible). Finally, the Germans did not dare to imprison him. Source: Bernard Berthod (Lyon), biographer of Cardinal Gerlier, conversation with the author, December 2002.

large store in Strasbourg: Robert Jung managed a large store in Strasbourg. He was criticized after the war for doing business with the occupying forces. Source: Francis Rosenstiel, Strasbourg.

had to work together: Personal notebooks of Adolphe Jung written in Berlin during the war. Unpublished document kindly made available by Frank and Marie-Christine Jung in Strasbourg.

Sauerbruch's staff in Berlin: This assignment was probably secured through the recommendation of the French surgeon René Leriche, who had a position in France comparable to Sauerbruch's. Adolphe Jung had been one of René Leriche's closest colleagues in Strasbourg. Source: Jung family, Strasbourg.

Wilhelmstrasse 74–76: The file on Gertrud von Heimerdinger disappeared from the Foreign Ministry archives, probably in the course of Allied bombing at the end of the war.

she shared his opinions: "One got so one could almost smell the difference between enemy and friend," Fritz told Edward P. Morgan, "The Spy the Nazis Missed."

had been cut adrift: Fritz learned much later that Gertrud von Heimerdinger was close to Adam von Trott zu Solz, a diplomat associated with the Kreisau Circle (von Trott was executed the following year, after the July 20, 1944 assassination attempt against Hitler). She was also close to other figures opposed to the regime (Beppo Roemer, Richard Kuenzer, Albrecht Graf von Bernstorff, Herbert Mumm von Schwarzenstein). Rudolf Pechel, *Deutscher Widerstand*. After the war, she worked for the American occupation administration in Wiesbaden. German Federal Archives, Koblenz, Rudolf Pechel file.

the opportunity might arise: Fritz Kolbe reviewed approximately 250 diplomatic cables a day. Biographical document by Gerald Mayer and Fritz Kolbe.

danger and disillusionment: "People no longer cared how the war ended, just as long as it ended. They didn't care who won," according to Mary Bancroft's German housekeeper (Bancroft was an agent and Allen Dulles's mistress in Switzerland) in the summer of 1943. Mary Bancroft, *Autobiography of a Spy* (New York: Morrow, 1983), p. 178.

"one of the last times": Account by August von Kageneck, wounded on the Russian front in the summer of 1942, in *Examen de conscience* (Paris: Perrin, 1996), p. 81.

finally near Tempelhof airport: Foreign Ministry, Fritz Kolbe file.

telephone number was 976.981: Portrait of Fritz Kolbe (2 pages), August 19, 1943, OSS Bern, National Archives. A few months later the Americans corrected the telephone number, which ended in 0, not 1. But they never used it.

of being "taken away": Abgeholt: the word alone summed up the terror inspired by the Gestapo.

thoroughly, nothing more serious: Autobiographical document, May 15, 1945.

Chapter 6

by a personal chauffeur: Allen Dulles's chauffeur was a Frenchman named Édouard Pignarre, totally loyal and extraordinarily discreet. Source: Cordelia Dodson-Hood, conversation with the author, Washington, March 21, 2002.

ambassador to Switzerland: The details about Allen Dulles and the Bern office of the OSS are drawn from several sources. An internal undated 36-page OSS document describes in detail the activities of the Bern office during the war (titled *Bern,* National Archives). The two standard biographies of Allen Dulles (by James Srodes and Peter Grose) as well as extensive correspondence with James Srodes, have also been very helpful. The memoirs of Mary Bancroft, colleague and mistress of Allen Dulles in Switzerland during the war (*Autobiography of a Spy*), are full of descriptions and anecdotes.

a few decades earlier: Dulles was "well born, well bred, well connected." John Waller, *The Unseen War in Europe* (New York: Random House, 1996), p. 272.

a Wall Street lawyer: Allen Dulles worked at Sullivan & Cromwell, a firm founded in 1879 that still exists. According to Peter Sichel, "he was a rainmaker." Interview, May 25, 2002, New York.

a friend to Germany: This reputation injured Dulles, who was often accused after the Second World War of having been close to certain German financial interests compromised with Nazism (notably the Schrœder Bank in London, connected to the banker Kurt von Schrœder in Cologne, who had helped finance Hitler's rise to power).

seizing the southern zone: Since June 1941, there had been a German customs control station at Annemasse. Its mission was to exercise control over goods and people moving between Switzerland and France. It frequently moved along the border. On November 11, 1942, three days after the Allied landing in North Africa, the Wehrmacht did away with the unoccupied zone. The French-Swiss border was thenceforth completely closed.

now based in Algiers: Lieutenant-Colonel Pourchot, head of the Deuxième Bureau in Switzerland, became one of Dulles's preferred informants. "Shortly after the Deuxième Bureau was suppressed by Vichy its financing was taken over jointly by OSS and the American Military Attaché, General Legge." Internal OSS Bern report on France (*French Intelligence*), undated, National Archives.

disposal in occupied France: Pierre de Bénouville, of the Combat network, was a regular visitor to Herrengasse 23, where he was fed and lodged.

mistress of Admiral Canaris: Wilhelm Canaris (1887–1945) was one of the most enigmatic figures of the Third Reich. An ultraconservative nationalist, he nevertheless tried discreetly to counter Hitler's belligerent plans. His double game finally came into the open and he lost his post in February 1944. He was executed in April 1945. See Heinz Höhne, *Canaris,* tr. J. Maxwell Brownjohn (New York: Doubleday, 1979).

military intelligence (Abwehr): The Abwehr, which designated all the intelligence services of the German army, was expert in counterespionage. The agency was established by Prussia in 1866, during the war with Austria.

also became preferred sources: In a letter of December 10, 1943, Hugh R. Wilson (a high official in the OSS) wrote to Assistant Secretary of State Adolf Berle: "On the second of November we informed our representative in Bern that the Joint Chiefs of Staff had instructed us to do what we could to detach the satellite countries, Bulgaria, Hungary and Rumania immediately from the Axis." *Foreign Relations of the United States* 1943, vol. 1.

Lieutenant-Colonel Roger Masson: Lieutenant-Colonel Masson's services had several irons in the fire: their contacts with the Americans did not keep them from sustained dialogue with the German intelligence services, headed by Walter Schellenberg, who went to Switzerland several times in 1943.

a large German community: The Swiss NSDAP had been banned since the assassination of its leader Wilhelm Gustloff by the Yugoslavian student David Frankfurter in February 1936 in Davos. Nazi Germany attached little importance to the country's neutrality, as demonstrated by the 1935 kidnapping of the German pacifist militant Berthold Jacob by German agents in Basel.

(Sicherheitsdienst, foreign intelligence services): Headed by Walter Schellenberg, the SD was under the Central Security Service of the Reich, the Reichssicherheitshauptamt (RSHA), another name for Heinrich Himmler's police empire. The SD was Department VI of the RSHA, the Gestapo Department IV.

"unconscious" of the Germans: See Bancroft, *Autobiography of a Spy.*

Ecumenical Council of Churches: Willem Visser't Hooft: his friends called him simply Wim, and in Dulles's secret correspondence with Washington, he was merely number 474. Sauerbruch had number 835 for the OSS, while Kocherthaler seems not to have had a number.

Dulles's close collaborators: This visit was full of meaning for Dulles: The threat of a shift of German liberal elites toward communism was very real. This appeal was all the more troubling because it came from a man, von Trott, who had had some of his schooling in England and knew the United States well.

"unconditional surrender" of Germany: Policy defined at the Casablanca conference between Roosevelt and Churchill, from January 24 to 26, 1943. This strategy seemed dangerous to Allen Dulles because in his view it risked humiliating the Germans and driving them into the arms of the Russians. "We rendered impossible internal revolution in Germany and thereby prolonged the war and the destruction," Dulles wrote after the war. Letter of January 3, 1949 to Chester Wilmot (Australian war correspondent), Allen W. Dulles papers, Seeley G. Mudd Manuscript Library, Princeton.

contact for the future: Relations between Allen Dulles and Prince Hohenlohe were used after the war by Soviet propaganda to discredit after the fact American policy during the war. See James Srodes, *Allen Dulles, Master of Spies* (Washington, DC: Regnery, 1999), pp. 261–67.

rest of the world: Connections by air between Switzerland and the rest of the world had been practically nonexistent since the beginning of the war, except for flights to Germany. Source: Rudolf J. Ritter, Grub, Switzerland.

postal and telecommunications service: Allen Dulles, *The Secret Surrender* (New York: Harper & Row, 1966). Dulles telephoned Washington four or five times a week to provide general political analyses and news summaries without operational implications.

numbered only about fifteen: The two permanent agents assigned as cipher clerks received reinforcements from American aviators blocked in Switzerland after forced landings. Source: *Bern,* summary of the OSS Bern office during the war, National Archives. In Bern, Dulles had four intelligence officers (Gero von Schulze-Gaevernitz, Gerald Mayer, Frederick Stalder, and Royall Tyler), and about ten cipher clerks, not counting about one hundred informants working regularly for him.

concerned sensitive information: The series of dispatches dealt with the political situation in Italy and the rise of anti-German feeling in Mussolini's entourage. Soon thereafter (was this coincidental?), they learned of the disgrace of Count Ciano, the Italian Foreign Minister, and of several of his friends who wished to end the German alliance. Source: *Bern.*

the German Enigma code: "Thanks to the extraordinary efforts of British crypt-analysts, and the cooperation of Polish, Czech, and French liaison colleagues, and a lone German spy [Hans-Thilo Schmidt], the Nazi military and intelligence ci-phers had been broken sometime before Kolbe became active. This success—code name ULTRA—rivaled only by the American triumph of breaking Japanese ciphers (code name MAGIC), was one of a handful of the great secrets of World War II. The Ultra information made a vital contribution to the Allied victory in Europe and Africa." Richard Helms, *A Look Over My Shoulder.* "Enigma" was the name of the sophisticated machine used to encrypt the secret messages of the German army. "Ultra," the system for decoding Enigma messages set up in England during the war, was located in Bletchley Park, not far from London, and employed dozens of expert mathematicians working in absolute secrecy.

and to General Oster: General Hans Oster (1887–1945) was number two in the Abwehr. He informed the Dutch of the imminent invasion of their country by the troops of the Wehrmacht in the spring of 1940. He played an initiating role in sev-eral seditious anti-Nazi plots but was placed under Gestapo surveillance by 1943 and was relieved of duty in the spring of 1944. He was executed in April 1945 in the Flossenbürg concentration camp.

explained that these rockets: "V" was the abbreviation for *Vergeltungswaffe,* retalia-tory weapon. The V-1 rocket was made up of an aerodynamic fuselage with two small wings propelled by a jetpulse engine in the rear. This was the first cruise missile in history. This flying bomb loaded with explosives was launched from an inclined ramp and was not very precise. The V-2 (or A4), developed and built at Peenemünde (a Baltic Sea resort), was a veritable rocket, having a range of about 320 kilometers and capable of being launched from mobile ramps that were easily camouflaged. This rocket and its principal inventor, Wernher von Braun, made possible the development of American space research after the war. The first V-1 missile was fired on London in June 1944. In September, it was the turn of the V-2 to enter into action. Thousands of V-2s were launched in 1944 and 1945, chiefly on London and Antwerp, causing tens of thousands of deaths. Thanks to Philippe Ballarini and Michel Zumelzu for their invaluable web sites (*www.aerostories.org* and *www.perso.club-internet.fr/mzumelzu/home.htm*).

a Baltic Sea resort: Allen Dulles learned of the existence of Peenemünde in sev-eral stages: first from the Swiss industrialist Walter Boveri (February 1943), then from Hans-Bernd Gisevius (May 1943), then from Franz Josef Messner (chief executive of a company in Vienna). Peenemünde was bombed on August 17, 1943. *Bern*, National Archives.

bad with utmost confidence: Srodes, *Allen Dulles, Master of Spies*, p. 268.

Chapter 7

given to a woman: Circular of June 10, 1941 on the organization of diplomatic mail, Foreign Ministry archives, Berlin.

offices throughout the world: Excerpt from the circular of June 10, 1941: "We have recently noticed an abusive increase in missions to our offices abroad [*Kurierausweis*]. In many cases, these are merely documents of convenience used primarily to offer the beneficiary the opportunity to travel comfortably and to pass easily through customs. This is not acceptable."

between Himmler and Ribbentrop: "We encounter constant difficulties because of the inopportune activities of your services abroad," Ribbentrop wrote to Himmler on June 11, 1941. Foreign Ministry archives.

packages, stamped "official dispatch": In German, *völkerrechtlich immun*. The stamp had both French and German phrases.

envelope containing diplomatic cables: "Since he traveled on a diplomatic passport, the border controls never thought once to inspect closely the large envelope which he carried." Unpublished, undated memoir by Allen Dulles, Allen W. Dulles Papers (box 114, file 11), Seeley G. Mudd Manuscript Library, Princeton.

despite official warnings: Internal circular of the Foreign Ministry (February 27, 1943) concerning the organization of diplomatic mail, Foreign Ministry archives.

with sturdy string: Biographical document by Gerald Mayer and Fritz Kolbe.

as a diplomatic courier: Fritz Kolbe had been trying unsuccessfully to secure an assignment as diplomatic courier to Switzerland since 1940. "The fact that he did not belong to the party kept him from being placed on the lists." Biographical document by Gerald Mayer and Fritz Kolbe.

semivacation in Switzerland: The circle of the "privileged" was rather large, because the transport of diplomatic mail between Berlin and Bern took place every day, at least in the first years of the war. Those charged with carrying diplomatic mail were not supposed to have to high a rank in the ministry hierarchy.

his political reliability in writing: Autobiographical document written by Fritz Kolbe in Berlin in early January 1947.

the Ministry of Propaganda: Propaganda Ministerium, or Promi in common speech.

not repress a shiver: The Central Security Office of the Reich, Reichssicherheitshauptamt (RSHA).

the Askanischer Platz: The names are references to German history. The old princely house of Askania reigned over the duchy of Anhalt until 1918.

not bang into them: Source: Alfred Gottwaldt, Berlin, January 10, 2002. All the technical details on trains (including the schedules) were kindly provided by Mr. Gottwaldt, curator of the railroad department in the Technical Museum in Berlin.

front of the train: In 1939, the diplomat Theo Kordt traveled from Bern to Berlin in first class "because he was carrying dispatches" (Foreign Ministry, Theo

Kordt file). During the war, first class was abolished on German trains (Alfred Gottwaldt).

Berlin (*visa no. 519*): Fritz Kolbe's diplomatic passport has been kept by his son, Peter Kolbe, in Sydney. See illustrations.

Italian, and Austrian deserters: One of Fritz Kolbe's friends had wanted to desert and go secretly to Switzerland. Kolbe had succeeded in dissuading him and brought him back to his barracks before his absence was noticed. Morgan, "The Spy the Nazis Missed."

not display a Nazi flag: German diplomats feared hostile reactions from the Swiss population and made themselves as discreet as possible.

concealed beneath his pants: Where were the documents hidden? It is impossible to say. The hotel was not a secure place, because the owners had good relations with the German authorities (reservations were made by the Foreign Ministry).

known well since Spain: Otto Köcher had the title "envoy" (*Gesandte*), not ambassador (*Botschafter*, which was reserved for diplomats serving in the major capitals; see ch. 1, n. 2) Otto Köcher was born in Alsace in 1884. He joined the Foreign Ministry in 1912, was vice-consul in Naples, then first secretary in Bern; legation adviser in Mexico City in 1924; consul general in Barcelona in 1933. Joined the NSDAP on October 1, 1934 (number 2,871,405). Head of the German legation in Switzerland from March 29, 1937. Very favorably evaluated by the hierarchy of the National Socialist Party. Also very much appreciated by the Swiss authorities (note that Köcher's mother was Swiss). "George, from his Spanish times, was well acquainted with . . . Herr Köcher, who had been formerly Consul general in Barcelona" (Ernst Kocherthaler, "The Background of the George Story").

nature of the place: "Everywhere, only happy people could be seen," wrote Klaus Mann in his novel *The Volcano*.

south of the capital: Ernst Kocherthaler had settled in the heart of the Bern Oberland in September 1936 after fleeing from the Spanish Civil War. All his movements were closely scrutinized. His mail was opened. "Mr. Kocherthaler spends his time taking photos of the region," "he receives many letters from abroad," "he lives in the same chalet as Dr. Hans Schreck, a Bavarian who spied for Germany in 1916." These are some of the observations noted down in police reports of the time, now preserved in the Ernst Kocherthaler file of the Swiss public archives (Federal Archives, Bern).

to many different versions: The first meeting among Fritz Kolbe, Allen Dulles, and Gerald Mayer is described in several archival documents: Memorandum of Gerry Mayer and Allen Dulles of August 28, 1943, National Archives; memorandum of OSS Bern of August 31, 1943, National Archives; biographical document by Gerald Mayer and Fritz Kolbe; various undated documents written by Allen Dulles (Allen W. Dulles Papers, Seeley G. Mudd Manuscript Library, Princeton).

attaché since September 1939: Cartwright was a man of action. He had escaped dozens of times from German internment camps during the First World War. Srodes, *Allen Dulles, Master of Spies*, p. 280.

in Bern that day: On the British intelligence network in Switzerland during the war, see the article by Neville Wylie in *Intelligence & National Security*, vol. 11, no. 3 (July 1996).

Alpenstrasse 29 and 35: This scene is described in the memorandum of Gerry Mayer and Allen Dulles of August 28, 1943, National Archives.

his office on Dufourstrasse: The OSS offices in Bern (officially the offices of the "special assistant to the American envoy") occupied the second, third, and fourth floors of two residential buildings in the Kirchenfeld district. The ground floor was occupied by the offices of the Office of War Information (OWI) headed by Gerald Mayer, "press attaché" of the American legation. The premises were covered by diplomatic immunity. *Miscellaneous Activities OSS Bern,* undated internal document of the OSS Bern office, National Archives.

at nine that morning: Memorandum of August 28, 1943 by Gerry Mayer and Allen Dulles, National Archives.

War Information (OWI): Gerald Mayer sent thousands of leaflets, pamphlets, newspapers, brochures, and other printed matter into enemy territory during the war. "Mr. Mayer worked closely with Mr. Allen Dulles . . . and was of inestimable help to him, particularly in developing a contact which went into the heart of the German Foreign Office. This contact was generally recognized as being one of the outstanding intelligence sources of the war." Statement of War Services of Mr. Gerald Mayer, sent April 24, 1947 by Allen Dulles to General Donovan, Allen W. Dulles Papers, Seeley G. Mudd Manuscript Library, Princeton. See also *Miscellaneous Activities OSS Bern,* National Archives.

"is okay with me": Anthony Cave Brown, *Bodyguard of Lies* (New York: Harper & Row, 1975).

in the Kirchenfeld district: Gerald Mayer's apartment was at Jubiläumsstrasse 97. Swiss Federal Archives, Gerald Mayer file.

"Mr. Douglas, Mayer's assistant": Morgan, "The Spy the Nazis Missed."

"Dulles considered honest determination": Unpublished, untitled document of 1954 in the personal archives of Allen Dulles. Allen W. Dulles Papers.

out of the envelope: How many documents were there in this first "delivery" from Fritz Kolbe? The figure of 186 cables is commonly put forward. Correspondence between Allen Dulles and Gerald Mayer, Allen W. Dulles Papers. But in an unpublished and undated memorandum, Allen Dulles speaks of only "20 copies of documents." Allen Dulles/Fritz Kolbe correspondence, Allen W. Dulles Papers.

State Secretary Martin Luther: Martin Luther, Fritz Kolbe's former superior, tried to provoke Ribbentrop's fall in early February 1943. The "coup" just failed, and Martin Luther was arrested and sent to the concentration camp of Sachsenhausen. Behind Luther was probably Walter Schellenberg, Himmler's chief of foreign intelligence, who had been trying to initiate negotiations with the Allies since the summer of 1942 and wanted to take over the reins of German foreign policy himself. For Schellenberg and Himmler, Ribbentrop remained the man of the Nazi-Soviet pact, in short the "friend of Moscow." He was known to be opposed to any separate peace with the West, and his hatred for England was boundless.

"meters to the north": Kappa message of August 26, 1943, National Archives. See also memorandum of August 19, 1943, OSS Bern, National Archives.

on August 7, 1943: On the August 7 Cairo cable, see Kappa message of August 25, 1943, National Archives.

out of his sleeve: "He had information that literally came out of his sleeve." Biographical document by Gerald Mayer and Fritz Kolbe.

"tungsten to the Germans": Memorandum of August 20, 1943, OSS Bern, National Archives. Tungsten, a metal that serves to harden steel, is indispensable for the arms industry.

"for days on end": Memorandum of August 19, 1943, OSS Bern, National Archives.

minister of aeronautic production: Ibid.

in the Irish capital: Ireland had declared its neutrality in 1939. Berlin, which supported the Irish independence forces, wished to use the island as a base for observation and clandestine operations against England. The Reich had parachuted several secret agents in 1940, including Hermann Görtz. The United States vigorously protested to Eamon de Valera, head of the Irish government, against the presence of a clandestine German transmitter in Dublin, which was finally seized and neutralized during the winter of 1943–44. See Kappa message of April 12, 1944 and Boston documents nos. 12 and 124, National Archives. See also Enno Stephan, *Spies in Ireland,* tr. Arthur Davidson (Harrisburg: Stackpole, 1965).

ships in the southern oceans: On Lourenço Marques, see Kappa message of August 26, 1943, National Archives. A few months later, Fritz Kolbe provided information making it possible to trap Leopold Wertz, the German consul in Lourenço Marques: "Dr. Wertz has a weakness for women." Kappa message of October 22, 1943.

"and original cipher results": Memorandum of August 19, 1943 OSS Bern, National Archives.

to talk about himself: Portrait of Fritz Kolbe, August 19, 1943, OSS Bern, National Archives.

serve as a guarantee: Biographical document by Gerald Mayer and Fritz Kolbe.

"reimbursement of modest expenses": "George answered that he would refuse any money for his collaboration, as he was driven by the conviction that only by helping now the Americans, Germany would merit a backing by the U.S., which tomorrow would prove necessary against the Russian threat." Kocherthaler, "The Background of the George Story."

"joke?" they both said: Morgan, "The Spy the Nazis Missed."

Fritz felt "deep satisfaction": Biographical document by Gerald Mayer and Fritz Kolbe.

Fritsch ("nicknamed 'little rabbit'"): Häschen in German.

"just sense of reality": Fritz Kolbe's mother was opposed to the Nazis. In the early 1930s, she had moved out of her Berlin apartment because its windows overlooked an SA barracks and she could not bear the sight of the paramilitary uniforms. Anecdote recounted by Peter Kolbe, Sydney, November 2001; also in Morgan, "The Spy the Nazis Missed."

"still a good brother": Hans was an electronic engineer employed by the Loewe firm in Berlin and was not a member of the Nazi Party. Biographical document by Gerald Mayer and Fritz Kolbe.

"the last few years": Manuscript will (dated August 19, 1943) and typewritten transcript, personal archives of Fritz Kolbe, Peter Kolbe collection, Sydney.

eight in the morning: Memorandum of August 28, 1943, Gerry Mayer and Allen Dulles, National Archives.

"also a lukewarm Nazi": Memorandum of August 20, 1943, OSS Bern, National Archives.

two hundred Swiss francs: Biographical document by Gerald Mayer and Fritz Kolbe. The sum of two hundred Swiss francs was rather large, considering that the monthly salary of a high school teacher was seven hundred Swiss francs during the war. Source: Antoine Bosshard, Lausanne.

feeling of great success: "He felt the same exhilarating sensation he remembered having when he made his first successful ski jump after long and careful practice." Morgan, "The Spy the Nazis Missed."

he asked himself anxiously: Biographical document by Gerald Mayer and Fritz Kolbe.

Chapter 8

"roasting in the sun": Words from the anthem of the Germans of the "Südwest," the "Südwesterlied." Source: Peter Kolbe.

X-2 of the OSS: "The only element of OSS known to me to have had access to ULTRA on a continuing basis was the London office of X-2, the OSS counterespionage section in England. Although General Donovan was 'indoctrinated'—the term for having been briefed and granted access to the ULTRA material—he was rarely in a position to follow it on a regular basis. To my knowledge James Murphy, chief of X-2, was the only OSS officer based in Washington who was indoctrinated and fully informed. It was his responsibility to keep General Donovan briefed on the most important ULTRA data." Helms, *A Look Over My Shoulder*, p. 37.

name is a mystery: "Nobody remembered later just how the name George Wood was invented." Morgan, "The Spy the Nazis Missed."

being better than one: In the internal nomenclature of the OSS, Allen Dulles was number 110. He was also called "Burns."

description of the man: Portrait of Fritz Kolbe, August 19, 1943, OSS Bern, National Archives.

Secret Intelligence Service (SIS): The Secret Intelligence Service (SIS), or MI6 (for Military Intelligence 6), had been headed since 1939 by Lieutenant-Colonel Stewart Menzies. It was subdivided into ten sections, including section V, which specialized in counterespionage.

assessment of the file: The note from Dansey to David Bruce was dated August 25, 1943, only five days after Fritz's return to Berlin. Everything had gone very quickly. Source: National Archives.

"a fierce proprietary obsession": Kim Philby, *My Silent War* (New York: Grove Press, 1968), p. 103.

unknown figure, Kim Philby: Ibid., pp. 103–04. Kim Philby (1912–88) was, with Guy Burgess and Donald Maclean, one of the most famous spies and "traitors" in British and European history.

"674" (Fritz Kolbe): Message from Russell G. D'Oench to Whitney Shepardson, September 1, 1943, National Archives.

on the wrong track: Srodes, *Allen Dulles, Master of Spies*, p. 286.

work for the Americans: If there had been a separate peace with the West, the Soviets would have been left alone in the face of the enemy. Kim Philby, therefore, had to do everything in his power to prevent these discussions from coming to fruition.

"cause," explained Kim Philby: Philby, *My Silent War*, p. 50.

"hatred, passion, or revenge": Peter Grose, *Gentleman Spy, The Life of Allen Dulles* (Boston: Houghton Mifflin, 1994), p. 320.

Austria-Hungary had demonstrated: Colonel Alfred Redl, one of the principal intelligence officers of the Austro-Hungarian Empire, betrayed his country to Russia, but also to France and Serbia on the eve of the First World War. He was unmasked and committed suicide in 1913.

"things in the world": These words are those of John Foster Dulles, Allen's brother, secretary of state under President Eisenhower. Allen W. Dulles Papers.

Berlin in the 1920s: The facts about Gero von Schulze-Gaevernitz come from a four-page biographical document in the National Archives. Gerhart von Schulze-Gaevernitz, his father, was involved in the Quaker movement in support of peace and had great admiration for the Anglo-American world. He had sent his son Gero, when he was barely of age, to make his way in the United States with $100 in his pocket. He was also a friend of Max Weber.

of the Stinnes family: The Stinnes family was one of the most powerful industrial dynasties in Germany, dominated by the figure of the founding father, Hugo Stinnes (1870–1924), who had created a coal and steel empire in the Ruhr.

in one of his memoirs: Allen Dulles, *The Secret Surrender* (New York: Harper & Row, 1966), p. 17.

had come from Berlin: That summer, he had been visited in particular by the German lawyer Carl Langbehn, a personal friend of Heinrich Himmler (who was already considering the idea of a separate peace with the Anglo-American forces, hoping to save the Nazi regime by means of a grand alliance against the Soviets). Langbehn paid a visit to Bern in August 1943 but was arrested by the Gestapo on his return to Berlin and "dropped" by Himmler, who pretended not to know him in order not to compromise himself in the führer's eyes.

Warburg & Co, Hamburg: Sigmund Warburg (1902–82) had left Hamburg for London in 1933. He is considered one of the founding fathers of modern finance. See Jacques Attali, *Un homme d'influence* (Paris, 1985).

"education of German teachers": Memorandum of August 31, 1943, OSS Bern, National Archives.

assist the ongoing investigation: Dulles seems not to have wondered about the reasons that could explain why Kocherthaler, when he wanted to approach the Americans to talk to them about Fritz Kolbe, had not spoken directly to Gero von Schulze-Gaevernitz. Why had he asked for advice from Paul Dreyfuss, his banker friend in Basel, about making contact with the Americans? The mystery remains.

Kolbe, Fritz's only brother: Biographical document by Gerald Mayer and Fritz Kolbe.

Fritz's real intentions: Letter from Fritz Kolbe to Walter Bauer, November 15, 1949, personal archives of Fritz Kolbe, Peter Kolbe collection, Sydney.

his visit to Bern: Biographical document by Gerald Mayer and Fritz Kolbe.

not said his last: Anthony Quibble, "Alias George Wood," *Studies in Intelligence,* 1966.

sent books, radios, phonographs: "We have noted increased abuse of the diplomatic mail service for the purpose of transporting private letters. It is absolutely indispensable to limit this phenomenon," according to a circular from the German minister in Bern, Otto Köcher, in November 1941. Source: German Foreign Ministry.

Sport Club of Sélestat: Article by Maurice Kubler in the *Nouveau dictionnaire de biographie alsacienne.*

travel secretly to London: Biographical document by Gerald Mayer and Fritz Kolbe.

Bur was a rare jewel: "With the agreement of Allen Dulles, I gave Albert Bur documents concerning France (activities of collaborators), but also information concerning German espionage activities in the entourage of Winston Churchill," Fritz wrote in an autobiographical document in January 1947 in Berlin.

meant Wood's cross-examination: Kappa messages of October 8 and 9, 1943, National Archives.

assignment as diplomatic courier: Fritz's second meeting with the Americans in Bern is described in several documents, particularly the biographical document by Gerald Mayer and Fritz Kolbe.

for making "defeatist" statements: "The climate is one of pure terror," wrote Ulrich von Hassell in his diary on October 9, 1943, *Die Hassell Tagebücher* (Berlin, 1988). "Nothing in Germany any longer has a face, neither streets nor men," wrote Jean Guéhenno on October 6, 1943, following the account of a friend who had come back from the other side of the Rhine. *Journal des années noires* (Paris: Gallimard, 1947).

warden smiled with pleasure: This episode is recounted in the biographical document by Gerald Mayer and Fritz Kolbe. See also Morgan, "The Spy the Nazis Missed."

a pouch with a false top: "When the sealed envelope was handed him in Berlin, Kolbe merely placed it, together with the documents scooped out of his private safe, in a larger official envelope to which he affixed a Foreign Office seal." Unpublished memoir by Allen Dulles, Allen W. Dulles Papers (box 114, file 11).

turned into a disaster: Biographical document by Gerald Mayer and Fritz Kolbe.

day from his schedule: This episode is reported in Morgan, "The Spy the Nazis Missed."

them in his coat: Unpublished memoir by Allen Dulles, Allen W. Dulles Papers (box 114, file 11).

ashes down the bowl: Morgan, "The Spy the Nazis Missed."

"because of the curfew": Ibid.

easy to pass unseen: Biographical document by Gerald Mayer and Fritz Kolbe.

was in Herrengasse 23: "Meetings with secret agents were held in Mr. Dulles's private house after blackout. This house, in addition to its entrance on the street, had a private entrance in the rear, which went through a garden into a back street where surveillance was almost impossible." *Miscellaneous Activities OSS Bern*, National Archives.

armaments industry desperately needed: The deliveries of Spanish tungsten to the Reich were handled in secret by a company called Sofindus (Sociecad Financiera y Industrial). The Americans subjected Franco Spain to an oil embargo after learning of these deliveries of strategic raw materials to the Reich, contrary to Franco's promises. Morgan, "The Spy the Nazis Missed."

U-boats in the Atlantic: Several secondary sources indicate that the information provided by Kolbe enabled the Americans to save a maritime convoy that was going to be attacked by German submarines. See, for example, Andrew Tully, *CIA, the Inside Story* (New York: Morrow, 1962).

housing the Leibstandarte SS: Hitler's personal guard (*Leibstandarte SS Adolf Hitler*) had been established as early as March 1933 by Josef "Sepp" Dietrich, the führer's chief bodyguard. Its strength was that of a division (20,000 men in December 1942). It participated in most of the major military operations of the war.

"Hitler's personal guard": Document of OSS Bern, October 9, 1943, National Archives.

his family, his opinions: "This time we had more time to talk," Fritz said about his October visit. Biographical document by Gerald Mayer and Fritz Kolbe.

course of the conversation: Message from OSS Bern to Washington, October 4, 1943, National Archives.

door of Herrengasse 23: Biographical document by Gerald Mayer and Fritz Kolbe.

colleagues in the legation: Ibid.

connection might attract suspicion: Ibid.

specialized in venereal diseases: Ibid.

of a later interrogation: Fritz Kolbe recounts that he was indeed interrogated by a security officer on his return from Bern. "We know that you were absent from your hotel on the night of 9 October. What do you have to answer?" The doctor's bill enabled him to calm the suspicions of the interrogator, and Kolbe escaped with a verbal warning. Morgan, "The Spy the Nazis Missed." Morgan places the scene in August 1943, apparently mistakenly.

"apartment on Kurfürstendamm": Documents from OSS Bern, October 8 and 9, 1943, National Archives.

came to arrest him: "The Story of George." Fritz Kolbe intended to shoot himself in the head if he were arrested. Morgan, "The Spy the Nazis Missed."

Kolbe ("Subject: Wood case"): Note from Norman Holmes Pearson (OSS London, chief of the counterespionage branch) to Colonel David K. E. Bruce, chief of the OSS in London, November 23, 1943, National Archives.

and the Ultra machine: See Chapter 6, note 20.

of the Royal Navy: Correspondence of the author with Nigel West, an English historian of espionage, and with David Oxenstierna in Boston, grandson of Johann Gabriel Oxenstierna.

"Josephine," were disciplined: Count Oxenstierna was replaced in the spring of 1944 by another member of the Swedish aristocracy, Count Bertil. Among the high British officials who had to explain themselves on this matter was notably Sir William Strange, Assistant Undersecretary of State at the Foreign Office.

"course of the war": Letter from Claude Dansey to OSS London, November 5, 1943, National Archives.

which Kolbe had revealed: Kappa message of December 30, 1943, National Archives.

"factory was not hit": Kappa message of October 11, 1943, National Archives.

"correct," and so on: Messages from OSS London to Washington, Kappa series, November 19, 1943 and January 22, 1944, National Archives.

Chapter 9

the pay of Germany: Elyeza Bazna was born in 1904 in Pristina, in the western part of the Ottoman Empire. He came from a modest Muslim family. The British ambassador in Ankara hired him as a valet in 1942.

combining diplomacy with espionage: Von Papen had been expelled from the United States in 1915 for engaging in secret activities incompatible with his position as military attaché at the German embassy.

Schellenberg, head of foreign espionage: Department VI of the RSHA, the SD.

so, at what price?: Officially, Turkey was tied to England by a treaty of alliance dating from October 1939.

the German secret services: Ernst Kaltenbrunner had taken charge of the Reichsicherheitshauptamt after the assassination of Reinhard Heydrich in Prague in May 1942.

memoirs after the war: Franz von Papen, *Memoirs* (London: André Deutsch, 1952).

this mysterious source: Kappa message, December 29, 1943, National Archives.

"source designated as Cicero": Kappa message from OSS Bern, December 30, 1943. The next message was dated January 1, 1944. These documents were summarized to constitute the very first documents of the "Boston series," a shorter version of the Kappa messages. Document number 5 of the Boston series—intended for distribution to the top leadership of the United States—was concerned with the procurement of British documents by the German embassy in Ankara. Source: National Archives.

"from the Cicero sources": Message from OSS London to OSS Bern, January 25, 1944, National Archives.

of the November cables: Message from OSS London to OSS Bern, February 19, 1944, National Archives.

"the identity of Cicero": Kappa message, January 10, 1944, National Archives.

"with him to Cairo": Kappa message received in Washington on February 22, 1944.

source of the leak: Allen Dulles gives his version of the events: "Of direct practical value of the very highest kind among Wood's contributions was a copy of a cable in which the German Ambassador in Turkey, von Papen, proudly reported to Berlin (in November 1943) the acquisition of top secret documents from the British Embassy in Ankara through 'an important German agent.' . . . I immediately passed word of this to my British colleagues, and a couple of British security inspectors immediately went over the British Embassy in Ankara and changed the safes and their combinations, thus putting Cicero out of business. Neither the Germans nor Cicero ever knew what was behind the security visit, which was, of course, made to appear routine and normal." *The Secret Surrender*, p. 24.

wrote after the war: The Secret Surrender. After the war, the British secret services claimed that they had "turned" Cicero between January and March 1944 and used him to disseminate false intelligence to the Germans. For his part, Allen Dulles explained at the end of his life that "[i]t was obvious to me that the British were playing some sort of game with Cicero." But the most current explanations are of a different nature: there is hardly any doubt about the negligence of the British ambassador. See Nigel West, "Cicero; A Stratagem of Deception?" in *A Thread of Deceit: Espionage Myths of World War II* (New York: Random House, 1985).

began to resemble fountains: Paul Seabury, *The Wilhelmstrasse, A Study of German Diplomats under the Nazi Regime* (Berkeley: University of California Press, 1954).

were evacuated to Silesia: The ministry retreated to Krummhübel (now Karpacz in Poland), in the Ricsengebirge, or "mount of giants" region. See Kappa message, December 30, 1943, National Archives.

"soldiers all mixed together": Unpublished notebooks of Adolphe Jung in the possession of Frank and Marie-Christine Jung, Strasbourg.

was in short supply: The "coal thief," *Kohlenklau*, was denounced as a dangerous public enemy.

your civil defense kit: In German, *Luftschutzkoffer*. In every air raid, Fritz Kolbe put in this case the "hot" documents that he did not want to fall into the wrong hands. Biographical document by Gerald Mayer and Fritz Kolbe.

Rome, Ulrich von Hassell: Ulrich von Hassell (1881–1944) belonged to the nationalist political persuasion, but he was also one of the strongest opponents of Hitler. German ambassador to Italy from 1932 to 1938, he then took refuge in internal exile and participated in the plot of July 20, 1944. Arrested after the failure of the assassination attempt against Hitler, he was tried by a "People's Court" and executed on September 8, 1944. His diaries, published in Berlin in 1988, are among the richest and most interesting documents concerning the period.

singing old student songs: Klaus Scholder, *Die Mittwochsgesellschaft* (Berlin, 1982).

journalist Ursula von Kardorff: Ursula von Kardorff, *Berliner Aufzeichnungen* (Munich, 1997).

"catastrophe" from their vocabulary: The word "catastrophe" was also eliminated from civil defense vehicles (formerly *Katastropheneinsatz*), which were now given the label "Emergency Help" (*Soforthilfe*). This observation comes from Victor Klemperer, who wrote in his diary on December 25, 1943: "The Nazis' military reserves may be exhausted, their propaganda reserves are far from exhausted." Victor Klemperer, *I Will Bear Witness: A Diary of the Nazi Years 1942–1945*, tr. Martin Chalmers (New York: Random House, 1999), p. 281.

"which is not likely": Message from Allen Dulles to John Magruder, November 4, 1943. See also Kappa message, October 27, 1943: "805 is in no position to secure such information without risking his own security and thus causing a stoppage of information." National Archives.

passed through his hands: Morgan, "The Spy the Nazis Missed."

"his family. Merry Christmas!": This letter is in the National Archives.

to Bern since August: This third visit is reported in particular in the biographical document by Gerald Mayer and Fritz Kolbe.

as usual, in advance: Biographical document by Gerald Mayer and Fritz Kolbe.

Messerschmitt 262 were assembled: "About a month and a half ago production on a new fighter plane, having a top speed of almost 1000 kilometers an hour, was begun. Reports on this plane by Gallant, leading test pilot in the Reich, were enthusiastic." Kappa message, December 30, 1943, National Archives. The Messerschmitt Me-262 in question here was flown for the first time in July 1942. It was the first operational jet plane in history. Hitler had it presented to him in December 1943 and asked whether the plane could carry bombs (he was dreaming of a fast bomber). But the Luftwaffe pilots needed a fighter plane. Hitler prohibited this two-engine jet from being used as anything but a light bomber. The plane might have modified the course of the end of the conflict, but it was a victim of Hitler's obsession with offensive materiel to the neglect of defensive armaments. Source: Philippe Ballarini.

was traveling in Belgium: Debriefing of Fritz Kolbe on the night of December 27, 1943, OSS Bern, National Archives.

bombed in August 1943: Kappa message, January 1, 1944, National Archives.

"fighting alongside the Nazis": Kappa message, October 11, 1943.

"military developments from HQ": Kappa message, October 13, 1943.

than seven hundred tons: Kappa message, January 7, 1944.

shipped to Germany: Kappa message, January 8, 1944.

"he take a rest": Kappa message, October 20, 1943. The Japanese were very well informed about the Soviet Union. Fritz Kolbe transmitted several messages about

Russia coming from Tokyo, notably a very precise evaluation of Russian military potential made by the Japanese (November 1943).

"Guarantee our borders?": The cables about Bulgaria, Rumania, and Hungary are in the National Archives.

of a "militia state": On the notion of "militia state," see Jean-Pierre Azéma and Olivier Wieviorka, *Vichy 1940–1944* (Paris: Perrin, 2000). In December 1943, Himmler demanded that René Bousquet be dismissed and replaced by the head of the Milice, Joseph Darnand. Bousquet was criticized, among other things, for having allowed the underground to develop.

part of the Germans: The following people were designated as suspect: Bernard Ménétrel, Jean Jardel, General Campet, and Lucien Romier. Kappa message, January 16, 1944 and Boston document no. 91, National Archives.

for influence against Pétain: Boston document no. 1067.

"Pétain's group of associates": Boston document no. 91.

"national stagnation and reaction": Kappa message, January 8, 1944.

of a continuous increase: "Statistics for November 1943 (with the figures for November 1942 in parentheses); assassinations: 195 (15), destruction of rail lines: 293 (24), acts of sabotage using explosives: 443 (56), cable cutting: 48 (10), criminal arson: 94 (32)." National Archives.

former minister, Lucien Lamoureux: Lucien Lamoureux (1888–1970) represented the Allier department between the wars. He was a minister several times, of the budget (1933), of labor (1933–34), of colonies (1934), and of finance (1940). He voted in favor of granting full authority to Marshal Pétain.

such as Henri Ardant: On Henri Ardant, see Renaud de Rochebrune and Jean-Claude Hazéra, *Les Patrons sous l'Occupation* (Paris: Odile Jacob, 1995), pp. 693–722. Henri Ardant, as president of the *Comité d'organisation des banques,* was the principal spokesman for French private banks to the Germans and Vichy. He was convicted at the Liberation and spent thirteen months in prison from November 1944 to December 1945.

Yves Bréart de Boisanger: At the liberation of Paris in August 1944, the provisional government of General de Gaulle dismissed Yves Bréart de Boisanger from his post and replaced him with Emmanuel Monick. See Annie Lacroix-Riz, *Industriels et banquiers sous l'Occupation* (Paris: Armand Colin, 1999).

Marie Bell, Béatrice Bretty: Marie Bell (1900–85) was known primarily for her major roles in the theater (*Phèdre* at the Comédie-Française), but she also acted on screen (*Carnet de Bal, Le Grand Jeu*).

stronger than the Gestapo: This list of French personalities is preserved on microfilm in the National Archives (original German document of December 24, 1942).

"always a little nervous": Biographical document by Gerald Mayer and Fritz Kolbe.

though nothing had happened: It was a miracle that the Gestapo did not discover George's activities." "The Story of George."

by Fritz, the Kappa: It is not known why the name "Kappa" was chosen to designate the information supplied by Fritz Kolbe. As for the term "Boston series," this is probably a name chosen at random.

of Corsica in October: The liberation of Corsica took place from September to October 4, 1943. It was the first French department to be liberated. Corsica had been annexed by Italy on November 11, 1942. Four Italian divisions had occupied it, joined in July 1943 by a brigade of the Waffen-SS and in September 1943 by a German division transferred from Sardinia.

twelve days went by: Bern, undated internal document of the OSS, probably from immediately after the war, on the activities of the Bern office, National Archives.

correspondents in the OSS: National Archives.

cables to President Roosevelt: "From early July 1944 forward, General Donovan sent many of the Dulles reports to President Roosevelt verbatim, but aside from the case of Sunrise [the Wehrmacht surrender in Italy], there is scant record of White House reaction. Nor was Dulles's input discussed by FDR and Churchill. One searches in vain for a single instance in which the riches of Bern's intelligence on Germany made a difference on the high policy level." Neal H. Petersen, "Allen Dulles and the Penetration of Germany," in George Chalou, ed., *The Secrets War: The Office of Strategic Services in World War II* (Washington, DC: National Archives and Records Administration, 1992), p. 287.

revelations from "George Wood": Document no. 1 of the Boston series, National Archives.

qualities for the position: "Although officially a member of the party, Pohle agreed to transmit my messages to Ernst Kocherthaler. Beginning in the spring of 1944, he went to Bern six or eight times," Fritz wrote in an autobiographical document composed in Berlin in January 1947. "Several German diplomatic officials had to help. Most of them did it by friendship for George and by hatred against the Nazis, others because they liked George's presents of cigars and chocolate which he brought home from his trips to Switzerland." "The Story of George."

some to Karl Ritter: Biographical document by Gerald Mayer and Fritz Kolbe.

the surgeon the truth: "Sauerbruch was never in the inner circle. I had always his whole confidence and trusted him completely, but it was not necessary to let him into my affairs. Of course he knew that I was dealing with the Allies, but I gave him neither details nor names except the name of Dr. Kocherthaler." Letter from Fritz Kolbe to Allen Dulles, May 29, 1945 (written in Hegenheim), personal archives of Fritz Kolbe, Peter Kolbe collection.

one typed single-spaced: Kappa message received in Washington February 23, 1944. See also Anthony Quibble, "Alias George Wood," *Studies in Intelligence* (a CIA publication), Spring 1966, vol. 10.

confessed after the war: Autobiographical document, May 15, 1945.

"may explain the inconsistencies": Kappa message, February 25, 1944.

"April and June 1944": Kappa message, April 17, 1944 and Boston document no. 284. The source was Hans Thomsen, envoy of the Reich in Stockholm.

spies based in Ireland: Boston document no. 154.

"no other card available": Biographical document by Gerald Mayer and Fritz Kolbe. The postcard is preserved in the National Archives.

his personal secret code: Fritz Kolbe had devised a secret code that he considered very secure and he had shown it to a specialist in the Foreign Ministry. Biographical document by Gerald Mayer and Fritz Kolbe.

German legation in Switzerland: The Americans were very surprised at receiving this postcard, which had taken three weeks to reach them. After some investigation, it was confirmed that an Edgar H. Yolland, who had worked for the American intelligence services in Turkey until August 1943 (when he had been dismissed), was in the process of approaching the Germans in order to obtain a German passport. In exchange, he offered to reveal the information in his possession. It is impossible to tell whether Edgar Yolland was neutralized in time. For Berlin, Yolland's defection could not have come at a better time. A few weeks earlier, the Vermehrens, a couple of Abwehr agents based in the Reich's consulate in Istanbul, had defected to the Allies. The event had brought about the definitive disgrace of Admiral Canaris in Germany, a prelude to Himmler's seizure of control over the Abwehr.

Soviet regime in Germany: Kappa message, April 27, 1944 and Boston document no. 259. A little later, in November 1944, the Germans regretted the departure of Marcel Pilet-Golaz, whom they considered "their last support in the Swiss Federal Council." Boston document no. 604.

letter received in February: German diplomatic cable, January 22, 1944, microfilm, National Archives.

the fall of 1943: A month later, in late February 1944, Jean Jardin tried to meet Allen Dulles, who at first refused to see him. On Jean Jardin, see the biography by Pierre Assouline, *Une éminence grise* (Paris: Balland, 1986), p. 125: "Laval and Pétain intended to make Jean Jardin into a veritable go-between with Allen Dulles."

(the Abwehr) in Switzerland: Kappa message, March 13, 1944.

was located in Zurich: Biographical document by Gerald Mayer and Fritz Kolbe.

Chapter 10

on January 22, 1944: National Archives.

we know the answers: Message from London to Bern and Washington, Kappa series, January 28, 1944.

document into the wastebasket: Quibble, "Alias George Wood."

a former Chicago lawyer: The department headed by Alfred McCormack (Special Branch) had nearly four hundred employees. It was the largest military espionage unit, specializing in the interception of enemy signals (SIGINT). McCormack's investigation was carried out in close cooperation with the British. See Quibble, "Alias George Wood."

intelligence and counterespionage: Memorandum Re Procedure for Handling Kappa Intelligence, August 7, 1944, and *Method of Control of Boston Series Material,* February 29, 1944, National Archives. See also Quibble, "Alias George Wood."

in late February 1944: Boston document no. 111 and Kappa message, March 29, 1944.

and the Far East?: Message from OSS Washington to Allen Dulles, March 22, 1944, National Archives.

of the Japanese administration: In August 1940, American military espionage had succeeded in cracking the Japanese diplomatic code. This decoding system was given the name Magic. Thanks to Magic, the imminence of a diplomatic break between the United States and Japan was known before the attack on Pearl Harbor on December 7, 1941. But the information was not treated as it might have been, for want of relevant analysis.

when the opportunity arose: The episode of the Japanese postcard is recounted in detail in the following: "The Story of George"; the biographical document by

Gerald Mayer and Fritz Kolbe; Morgan, "The Spy the Nazis Missed." Allen Dulles
often told the story in his postwar writings. See, for example, *The Craft of Intelligence* (New York: Harper & Row, 1963).

prime minister of Hungary: Unpublished memoir by Allen Dulles, Allen W. Dulles
papers (box 114, file 11).

on March 22, 1944: Ruth Andreas-Friedrich, *Der Schattenmann* (1947; Berlin:
Suhrkamp, 1984).

breakdown over the incident: Biographical document by Gerald Mayer and Fritz
Kolbe.

good offices of Fritz: Boston document no. 1166.

maybe pulling our legs: Kappa message, December 29, 1943.

trap with terrible consequences: This is the analysis of Timothy Naftali, an American historian specializing in intelligence and the Second World War. Interview on
Fritz Kolbe produced by Linda Martin for The History Channel in September 2003
with the title "The Too Perfect Spy." Available in The History Channel Store:
http://store.aetv.com/html/product/index.jhtml?id=43836.

to Berlin for interrogation: Bern, a summary of OSS Bern activities during the
war, National Archives.

in the Hungarian capital: Questioned by the Americans after the war, Ritter
claimed to have worked with Veesenmayer for only a few weeks. He claimed not
to have been aware of the program for the extermination of the Jews of Hungary
(he thought they were being sent to "work camps") and said that Veesenmayer
was overwhelmed by the actions of the SS. Interrogation of Karl Ritter, July 24,
1947 (*US Chief Counsel for War Crimes* document in the collection of Hans-Jürgen
Döscher, Osnabrück).

spreading through neutral countries: In October 1942 and January 1943, warning
messages on this subject were circulated in the Foreign Ministry. Source: German
Foreign Ministry.

and goings in Switzerland: Biographical document by Gerald Mayer and Fritz
Kolbe.

determined to take action: Walter Bauer came from Heilbronn in southern Germany.
This industrialist was close to Christian intellectual circles in Freiburg who were
thinking about the democratic future of Germany. As the assassination attempt of
July 20, 1944 approached, he frequented Carl Goerdeler, who was supposed to become chancellor after the putsch. Bauer drafted the cultural segment of the policy
speech that Goerdeler intended to deliver if he became chancellor.

by a Jewish family: The coal conglomerate of the brothers Ernst and Ignatz
Petschek was at the time one of the most powerful companies in the sector in
central Europe.

came to recognize them: After the failure of the July 20, 1944 plot, Fritz Kolbe
volunteered to help Carl Goerdeler escape to Switzerland, but the plan was not
carried out in time. Morgan, "The Spy the Nazis Missed."

"too old" for his taste: Sauerbruch proposed to Fritz Kolbe not that he become a
member of the Wednesday Club but that he address it. Biographical document by
Gerald Mayer and Fritz Kolbe.

of the Weimar Republic: Paul Löbe was born near Breslau in 1875. He was
trained as a typesetter. A deputy beginning in 1920, he was president of the
Reichstag between 1920 and 1932. In June 1933, he took the head of the Social

Democrats who had decided to remain in Germany, as opposed to those who had taken refuge in Prague. After the SPD was banned by the Nazis on June 22, 1933, he lived in hiding and was sent to a concentration camp. Friedrich Ebert Foundation, Bonn.

a comrade in arms: There is no indication that Fritz crossed paths with other major figures of the underground Social Democrats of the time, such as Julius Leber and Wilhelm Leuschner.

after the fall of Nazism: Kappa message, June 13, 1944.

individualism of Western civilization: National Archives.

in Post-War Europe: The Jewish Question in Post-War Europe, dated March 6, 1944, National Archives.

terror of being arrested: "Fritz's heart was beating so hard as he went through customs that he was afraid it would give him away." Morgan, "The Spy the Nazis Missed."

for a handsome tip: Biographical document by Gerald Mayer and Fritz Kolbe.

headquarters cabled back: Kappa message, April 11, 1944.

quality of the document: Apparently only the military attaché and his Air Force colleague sent their cables to the Foreign Ministry, which was not the case for the naval attaché, according to a remark in a notarized document written by Allen Dulles in January 1948 to facilitate Fritz Kolbe's immigration to the United States. Allen W. Dulles Papers.

the Thai prime minister: In December 1938, Pibul Songgram became prime minister of Thailand and implemented a "pan-Thai" policy that was nationalist, expansionist, and racist (anti-Chinese). Siam at that time adopted the name Thailand. In 1941, Songgram drew his country, initially neutral, onto the side of Japan. In recompense, he received part of Laos and Cambodia, the northern part of Malaya, and part of Burma. But in Washington and London the Free Thai movement of Seni Pramoj and, in the country, the network of Pridi Phanomyong, then regent, organized the resistance. Thanks to the contacts the resistance made with the Allies starting in 1944, Thailand was not treated as an enemy by the United States after the Japanese capitulation in 1945.

transmitted to Washington: Bern, National Archives.

more than ten sections: Kappa messages, April 19 and 21, 1944.

espionage network in Sweden: Kappa message, April 17, 1944, list of the principal members of the Abwehr in Sweden.

same kind for Spain: Kappa message, April 18, 1944.

on the Russian front: Kappa message, April 12, 1944.

Antwerp, or maybe Norway: Ibid.

Reich's envoy in Dublin: See, for example, Kappa message, April 12, 1944, and Boston document no. 154 ("there is a tank arsenal and a sizeable airfield for heavy bombers located at Hatfield. . . . Most of the tanks are reported to be of the Sherman type. Ninety per cent of the total number of pursuit planes are said to be built in this general neighborhood. . . . American forces are reaching Bristol constantly, night and day.")

used by the Allies: Germany had been working since late 1943 on the development of the technology of miniaturized submarines, like the *Biber* (Beaver), which had a one-man crew. The use of these submarines beginning in the spring of 1944 produced mixed results because of many technical problems.

the invasion even starts: Kappa message, April 12, 1944.

their arms for liquor: Kappa message, April 13, 1944.

gathered around Marthe Bibesco: Marthe Bibesco (1889–1973) was a figure in literary and social life in Paris and Bucharest. The author of many books, she was surrounded by crowned heads and famous writers.

alone win him over: Kappa message, April 12, 1944, reprinted in Neal H. Petersen, ed., *From Hitler's Doorstep: The Wartime Intelligence Reports of Allen Dulles, 1942–1945* (University Park: Penn State University Press, 1996), pp. 267–68.

they are more severe: Kappa message, April 15, 1944.

the object of pity: Ibid.

at 60% of capacity: Kappa message, April 14, 1944.

Chetniks and the Germans: "The Chetnik leaders have decided to join the further movements of the German Wehrmacht. They wish to continue the struggle against communism under all circumstances. . . . They are also ready to enter into action frontally with the German Wehrmacht against the Russian Army." Boston document no. 553.

"favoring Muslim autonomy": Kappa messages, April 15 and 18, 1944. After the invasion of Yugoslavia in April 1941, puppet states under the boot of the Reich had been set up in Croatia (Ante Pavelic) and in Serbia (Milan Nedic). Beginning in February 1943, the British chose to give increased support to Tito's resistance at the expense of Mihailovich's Chetniks, who then turned to the Germans.

"Peter," his son's name: Kappa message, April 11, 1944.

a few years later: Biographical document by Gerald Mayer and Fritz Kolbe.

comments and photograph them: "I sent undeveloped film. There were up to sixty exposures per roll and two to four rolls in each shipment. . . . I took the photographs in Maria Fritsch's on-site apartment in the Charité hospital. This was where the documents were kept, which was not without danger with the bombing," Fritz wrote in an autobiographical document in Berlin in January 1947. The sending of photographic documents did not really begin to function until the fall of 1944. *Bern*, National Archives.

of cables every time: See, for example, Boston document no. 163. It is one of the longest of the series: twelve pages entirely devoted to deliveries of Spanish tungsten to Germany.

the situation is ripe: Document of April 25, 1944 (*Germany in April 1944*), based on a conversation with Fritz Kolbe, OSS Bern, National Archives.

friends in the Abwehr: Among the few regular informers of the OSS coming from the Reich, there was notably Eduard Wätjen, a colleague of Hans-Bernd Gisevius at the German consulate in Zurich, a member of the Abwehr who had been trained as a lawyer. His mother was American, and his sister had married a Rockefeller.

an occasional businessman: Notably Eduard Schulte, a German industrialist who was one of the first to inform the Allies of the existence of Auschwitz, in the first months of 1942.

the cafés of Basel: Message from OSS Bern to Washington, October 30, 1943, National Archives.

and without Festung Europa: Kappa message, April 12, 1944. Document sent to the White House: Memorandum for the President, April 15, 1944, microfilm (entry 190c, MF1642, roll 18). Document sent to the military leadership: letter from

Edward Buxton to the secretary of the Joint US Chiefs of Staff, April 18, 1944, microfilm (entry 190c, MF1642, roll 18), National Archives.

gaining the victory now: Franklin D. Roosevelt Presidential Library and Museum. The document can be found online at: *www.fdrlibrary.marist.edu/psf/box4.*

defense against invasion: Kappa message, April 17, 1944; Memorandum for the President, April 19, 1944. This continuation of the story was also distributed to the military leadership, letter from Edward Buxton to the secretary of the Joint Chiefs of Staff, April 19, 1944, microfilm (entry 190c, MF1642, roll 18), National Archives.

any hot invasion material: Quoted in Petersen, ed., *From Hitler's Doorstep.*

"in Burma," he wrote: Final report of Alfred McCormack on the Boston series, May 6, 1944, National Archives.

was false or incorrect: Quibble, "Alias George Wood."

the material on Japan: Message from David Bruce, May 12, 1944, quoted by Srodes, *Allen Dulles, Master of Spies,* p. 296.

with his useful suitcase: Philby, *My Silent War,* pp. 107–08.

Shepardson, known as "Jackpot": Whitney H. Shepardson had headed the espionage branch of the OSS (Secret Intelligence Branch or SI) since 1943. Shepardson, a businessman and lawyer, was an old friend of Allen Dulles. They had both been members of the American delegation to the Versailles treaty negotiations in 1919.

quite usual in conspirators: Kappa message, April 26, 1944.

of the Weimar Republic: The largest league for the defense of republican institutions was the *Reichsbanner Schwarz-Rot-Gold,* established in 1924, which had three million members in the late 1920s.

this small underground army: There are several sources on the "militia" of Fritz Kolbe, notably a document of April 25, 1944 (*Germany in April 1944*) based on a conversation with Fritz Kolbe (OSS Bern, National Archives), as well as the biographical document by Gerald Mayer and Fritz Kolbe.

Alfred Graf Waldersee: This list was transmitted to Washington in April 1944. Kappa message, April 26, 1944.

most useful for us: "It was not easy to persuade George, and we argued it back and forth for many hours. Finally, he agreed to stay on the job, and I breathed a sigh of relief." Allen Dulles commenting on Edward P. Morgan's article in the anthology Dulles edited, *Great True Spy Stories* (New York: Harper & Row, 1968), p. 29.

authorized to travel abroad: Autobiographical document written by Fritz Kolbe in Berlin in January 1947.

at Pentecost in 1944: "Sauerbruch was going to Switzerland, to Zurich, to operate on a diplomat from South America who was staying there for a while. He got permission from the government to travel there by car and also received enough fuel for a round trip to the Swiss border." (Adolphe Jung, unpublished notebooks, private archive, Strasbourg.) "Sauerbruch went to Switzerland three or four times, each time taking with him material for Bern on my behalf," Fritz wrote in the autobiographical document of January 1947.

to leave the ministry: Wilhelm Mackeben (b. 1892) had joined the Foreign Ministry in 1919. He had had trouble with the Nazis as early as 1933. At the time, he was representing Germany in Guatemala as chargé d'affaires. His work consisted of negotiating commercial contracts. He could not stand being challenged and even violently criticized by the parallel diplomacy of the Nazi Party, and he was forced to return to Germany. Foreign Ministry, Wilhelm Mackeben file. Fritz Kolbe considered Mackeben an "eccentric." Morgan, "The Spy the Nazis Missed."

a former Norwegian consul: Boston document no. 332.

Eberswalde (northeast of Berlin): See Boston document no. 296. Eberswalde, near Berlin, harbored an important communications center for the Navy. In particular, it provided guidance for the operations of German submarines.

'are you still asleep?'": Kappa message, May 4, 1944.

"yet I love her!": Letter from Fritz Kolbe to his "friends in Bern," May 10, 1944, National Archives.

"no cigarettes," signed "Georg": This telegram, received by Ernst Kocherthaler on May 20, 1944, is in the National Archives.

philosopher Eduard Spranger: Klaus Scholder, *Die Mittwochsgesellschaft* (Berlin, 1982).

Army Supply Services: Colonel Claus Schenk Graf von Stauffenberg was chief of staff of the Army Supply Services (the Allgemeines Heeresamt, in charge of supervising the arming and equipment of the Wehrmacht) and was soon to be appointed Chief of Staff of the Home Army. The unit to which he belonged was the 17th Cavalry Regiment of Bamberg, in which Peter Sauerbruch, the surgeon's son, also served; he was supposed to participate in plans for the assassination attempt but was sent to the Russian front in February 1944. Thanks to August von Kageneck.

decline; quite the contrary: Once again, the documents were sent on paper. Apparently, Fritz had not yet mastered the operation of the camera.

vicinity of St. Valentin: "Lower Danube": perhaps the Zipf camp, an annex of Mauthausen.

days at the outside: Boston documents nos. 339 and 360. These documents were transmitted to President Roosevelt and to the Joint Chiefs of Staff. Memorandum for the President, July 10, 1944, microfilm (entry 190c, MF1642, roll 18). In *The Secret Surrender* (p. 29), Dulles writes: "He turned in to us some of the best technical and tactical information on the V-weapons."

enter the production phase: Boston documents nos. 341 and 607. These details were also transmitted to President Roosevelt and to the Joint Chiefs of Staff. The site in Kahla where the Me-262 plane was to be built, was an old mine (See Chapter 9, note 29).

to have been untouched: Boston document no. 380.

were to be executed: Several documents mention this story—for example, "The Story of George"; also "The Spy the Nazis Missed"; and the biographical document by Gerald Mayer and Fritz Kolbe. According to Edward P. Morgan, Maria Fritsch intentionally failed to inform Fritz of the meeting out of fear of the danger.

Chapter 11

world and of history: Henning von Tresckow, speaking shortly before the assassination attempt, quoted in Michael Burleigh, *The Third Reich: A New History* (New York: Hill and Wang, 2000), p. 716.

silence scorn its leaders: Albert Camus, editorial of August 24, 1944, in *Camus à Combat. Éditoriaux et articles d'Albert Camus, 1944–1947* (Paris, Gallimard, 2002).

decision had been ratified: Foreign Ministry, Fritz Kolbe file, official document sent by the ministry to the NSDAP on March 30, 1944.

his messages to Bern: Quibble, "Alias George Wood."

Max de Crinis: Max de Crinis (1889–1945): a neurologist and head of the department of psychiatry in the Charité hospital, he also held a high rank in the SS. He was one of the figures behind the euthanasia program implemented by the Nazi regime against the physically and mentally handicapped (70,000 victims between 1939 and the summer of 1941). He committed suicide by swallowing a cyanide capsule at the end of the war.

and with Professor Gebhardt: Karl Gebhardt (1897–1948) was one of the most honored doctors in the Nazi regime and held a high position in the SS. He was head of a hospital in Hohenlychen, about one hundred kilometers north of Berlin, where he carried out sinister experiments, such as tests with sulfonamides, on inmates of the nearby camp of Ravensbrück. Sentenced to death by an American military tribunal after the war, he was executed on June 2, 1948. He was a former student of Professor Sauerbruch, with whom he was in regular contact.

that followed the attempt: Unpublished notebooks of Adolphe Jung. Frank and Marie-Christine Jung collection, Strasbourg.

events of July 20: Wilhelm Hoegner had been the prosecutor in Hitler's trial after the failed Munich putsch of 1923. He had been living in exile in Switzerland since the early years of Nazism.

dated August 8, 1944: R. Harris Smith, *OSS, The Secret History of America's First Central Intelligence Agency* (Berkeley: University of California Press, 1972), p. 221.

finish off the job: From Hitler's Doorstep, p. 358.

now the Communist group: Ibid., p. 360.

to work with Volksmiliz: Kappa message, August 18, 1944.

in on the secret: Letter of August 14, 1944 to Ernst Kocherthaler, National Archives.

join in X/2 hours: Undated manuscript note of Ernst Kocherthaler (*Key for Wood*), National Archives.

legality on their side: See Boston document no. 358. The Germans intended to revive politically Édouard Herriot and a few other politicians of the Third Republic.

First Regiment of France: In November 1942, with the end of the unoccupied zone, the scuttling of the French fleet in Toulon, and the dissolution of the Armistice Army, the French Army had only one remaining regiment, christened the First Regiment of France.

his plan had failed: Memorandum of August 22, 1944 sent to the British secret services by Allen Dulles, National Archives.

had the changes been: Bern, National Archives.

spies had become professionals: The OSS hired the best experts from the major universities and law firms of the East Coast. It employed experts from many fields, including psychoanalysts asked to analyze the depths of the German soul, chemists working on sometimes lunatic plans (for example, adding various drugs to Hitler's food), and even writers, particularly Germans (including Carl Zuckmayer, Franz Neumann, Herbert Marcuse, and Erich Maria Remarque).

and their new hideouts: Letter from Allen Dulles to William Donovan, September 23, 1944, microfilm (MF1642, roll 81), National Archives.

lack of fuel coupons: Letter from Allen Dulles to his wife Clover, December 9, 1942, Allen W. Dulles Papers.

the envoy, Leland Harrison: "This situation did not fail to provoke the diplomats' jealousy," according to Cordelia Dodson-Hood, a colleague of Dulles in Bern in 1944 and 1945 (interview in Washington, March 21, 2002).

of the Weimar Republic: Miscellaneous Activities OSS Bern, undated internal document of OSS Bern, National Archives.

the July 20 plot: Hans-Bernd Gisevius, who had returned to Berlin to participate in preparations for the plot, lived underground for six months before returning to Bern with forged Gestapo papers fabricated by the OSS. *Bern,* National Archives.

"Dulles's prestige," Sichel recalls: Interview with Peter Sichel, December 1, 2001, Bordeaux. After the war, Peter Sichel headed the Berlin branch of the CIA (1949–52), later directed CIA operations in Eastern Europe, and then took over the Hong Kong office in 1956.

of narrow self-interest: Joseph Persico, *Piercing the Reich* (New York: Viking, 1979).

headquarters in East Prussia: This episode has been reconstructed in part on the basis of a letter of October 4 from Fritz Kolbe to Ernst Kocherthaler, National Archives, and the biographical document by Gerald Mayer and Fritz Kolbe.

"like Wilhelm Furtwängler's": Letter from Fritz Kolbe to Allen Dulles, June 28, 1962, Allen W. Dulles Papers.

to prescribe fictitious treatments: Fritz Kolbe relied more than once on the complicity of his medical friends. On one occasion, he had Adolphe Jung give him an injection causing a fever so that he could take a few days off to work on the files that he wanted to transmit to the Americans. Morgan, "The Spy the Nazis Missed," and biographical document by Gerald Mayer and Fritz Kolbe.

of the Ost Ministerium: In the fall of 1944, the Ministry of the Occupied Territories in the East (Reichsministerium für die Besetzten Ostgebiete or Ostministerium, headed by Alfred Rosenberg), was nothing but an empty shell, as most of the territory in question had been retaken by the Red Army.

agreement with the Soviets: Kappa message, October 7, 1944 and Boston document no. 426. The attempts at an approach to the Soviet Union by Peter Kleist had been mentioned in the American press in July 1944, but had been the subject of an official denial by the authorities of the Reich. Boston document no. 411.

a vast agricultural zone: Treasury Secretary Henry Morgenthau's plan, revealed in September 1944, was widely used by Nazi propaganda to denounce America's "criminal" intentions toward Germany.

prepared by Allen Dulles: Kappa message, October 7, 1944.

I should join you: Letter from Fritz Kolbe to Ernst Kocherthaler, November 14, 1944, National Archives.

supplied by the Americans: "With the camera, the volume of documents processed increased enormously." Biographical document by Gerald Mayer and Fritz Kolbe.

while I was working?: Unpublished notebooks of Adolphe Jung.

confessed many years later: This episode is recounted in detail in "The Story of George" and in the biographical document by Gerald Mayer and Fritz Kolbe. Fritz Kolbe had the habit of drinking a cognac after moments of great anxiety. Morgan, "The Spy the Nazis Missed."

population in the neighborhood: Episode recounted in the biographical document by Gerald Mayer and Fritz Kolbe and in "The Spy the Nazis Missed." The Blockwart's function was to be a liaison between the NSDAP and society. There were two million of these "little führers" in wartime. They observed the neighborhood, organized informing on deviant behavior, and the like.

caught him crossing Alexanderplatz: Biographical document by Gerald Mayer and Fritz Kolbe.

in the Dufourstrasse buildings: Complete Diary of Clandestine Radio Communications in Bern, Switzerland from November 24, 1944 through the Month of June 1945, National Archives.

carry out a search: Bern, National Archives.

a watch to be repaired: Biographical document by Gerald Mayer and Fritz Kolbe.

region for the present: Boston documents nos. 415 and 470. This information was transmitted by the OSS to President Roosevelt. Memorandum for the President, October 11, 1944, microfilm (entry 190c, MF1642, roll 18).

for a German defeat: Boston documents nos. 475, 478, and 479.

SS-Obersturmbannführer Eichmann: Boston document no. 471.

forced labor and "conscription": Boston document no. 534.

of the Boston series: Boston document no. 542.

amounted to 440,000 people: Boston document no. 733.

the Jews of Budapest: In late December 1944, Fritz Kolbe informed the Americans that "Obersturmbannführer Eichmann has been ordered back to Berlin," his mission accomplished. See Boston document no. 733.

dated December 1, 1944: Microfilm document (MF1642, roll 18).

the giving of guarantees: Ibid.

best deliveries of "Wood": Evaluation of Boston Series, December 28, 1944, National Archives.

to his Washington colleagues: Hansjakob Stehle, "Der Mann, der den Krieg verkürzen wollte," *Die Zeit,* May 2, 1986.

courier never traveled alone: Biographical document by Gerald Mayer and Fritz Kolbe.

legation in Bern, noted: Boston document no. 802.

"personal friend" of Emil Puhl: Boston document no. 355.

the IG Farben conglomerate: Boston document no. 804.

political asylum in Switzerland: In April 1945, several German diplomats left the legation in Bern and took refuge with Swiss friends. They returned to Germany after the fall of the Nazi regime. Handwritten notes of Ernst Kocherthaler, April 10, 1945, National Archives.

most of the trip: Biographical document by Gerald Mayer and Fritz Kolbe.

and the People's Court: The ignoble chief prosecutor of the Nazi regime, Roland Freisler, died that day after being hit by a projectile while crossing the building's courtyard.

close off the street: Unpublished notebooks of Adolphe Jung.

of the Foreign Ministry: Biographical document by Gerald Mayer and Fritz Kolbe. A large scale destruction of archives was to take place during the final weeks of the Nazi regime. Kappa message, April 5, 1945.

had not been obtained: Kappa message, February 5, 1945, in *From Hitler's Doorstep,* p. 444. The question does indeed arise as to why the Americans never bombed Hitler's headquarters in East Prussia, when Kolbe had indicated its precise location during his first visit in August 1943. According to the historian Klemens von Klemperer, the reason was the limited range of Allied aircraft, given the fact that the Soviets would not permit them to be refueled in the USSR.

decipher crossword puzzles: Kappa message, February 5, 1945.

Undersecretary, and President: Letter from Ferdinand L. Mayer to Whitney H. Shepardson, December 28, 1944, National Archives.

analyze the Kappa messages: OSS document dated February 20, 1945, entitled *Special Unit,* Kappa *Material Organization and Handling,* National Archives.

former right-hand man: Karl Wolff (1900–84) had been Heinrich Himmler's right-hand man beginning in the mid-1930s. He was sent to Italy in 1943 to take charge of SS troops and protect what remained of Mussolini's fascist regime. His role in the peaceful surrender of German troops in Italy in the spring of 1945 led to his being spared at the Nuremberg trials (at the time he benefited from the effective protection of Allen Dulles). He was again arrested in the early 1960s and sentenced to fifteen years in prison for his role in the deportation of hundreds of thousands of Jews to Treblinka. But he was released in 1970 for good behavior.

armed with improvised weapons: Fritz was enrolled for a few days in the Foreign Ministry brigade of the *Volkssturm.* Biographical document by Gerald Mayer and Fritz Kolbe.

singer of light music: Morgan, "The Spy the Nazis Missed."

our friend D. [Dulles]: Unpublished notebooks of Adolphe Jung.

the password 'George 25900': Biographical document by Gerald Mayer and Fritz Kolbe.

people in the car: The presence of Margot Sauerbruch on this journey is reported by Morgan, "The Spy the Nazis Missed." Morgan also indicates that Fritz Kolbe had proposed that Maria Fritsch come with him, but that she had refused, saying that her duty was to stay in the hospital. Margot Sauerbruch, the surgeon's second wife (thirty years younger than he, thus born around 1905) was among Fritz Kolbe's closest friends. Although she had been married to a close associate of Hitler in the Reich Chancellery, she was an anti-Nazi. She knew very precisely the nature of Fritz's activities, unlike the surgeon, who was never told of the details. Autobiographical document written by Fritz Kolbe in January 1947.

or by SS units: This traversal of Germany is reported in a document that is probably a debriefing of Kolbe by Ernst Kocherthaler in early April 1945, a ten-page document whose first page is missing, National Archives. See also Morgan, "The Spy the Nazis Missed."

who was passing through: Biographical document by Gerald Mayer and Fritz Kolbe.

leave without further trouble: This episode appears in several documents, notably "The Story of George." According to this document, the arrest by the Gestapo was provoked by Fritz's visit to the Ottobeuren monastery, which was under surveillance. See also Morgan, "The Spy the Nazis Missed."

long nighttime conversation: Morgan, "The Spy the Nazis Missed."

the war was over: These men were in the espionage department of the Wehrmacht that specialized in Russia (Fremde Heere Ost), headed by Reinhard Gehlen. He managed to sell his knowledge to the Americans, who seem to have heard of him for the first time from Fritz Kolbe. Gehlen became one of the most important figures in the cold war. He created the foreign intelligence services of the new German Federal Republic and became the first head of the Bundesnachrichtendienst (BND). Debriefing of Fritz Kolbe by Ernst Kocherthaler, April 1945.

nor smallpox, nor scabies: Biographical document by Gerald Mayer and Fritz Kolbe.

on April 4, 1945: Kappa message, April 4, 1945.

his conversations with Fritz: Message from Allen Dulles to Whitney H. Shepardson, April 5, 1945, National Archives.

developments in Japanese aviation: This information on Japan was the subject of two Kappa messages on April 6, 1945. See also Boston document no. 609.

believed in this scenario: The Germans knew that the Americans were very interested in the possibility of the "Alpine Redoubt" and succeeded in fostering their illusion for many long weeks. This maneuver had a decisive effect on the course of military operations. On April 14, 1945 (two days before Roosevelt's death), American troops halted on the Elbe and stopped advancing toward Berlin in order to secure southern Germany. At the same time, on the night of April 15, the Russians launched their final great offensive against Berlin. See Antony Beevor, *The Fall of Berlin, 1945* (New York: Viking, 2002) and Persico, *Piercing the Reich.*

protection of Allen Dulles: Fritz Kolbe had had the good fortune never to be suspected by the Gestapo. He was very grateful to the Americans for having done everything to protect him during the war. "I had the privilege to collaborate now during years with two of your most distinguished diplomates [*sic*]. I have found them so cautious and discreet that none of the secrets my life depended on has been divulged." "The Story of George." "I am very grateful to my 'partners' in Bern for having done everything to prevent my being discovered. It must not always have been easy." Autobiographical document written by Fritz Kolbe on May 15, 1945.

Fritz—came out of prison: Walter Bauer's name had been found in the private diaries of some of the July 20 conspirators, such as Carl Goerdeler. He was jailed in the prison on Lehrterstrasse (Berlin-Moabit) and tortured. "Will he talk?" Fritz wondered anxiously. Biographical document by Gerald Mayer and Fritz Kolbe.

he could go home: Konrad Adenauer Foundation, Sankt Augustin. Walter Bauer Archives.

"emptied like toothpaste tubes": Report by Vassili Grossman, quoted by Antony Beevor in *The Fall of Berlin, 1945.*

"be hit?" (April 24): Unpublished notebooks of Adolphe Jung.

Chapter 12

the destruction of documents: Episode reported in various documents, notably a memorandum written by Fritz Kolbe for the Swiss police, July 12, 1945 (personal archives of Fritz Kolbe, Peter Kolbe collection, Sydney) and the record of the hearing of Fritz Kolbe by the Swiss authorities, April 26, 1948 (Swiss Federal Archives, document kindly supplied by Peter Kamber). See also Morgan, "The Spy the Nazis Missed."

secretly shipped to Bern: These secret shipments of gold to Bern are mentioned by Robert Kempner, American prosecutor at the Nuremberg trials, in *Das III. Reich im Kreuzverhör* (p. 282): "700 kilos of gold were transferred to the German legation in Bern, with Ribbentrop's approval, in the form of coins, in March 1945." The building housing the German legation in Bern was placed under seal in May 1945. Swiss Federal Archives.

door in Fritz's face: This series of visits to Otto Köcher is set out in detail in several documents from the personal archives of Fritz Kolbe: "The Background of the George Story"; letter from Fritz Kolbe to Walter Bauer, May 9, 1948; memorandum from Fritz Kolbe to Walter Bauer, August 4, 1950. Peter Kolbe collection, Sydney.

Ludwigsburg, north of Stuttgart: Ludwigsburg had been liberated by the French in April 1945, but had soon come into the American occupation zone, like the entire northern part of Würtemberg.

"His name: Fritz Kolbe": "Köcher supposed that [the withdrawal of Swiss protection] was due to American influence provoked by George. This suspicion was told by him as a fact to the many German diplomats concentrated with him in the camp, and this was the reason for considering George responsible for the death of Köcher in the eyes of many of his colleagues." "The Background of the George Story."

confident about his future: "How full of confidence he was about the future after the war!" wrote Maria Fritsch many years later. Letter from Maria Fritsch to Peter Kolbe, May 31, 1978. Peter Kolbe collection, Sydney.

again at the ministry: Memorandum from "George Wood," April 17, 1945, National Archives. Opinion of Fritz Kolbe on the members of the Foreign Ministry in late March 1945. Kolbe had filled several sheets of paper with the names of the principal diplomats in the ministry. A red star in front of a name meant "particularly dangerous" (*besonders gefährlich*). A blue star meant "not a member of the Nazi Party" (*nicht Pg*). A classification into four categories specified matters. The figure 1 meant "immediate expulsion desirable (*sofortige Entfernung erwünscht*), affecting 79 people. The figure 2 meant "expulsion in the near future desirable" (54 people). 3: "can be employed again on a trial basis after a warning" (84 people). 4: anti-Nazi (24 people mentioned, including Willy Pohle, Karl Dumont, Gertrud von Heimerdinger, and a few people in the ciphering office and the diplomatic courier service). Karl Ritter was in category 1 with a red star.

"The Story of George": This undated document is sometimes in the first person, sometimes in the third. It recounts the principal events in Fritz Kolbe's life as a spy. It contains the following noteworthy passage: "All these details of his adventures in fighting the Nazis we had to extract from his friends, because George himself dislikes publicity and surrounds himself by a wall of modesty." The document is in Fritz Kolbe's personal archives as well as in the National Archives.

banks of the Tegernsee: Eva Braun committed suicide on April 30, 1945 with Adolf Hitler, whom she had married the day before, in the underground bunker of the Reich Chancellery in Berlin.

headed toward Kreuth: Memorandum of prelate Schreiber about a trip to Bavaria from June 2 to 6 with Fritz Kolbe and an American officer. See also memorandum from Ernst Kocherthaler to Allen Dulles, June 8, 1945, National Archives. The Gauleiter of Munich was Paul Giesler, designated by Hitler as the successor to Heinrich Himmler in the final hours of the war.

June 14, 1945: The circumstances of Ribbentrop's arrest were bizarre. In Hamburg, the British had arrested someone who they were not sure was the former foreign minister. They confronted him with his sister, Ingeborg Ribbentrop, who immediately recognized him and could not help crying out "Joachim!" Hans-Jürgen Döscher, *Verschworene Gesellschaft* (Berlin, 1995).

the OSS in Germany: Peter Sichel, interview in New York, May 25, 2002.

time to General Donovan: General Donovan met "George Wood" several times thereafter and seemed to appreciate him. In a letter of March 16, 1949 to Allen Dulles, he wrote: "I am returning your letter from 'George.' I would like to see him again when he gets there." Allen W. Dulles Papers.

the British secret services: "Usually skeptical and conservative British officials rated this contact as the prize intelligence source of the war." Memorandum for the President, June 22, 1945, sent to President Truman by General Donovan, National Archives (entry 190c, MF1642, roll 83).

the plot against Hitler: Letter from Fritz Kolbe to Ernst Kocherthaler, July 2, 1945, Wiesbaden. Personal archives of Fritz Kolbe. Gerstenmaier was the representative of the Protestant bishop of Würtemberg in Berlin. He frequented the Kreisau Circle, one of the centers of opposition to the Nazi regime implicated in the July 20 plot. "Gerstenmaier was the kind of man who would have a Bible in one hand and a revolver in the other." Peter Sichel, interview in Bordeaux, December 1, 2001.

hesitation in saying so: "The role played by the Protestant and Catholic Churches in the fight against Hitler was large but should not be overestimated. In no sense did the Churches have a monopoly in the combat against fascism. To grant them that role today would amount to favoring the creation of a clerical government in Germany," Fritz Kolbe wrote in a document on the "question of the Churches" (*zur Kirchenfrage*) written in Wiesbaden, July 9, 1945. Personal archives of Fritz Kolbe.

of the Nazi regime: Hans-Bernd Gisevius went to live in the United States after the war. He worked for a think tank in Dallas, the Dallas Council on World Affairs. Presented as a great German resistance figure in the American press, he was considered an inveterate liar by the German press. *Der Spiegel* no. 18 (1960); Allen W. Dulles Papers.

US Army C-47: Letter from Fritz Kolbe to Ernst Kocherthaler, Wiesbaden, July 2, 1945, personal archives of Fritz Kolbe. See also Morgan, "The Spy the Nazis Missed."

at the Charité hospital: In March and April 1945, "we lived on Scotch whiskey and Swedish crackers in the Charité shelter," according to the memoirs of Ferdinand Sauerbruch.

in the Soviet zone: In May 1945, Professor Sauerbruch was named by the Soviets as director of health in the city administration. But in October of the same year, he was dismissed from all his political offices. In December 1949, he was removed from his medical and teaching posts in the Charité and in Humboldt University. Afflicted with a cerebral ailment, he nevertheless continued to operate almost until the end of his life. Several patients did not survive in the operating room. He died on July 2, 1951 at the age of seventy-six after publishing a book of memoirs that was a best-seller in Germany.

had returned to France: Adolphe Jung returned to Strasbourg, where he had a great deal of difficulty in reestablishing himself, because he was suspected of collaboration with the Germans. He asked for help from the Americans, but they could not do much to help the surgeon save his reputation. The wounds of the past are still very much alive in Strasbourg. Postwar correspondence between Adolphe Jung and Allen Dulles, Allen W. Dulles Papers; interview with Frank and Marie-Christine Jung and Pierre Kehr, Strasbourg, January 2003.

had not completely disappeared: Throughout 1945, Nazi commandos continued to create anxiety and insecurity in Germany. The terrorist groups were known as Werewolves. See handwritten notes of Ernst Kocherthaler, April 10, 1945, National Archives.

recalling the year 1945: Document written by Maria Fritsch in October 1972, private archives of Martin and Gudrun Fritsch, Berlin.

CARE packages containing food: CARE (Cooperative American Remittance for Europe) packages made it possible to avoid the rationing in force in Germany. They were distributed in Europe beginning in the spring of 1946.

medicine, or a job: Getting a pass required going through an obstacle course for everyone who did not have connections with the occupation authorities. To go from Berlin to Hamburg, for example, one needed an "interzone" pass, which was good for only one round trip and could not be obtained without a "favorable opinion" from the military authorities.

working for the conquerors: The details of Fritz's work for the OMGUS are found in a letter from Fritz Kolbe to Ernst Kocherthaler, December 29, 1945, personal archives of Fritz Kolbe.

become common insults: In German, *Aliiertenknecht* and *Vaterlandsverräter*.

she was deeply hurt: The family of Maria Fritsch (from the petite bourgeoisie; one of her brothers owned a grocery store in Berlin) were hugely suspicious of Fritz but nonetheless came to see him for provisions supplied by the Americans, which they sold on the black market. Interview with Maria's nephew Martin Fritsch, Berlin, January 5, 2002.

"transportation firms," he said: Letter from Fritz Kolbe to Allen Dulles, National Archives.

major German political figures: For example, Fritz Kolbe interviewed Kurt Schumacher for *Tagesspiegel* in the spring of 1946. Letter from Fritz Kolbe to Ernst Kocherthaler, April 1, 1946, personal archives of Fritz Kolbe.

von Hornstein, a painter: "Fritz Kolbe was a mysterious person but he was full of life and spirit. There was incredible energy in his face. We knew that he was working for the CIA. He helped me get a pass so I could go to Bavaria with my two year old baby, who was ill with tuberculosis." Interview with Erika von Hornstein, October 27, 2001, Berlin.

Felicitas von Reznicek: Letter from Fritz Kolbe to Allen Dulles, July 28, 1945, National Archives. Felicitas von Reznicek, a friend of Gertrud von Heimerdinger, was a journalist and the author of successful novels and screenplays for crime films.

him with electric trains: Letter from Tom Polgar, May 13, 2002. Tom Polgar was to spend the rest of his career in the CIA, notably directing the Vietnamese branch during the war years. He was one of the last American citizens to leave Saigon in April 1975.

Party in the East: The forced merger of the SPD and the SED took place on April 21 and 22, 1946.

war against the USSR: Erika von Hornstein, interview, October 27, 2001, Berlin.

and several broken ribs: Letter from Maria Fritsch to Ernst Kocherthaler, August 23, 1945, personal archives of Fritz Kolbe; Morgan, "The Spy the Nazis Missed."

by DeWitt C. Poole: Like Dulles, DeWitt C. Poole was a Princeton graduate. Posted as a diplomat to Moscow during the Russian Revolution, he had been involved in a planned assassination attempt against Lenin. He was violently anticommunist and also adopted a hard line against Germany.

to begin in Nuremberg: The trial of the Nazi leaders had been in preparation since late 1942. The establishment of a commission called on to judge the German leaders was announced in November 1943. In August 1945, the statute for the tribunal was adopted in London by the three principal Allies: the United States, England, and the USSR. The Nuremberg tribunal opened its doors in November 1945 and sentences were pronounced on October 1, 1946. Among other Nazi leaders, Joachim von Ribbentrop was executed by hanging on October 16, 1946 in a Nuremberg gymnasium.

"pride," Peter Sichel recalled: This testimony mildly contradicts Edward P. Morgan, who quotes the following statement by Fritz Kolbe: "I won a lot of trophies, but I never took one of them. I do things for the sake of doing them. That is enough. I don't like trophies or medals or uniforms." "The Spy the Nazis Missed."

of the Poole commission: Fritz Kolbe was questioned by Harold C. Vedeler. The transcripts of the conversations, declassified since 1963, are on microfilm in the National Archives (M679, roll 2).

had to remain secret: An official document of the Nuremberg tribunal attests that Fritz Kolbe "has worked as an investigator for the War Crimes Commission from July 23, 1945 until this date. Subject has given outstanding service and is to be highly commended for the efficient and tactful manner in which he handled his assignments." War Crimes Commission, document dated December 15, 1945, Peter Kolbe collection, Sydney.

Allies during the war: Letter of William Donovan to Allen Dulles, June 29, 1946, Allen W. Dulles Papers. At the time, Allen Dulles had left the OSS to return to the practice of law in New York. The OSS itself no longer existed. The office had been renamed SSU (for Strategic Services Unit) before becoming the CIA in September 1947. The OSS had been dismantled in October 1945 by President Truman, who feared the rise to power of an American-style "secret police."

is no longer safe: Letter from Allen Dulles to William Donovan, July 8, 1946, Allen W. Dulles Papers. The possibility of a kidnapping of Fritz Kolbe can be understood in the context of the time. It was not infrequent in postwar Berlin for people to "disappear" mysteriously. The journalist Dieter Friede was kidnapped in the fall of 1947. Walter Linse, a jurist and defender of human rights, was kidnapped in July 1952 and executed by the Soviets a few months later

the Americans in Berlin?: Peter Sichel believes that this evaluation by Dulles "was probably a little exaggerated." Interview with Peter Sichel, May 25, 2002, New York.

in the State Department: Letter from Fritz Kolbe to Ernst Kocherthaler, June 1947, personal archives of Fritz Kolbe.

from the United States: Letter from Fritz Kolbe to Allen Dulles, March 1, 1948, Allen W. Dulles Papers.

the American immigration authorities: After the German surrender, Allied soldiers did not have the right to communicate with German civilians. This policy of "non-fraternization" was not rescinded until mid-July 1945.

the course of 1947: Allen Dulles wondered what "George" could possibly be able to do in the United States, but he was prepared to help him in his plans. Correspondence between Fred Stalder and Allen Dulles, Allen W. Dulles Papers. The questions about Fritz were sent to Dulles by his Washington colleagues on November 21, 1947. National Archives.

submitted in New York: Affidavit notarized on January 15, 1948 by John. W. P. Slobadin, Allen W. Dulles Papers.

event of any difficulties: Affidavit notarized on April 26, 1948, same notary, Allen W. Dulles Papers. See also a letter from Richard Helms to Allen Dulles, April 21, 1948: "For your information, George has earned from us since 1945 the sum of $6,199.25. This is in addition to the 20,000 Swiss Francs which you left for him in Switzerland." Allen W. Dulles Papers.

days of the war: Letter from Ernst Kocherthaler to Allen Dulles, October 8, 1945, National Archives.

just established in Zurich: Curriculum vitae prepared by Fritz Kolbe after the war, personal archives of Fritz Kolbe.

was in full swing: The Berlin blockade lasted from June 1948 to May 1949.

or a research assistant: Letter from Allen Dulles to Fritz Kolbe, April 1949, personal archives of Fritz Kolbe.

"difficulties," he told him: Letter from Walter Bauer to Fritz Kolbe, May 21, 1949, personal archives of Fritz Kolbe.

Standard Oil or Texaco: Letter from Ernst Kocherthaler to Fritz Kolbe, June 7, 1949, personal archives of Fritz Kolbe.

Fritz's capital of $25,000: Correspondence between Fritz Kolbe and Allen Dulles, personal archives of Fritz Kolbe; correspondence between Allen Dulles and Ernst Kocherthaler, Allen W. Dulles Papers. The CIA had offered Fritz the sum of $25,000 on his arrival on American soil (in addition to the 20,000 Swiss francs deposited by Allen Dulles in a trust account in Switzerland). Hansjakob Stehle, "Der Mann, der den Krieg verkürzen wollte," *Die Zeit*, May 2, 1986.

a few months later: Letter from Allen Dulles to Ernst Kocherthaler, November 28, 1949, Allen W. Dulles Papers.

not a businessman type: Letter from Ernst Kocherthaler to Allen Dulles, January 27, 1953, Allen W. Dulles Papers.

on May 9, 1949: Personal archives of Fritz Kolbe.

based in Frankfurt: Walter Bauer had a leading position in the embryonic economic administration in the land of Hesse, and he participated in the European negotiations on coal and steel. He was an insider who knew everyone. On several occasions, Chancellor Adenauer offered him a ministerial position, which he refused. He was one of the important figures in the employers' organizations (the BDI), where he represented the interests of the textile industry. Konrad Adenauer Foundation, Sankt Augustin, Walter Bauer file.

the Social Democratic Party: Letter from Fritz Kolbe to Carlo Schmid, June 13, 1949 (and answer from Schmid's office, August 17, 1949); letter of application to the Marshall Plan administration, July 11, 1949; letter from the head office of the SPD to Fritz Kolbe, October 18, 1949. Personal archives of Fritz Kolbe.

be "absolutely politically clean": Newspaper article of July 1949. The quotation from Governor Robertson was underlined by Fritz Kolbe; personal archives of Fritz Kolbe.

a member of the party: Letter from Fritz Kolbe to Rudolf Pechel, August 11, 1949. German Federal Archives, Koblenz, Rudolf Pechel file.

But me he kept: Letter from Fritz Kolbe to Walter Bauer, November 15, 1949, personal archives of Fritz Kolbe.

his house in Bavaria: In January 1948, the "Wilhelmstrasse" trial began against twenty-one former high-ranking diplomats, including Karl Ritter. He was sentenced in April 1949 to four years in prison for "war crimes" because of his decision-making responsibilities in the treatment of Allied prisoners of war. He was acquitted on other charges (notably of "crimes against humanity" in connection with the occupation of Hungary after March 1944). Karl Ritter had already served his sentence. He returned to his chalet in Bavaria and lived away from public life. (Fritz heard that Ritter was going back to Brazil in 1950 to marry a rich heiress. Morgan, "The Spy the Nazis Missed").

the new Germany: Personal archives of Fritz Kolbe.

Federal Chancellery in Bonn: Fritz Kolbe had never officially left the ministry, as he had a life appointment; he was simply "on a leave of absence." He was waiting for a new administration to be put in place. In 1950, the Foreign Ministry had still not been authorized by the occupying authorities to rise from its ashes. In September 1945, the Allies had officially put an end to the existence of the ministry, the embassies, and the consulates and other German representatives abroad. However, at the Chancellery in Bonn, a new diplomatic apparatus was being set up. "In late 1949 and early 1950, three months after the establishment of the federal government, the organization of the ministry and above all the attribution of positions was essentially settled. . . . The former Wilhelmstrasse diplomats occupied all the key positions in the ministry. Döscher, *Verschworene Gesellschaft.* The Allies did not try to influence appointments, except for the German embassies in Washington, London, and Paris. The Foreign Ministry of the new German Federal Republic was established in March 1951, and Chancellor Adenauer appointed himself head of the German diplomatic service.

the chancellery in Bonn: Letter of application from Fritz Kolbe to Hans-Heinrich Herwarth von Bittenfeld, October 15, 1949, personal archives of Fritz Kolbe. Herwarth was chief of protocol at the Chancellery in Bonn. His past was spotless: because he was one-fourth Jewish, he had had to leave the Foreign Ministry in 1939. He was not a member of the Nazi Party and he owed his life to the protection he enjoyed in high places. To thank all those who had helped him during the war, he used his position of power after 1945 to distribute certificates of good conduct to his friends, most of whom were former Nazis. Döscher, *Verschworene Gesellschaft.*

Chancellor Adenauer, Herbert Blankenhorn: Herbert Blankenhorn (1904–91) probably played a major role in blocking Fritz Kolbe's career after the war. In March 1950, when Fritz was trying to get hired by the new German consul general in Washington, Ernst Kocherthaler wrote to Allen Dulles: "George is trying to get included into the staff of the new Consul General to Washington, Herr von Schlange-Schöningen, but I doubt that Herr Blankenhorn, who is Adenauer's actual manager for foreign affairs, might tolerate him. Blankenhorn was one of Köcher's assistants and Köcher attributed his personal catastrophe to George, who therefore is considered something like a traitor by this special group." Letter from Ernst Kocherthaler to Allen Dulles, March 28, 1950, Allen W. Dulles Papers. Herbert Blankenhorn was the "strong man" of the new Foreign Ministry (director of political affairs from 1951, he was subsequently ambassador to NATO, Paris, Rome, and London). But he was not a man without a past: he had been in charge of culture and propaganda at the German legation in Bern between 1940 and July 1943. He had of course been a member of the Nazi Party. But above all he had worked every day with Otto Köcher, whose hatred for Fritz Kolbe dated at least from the early days of May 1945.

this interview in Bonn: Letter to Fritz, May 20, 1950, Peter Kolbe collection. Ludwig Erhard (CDU) was Adenauer's economics minister from September 1949 to October 1963.

activity during the war: Personal archives of Fritz Kolbe.

"my favor," he explained: Ibid.

"me more about this?": Letter from Walter Bauer to Fritz Kolbe, Fulda, July 30, 1950, personal archives of Fritz Kolbe.

out of the conversation: Letter from Fritz Kolbe to Walter Bauer, August 4, 1950, personal archives of Fritz Kolbe.

position in the ministry: "Perhaps it's just as well that I was not rehired by the ministry, because I might have greeted people in the corridors by saying 'Heil Hitler!' to them," Fritz is supposed to have said. *"Der Mann, der den Krieg verkürzen wollte."* There is no document in the archives in which Fritz was told that he would not be rehired by the ministry.

plans to publish them: "It seems that great things are afoot. Allen has asked me to speak at a little greater length about my motives. . . . You can imagine how little pleasure I take in continuing this exercise, which consists of talking about myself." Letter from Fritz Kolbe to Ernst Kocherthaler, May 29, 1945, personal archives of Fritz Kolbe. In the books that he published after the war, Allen Dulles mentioned "George Wood" several times.

("The Story of George"): "Allen Dulles asked me for a 'story' about George. He says that you are too modest to write it yourself." Letter from Ernst Kocherthaler to Fritz Kolbe, July 4, 1945, personal archives of Fritz Kolbe.

in the German resistance: Letter from Fritz Kolbe to Toni Singer, September 30, 1946, personal archives of Fritz Kolbe.

Ernst Kocherthaler in July: Letter to Ernst Kocherthaler, written in Wiesbaden, July 2, 1945, personal archives of Fritz Kolbe.

enterprise of collective mystification: "Everybody and his brother, it seems, are writing their memoirs of the Hitler era." Morgan, "The Spy the Nazis Missed."

film or a book: In the late 1960s, Gerald Mayer began working seriously with Fritz Kolbe on a proposed book. He had the CIA in Washington send him a complete file on the activities of "Wood" during the war. Fritz's death in 1971 put an end to the work. "I have seen George Wood in Bern on several occasions. He looks very fit and I hope to be of help to him in the writing of his memoirs," Mayer wrote to Allen Dulles on July 14, 1968. Allen W. Dulles Papers. In October 1972, Maria Fritsch wrote a memo in which she said that "death struck Fritz down at a time when he was ready to write his memoirs as he had hoped to do for a long time." Private archives of Martin and Gudrun Fritsch, Berlin.

for the magazine True*:* Correspondence between Gerald Mayer and Fritz Kolbe, September 1949 to January 1950, personal archives of Fritz Kolbe. *True* was an abundantly illustrated mass market men's magazine owned by the Fawcett group. Edward P. Morgan later had a career as a political journalist and television commentator.

Game of a Diplomat: Personal archives of Fritz Kolbe; Allen W. Dulles Papers.

unsuccessfully attempted to prevent: "I am sorry about George's article as I fear the publication in Switzerland at this time will do him a good bit of harm and this is really very tragic." Letter from Allen Dulles to Ernst Kocherthaler, April 20, 1951, Allen W. Dulles Papers.

major intellectual, Rudolf Pechel: Rudolf Pechel had been arrested in 1942 because of an article that had displeased Goebbels. He was born in Güstrow in 1888. He had been a naval officer before the First World War. Close to Moeller van den Bruck in the 1920s, he had later moved away from nationalism. During the war, he frequented the most active members of the German opposition (Carl Goerdeler, Wilhelm Leuschner). In 1947, Pechel wrote a book titled *German Resistance* (*Deutscher Widerstand*) in order to prove that there had been forms of rebellion in his country. He spent the end of his life in Switzerland, where he died in 1961.

journal circulated in secret: German Federal Archives, Koblenz, Rudolf Pechel file.

Golo Mann, Wilhelm Röpke: Carlo Schmid (1896–1979): major postwar Social Democratic leader, he was also an activist for Franco-German reconciliation and the construction of Europe. Golo Mann (1909–94): historian, son of Thomas Mann. Wilhelm Röpke (1899–1966): economist, one of the spiritual fathers of the "social market economy."

been a patriotic gesture: In their democratic and pro-Western declarations of faith, Rudolf Pechel, and Ernst Kocherthaler as well, were in sympathy with the Moral Rearmament movement founded by the American minister Frank Buchman, who promoted a "world without hatred, without fear, without egotism," and who had committed himself to a "moral and spiritual reconstruction" of Europe, with the reconciliation of old enemies, particularly France and Germany, as a priority.

acted as a patriot: "I am convinced to have acted as a German patriot in having proved to some Allied personalities I got acquainted with that even in Germany the front of goodwill has existed and still exists." "The Story of George."

Republic only in 1968: Article 20, paragraph 4 of the Fundamental Law of the FRG, added to the 1948 Constitution in 1968, stipulated that "all Germans have the right to resist against anyone who undertakes to remove the democratic order, if no other means is possible."

Lisbon, Stockholm, or Madrid: Mary Alice Gallin, *German Resistance to Hitler: Ethical and Religious Factors* (Washington, DC: Catholic University of America Press, 1962). Hasso von Etzdorf was a conservative diplomat opposed to the Nazis during the Second World War.

aim of saving lives: Bancroft, *Autobiography of a Spy*, p. 195.

soldier would have done: In a speech delivered on July 20, 1964 for the twentieth anniversary of the plot against Hitler, Eugen Gerstenmaier pointed out that the Germans who resisted Nazism had had "constantly to weigh the balance between rebellion against the government and loyalty to the people and the army." Hans-Jakob Stehle, "*Der Mann, der den Krieg verkürzen wollte.*" "They'll die, that's what they deserve," Fritz had said to Adolphe Jung about the Germans. See Chapter 5.

were particularly compromised: Among them was Werner von Bargen, former envoy of the Reich to Belgium, who shared responsibility for the deportation of Jews from Belgium during the war. Döscher, *Verschworene Gesellschaft.*

was already too late: Ibid.

Berlin in April 1948: According to Richard Helms and William Hood, Fritz Kolbe received a monthly pension from the CIA starting a few years later when he settled in Switzerland in the mid-1950s. *A Look Over My Shoulder.* According to Peter Kolbe, Fritz also received a pension from the Foreign Ministry in the last years of his life.

employer terminated discussions: Letter from Ernst Kocherthaler to Allen Dulles, February 20, 1953, Allen W. Dulles Papers.

life and never complained: "He was not plaintive in any sense. It was just those little things that an individual lets out, that shows that you were hurt by the fact that you have been thrown aside." Richard Helms, interview with Linda Martin for The History Channel, September 2003. "Kolbe never expressed any feelings of bitterness or regret about his post-war fate." Tom Polgar, letter to the author, May 13, 2002.

see his son again: Handwritten document written by Maria Fritsch in October 1972. Collection of Martin and Gudrun Fritsch.

him which never came: All these details come from an interview of Peter Kolbe in Sydney, November 2001.

Hermsdorf of the CIA: Relations between Fritz and his third wife, Maria, seem to have gone through some rough times in the 1950s. In her private diaries of the time, Maria confided her romantic unhappiness. At the end of her life, she admitted never having fully penetrated Fritz's personality: "he came from another planet," she said. Interview with Gudrun and Martin Fritsch, Berlin, January 2002.

the language very well: Even though he has never lived in Germany, Peter Kolbe speaks unaccented German and has a slight German accent when he speaks English.

Africa in January 1954: Peter returned to Germany several times and relations with his father grew a bit smoother over time. He studied science in South Africa and Australia and became a geologist. After post-doctoral studies at MIT and a position with an American company based in Canada, he moved to Australia, where he took up a position as professor of geology and geochemistry at Sydney University, where he spent the rest of his career. With the passage of time, Peter Kolbe has inwardly reconciled himself with his father and is finally grateful to him for not bringing him back to Germany in September 1939.

cement market in South Africa: Correspondence between Fritz Kolbe and his son, September 1953. "My father sent me letters in which he asked me for stacks of information about the economic needs of South Africa: concrete poles for telephone lines, wooden ties for railroad lines. . . . I found this completely ridiculous and I said to myself, what a loser!" Peter Kolbe, Sydney, November 2001.

to join the Masons: Peter Kolbe joined a lodge in Durban, but set foot in it only once or twice.

on February 26, 1953: "Without Kolbe, Allen Dulles would never have become head of the CIA," according to Mary Bancroft, former informal collaborator and mistress of Allen Dulles, in an article by Barbara Ungeheuer in *Die Zeit,* May 1986.

influential New York organization: The Council on Foreign Relations was established after the First World War by young disciples of President Wilson, among them Allen Dulles. The organization saw the light of day at the Hotel Majestic in Paris in May 1919, during the negotiations on the Versailles treaty. Over time, the forum became a nursery for the upper echelons of the American leadership.

the Nazi Foreign Ministry: Allen W. Dulles Papers. On the death of Allen Dulles on January 30, 1969, all the obituaries in the American press mentioned the existence of "George Wood."

the Kappa-Wood material: Letter from General John Magruder to Allen Dulles, December 6, 1945, Allen W. Dulles Papers.

raids on German cities: Speech of President Truman reprinted in the press release from Macmillan in presentation of the book by Allen Dulles on German resistance to Nazism, *Germany's Underground* (1947). Allen W. Dulles Papers.

by the United States: Among other sources, we may cite a letter from Fritz Kolbe to his son, dated May 1968, in which he criticizes Western consumer society and exhibits understanding for the rebellion of young people in France and around Europe, personal archives of Fritz Kolbe.

had never dropped him: The two men remained in touch until the death of Allen Dulles. In the 1960s, they continued to meet in Bern or in the United States whenever the opportunity arose.

Fritz secure this position: From the mid-1950s on, Fritz was not content to be merely a sales representative for a chain saw company. He also represented in Switzerland the interests of his friend Walter Girgner, owner of a large clothing company in Germany (Trumpf shirts), and accumulated assignments for sales canvassing in all areas (steel, machinery, textiles, etc.).

were infested with snakes: German Federal Archives, Koblenz, Rudolf Pechel file, correspondence with Fritz Kolbe, April 1954.

$250 a month: The contract is in the personal archives of Fritz Kolbe.

what he could do: Peter Sichel, interview, Bordeaux, December 1, 2001.

Epilogue

that of Fritz Kolbe: See the illustrated volume *100 Jahre Auswärtiges Amt (1870–1970)*, published by the German Foreign Ministry in 1970, and *Widerstand im auswärtigen Dienst*, published by the ministry in 1994. The names of the martyrs of July 20, 1944 engraved in marble in the ministry were (and remain) the following: Albrecht Graf von Bernstorff, Eduard Brücklmeier, Hans-Bernd von Haeften, Ulrich von Hassell, Otto Kiep, Herbert Mumm von Schwarzenstein, Friedrich-Werner Graf von der Schulenburg, Adam von Trott zu Solz, Herbert Gollnow, Richard Kuenzer, and Hans Litter, to which was added a few years later Rudolf von Scheliha. All these diplomats were executed between 1942 and 1945.

list of the "just": Ludwig Biewer, director of archives for the Foreign Ministry.

to his friend intolerable: "The ironic result of the story is that a valiant patriot could have been considered a traitor to his country, when he really was one of the few who helped that in the decisive moments of German history a responsible American set of politicians could stop the Morgenthau policy and back Germany against Soviet Russia's domination." Ernst Kocherthaler, "The Background of the George Story."

years left to live: Ernst Kocherthaler died in Bern on September 6, 1966.

suspicions weighing on him: Letter from Eugen Gerstenmaier, March 10, 1965, personal archives of Fritz Kolbe.

to me my honor: Letter from Fritz Kolbe to Ernst Kocherthaler, January 10, 1965, personal archives of Fritz Kolbe.

February 16, 1971 in Bern: "He did not die peacefully," says his son, who was present for his last moments in a Bern hospital. His last words were to ask his son whether he "had been a good father." His estate, inventoried by a Bern notary, included among assets 47,746 Swiss francs, a 1968 Opel Commodore GS, and a guitar. Fritz Kolbe's personal indebtedness amounted to 7882 Swiss francs.

director of the CIA: Richard M. Helms (1913–2002) was director of the CIA from 1966 to 1973. A former journalist, he had covered the 1936 Berlin Olympic Games for United Press and had interviewed Hitler. He joined the OSS in 1943 and continued his career in the CIA after the war. He succeeded Allen Dulles as chief of American intelligence in Germany after October 1945. After his return to Washington, Allen Dulles asked him to handle Fritz Kolbe's immigration file between 1947 and 1949. He was appointed director of the CIA in 1966 under the presidency of Lyndon Johnson. In 1977, after refusing to testify before Congress on the role of the CIA in the 1973 coup d'état in Chile, he was given a suspended sentence of two years in prison and fined $2,000. The memoirs of Richard Helms, written in collaboration with William Hood, were published in the United States in the spring of 2003, with the title *A Look Over My Shoulder*.

in his own country: Unused material for *Great True Spy Stories* (1967), Allen W. Dulles Papers.

ACKNOWLEDGMENTS

My special thanks go to Peter Kolbe (Sydney), the son of Fritz Kolbe, who welcomed me to his home, opened his father's archives to me, and answered all my questions. Without him, this book would not have been possible.

I would also like to thank Peter Kolbe for having made available the photographic documents, some of which are reproduced in this book.

Thanks also to: Peter Sichel (New York, Bordeaux), head of the CIA in Berlin after the war, who greatly helped me at all stages of this book.

Hans-Jürgen Döscher (Osnabrück), historian of the German Foreign Ministry, who granted me the benefit of his incomparable knowledge of the German diplomatic administration and its history.

Axel Frohn and Hans-Michael Kloth (*Der Spiegel*), who made me want to write this book.

Philippe Garnier (Denoël, Paris), for his patience and encouragement.

Florence and all the children: Juliette, Jean-Baptiste, Milán, Benjamin, Eléna, and Mateo, for their infinite patience.

George Holoch, for his great translation and his personal dedication to all the details.

* * *

For their invaluable testimony, I would also like to thank Gudrun and
Martin Fritsch in Berlin, Sylvia and Gerald Roth in Geneva, and Marie-
Christine and Frank Jung in Strasbourg. I would like to thank each
of them as well for kindly making available important unpublished
documents, notably some photographs reprinted here, as well as notes
and diaries that were used extensively.

My thanks finally, to all those who have in one way or another made
valuable contributions to the writing of this book.

Yves-Marc Ajchenbaum, Paris.

Fabrice d'Almeida, Paris.

Nickie Athanassi, Paris.

Hervé Audibert, Joinville-le-Pont.

Lucienne Bastien, Paris.

Gerhard A. Bayer, Bundesverband Deutscher Eisenbahn-Freunde
e. V., Füssen-Weisensee.

Ludwig Biewer, archives of the German Foreign Ministry, Berlin.

Dennis E. Bilger, Harry S. Truman Library.

Antoine and Madeleine Bosshard, Lausanne.

Marie-Françoise Bothorel, Paris.

Daniel Bourgeois, Swiss Federal Archives, Bern.

Greg Bradsher, United States National Archives, College Park.

Pierre Braunschweig, Paris.

Jacques Bureau, Paris.

Marianne Brück, Ottobeuren.

Didier Cantarutti, Paris.

Danielle Delattre, Paris.

Micheline Delattre, Noisy-le-Roi.

Cordelia Dodson-Hood, Washington.

Louis-Marie and Nicole Duchamp, Paris.

Wolfgang U. Eckart, Heidelberg.

Bruce Edwards, Rutland, Vermont.

François Fejtö, Paris.

Louis de Fouchécour, Neuilly-sur-Seine.

Mark Fritz, New York.
François George, Paris.
Alfred Gottwaldt, Museum of Science and Technology, Berlin.
Hélène Gournay, Service pédagogique La Coupole.
Jean-Paul Guilloteau, Paris.
Peter Hantke, August Horch Museum, Zwickau.
A. Herrbach, Sélestat.
Stefan Hausherr, Winterthur.
Christine Herme, Paris.
Ronald Hermsdorf, New Boston, New Hampshire.
William Hood, Amagansett, New York.
Erika von Hornstein, Berlin.
Brigitte Kaff, Konrad-Adenauer-Stiftung, Sankt Augustin.
Peter Kamber, Bern.
Dr. Pierre Kehr, Strasbourg.
Professor Klemens von Klemperer, Northampton, Massachusetts.
Karin Kolbe, Sydney.
Ursula Kolbe, Sydney.
August von Kageneck, Neuilly-sur-Seine.
Arnold Kramish, Reston, Virginia.
Dr. Ursula Krause-Schmidt, Studienkreis deutscher Widerstand, Frankfurt.
Dominik Landwehr, Kollbrunn, Switzerland.
Linda Martin, CBS News Productions, New York.
Christof Mauch, Washington.
Gerald M. Mayer, Jr., Newbury, New Hampshire.
Fritz Molden, Vienna.
Beth Montandon, Lausanne.
Professor Dr. Rudolf Morsey, Neustadt.
Melissa Müller, Munich.
David Oxenstierna, Boston.
Anne Perfumo, Paris.
Serge Pétillot-Niémetz, Paris.
Gregor Pickro, German Federal Archives, Koblenz.
Tom Polgar, Maitland, Florida.

Norbert Prill, Strasbourg and Bonn.

Rudolf J. Ritter, Grub, Switzerland.

Constantin Roman, London.

Francis Rosenstiel, Strasbourg.

Olivier Rubinstein, Paris.

Ulrich Sahm, Bodenwerder.

Serguei, Paris.

Thomas Sparr, Siedler Verlag, Berlin.

James Srodes, Washington.

Olivia Stasi, Paris.

Dr. Christoph Stamm, Friedrich-Ebert-Stiftung, Bonn.

Hansjakob Stehle, Vienna.

Ute Stiepani, Gedenkstätte Deutscher Widerstand, Berlin.

Jean-Pierre Tuquoi, Paris.

Professor Klaus Urner.

Professor Jean-Marie Vetter, Strasbourg.

Dr. Bernhard Weber-Brosamer, Franz Haniel & Co., Duisburg.

Abbot Paulus Weigele, Ottobeuren.

Professor Gerhard Weinberg, Chapel Hill, North Carolina.

Nigel West, Berkshire, England.

Neville Wylie, School of Politics, University of Nottingham.

SOURCES AND BIBLIOGRAPHY

Archives

1. Personal archives of Fritz Kolbe, Sydney

Peter Kolbe graciously made available his father's archives, which he has preserved in Sydney. Fritz Kolbe kept a written record of most of the events of his life. His correspondence is extraordinarily rich (he even kept copies of letters he sent to his correspondents). A large number of documents covering the entire life of Kolbe was available for consultation. For several decades, these documents had been held in Bad Dürrheim, in the Black Forest region, by Maria Fritsch, Kolbe's third wife, who died in June 2000 at the age of ninety-eight. The widow had not wanted to divulge them. Several historians and journalists vainly attempted to persuade her to open the files in her possession (for example, Klemens von Klemperer in the late 1970s, and Hansjakob Stehle of the weekly *Die Zeit* in 1986). She preferred to turn over all the documents in her possession to Peter Kolbe in Australia, to whom she sent, bit by bit, in the mail, the documents that she had preserved in the cellar of her house.

I have been able to consult all these documents—all previously unpublished— at the home of Peter Kolbe. Most of them were typed. When this was not the case (for example, the postwar correspondence between Fritz Kolbe and Ernst Kocherthaler), Peter Kolbe kindly took the trouble to decipher his father's handwriting (very difficult to read because of old German script).

Among the most useful items was a fifty-nine-page typed document in German written by Gerald Mayer and Fritz Kolbe, unfortunately undated. Perhaps it was a sketch for the autobiography that Fritz Kolbe intended to write in the

late 1960s. It is impossible to say. The text is written in the third person, and
Kolbe is named in it "König." Mayer's and Kolbe's points of view are blended
together. The text is a bit novelistic (it begins: "On 18 August 1943, we meet
him for the first time . . .").

"The Story of George" (seven typed pages in English), written by Ernst Kocherthaler in the spring of 1945, was also of great help in reconstructing the life of Fritz
Kolbe, along with various autobiographical documents that Kolbe wrote after the
war (notably a ten-page autobiographical text in German, dated May 15, 1945). In
the 1960s, Ernst Kocherthaler wrote another summary, "The Background of the
George Story" (four typed pages in English, November 1964) to assist in the rehabilitation of his friend.

The problem with all these documents is that they present the point of view of
a man on his own story, with all the distortions (voluntary or not) that that pre-
supposes. "Human history is made up of many fables mixed with a few truths"
(Chateaubriand). In every autobiographical narrative, the author seeks to justify
his actions and to explain the coherence of his acts after the fact.

Hence the importance of all the dry and factual administrative documents, which
are also found in abundance in Fritz Kolbe's personal archives. Private and public
correspondence, orders, passports, photographs . . . This type of document, which is
invaluable, makes it possible to provide a multiplicity of perspectives on the picture.

2. United States National Archives, College Park

The U.S. National Archives (National Archives and Records Administration [NARA]
announced in June 2000 the opening to the public of documents from the Office
of Strategic Services (OSS), predecessor of the CIA. This major declassification
procedure was the result of the Nazi War Crimes Disclosure Act, a law passed by
Congress in 1998 intended to facilitate informing the public about still-hidden aspects of the Second World War, at a time when there was a renewed wish for truth
and transparency about a past still open to debate and polemic ("Nazi gold," "in-
demnification for slave labor in the Third Reich," etc.).

This huge mountain of declassified documents (400,000 pages of text) contained a subset that did not go without notice: the totality of the 1,600 documents
provided to the Americans by Fritz Kolbe, alias "George Wood," commonly presented as the best source of information to the Allies during the war. These declassified documents (the entire Boston series) contain all the transcriptions in
English of the German diplomatic cables classified "top secret" that Fritz Kolbe
brought to Bern between 1943 and 1945. Other documents supplied by "Wood"
(copies of originals in German, Kappa messages sent by OSS Bern to Washington,
various memoranda of the Bern office of the OSS, etc.) had already been open to
the public for several years. These files can be consulted in the National Archives
building in College Park, MD, near Washington.

All the OSS documents are filed in the category Record Group 226 (RG 226),
and in many subcategories that require patience to explore (entries 210 to 220,
190c, 134, 121, 138, 162, et al.).

Thanks to the OSS archives, Fritz Kolbe's activities can be observed from the
outside: it is possible to retrace with relative precision the deeds of the spy beginning in August 1943, the date of his first meeting with Allen Dulles in Bern. The

problem is that the OSS documents are not always dated—the Kappa messages are, but not the documents of the Boston series—and they are scattered through many boxes with no apparent order.

3. Allen W. Dulles Papers, Princeton

The private archives of Allen Dulles were bequeathed to Princeton University by his widow, Clover Todd Dulles, in 1973. They contain many very valuable items, notably Dulles's personal correspondence (for example, with Fritz Kolbe, Gerald Mayer, and Ernst Kocherthaler), as well as unpublished manuscripts in which the story of "George Wood" appears. Allen Dulles accumulated many documents on Fritz Kolbe, items that have never been published. Unfortunately, these documents are often undated.

4. Archives of the German Foreign Ministry, Berlin

The German Foreign Ministry in Berlin lost some of its archives during the bombings between 1943 and 1945. Part of the Fritz Kolbe file (nos. 007680 and 007681) was destroyed. The entirety of some files (Gertrud von Heimerdinger, for example) has completely disappeared. But there is a great deal of information on Fritz Kolbe's colleagues, and particularly his superiors (files on Johannes von Welczeck, Karl Ritter, and Rudolf Leitner). The archives of the German legation in Bern are particularly well preserved. Many internal ministry circulars, full of information, were also consulted.

5. Swiss Federal Archives, Bern

Several files of the "public ministry" (files comparable to those of the French security services) were consulted, notably those on Ernst Kocherthaler and Gerald Mayer. The Swiss Federal Archives also contain several police documents relative to the mysterious encounter between Fritz Kolbe and the head of the German legation, Otto Köcher, in late April 1945.

6. German Federal Archives, Koblenz

Rudolf Pechel's archives are kept in Koblenz. Fritz Kolbe's participation in the *Deutsche Rundschau* from 1950 to 1954 would have been unknown were it not for these files.

7. Konrad-Adenauer-Stiftung, Sankt Augustin

Here can be found original documents concerning the life of Walter Bauer (1901–68), an industrialist who was a close friend of Fritz Kolbe.

8. Friedrich-Ebert-Stiftung, Bonn

This institution has a file of original documents concerning Paul Löbe (1875–1957), former president of the Reichstag and friend of Fritz Kolbe during the war.

Documents on the history of the labor movement were also consulted (notably publications of the guild of saddle makers in Berlin from the early years of the twentieth century).

9. Various private and unpublished archives

In Berlin, Martin and Gudrun Fritsch recounted their memories of Fritz and allowed me to consult unpublished documents (notebooks, letters, photographs) having belonged to Maria Fritsch, Fritz Kolbe's third wife and Martin Fritsch's aunt.

In Geneva, Gérard and Sylvia Roth graciously allowed me to consult the notebooks of memoirs by Ernst Kocherthaler, their father and father-in-law, and told me some of their own memories.

In Strasbourg, Frank and Marie-Christine Jung, son and daughter-in-law of the surgeon Adolphe Jung, kindly allowed me to use a document written by him in Berlin during the war. It was a long diary full of very concrete observations on life in the capital of the Reich between 1942 and 1945. The original manuscript was transcribed and typed by Marie-Christine Jung.

It was not possible to consult the private archives of Ferdinand Sauerbruch, given by the family to the Prussian Cultural Foundation (Preussischer Kulturbesitz), which will not be open to the public until 2006 (as I was told by Tilman Sauerbruch, the surgeon's grandson).

Personal Testimony

Witnesses are rare, as not many contemporaries of Fritz Kolbe are still alive.

Aside from the people already mentioned, these are the witnesses who were willing to talk to me:

Peter Sichel (New York/Bordeaux), head of the CIA post in Berlin (1949–52), then in charge of operations for all of Eastern Europe, and head of the Hong Kong office in the late 1950s. He knew Fritz Kolbe well between 1945 and 1955.

William Hood (Amagansett, NY), head of the CIA office in Bern during the 1960s. He frequently saw Fritz Kolbe in Bern.

Cordelia Dodson-Hood (Washington), worked with Allen Dulles in Bern at the end of the Second World War.

Tom Polgar (Maitland, FL), headed the CIA offices in Austria, Argentina, Vietnam, Mexico, and Germany. He knew Fritz Kolbe well in Berlin between 1947 and 1949.

Beth Montandon (Lausanne), worked for the CIA in Switzerland. She knew Fritz Kolbe well in Bern in the 1960s.

Erika von Hornstein (Berlin), painter and writer. She frequented Fritz Kolbe and Maria Fritsch in Berlin in the early postwar years.

Ronald Hermsdorf (New Hampshire), son of Harry Hermsdorf, CIA officer posted in Germany after the war, very close to Fritz Kolbe.

Gerald M. Mayer, Jr. (Newbury, NH), son of Gerald Mayer.

Articles

Fritz Kolbe has never been the subject of a book, but several magazine and newspaper articles have been published about him since the early 1950s:

Edward P. Morgan, "The Spy the Nazis Missed," *True*, July 1950. Based on the direct testimony of Fritz Kolbe, interviewed in his home near Frankfurt. Translated into German in the Swiss weekly *Die Weltwoche*, a year later (July 1951). The article was also reprinted in Allen Dulles, ed., *Great True Spy Stories* (New York: Harper & Row, 1968).

Anthony Quibble, "Alias George Wood," *Studies in Intelligence* (CIA publication), vol. 10 (Spring 1966). Internal OSS documents, previously unpublished, were used to write this groundbreaking article.

Articles by Hansjakob Stehle and Barbara Ungeheuer in *Die Zeit*, May 2, 1986. Hansjakob Stehle, then Rome correspondent for *Die Zeit*, interviewed Maria Fritsch, who showed him some original documents. Gerald Mayer and Gertrud von Heimerdinger were also questioned. The article was based essentially on OSS documents obtained in 1985 by an American Jesuit priest, Robert A. Graham. Some excerpts from these documents appeared in the Jesuit publication *Civilta Cattolica* before their publication in *Die Zeit*.

Mark Fritz, "The Perfect Spy," *Boston Globe*, March 11, 2001. The journalist relied on declassified OSS documents and interviewed Peter Kolbe in Sydney.

Axel Frohn and Hans-Michael Kloth, "Der Bote aus Berlin," *Der Spiegel*, September 2001. The two others relied on documents declassified in Washington and brought Fritz Kolbe out of the shadows for the first time since the articles in *Die Zeit* in 1986.

Greg Bradsher, "A Time to Act," *Prologue* (journal of the NARA), Spring 2002. The author, an archivist in College Park, MD, made a thorough study of the recently declassified documents concerning Fritz Kolbe and compared them with various other OSS archives, about whose subtle complexities he is thoroughly knowledgeable.

Thematic Bibliography

The Second World War

Andreas-Friedrich, Ruth. *Der Schattenmann. Tagebuchaufzeichnungen 1938–1948*. Frankfurt, 2000.

Beevor, Antony. *The Fall of Berlin*. New York, 2002.

Dear, I. C. B. and M. R. D. Foot, eds. *The Oxford Companion to World War II*. Oxford, 1995.

Kageneck, August von. *Examen de conscience*. Paris, 1996.

Kardorff, Ursula von. *Berliner Aufzeichnungen. 1942 bis 1945*. Munich, 1997.

Laqueur, Walter and Richard Breitman. Breaking the Silence. New York, 1986.

Read, Anthony and David Fisher. *The Fall of Berlin*. London, 1999.

Nationalism and the Third Reich

Bedürftig, Friedemann and Christian Zentner. *Das Grosse Lexikon des Dritten Reiches.* Munich, 1985.

Burleigh, Michael. *The Third Reich: A New History.* New York, 2000.

Cookridge, Edward Henry. *Gehlen: The Spy of the Century.* London, 1971.

Focke, Harald and Uwe Reimer. *Alltag unterm Hakenkreuz.* Hamburg, 1999.

Haffner, Sebastian. *Anmerkungen zu Hitler.* Berlin, 1978.

Heims, Heinrich. *Monologe im Führerhauptquartier, 1941–1944.* Hamburg, 1980.

Johnson, Eric A. *Nazi Terror: The Gestapo, Jews and Ordinary Germans.* New York, 1999.

Junge, Traudl, in collaboration with Melissa Müller. *Bis zur letzten Stunde. Hitlers Sekretärin erzählt ihr Leben.* Munich, 2002.

Kahn, David. *Hitler's Spies: German Military Intelligence in World War II.* London, 1978.

Kershaw, Ian. *The "Hitler Myth": Image and Reality in the Third Reich.* New York, 1987.

———. *The Nazi Dictatorship: Problems and Perspectives of Interpretation.* New York, 1989.

Klemperer, Victor. *The Language of the Third Reich: LII: Lingua Tertii Imperii,* tr. Martin Brady. London, 2000.

Neumann Franz. *Behemoth: The Structure and Practice of National Socialism.* London, 1942.

Schellenberg, Walter. *The Labyrinth: Memoirs,* tr. Louis Hagen. New York, 1956.

Shirer, William L. *Berlin Diary: The Journal of a Foreign Correspondent 1934–1941.* New York, 1941.

Smelser, Ronald, Enrico Syring, and Rainer Zittelmann, eds. *Die braune Elite,* vol. 2. Darmstadt, 1993.

Wistrich, Robert. *Who's Who in Nazi Germany.* New York, 1982.

Diplomacy, German Foreign Ministry

100 Jahre Auswärtiges Amt 1870–1970. Published by the German Foreign Ministry. Bonn, 1970.

Akten zur deutschen auswärtigen Politik, 1918–1945. Aus dem Archiv des Auswärtigen Amts. Göttingen, 1969–79.

Bloch, Michael. *Ribbentrop.* New York, 1993.

Browning, Christopher. *The Final Solution and the German Foreign Office.* New York, 1978.

Döscher, Hans-Jürgen. *Das Auswärtige Amt im Dritten Reich.* Berlin, 1987.

———. *Verschworene Gesellschaft. Das Auswärtige Amt unter Adenauer zwischen Neubeginn und Kontinuität.* Berlin, 1995.

Halcomb, Jill. *Uniforms & Insignia of the German Foreign Office & Government Ministries, 1938–1945.* Agincourt, 1984.

Hassell, Ulrich von. *Die Hassell-Tagebücher, 1938–1944.* Berlin, 1988.

Hill, Leonidas E., ed. *Die Weizsäcker-Papiere, 1900–1932,* 2 vols. Berlin, 1974 and 1982.

Kleist, Peter. *Zwischen Hitler und Stalin, 1939–1945.* Bonn, 1950.

Papen, Franz von. *Der Wahrheit eine Gasse.* Munich, 1952.

Sahm, Ulrich. *Rudolf von Scheliha 1897–1942: ein deutscher Diplomat gegen Hitler.* Munich, 1990.

Schmidt, Paul. *Statist auf diplomatische Bühne, 1923–45. Erlebnisse des Chefdolmetschers im Auswärtigen Amt mit den Staatsmännern Europas.* Bonn, 1949.

Seabury, Paul. *The Wilhelmstrasse: A Study of German Diplomats Under the Nazi Regime.* Berkeley, 1954.

Thielenhaus, Marion. *Zwischen Anpassung und Widerstand: Deutsche Diplomaten 1938–1941: die politischen Aktivitäten der Beamtengruppe um Ernst von Weizsäcker im Auswärtigen Amt.* Paderborn, 1985.

Weinberg, Gerhard L. *The Foreign Policy of Hitler's Germany*, 2 vols. Chicago, 1970.

The German Resistance

Badia, Gilbert. *Ces Allemands qui ont affronté Hitler*, Paris, 2000.

Boveri, Margaret. *Der Verrat im 20. Jahrhundert.* Hamburg, 1961.

Dulles, Allen. *Germany's Underground.* 1947. Cambridge, MA, 2000.

Gallin, Mary Alice. *German Resistance to Hitler: Ethical and Religious Factors.* Washington, DC, 1962.

Grossmann, Kurt R. *Die unbesungenen Helden.* Berlin, 1957.

Heideking, Jürgen, Marc Frey, and Christoph Mauch. *American Intelligence and the German Resistance to Hitler: A Documentary History (Widerstand, Dissent and Resistance in the Third Reich.* Boulder, CO, 1996.

Heuss, Theodor. *Dank und Bekenntniss. Gedenkrede zum 20 Juli 1944.* Tübingen, 1954.

Kern, Erich. *Verrat an Deutschland: Spione und Saboteure gegen das eigene Vaterland.* Preußisch-Oldendorf, 1972.

Klemperer, Klemens von. *German Resistance Against Hitler: The Search for Allies Abroad 1938–1945.* Oxford, 1992.

Levisse-Touzé, Christine and Stefan Martens, eds. *Des Allemands contre le nazisme: oppositions et résistances, 1933–1945.* Paris, 1997.

Mommsen, Hans. *Alternatives to Hitler: German Resistance Under the Third Reich*, tr. Angus McGeoch. Princeton, 2003.

Pechel, Rudolf. *Deutscher Widerstand.* Zurich, 1947.

Steinbach, Peter. *Widerstand im Widerstreit.* Paderborn, 2001.

Steinbach, Peter and Johannes Tuchel, eds. *Widerstand gegen den Nationalsozialismus.* Bonn, 1994.

OSS, United States, Espionage

Casey, William J. *The Secret War Against Hitler.* Washington, DC, 1988.

Cave Brown, Anthony. *Bodyguard of Lies.* New York, 1975.

———. *The Last Hero: Wild Bill Donovan.* New York, 1982.

Chalou, George C., ed. *The Secrets War: The Office of Strategic Services in World War II.* Washington, DC, 1992.

Helms, Richard, with William Hood. *A Look Over My Shoulder.* New York, 2003.

Mauch, Christoph. *Schattenkrieg gegen Hitler. Das Dritte Reich im Visier der amerikanischen Geheimdienste 1941–1945.* Stuttgart, 1999.

Persico, Joseph E. *Piercing the Reich: The Penetration of Nazi Germany by American Secret Agents during World War II.* New York, 1979.
Persico, Joseph E. *Roosevelt's Secret Wars: FDR and WW II Espionage.* New York, 2001.
Petersen, Neal H., ed. *From Hitler's Doorstep: The Wartime Intelligence Reports of Allen Dulles, 1942–1945.* University Park, PA, 1996.
Simpson, Christopher. *Blowback: America's Recruitment of Nazis and Its Effects on the Cold War.* New York, 1988.
Smith, Bradley F. *OSS: The Secret History of America's First Central Intelligence Agency.* Berkeley, 1972.
Tully, Andrew. *CIA: The Inside Story.* New York, 1962.
Waller, John H. *The Unseen War in Europe.* New York, 1996.

German Social History

Bergmann, Jürgen. *Das Berliner Handwerk in den Frühphasen der Industrialisierung.* Berlin, 1973.
Frei, Norbert. *Karrieren im Zwielicht. Hitlers Eliten nach 1945.* Frankfurt, 2001.
Ritter Gerhard A. *Arbeiter, Arbeiterbewegung und soziale Ideen in Deutschland: Beiträge zur Geschichte des 19. und 20. Jahrhunderts.* Munich, 1996.
——. *Arbeiter im deutschen Kaiserreich (1871–1914).* Bonn, 1992.
Ruppert, Wolfgang, ed. *Die Arbeiter: Lebensformen, Alltag und Kultur von der Frühindustrialisierung bis zum 'Wirtschaftswunder.'* Munich, 1986.
Wehler, Hans-Ulrich. *Deutsche Gesellschagtsgeshichte (1849–1914).* Munich, 1995.

Youth, *Wandervogel*

Blüher, Hans. *Wandervogel: Geschichte einer Jugendbewegung.* Berlin, 1913.
Höffkes, Karl. *Träumer, Streiter, Bürgerschreck. Aus der Geschichte der deutschen Jugendbewegung.* 1983.
Ille, Gerhard. *Der Wandervogel. Es begann in Steglitz.* Berlin, 1987.
Klönne, Arno. *Hitlerjugend. Die Jugend und ihre Organisation im dritten Reich.* Hanover, 1957.
Völpel, Christiane. *Hermann Hesse und die deutsche Jugendbewegung: eine Untersuchung über die Beziehungen dem Wandervogel und Hermann Hesses Frühwerk.* Bonn, 1977.

Switzerland in the Second World War

Bonjour, Edgar. *Schweizerische Neutralität. Kurzfassung der Geschichte in einem Band.* Basel, 1978.
Bourgeois, Daniel. *Le Troisième Reich et la Suisse: 1933–1941.* Neuchâtel, 1974.
Braunschweig, Pierre-Th. *Geheimer Draht nach Berlin: die Nachrichtenlinie Masson-Schellenberg und der schweizerische Nacrichtendienst im Zweiten Weltkrieg.* Zurich, 1990.
Garlinski, Josef. *The Swiss Corridor: Espionage Networks in Switzerland during World War II.* London, 1981.
Jacquillard, Colonel R. *La Chasse aux espions en Suisse, choses vécues, 1939–1945.* Paris/Lausanne, 1948.

Loeff, Wolfgang. *Spionage. Aus den Papieren eines Abwehroffiziers.* Stuttgart, 1950.
Lüönd, Karl. *Spionage in der Schweiz*, 2 vols. Zurich, 1977.
Read, Anthony and David Fisher. *Operation Lucy: The Most Secret Spy Ring of the Second World War.* New York, 1981.
Urner, Klaus. *Die Schweiz muss noch geschlukt werden! Hitlers Aktionspläne gegen die Schweiz.* Zurich, 1990.

British Secret Services in the Second World War

Hinsley, F. H. and Alan Stripp, eds. *Codebreakers: The Inside Story of Bletchley Park.* Oxford, 1993.
Philby, Kim. *My Silent War.* New York, 1968.
West, Nigel. *MI5: British Security Service Operations, 1909–1945.* London, 1988.
West, Nigel. *MI6: British Secret Intelligence Service Operations, 1909–1945.* London, 1988.
Winterbotham, Frederick. *The Ultra Secret.* New York, 1974.

The Cicero Affair

Bazna, Elyesa and Hans Nogly. *Ich war Cicero.* Munich, 1964.
Denniston, Robin. *Churchill's Secret War: Diplomatic Decrypts, the Foreign Office and Turkey 1942–1944.* New York, 1997.
Moyzisch, Ludwig C. *Der Fall Cicero.* Saarbrücken, 1949.
West, Nigel. *A Thread of Deceit: Espionage Myths of World War II.* New York, 1985.
Wires, Richard. *The Cicero Spy Affair: German Access to British Secrets in World War II.* Westport, CT, 1999.

Peenemünde, V-1, and V-2

Bergier, Jacques. *Agents secrets contre armes secrètes.* Geneva, 1970.
Dornberger, Walter. *Peenemünde. Die Geschichte der V-Waffen.* Berlin, 1997.
Longmate, Norman. *Hitler's Rockets: The Story of the V-2s.* London, 1985.

Hungary in the Second World War

Biss Andreas. *Der Stopp der Endlösung. Kampf gegen Himmler und Eichmann in Budapest.* Stuttgart, 1966.
Braham, Randolph L. *The Politics of Genocide: The Holocaust in Hungary*, 2 vols. New York, 1981.
Braham, Randolph L., ed. *Studies on the Holocaust in Hungary.* New York, 1990.

Ireland in the Second World War

Hull, Mark M. *Irish Secrets: German Espionage in Wartime Ireland.* Dublin, 2002.
Stephan, Enno. *Geheimauftrag Irland.* Hamburg, 1961.

Vichy

Azéma, Jean-Pierre and Olivier Wieviorka. *Vichy, 1940–1944.* Paris, 2000.
Lacroix-Riz, Annie. *Industriels et banquiers sous l'occupation.* Paris, 1999.
Rochebrune, Renaud de and Jean-Claude Hazéra. *Les Patrons sous l'occupation.* Paris, 1995.

The Nuremberg Trials

Kempner, Robert M. W. with Jörg Friedrich. *Ankläger einer Epoche: Lebenserinnerungen.* Frankfurt, 1983.
Taylor, Telford. *Anatomy of the Nuremberg Trials.* New York, 1992.

Allen Dulles

Assouline, Pierre. *Une Éminence grise: Jean Jardin, 1904–1976.* Paris, 1986.
Bancroft, Mary. *Autobiography of a Spy.* New York, 1983.
Dulles, Allen W. *The Craft of Intelligence.* New York, 1963.
———. *The Secret Surrender.* New York, 1966.
Grose, Peter. *Gentleman Spy: The Life of Allen Dulles.* Boston, 1994.
Hersh, Burton. *The Old Boys: The American Elite and the Origins of the CIA.* New York, 1992.
Srodes, James. *Allen Dulles: Master of Spies.* Washington, DC, 2000.
Wala, Michael. *The Council on Foreign Relations and American Foreign Policy in the Early Cold War.* Oxford, 1994.

Ernst Kocherthaler

Attali, Jacques. *Un Homme d'influence.* Paris, 1985.
Chernow, Ron. *The Warburgs: A Family Saga.* London, 1993.
Kocherthaler, Ernst. *Das Reich der Antike.* Baden-Baden, 1948.

Ferdinand Sauerbruch

Eckart, Wolfgang U. "Mythos Sauerbruch," *Frankfurter Allgemeine Zeitung,* July 15, 2000.
Hammerstein, Notker. *Die deutsche Forschungsgemeinschaft in der Weimarer Republik und im Dritten Reich: Wissenschaftspolitik in Republik und Diktatur 1920–1945.* Munich, 1999.
Kater, Michael H. *Ärzte als Hitlers Helfer.* Munich, 2000.
Klee, Ernst. *Deutsche Medizin im Dritten Reich. Karrieren vor und nach 1945.* Frankfurt, 2001.
Kudlien, F. and Chr. Andree. "Sauerbruch und der Nationalsozialismus," *Medizinhistorisches Journal* vol. 15 (1980), pp. 201–22.
Mitscherlich, Alexander and Fred Mielke. *Medizin ohne Menschlichkeit: Dokumente des Nürnberger Ärzteprozesses.* Frankfurt, 1997.
Sauerbruch, Ferdinand. *Das war mein Leben.* Bad Wörishofen, 1951.

Scholder, Klaus, ed. *Die Mittwochs-Gesellschaft: Protokolle aus dem geistigen Deutschland 1932 bis 1944.* Berlin, 1982.

Karl Ritter

Hilton, Stanley E. *Brazil and the Great Powers, 1930–1939: The Politics of Trade Rivalry.* Austin, TX, 1975.
————. *Hitler's Secret War in South America, 1939–1945: German Military Espionage and Allied Counterespionage in Brazil.* Baton Rouge, LA, 1981.

Adolphe Jung

Clément, G.-R. *Avec l'Alsace en guerre, 1940–1944.* Paris/Strasbourg, 1945.
Histoire de la médecine à Strasbourg. Published by the Faculty of Medicine of the University of Strasbourg. Strasbourg, 1998.
Hollender, Louis-François and Emmanuelle During-Hollender. *Chirurgiens et chirurgie à Strasbourg.* Strasbourg, 2000.

Rudolf Pechel

Knesebeck, Rosemarie von dem. *Rudolf Pechel un die 'Deutsche Rundschau' 1946–1961: Zeitgeschehen und Zeitgeschichte im Spiegel einer konservativen politischen Zeitschrift: eine Studie zur konservativen Publizistik in Deutschland nach dem Zweiten Weltkrieg.* Göttingen, 1975.
Mauersberger, Volker. *Rudolf Pechel und die 'Deutsche Rundschau'. Eine Studie zur konservativ-revolutionären Publizistik in der Weimarer Republik, 1918–1933.* Bremen, 1971.
Mohler, Armin. *Die konservative Revolution in Deutschland 1918–1932. Grundriß ihrer Weltanschauungen.* Stuttgart, 1950.

Hans-Bernd Gisevius

Gisevius, Hans-Bernd. *Bis zum bittern Ende.* Zurich, 1946.

Georg Schreiber

Morsey, Rudolf. *Der Untergang des politischen Katholizismus: die Zentrunspartei zwischen christlichen Selbstverständnis und "Nationaler Erhebung" 1932–33.* Stuttgart/Zurich, 1977.

Other Works Cited

Camus, Albert. *Camus à Combat. Éditoriaux et articles d'Albert Camus, 1944–1947.* Paris, 2002.
Guéhenno, Jean. *Journal des années noires. 1940–1944.* Paris, 1947.
Hesse, Hermann. *Steppenwolf,* tr. Basil Creighton (1929). New York, 1962.
Huth, Oskar, ed. Alf Trenk. *Überlebenslauf.* Berlin, 2001.

Kästner, Erich, *Als ich ein kleiner Junge war.* Munich, 1999.

Klemperer, Victor. *I Will Bear Witness: A Diary of the Nazi Years 1942–1945,* tr. Martin Chalmers. New York, 1999.

Mann, Klaus. *Mephisto,* tr. Robyn Smyth. New York, 1977.

Maugham, W. Somerset. *Ashenden.* London, 1928.

Schiller, Friedrich. *Wallenstein,* tr. Charles Passage. New York, 1958.

Towarnicki, Frédéric de. *Ernst Junger, récit d'un passeur de siècle.* Paris, 2000.